Britain's Maritime Heritage

Britain's Maritime Heritage

Robert Simper

DAVID & CHARLES

Newton Abbot   London   North Pomfret (Vt)

British Library Cataloguing in Publication Data

Simper, Robert
    Britain's maritime heritage.
    1. Shipping—Great Britain—History
    I. Title
    387.2′0941   HE824

    ISBN 0–7153–8177–6

Filmset in Monophoto Plantin by
Latimer Trend & Company Ltd, Plymouth
and printed in Great Britain
by Butler & Tanner Limited, Frome and London
for David & Charles (Publishers) Limited
Brunel House   Newton Abbot   Devon

Published in the United States of America
by David & Charles Inc
North Pomfret   Vermont 05053   USA

Contents

Acknowledgements

No one living in the British Isles is ever far away from the sea, and numerous rivers and estuaries push far inland so that even inland towns and villages often have strong maritime connections. Within the British Isles there is a tremendous variety in the types of coastline; to cover this diversity, I have had to call upon the advice of many people with specialist knowledge. A tremendous number of people have helped with this book, but I would particularly like to thank the following:

In Scotland, Hobson Rankin of Newport-on-Tay, David Gerrard of Arbroath, Joe Buchan of Fraserburgh, George Watt of Macduff, and Gordon Clarkson and Garth Sterne of the Scottish Fisheries Museum, Anstruther. P. R. Logue, the District Fishery Officer of the Department of Agriculture & Fisheries for Scotland, also supplied information.

In the north-east of England, Hector Handyside of Amble, Adrian Osler, Keeper of Shipping for the Tyne & Wear Museum Service, Dr Fraser, Secretary of the Society of Antiquaries, Newcastle, and Miss D. Johnson of the South Shields Central Library were all most helpful. On the north-west coast of England, Michael Stammers, Keeper of Maritime History at the Merseyside Maritime Museum, the Barrow-in-Furness historian, Alan Lockett, and the Cunard Archives at the University of Liverpool were all most helpful. Specialist knowledge was given by Bob Todd, Mr Hodge and Judith Watt at the National Maritime Museum, Greenwich. In Wales, J. Geraint Jenkins and the photograph archivist at the Welsh Industrial & Maritime Museum, Cardiff, helped a great deal, as did Heather Dalton at the Fishing Museum of Cenarth Falls and Roger and Lynn Danby.

In western England, thanks must go to John Powell, Librarian at the Ironbridge Gorge Museum, John Corin of the Port of Bristol Authority, the Bristol maritime artist, Peter Stuckey, and F. W. Greenacre of the Bristol Museum and Art Gallery. In Cornwall, Terry Heard, and in the Isles of Scilly, Alf J. Jenkins.

On sailing ships, guidance came from Hilton Mathews of the Isle of Wight, Norman Brouwer of New York, Anthony Davies of Brightlingsea, Robin Davies of Colchester and Rick Hogben of London. On local craft, assistance came from Chris Waddington of the Solent Smack Society. W. T. Rose gave material on Pollock of Faversham, while Hugh

Perks came up with some valuable assistance. William Honey of Deal was most informative about the Deal beach boats. On yachts, Gordon and Caroline Waller were most helpful, and so too was Brian Hillsdon of The Steam Boat Association of Great Britain. I also had help from Craig J. M. Carter of Liverpool, Stephen Rabson of P & O, R. D. Johnson of The Port of London Authority, R. J. Adie of the British Antarctic Survey, Lt Snetton, the British Waterways Board and Mrs Kimble of Brixham. For illustrations and photographic work thanks must go to Graham and Honor Hussey of Butley and Geoff Cordy of Felixstowe; and on books to John Cook.

The people who have had to do the most to steer this book into a worthwhile conclusion are Anthony Lambert of David & Charles, my wife Pearl and my daughter Joanna, who was also co-opted for some of the typing. Thank you to all these people.

R.S.
Ramsholt, 1981

Introduction

Britain has a rich and fascinating heritage of maritime enterprise. It is a heritage born out of necessity for, as an island race, the control and mastery of the sea has been of vital importance. There are other similar groups of islands elsewhere in the world which do not have such a strong maritime heritage. The reasons why Britain became a major maritime power are complex. The attitudes of kings, political leaders and the people generally, towards the sea, and what use Britain made of this natural resource has changed constantly over the centuries.

The Romans were the first to make organised defences to guard the territory they held in Britain against invasion. Sea raiders from northern Europe were such a menace that the Romans built a chain of forts along the coast of East Anglia and down the south coast of England. Besides these were other forts guarding the coast of Cumbria from attacks by bellicose tribes to the north. When the Romans withdrew, the whole of Britain at once became open to attack. This reached a peak in the ninth century with the Viking raids virtually destroying the Christian Anglo-Saxon society. It was Alfred, King of Wessex, who set out to defend his kingdom by controlling the sea. Instead of waiting for the attackers to land, Alfred built ships, manned them with Friesian mercenaries and Anglo-Saxon levies, and went out to fight the Vikings at sea.

Alfred's policy was successful and the Viking attacks were eventually controlled, but the maintenance of a regular naval force was beyond the resources of the looseknit Anglo-Saxon social structure. When William the Conqueror sailed with his invasion force from Normandy in 1066, there was no fleet to prevent his landing on the Sussex coast and he was only opposed when his army landed. The subsequent medieval kings of England either held, or attempted to hold, territory in northern France, so there had to be a constant seaborne link between the two coasts. These ships were often sold or laid up during periods of peace, but royal ships were used as front line defence in the protection of the kingdom and also to guard the merchant routes.

Although trade between the British Isles and European neighbours, particularly in wine from France, necessitated the growth of a merchant fleet, it was the wool trade which brought a great upsurge in commercial traffic. Ships were also going to Icelandic fishing grounds so there was a need to produce larger vessels, capable of staying at sea longer than the open longships and keeping larger cargoes dry.

In the medieval period open ships were gradually replaced by decked vessels, the inspiration for which was drawn from the Low Countries and northern France. The influence of the Mediterranean countries came through France and the Low Countries, prompting the replacement of easily built clinker hulls by carvel-planked hulls on larger vessels. Rudders were fixed on the stern by about 1200 instead of steering oars on either side of the stern, which meant that even larger ships could be introduced. Many continental master shipbuilders were hired by England and Scotland. Most were drawn from the Italian states but there were also French, Dutch and Germans willing to sell their skills to the highest bidder. There were also skilled gunfounders who moved around working for whichever country was currently on a war footing.

The rejection of the authority of the Church of Rome by King Henry VIII in the early 1530s isolated England from Europe, some Protestant states in northern Europe excepted. After the final break with Rome, native shipbuilding skills had to be developed, although some foreigners were still available for hire. The break with the Church of Rome led to the intensely nationalistic Elizabethan age. The European mainland powers, Spain and France, could not countenance a Protestant monarchy in England. France attempted to encourage Scotland to harass England, but the skilful diplomacy of Queen Elizabeth I succeeded in maintaining peace with her northern neighbour.

Queen Elizabeth I connived at acts of piracy on Spanish ships by her sea captains but at the same time tried to prevent this developing into open war. Philip, King of Spain, had a deeply religious belief that England should be brought back under the Church of Rome, besides wanting to end the raids by English pirates. The Spanish Armada was sent to achieve this aim, but was defeated, although not through tactical inferiority.

Before the Elizabethan age, the British Isles had been on the fringe of European culture and wealth, but the position changed with the opening up of ocean sea routes. Britain's seamen acquired the skill and aggressive outlook needed to make long voyages in small ships. In country houses and taverns gentlemen, merchants and sea captains discussed the possibility of finding great wealth by reaching distant places. It was impossible for Britain to completely disassociate herself from European power struggles, but great energy was devoted to creating an overseas trading empire. This was not usually done by conquest, but by the creation of individual trading ventures which grew into settlements and in time became recognised colonies.

The official title of the United Kingdom of Great Britain and Ireland was not adopted until the Act of Union in 1801, but Britain had effectively been one political unit for the previous two hundred years. This unity was established when Elizabeth I was succeeded in 1603 by her nephew, James VI of Scotland, who became James I of England and head of state of all the British Isles. Although James I lacked political ability, the growth of the merchant sphere of influence continued, despite neglect of the Royal Navy.

Britain's earliest overseas expansion was along the coast of North America and in the West Indies. The Far East held a great fascination for the British, but the voyages there took months of extreme discomfort and danger. Elizabeth I had thoroughly understood and controlled the merchants, and in 1600 had granted a charter to the East India Company, allowing them the sole right to trade with lands east of the Cape of Good Hope. In the Stuart period the East India Company made huge profits which encouraged an increasing number of men and women to risk the dangers of disease and war in the East. Many of the ships on voyages to the East were away for years. A fast passage for an East Indiaman was made by the *Thomas Coutts* which in 1826–7 went out and back to China via Bombay and Singapore in ten days under a year. The value of an East Indiaman was incredible; for instance, in 1804 a homeward-bound East India Company fleet which beat off an attack by a French squadron was reported to be worth £6 million.

Sea travel affected the whole way of life in Britain. Foreign customs, habits and words were constantly being introduced by men and women who visited every part of the globe. From China came porcelain and lacquered furniture, silk and tea, from South America came the potato, from North America came furs and tobacco, from the West Indies came sugar and pineapples and from the Mediterranean countries came citrus fruits. World trade improved the quality of life in Britain and gave employment to countless craftsmen who produced goods for exchange.

With so many overseas interests, conflict within some part of the huge trading empire became inevitable. The first and perhaps the most disastrous of the colonial wars was the War of American Independence which led to the establishment of the United States of America in 1776. Fighting a war so far away from the home country called for a highly effective Royal Navy, but the general incompetence of the administration of the land forces was no match for the determination of the American settlers, and mastery of the sea proved to be of little use on its own.

The secession of the American colonies was a major blow to the British economy, but the acquisition of other overseas territories mitigated the loss. The development of the empire was, from the early seventeenth century to the early twentieth century, a cornerstone of British foreign policy. In the seventeenth century the Dutch had been a rival to British seapower, but in the constant struggles for colonial territory in the late eighteenth and nineteenth centuries, France was the chief rival. The French Revolution in 1789 caused great concern in Britain with the proximity of the terrible reign of the guillotine. The sea as a barrier to impede ideas of social revolution and to thwart the personal ambitions of Napoleon became immensely important.

The long Napoleonic Wars did little to stop the well-established smuggling links between Britain and France. The high duty on silks, spirits and tobacco, and the virtual impossibility of continually patrolling the whole coast, caused smuggling to continue on a large scale. The revenue cutters attempted to intercept the smuggling luggers as they came in from France or Holland with gin, but they had only limited success. The goods were landed by gangs at night on lonely stretches of the coast and were then taken inland on pony trains guarded by armed men. Even on land the customs were, until they were given military assistance, unable to stop the smugglers. Soldiers were frequently aiding customs officers in the 1780s, but it was not until after the Napoleonic Wars that the government used the surplus manpower to suppress smuggling gangs. This proved effective in the 1820s when the Coast Guard Service was formed. In the nineteenth century, this service built groups of cottages all round the coast so that every possible landing beach was under their watchful eyes.

The Industrial Revolution, fuelled by the natural coal resources, resulted in a productive capacity far in excess of the needs of the home market. Colonisation eased the dilemma by establishing secure markets for British products and enabling emigration to act as a safety valve when unemployment threatened social unrest. Many emigrants from the British Isles and other European countries flocked to the United States, but the colonial countries of Australia, New Zealand and Canada were largely populated from Britain. Within the Empire many small places such as the Falkland Islands were entirely populated with settlers from Britain.

Despite fierce competition from all the industrial nations, particularly France, The Netherlands, the United States and Germany, Britain retained its maritime supremacy until World War I. From London, Southampton, Liverpool, Glasgow, Belfast and other ports, ran regular liner services which connected most of the world's countries. They ranged from cargo ships with only a few cabins for passengers on the more remote routes to the luxurious and prestigious liners of the North Atlantic route to New York which was by far the most lucrative trade.

Travel to the East was made a great deal easier by the opening of the Suez Canal in 1869. It was built largely by de Lesseps, a Frenchman, with the backing of his country, but the British Government gained a controlling interest in the Canal Company which was exploited to make Egypt part of the Empire. Control of the Suez Canal became vital because it became the gateway to India, Malaya, Australia and many other colonial outposts; one of Britain's last 'Imperial' acts was to try, unsuccessfully, to regain control of the Suez Canal by military force after it had been taken over by the Egyptian Government in 1956.

Many of the small colonial outposts were acquired in the nineteenth century as a result of the use of steamers. Sailing ships wandered for months across the world's surface propelled by the trade winds, but the steamers had to keep going into port for coal bunkering. The Royal Navy, which maintained a large force 'East of Suez', was very keen to acquire small islands which might make useful bunkering ports. The Royal Navy was capable of coaling their warships at sea and had coal ships which could follow a fleet for this purpose, but the liners, troop ships and tramp steamers had to call into port for bunkering.

The wealth generated by the Industrial Revolution and the growth of the Empire added a new dimension to the British attitude towards the sea. Previously most people had only gone to sea out of necessity to fight, trade, fish or smuggle, but in the nineteenth century there was a growing band of yachtsmen who actually went to sea for pleasure. The countless men who wrested a very bare existence from fishing in tiny and often worn out craft, were amazed that wealthy people should go to sea for pleasure. There were yacht clubs and regattas at most good sailing centres by the 1920s, but the real growth of this leisure activity took place after World War II. The coastal waters are no longer just a commercial highway; they have become Britain's largest leisure area. While most estuaries now suffer from overcrowding as leisure areas, the solitude and challenge of the open sea is still an irresistible challenge to many.

By the late nineteenth century, the coastal waters had been made a great deal safer by the steady introduction of buoys, lighthouses and lightships warning mariners of dangers. The first lighthouses had just coal fires which could be put out by rain or wind; however, the St Agnes lighthouse in the Isles of Scilly had an iron-cresset, coal-burning light which was in service from 1680–1911. The first lighthouse on the Eddystone Rock was built between 1695–1700, only to be washed away three years later. Smeaton's famous Eddystone lighthouse was completed in 1759 and lasted nearly 120 years, only being replaced by the present one because the rock foundations crumbled.

The world's first lightship was placed in the Thames Estuary at The

Nore in 1732. This was done by the Trinity House which was given its first charter in 1514 by Henry VIII, making it responsible for maintaining land marks and building lighthouses to aid mariners. However, many lighthouses remained private property and were a source of revenue for their owners who levied duty on passing merchant vessels. Many desperately poor fishing communities actively encouraged shipwrecks, and estate owners who claimed all the wreckage on their foreshores also did nothing to prevent wrecks. Trinity House was granted more power in an Act of Parliament in 1836 and were finally given responsibility for most navigation marks in England and Wales, while Scotland and the Isle of Man were made the responsibility of the Commissioners of the Northern Lighthouse; the Irish Coast came under the control of the Irish Lights Commissioners.

Navigation marks alone naturally did not make coastal waters totally safe. The loss of life in the age of sail remained high, partly due to the poor conditions of ships, but often due to ships being caught on a lee shore in a gale and being unable to sail clear. In one year, 1865, 2,607 British seamen died of drowning; some of these were on deep sea voyages, but most were in coastal wrecks. The creation of the Royal National Lifeboat Institution to set up lifeboat stations was a major contribution towards reducing the loss of life at sea. The unpaid lifeboatmen put to sea in the worst weather in open pulling lifeboats. Some of these had small lug sails, but to go out in such boats in winter gales was truly heroic. The Institution stationed its first steam lifeboat, the *Duke of Northumberland*, at Harwich in 1890. This could only lie afloat on moorings all the time as steam lifeboats were too heavy to launch from a beach. Six steam lifeboats served at stations round the coast for nearly forty years. The first motor lifeboat was used on station in 1904, but until the engines could be kept in watertight compartments, motors were not entirely successful! However, motor lifeboats were replacing the pulling and sailing lifeboats by the 1920s.

The Royal National Lifeboat Institution is one of the great British maritime achievements. It is entirely financed by donations and most lifeboats are manned solely by volunteers. There are exceptions such as Spurn Head at the entrance to the Humber where the lack of a community has necessitated the employment of professional lifeboatmen. The Institution was not set up to salvage vessels in distress although the lifeboatmen usually try to do so. This service is the model of many similar life-saving organisations throughout the world.

Britannia, in the late nineteenth century, ruled the waves in both naval strength and commercial enterprise. In the opening years of this century, Britain owned half of the world's shipping, and two-thirds of the world's merchant tonnage had been built in British shipyards. By 1914 other nations had expanded their mercantile fleets, reducing Britain's share of world trade to 38 per cent. By 1917 German U-boats had sunk about one-fifth of Britain's pre-war merchant fleet of 46 million tons. Shipowners in neutral countries, such as The Netherlands and Denmark, were quick to use the wartime boom in freight rates to increase their tonnage. The post-war boom lasted until 1921, followed by a long shipping slump during the Depression. Few new ships were built and most cargo vessels were only partly employed. The British Shipping (Assistance) Act of 1935 granted subsidies to help re-vitalise the tramp steamer and coastal shipping industries. In World War II Britain's merchant fleet was again savagely depleted by submarines. After the war British shipping companies made a determined effort to recapture world trade, but circumstances were against them. The Empire was replaced by the Commonwealth and most of the new nations tried to develop a merchant fleet under their own flag rather than the red ensign of British registered ships.

In the late 1950s, the pattern of world shipping changed. Until then shipowners had tended to have their ships built in, and their crews drawn from, their own country. However, because of the size of her merchant navy, Britain had never been able to man her fleet with her own nationals. This meant that for semi-skilled jobs, such as deck crew, in the last years of sailing ships, any nationality would be employed and many shipping lines operating to the East recruited Lascars in India. However, British seamen still took the better-paid jobs.

In the 1950s merchant ships under flags of convenience took over a large share of the world's trade, to the detriment of British shipping. The 1960s saw a steady rise in the number of merchant ships operated by Russia and Soviet bloc countries in international trade. Unlike the British shipping lines, which have to make a profit to survive, the Soviet mercantile marine is in a position to run at a loss simply to earn foreign currency.

The number of British ships has declined from 1,614 in 1975 to 1,130 ships in 1981. The decline of the number of ships and the number of men employed is not wholly due to competition from foreign-flag ships; it is also the result of the introduction of larger container ships and faster dock turn-rounds. For instance 26 container ships operated by Overseas Containers in 1981 were doing the work of 160 cargo ships of some twenty years before. However, much of the decline was due to low returns from ships sailing under the British flag. The shift of emphasis from the Empire to the British Commonwealth has meant that the Royal Navy has handed over the role of defence in many areas to new nations. However, the decline of Britain's industrial prosperity has meant less money to spend on warships and the Royal Navy's fleet has diminished.

Britain's maritime past has been a series of quite separate, although inter-dependent lines of development. For instance the Royal Navy has a quite different approach, and problems, to seafaring from that of the longshore fishermen, while the coastal seamen had totally different working lives to those on the liners. All the different branches of seagoing activities do however follow a certain similarity. There was an obvious break with the end of the age of sail and the beginning of the age of technology, starting with the first steamers. In the twentieth century there has been an almost continual stream of new technological inventions available to the mariner, making ships faster and safer.

This book is a survey of the different branches of seafaring, a reminder of just how much has been achieved in the evolution of Britain's maritime activities.

I

Britannia's Shield

The sea is a very difficult expanse of the world's surface for any nation to dominate. The British Isles, with a long coast line and numerous offshore islands has always been very vulnerable to attacks from the sea. The waves of raids by Vikings from Scandinavia prevented the establishment of a stable society, which exacerbated the difficulty of organization of a fighting force from the scattered groups of people living in Britain. The English King, Alfred the Great, was the first to successfully create a maritime force to meet the onslaught of the marauding Danes. In England, counties were originally divided up into 'hundreds', each area being occupied by a hundred families, but even by King Alfred's time most of these Anglo-Saxon areas supported a larger population.

Alfred instructed each of some 300 'hundreds' round the coast to provide at least one ship. Alfred also initiated a principle of naval strategy, which each successive generation followed, by ordering the construction of ships to be larger, and hopefully more powerful, than those of the enemy, which in this case was the Danish Vikings. With his ships divided into three groups, Alfred was able to beat back the Danes in a series of sea battles. However, the Danish Vikings were undeterred and continued their raids. Alfred's successor in 958 was Edgar who continued the policy of keeping a war fleet. Contemporary chroniclers were enthusiastic about Edgar's fleet and there are references to 3,600 and even 5,000 ships, although it is probable that even the lower figure is an exaggeration. If nothing else, the king's fighting ships did create a barrier which warded off the main attacks, but pirates continued to raid ships and coastal towns right through the medieval period.

Few of the medieval kings had a standing force organized to repulse pirate attacks, and since most of the attacks came from northern France, the Sussex coast was the most badly hit. The little towns and fishing villages here were forced to form a united defence and this confederation of towns became known as the Cinque Ports. In 1278 they were given legal privileges in return for the services they provided in defending the realm. It remained customary for medieval kings to raise a fleet in times of war and disperse them afterwards.

The idea of a fleet united for a national purpose would have been foreign to medieval people since loyalties were directed to a particular king, prince or lord. The predominant aspect of public life was an endless power struggle between rival monarchs, or between them and their feudal lords. English foreign policy was largely a question of trying to conquer and hold some part of northern France or the Low Countries. It was Edward III's claim to the throne of France which resulted in the naval Battle of Sluys in 1340. In order to press home his claim he hired merchant ships to carry his army across to Flanders (the coast of Belgium). This fleet assembled in the River Orwell, but when Edward III arrived there were only forty ships. These remained at anchor for several weeks while the king's followers went out to remind coastal ports to send their full quota of ships to the royal summons.

The royal fleet of some 200 ships finally sailed to the mouth of the River Schelde. Before the building of harbours this great river was the best place to gather a fleet for an invasion of England. For centuries the English kings' only real foreign policy, apart from the Crusades, had been to harry the French and make sure the mouth of the Schelde stayed in friendly hands. When Edward III arrived on the coast of Flanders in the middle of June they found the French fleet anchored off Sluys. The French stayed firmly at anchor waiting for the English fleet to come in on the flood tide. Edward III's ships, all merchantmen, with raised fighting tops in their bows and sterns for archers, ran alongside the ships of Philip de Valois and fighting was a brutal hand-to-hand affair with swords and battle axes.

The Battle of Sluys was a victory for Edward III and he succeeded in keeping the French feudal lords out of Flanders. The practical result of this encounter was that the Schelde remained open for English merchant ships to take wool to the markets at Ghent, Bruges and Ypres. After Sluys, Edward III claimed himself Lord of the English Sea and the fighting nobility had realised the vital importance of sea power. Sluys was also one of the opening struggles in what became the Hundred Years War between the English and the French kings. At the start this was a straightforward power struggle between feudal dynasties for land domination. Edward III and his nobles spoke French and it was only towards the end of this war against the French kings that the sense of national identity grew in the English people.

In 1360 Edward III, who was then fighting both the French and Spanish kings at sea, founded the Court of Admiralty of England which was responsible for administering the king's fighting ships. The need for some form of power to form a shield behind which England could live in peace was constantly being reinforced by French raids on the coastal towns and even the Thames. Well over a century later, King Henry VII clearly understood that sea power was vital to protect his kingdom and its trade. It was also realised that pressing merchantmen into service was not the best way to obtain good fighting ships. Because the royal ships were usually kept in the Thames off the Tower of London, then the strongest point of the realm, they were often referred to as being 'of the Tower' in records, to distinguish them from ordinary merchantmen. Henry VII raised the finance to build special fighting ships by import levies. These were called the King's Ships and the four largest were the *Sweepstake*, *Mary Fortune*, *Sovereign* and *Regent*. The high, built-up 'castles' in the bows and sterns and the fighting tops on the masts gave the archers the chance to fire down on enemy ships. Fighting was still largely hand-to-hand with spears, swords, pikes and bows. Crude cannons were carried, but had not yet been made effective.

The Tudor kings were thoroughly aware just how important a strong navy was if they were not to be overrun by the ambitious kings from the Continent. Henry VIII inherited a great naval force, but his expansion of the fleet gave him the largest permanent fleet in the world. While Alfred the Great had been the first to start a single fleet with the sole idea of protecting England, Henry VIII was the founder of the modern Royal Navy.

The responsibility of managing the King's Ships then rested with the Navy Board, created by Henry VIII, whose members met at a house on Tower Hill, London, and made their reports to the Lord High Admiral. The King's Ships were clearly a different type of ship from the merchant vessels which were roaming further and further afield in search of trade. However, between the wars, royal ships were still hired out to merchants. Guns were being developed rapidly to become the main fighting weapon. These muzzle loaded guns were increasing in size and weight, making them difficult to mount on the open deck. The first gun founders were recruited into the king's service from Flanders, and the important part of Henry VIII's policy was the gathering of experts, particularly Italians, into service at the royal dockyards. As gunnery techniques progressed, so there was need for a new type of ship. The larger cannon petroe, a long-range stone thrower, could hurl a 24lb stone 1,600 paces. Although this was not a very accurate weapon, a ship manned with these could prevent the old style warship coming alongside for hand-to-hand fighting. The next step was the introduction of iron round shot.

The weight of the new guns meant that they had to be placed lower down in the hull. The *Mary Rose*, built in 1513, was the first to have her sides pierced with ports for guns, but the *Henry Grâce à Dieu (Great Harry)* Henry VIII's great warship, built at Woolwich in 1514, also had guns on the lower deck which could only be fired sideways. She still had some 2,000 bows and arrows as an important part of her armoury, as close quarter fighting was still the usual form of sea battle. It was not until after 1568 that guns were used as much to destroy ships as to kill men. For the next 300 years, the 'broadside' was the main firing method for European ships and their overwhelming fire power gave them mastery of the seas.

The ships of Henry VIII sailed under the flag of St George, patron saint of England. Henry VIII's poor grasp of Scottish affairs allowed the French to use Scotland as a pawn to harass England. The old enmity between England and France now had a religious foundation. Henry VIII had firmly committed his kingdom to the new Protestant faith, while France and Spain remained even more firmly committed to the Catholic faith.

The friction led to raids and counter raids. The English took Boulogne in 1544, and in the following year the French sent some 235 ships across the Channel to capture and destroy the English fleet and the dockyard at Portsmouth. The French arrived at the Isle of Wight on 18 July and were forced to anchor off St Helens. The following morning they started off across Spithead to attack Portsmouth. Henry VIII watched from the newly completed Southsea Castle and saw his fleet, led by his flagship the *Mary Rose*, put out of Portsmouth to repulse the attack. As the great 600 ton carrack *Mary Rose* drew away from the land she listed over to starboard and then sank. Besides the crew of 200 sailors, she had soldiers and gunners aboard so that some 415 men were drowned before the king's eyes.

The king's vice-admiral, Sir George Carew, was amongst those drowned and his wife, who was watching from Southsea Castle, collapsed when she saw the ship go down. The king comforted her in person. Sir George's last message was to Sir Gawen Carew on the 600-ton *Matthew Gonson* when he shouted, 'I have the sort of knaves I cannot rule'. It is believed that poor discipline on the *Mary Rose* led to her gunports being opened when she turned and the water rushed in as she heeled. The French lost their flag ship, *La Maistresse*, when she sank on the St Helens shallows the previous day.

The existence of the great Tudor warship *Mary Rose* was dutifully recorded by historians, but the location was forgotten. However, historian Alexander McKee located the exact position from a nineteenth-century chart. Research under water started in 1965, although there were skirmishes with other diving groups wanting to raid the hulk for treasure. It was not until an unmistakable Tudor gun was raised in 1970 that the identity of the *Mary Rose* was confirmed and plans were started to bring her ashore at Portsmouth.

The guns of Southsea Castle had been recently installed and proved to be a vital element in helping to beat off the French. Much attention had been given to fortifying England's vital ports. The Thames was guarded by forts built at Gravesend and Tilbury, while other defensive castles were built at Portland and Cowes. Henry VIII's break with the Church of Rome had heightened fears of an invasion from the great Roman Catholic countries so forts were built at Deal, Sandown, Walmer, Sandgate, also in the West Country at Hurst, St Mawes, Pendennis and Calshot. A fort at Camber, guarding Rye in Sussex, was built with round walls which were better able to withstand cannon fire.

When in 1558 Elizabeth became Queen of England, the country was still in danger of invasion. Had the great Catholic powers united, they could soon have overrun Protestant England and Wales, and Ireland beyond, but France and Spain were bitter rivals. Elizabeth I played one off against the other while slowly building up the strength of her country. Scotland was very much a pawn of France and Elizabeth I spent much of her reign preparing the ground for the peaceful and honourable unity of the Tudor and Stuart kingdoms.

For Elizabeth to have openly challenged the might of France or Spain would have been suicidal. Instead of bringing about a mighty naval confrontation, she encouraged her subjects to plunder her enemies' ships. Throughout the Tudor period there had been a steady build up of national energy and Elizabeth channelled it to make England a major European power.

Elizabeth's principal maritime achievements were really to encourage merchant venturers such as Hawkins, Frobisher and Raleigh and explorers such as Drake. These men could never have been called naval officers: most of them, like Hawkins and Drake, were at times adventurers and at other times in service of the Crown, although even their actions in the Queen's service were often more like piracy than naval operations. However, Elizabeth wisely made Sir John Hawkins her Treasurer of the Navy. Elizabeth greatly disliked having to pay towards the upkeep of her ships and considered it far more profitable to allow Drake to go off raiding so long as she had a share of the takings.

Elizabethan England was playing a dangerous game: it was becoming progressively more established as a Protestant kingdom and at the same time it was openly flouting the great European Catholic powers. Such irritations were bound to provoke retaliation eventually. It was King Philip II of Spain who decided to invade England and bring her firmly back into the Catholic Faith. His early attempts to get together an invasion fleet were completely wrecked by Drake who, in 1587, boldly sailed into Cadiz and 'singed the Spanish King's beard' by sinking Spain's finest war galleys and also destroying their barrel staves so that they had no way of taking their provisions to sea.

This was only a temporary set-back to Philip of Spain's holy crusade and in 1588 the Spanish Armada sailed for the Spanish Netherlands to collect a waiting army before making the final invasion. There was no chance of the Spanish surprising the English because the whole country had been aware of this Armada for several years. When the Armada was sighted in the English Channel, beacons were lit warning of its approach and this signal was passed right along the south coast to Dover.

The main English fleet was commanded by Lord Howard of Effingham in *Ark Royal* who had joined forces with Drake and his fleet. The following day the ordinary merchantmen, converted to warships, came out of Plymouth to join forces. The English fleet consisted of 34 ships with probably over 100 hastily armed merchant ships, and these met around 124 Spanish ships, many of which were far larger than Howard's ships. On 31 July the two fleets came together for the first modern naval battle which did not follow the medieval pattern of immediate hand-to-hand fighting. Howard led his ships in single file but was careful only to attack the tip of the Spanish fleet's 7-mile-long crescent formation.

The English ships, small though they were, soon proved themselves faster and more manoeuvrable than the great Spanish ships. In the sixteenth century no monarch kept a fleet in commission between campaigns, but Elizabeth had allowed John Hawkins, the Treasurer of the Navy, to make some preparations for a major naval confrontation with the Spanish. The English gunnery was slightly better than the Spanish so the strategy adopted was to keep at a distance and bombard the Armada. As the Armada headed slowly up the English Channel, groups of English ships led by Drake in the *Revenge*, Hawkins in the *Victory* and Frobisher in the *Triumph* struck out at any stragglers. The English never attempted to meet the main Armada in battle, simply to weaken it by taking individual ships. Since Drake had spent the past fifteen years fighting a private war against the Spanish, it was hardly surprising that he continued his privateering by trying to capture rich prizes.

For four days as the Armada headed up the Channel, the English captains were greatly worried that the Spanish would try to seize a port to act as their base. However, the Armada's commander, the Duke of Medina Sidonia, had been given orders to wait until he had collected the army from The Netherlands. The English continued to worry the Armada, darting in to destroy or capture any Spanish ship which became separated from the main fleet. Finally the great Armada, still intact and formidable, anchored in Calais Roads. The English at once did the same and the two fleets lay watching each other. Long distance gunnery was out of the question because the cannons were unpredictable and gunpowder was already running very low.

The Spanish were supposed to collect The Netherlands' army from Dunkirk, but to reach it they had to navigate treacherous sandbanks in clumsy ships with the English biting their heels like a pack of terriers. Medina Sidonia was urged by some of his experienced commanders to give up the idea of an invasion of England, but he had had his orders from King Philip and adhered to them. When the English sent fire ships amongst the Armada, Medina Sidonia ordered anchor cables to be cut and the whole Spanish fleet headed north for Dunkirk.

Almost at once the strong North Sea tides broke up the Spanish crescent formation and the increasing wind strength caused many of the ships to get into difficulties. Besides, the delay at Calais had given the English time to assemble in one huge force of some 150 ships. It was Howard's intention to make the final assault on the Armada but this was delayed while English sailors looted a Spanish galley which had gone ashore. Indeed the whole English approach, by twentieth-century standards, was more like a privateering venture than calculated warfare. However, the commanders then and for centuries later regarded looting as being the simplest way to pay their sailors and soldiers. Often it was the only way.

The English now had the advantage of having been able to restock their ammunition after several days of running fighting. The weather was deteriorating and the Armada, through losses, was steadily weakening, with little hope of reaching a Dutch port. Medina Sidonia called off the invasion and decided to round the north of Scotland and return to Spain. The English followed them to the Firth of Forth. Then, satisfied that the Spanish were broken, they returned home. Many of the battered Armada galleys never reached Spain, being driven ashore in gales off Scotland and the west coast of Ireland. There, the Celtic people who knew nothing of and cared less for the ambitions of great kings, happily murdered the survivors and looted the wrecks.

The defeat of the Spanish Armada meant that much of northern Europe stayed Protestant and was an indication of the gradual shift in the centre of power from the Mediterranean to the northern countries. Queen Elizabeth remained at war with Spain until her death in 1603. The accession of James I unified the Kingdom of Scotland with the Kingdom of England which already included the Principality of Wales. James I made peace with Spain and privateering against her ships was outlawed. James I was not particularly interested in naval affairs, but construction of warships naturally continued. In the Stuart period British merchant ships were trading with new markets in Africa, India and China, while colonies were being developed in Virginia, New England, Barbados and Bermuda.

23

Cromwell, once his forces had crushed the Royalist armies and he had become Lord Protector, devoted considerable energy and skill to reorganising the dockyards and the fleet. The Dutch had emerged as Britain's main rival on the seas and all over the world British and Dutch traders were in competition. There was also rivalry over whether The Netherlands or Britain should control the North Sea fishery and trade. The Dutch wars were mainly a series of shore raids and naval battles fought in the English Channel and North Sea. These were not wars over territorial gains or religion but concern over world sea power. Both the Dutch and Royal navies were highly effective fighting forces. Even when King Charles II returned from exile in The Netherlands, the struggle for sea power erupted into a Third Dutch War. At the Admiralty Office, the industrious Samuel Pepys was pushing through many reforms to make sure that the King's fleet was always at top fighting strength. Pepys introduced an examination system for making sure that officers were competent and the Navy List which established an order of promotion. Also, in 1683, a Victualling Board was set up to fix the ration scale which sailors were allowed.

The end of the seventeenth century saw Britain again at war with the French. The crowning British sea victory of this hostility was the Battle of La Hogue in 1692 when Admiral Russell, with sixty-two sail, destroyed a French invasion fleet in the English Channel. In this war the Dutch allied with the British. Most of the fighting was over colonial possession and the Royal Navy was steadily laying the foundations for the growth of the British Empire. For rather uncertain reasons, a combined British and Dutch force under Admiral Sir George Rooke, captured the Rock of Gibraltar in 1704. Sir Cloudesley Shovel took over the Mediterranean command from Rooke and attacked the French naval base at Toulon. Returning to England, Shovell's flagship, the *Association*, and three other ships of his squadron were driven ashore on the Isles of Scilly. The Admiral was among those drowned.

By the time the Treaty of Utrecht was signed in 1713 the Royal Navy was master of the sea and the ambitions of the French King had been squashed. British warships of 100 guns and up to 2,600 tons were remaining at sea for long periods, independent of a land base. Since sugar was of vital importance to Europe, French and British warships spent a great deal of time in the West Indies. Both nations regarded these small sugar islands as being more important than their colonies on the North American mainland. However, what was crippling the efforts of the Royal Navy in foreign waters was not the French guns, but the bad health of her sailors.

The great killer on long ocean voyages was scurvy, the condition brought about by lack of fresh fruit and vegetables. During a voyage of HMS *Salisbury* in 1746–7, the ship's surgeon, James Lind (1716–94), tried to trace the origins of scurvy. He published his findings and recommended that a daily ration of lemon juice should be given to sailors on long voyages. This was not done until after his death when, in 1795, a Vitamin C substitute, lime, which was cheaper than lemon, was issued in the Royal Navy. The result was incredible: in 1760 the Haslar Hospital at Gosport admitted 1,754 cases of scurvy while in 1806 it had only one case. The outcome of Trafalgar might have been very different if the health of the British sailor had not been good. In spite of lime juice proving so successful in the Royal Navy, scurvy remained common in the Merchant Navy. It was not until 1844 that lime juice had to be served on merchant ships. Right to the end of the age of sail, British sailing ships were known all over the seven seas as 'lime juicers'.

Although serious attention was paid to the sailors' health, the Royal Navy did not prove a sufficiently attractive career to obviate the need for impressment. A few lower deck 'jolly jack tars' actually volunteered for service in the great wooden warships, but never enough. In the recruiting Act of 1795 every parish was supposed to supply a 'quota of men' for the Navy, but the men sent were usually petty criminals and the social misfits whom the local people wanted to be rid of. To make up the numbers still needed, the press gangs roamed the ports and raided merchant ships, literally dragging men off to serve in the Navy. The remainder were made up from the jails. Once aboard, the pressed men were not allowed ashore in case they deserted. The sailors seem to have accepted their enforced lot cheerfully. Only at times of gross neglect and harsh treatment did they refuse duty. This happened in 1797 when, largely because they had not been paid, the sailors in Sir Roger Curtis' squadron in Spithead and the North Sea fleet at the Nore mutinied and put their officers ashore. This was not out of disloyalty but frustration and once the grievances had been corrected the men returned to duty. There were plenty of revolutionary hot heads in the fleet intent on using the mutiny to create havoc, but the good humoured sense of the ordinary British seamen prevailed.

The Royal Navy had long carried Marines for short shore raids, and they were also useful to keep the impressed 'Jack Tars' under control. At the time of the revolution of the American colonists in 1775, the Marines were strong in number and the Navy used them as a kind of private army. The loss of the American colonies was not followed by any reduction in the size of the fleet. In 1783 the Royal Navy had about 112 ships-of-the-line divided into 1st, 2nd and 3rd raters. Of these only about 20 were 1st raters with 100 or more guns and there were frigates and smaller craft.

It was at this strength when yet another European war broke out.

Previously war had been fought for religious and territorial reasons, but the French Revolutionary Wars were ostensibly fought over ethical principles. Having swept away, with considerable help from the guillotine, the old order of government, the French continued the revolution by declaring war on other countries.

Like most revolutions, what started as a crusade soon turned into a struggle for power and the leaders distorted the original ideals for their own ends. The brilliant young soldier Napoleon Bonaparte quickly emerged as the leader of the new French Empire. On the European continent nearly every country was beaten in battle by Napoleon or reluctantly joined his armies. Whenever Napoleon reached the sea his progress was thwarted by the Royal Navy.

It was Horatio Nelson who finally ended Napoleon's attempt to vanquish the Royal Navy. Nelson was never a popular man with British royalty, politicians or his naval superiors, but his victories at sea and his just treatment of his men made him the popular hero of the Napoleonic Wars. With Admiral Lord St Vincent, Nelson was active in reforming conditions in the Navy. In 1798, Nelson's tactical plan captured and destroyed an entire French fleet in Egyptian waters, making the Battle of the Nile one of the most decisive naval victories ever achieved. The Battle of Copenhagen in 1801 was also won due to Nelson's brilliance. After putting a telescope to his blind eye so that he did not see a signal from his superior Admiral ordering him to withdraw, he led in a fleet and destroyed the ships which might have given Napoleon the upper hand in northern European waters.

After this, the Royal Navy slowly tightened its grip on Europe with a complete blockade which prevented most cargo ships reaching French-controlled ports. In 1805, Napoleon, in a desperate bid to break Britain's sea power, ordered the combined French and Spanish fleets to leave harbour and attack the British. When the combined fleet came out of Cadiz in southern Spain, Nelson was in the Atlantic with his fleet spread out looking for them. When they finally met off Cape Trafalgar the Royal Navy ships of the line closed in knowing that they were about to fight a decisive battle. On the *Victory* the coxswain found that the sloop carrying the mail had already sailed for England without a letter that he had written to his wife. Nelson heard of this and at once ordered, 'Hoist the signal to bring her back, who knows but that this man may fall in action tomorrow.'

This was part of the 'Nelson touch' and when the next day, 21 October, came, the British fleet used Nelson's revolutionary tactics to destroy the combined fleets of the French and Spanish. While walking openly on the *Victory*'s deck during the battle, Nelson was shot by a French marine from the fighting top on the mast of a French ship. He was carried below but died, aged forty-eight, at the height of his achievements. Trafalgar was the last major battle of the age of sail except for one in 1827 when the combined fleets of Britain, France and Russia destroyed the Turkish fleet in Navarino Bay. Although France's seapower was crippled by Trafalgar, Napoleon was not completely crushed on land until the Battle of Waterloo, by which time the Royal Navy was the most powerful in the world with some 700 ships all over the globe. Even before the Napoleonic Wars, a revolution in Britain was well under way. In this case it was the Industrial Revolution, based on the steam engine and coal. As the potential output of great iron foundries, factories and cotton mills increased, more overseas markets were needed for their products. Trading ports were set up all round the world and the Royal Navy's duty was to keep the high seas free so that British merchant ships were not attacked. To maintain ships over such a wide area, the Royal Navy needed new bases abroad, and the introduction of steam ships created a need for coaling stations along the ocean routes.

HMS Victory, *permanently on public display at Portsmouth, is there as a reminder of Nelson's victory at the Battle of Trafalgar in 1805. This remarkable man-of-war was also at the Battle of Ushant in 1778, the relief of Gibraltar in 1782, the capture of Toulon in 1792 and was flagship of Saumarez in the Baltic between 1808–12*
(Author)

What started as a collection of trading posts and naval bases snowballed into the British Empire. Many overseas rulers were willing to place themselves under the protection of the British Empire, but others resisted and had to be overcome by military intervention. The Royal Navy's vital role of keeping the sea lanes open was thoroughly understood by the public, and they were proud that Britain, with its comparatively small population, could be such a tremendous sea power.

It was in gratitude for the Royal Navy's role of keeping the seas open for commerce that Giffard Reade gave the Holbrook Estate on the banks of the River Stour, Suffolk, to the Admiralty in 1921. The Reade fortunes had come from trade with India and Giffard Reade felt that the wealth should go back to the Royal Navy to help them maintain their position at sea. The Lord High Admiral, faced with the decision of what to do with this gift, eventually gave it to the Royal Hospital School at Greenwich who then moved down to Holbrook in 1933, continuing their school for boys who intended making a career at sea.

Although there was no major conflict for forty years after the Napoleonic Wars, the Royal Navy was not short of work. Britain took on the role of policing the seas so that not just her own ships, but every merchant vessel, could move freely. This started with a British Naval Squadron bombarding the piracy stronghold at Algiers in 1816, and forcing the Bey to release his Christian slaves. The East India Company had its own warships to deal with pirates from the Persian Gulf, but the Navy joined in this action besides dealing with pirates on the Barbary coast, The Levant, Borneo and the China Sea. The Royal Navy was also used to stamp out the slave trade. Ships were stopped at sea, and the refuges of pirates and slavers on the west coast of Africa were raided.

For the first half of the nineteenth century, the Royal Navy remained firmly committed to the ship-of-the-line with three decks of guns. These were the 'wooden walls' which had won Trafalgar and the Admiralty and the public retained great faith in them. Even after regular transatlantic voyages had been made by passenger steamers, the Admiralty would still have little to do with steam engines. The reason was that in battle under gunfire, a steamer with paddles could have been put out of action quickly. In 1837 a screw steamer on the Thames towed an Admiralty barge from Somerset House to Limehouse at 10 knots and the Admiralty became aware of steam's potential. In 1845 the Admiralty had accepted steam and in order to decide which form of propulsion was the most powerful, a tug of war was held by the screw sloop *Rattler* and the paddle sloop *Alecto*. The *Rattler* won and the Navy decided to adopt the screw, although there was inevitably a long transitional period.

The HMS *Agamemnon*, launched at Woolwich in 1852, was the first

The introduction of shells made the wooden man-of-war very vulnerable. Between 1860–75 many wooden warships became 'ironclad' when the hull was encased by sheets of metal. Here HMS Royal Oak *is being clad with iron at Chatham in about 1862*
(National Maritime Museum)

battleship launched with an engine. Previously engines had been fitted to existing ships. There was nothing particularly revolutionary about this ship because she was still a wooden walled ship-of-the-line firing broadside, and she was still manned by men who signed on for one commission. The officers were in naval service in a semi-permanent way, but the Admiralty did not have a regular force. This was changed when sailors joined the Navy on a definite term of service. The long period of world peace ended in 1853 when Russia invaded Turkey around the Black Sea. Britain and France were alarmed that Imperial Russia had gained a naval base linked to the Mediterranean and sent forces to the Crimea to combat the Russian menace.

Both Britain and France had forgotten the art of large-scale military offensives and the Crimean War was a series of blunders with the Russians remaining on the Black Sea. The Crimean War also marked the end of men-of-war because they proved useless against shell fire from Russian shore batteries. In a wooden hull a hole from the old solid shot

HMS Warrior, *when launched on the Thames in 1860, outgunned every other warship afloat. To make her hull sides shell-proof, she had three skins, 1in of wrought iron, 18in of teak, a further 4in of wrought iron as an outer layer; she also had watertight bulkheads. Under engines she could make 14 knots, but she was credited with over 16 knots under sail and power. When she was under sail, the single screw, which weighed 10 tons, was lifted out of the water by some 600 men manning tackles. She is currently being refitted at West Hartlepool* (National Maritime Museum)

cannons could be quickly plugged, but exploding shells ripped a wooden hull to pieces. In 1855 both France and Britain completed new wooden-hulled ships which were protected by 4in iron plates. The Crimean War also hastened another change with the establishment of the Royal Naval Reserve in 1859, so that there was always a pool of trained sailors available in case of war. The system whereby the Navy's squadrons sailed under separate red, blue and white ensigns was ended in 1864, after which all ships sailed under the White Ensign. The Royal Naval Reserve, the Custom Service and later some yacht clubs, flew the Blue Ensign while the remaining merchant vessels and yachts flew the Red Ensign.

Once the Crimean War was over, Britain and France quickly returned to their old roles as rival empire builders in which control of the sea was a vital factor. The French took the lead by building *Gloire*, a wooden warship with iron armour propelled by steam and sail. Alarmed that they had been overtaken, the Lords of the Admiralty responded by building their first ironclad, HMS *Warrior*, launched in 1860. The *Warrior* had teak between iron plates, but the use of iron meant that she could be built much longer than wooden men-of-war. The Royal Navy described the revolutionary *Warrior* as a frigate, but she was more powerful than any battleship afloat. Napoleon III called *Warrior* the 'black snake amongst the rabbits' and although she was never used in serious action, she once again restored Britain's lead.

The day the *Warrior* was commissioned, all wooden men-of-war became useless against a shell-firing ship with a protected hull. The Navy used old ships-of-the-line as store hulls and training ships anchored in harbours. The *Victory*, because of her association with Nelson, was later preserved, and so was the 46-gun frigate *Foudroyant* which was built as the *Trincomalee* at Bombay in 1816. Both the *Victory* and the unrigged *Foudroyant* are still at Portsmouth. Another survivor of the days of sail is the 46-gun frigate *Unicorn*, built at Chatham Naval Dockyard. Her keel was laid in 1794 but she was not finally completed until 1824. Since the country was at peace she was never commissioned and, after long periods as a storage hulk, she became a Royal Naval Reserve Headquarters at the Earl Grey Dock, Dundee, in 1873.

Even if wooden walls could not withstand shell fire, they were still tough enough to last a long time. The 144-year-old *Implacable* was scuttled in the English Channel by the Navy in 1949. She had fought as the French *Duguay Trouin* at Trafalgar and been captured by Sir Richard Strachan's squadron three weeks later. In 1953, the 114-year-old, 94-gun *Conway*,

A group of officers aboard HMS Warrior *in about 1864. Standing on the right is Lt John Fisher who later, as an Admiral, was responsible for the introduction of the Dreadnought battleships* (National Maritime Museum)

The Royal yacht Victoria & Albert *at the Spithead Coronation Review in 1902. This was taken from HMS* Royal Sovereign *(National Maritime Museum)*

which had fought in the Crimean War, went ashore and broke her back while being towed through the Menai Straits.

Even the *Warrior* was soon outclassed and became a coal hulk and then an oiling platform at Pembroke Dock in Milford Haven. As a result of lessons learnt in building the *Warrior* and her sistership the *Black Prince*, the Admiralty had the 400ft ram-bowed HMS *Agincourt* built at Birkenhead in 1865. The *Agincourt* had a speed of 7½ knots from her 1,250hp engine, but was unusual for this period in having five masts. There is a story that in a fog another ship mistook her for a normal three master and tried to go under her stern, striking the *Agincourt* smartly amidships. The *Agincourt* was flagship for fifteen different Admirals, but in the long palmy days of British Naval supremacy, she fired more in salute than in anger. In 1909 she became a coal hulk and was at Sheerness until being towed away for breaking up on Trafalgar Day, 21 October, in 1960. On the same day Queen Elizabeth II launched the 3,500 ton *Dreadnought*, Britain's first nuclear submarine.

There was a steady development in the Victorian Navy. Nelson's *Victory* was armed with 3-ton guns while the *Warrior* carried 9-ton muzzle loading guns, but HMS *Captain* of 1869 was fitted with gun turrets protecting 25-ton shell firing guns. In 1871 came the first true mastless battleship, HMS *Devastation*, which was fitted with 35-ton guns in two central turrets. This layout was to prove the basis for future development, the weight of guns increasing to 110 tons.

The big gun era had arrived, but it was not these battleships which made the impact on colonial expansion; they were rarely used in the frequent colonial wars in which small gunboats predominated. The Navy was very active with its gunboats. Some gunboats were seagoing ship-rigged steamers while others were small shallow draft steamers with only a few guns, but they could travel up rivers to deliver troops, marines or even the 'blue jackets' themselves to subdue hostile rulers and chiefs.

British Naval policy during the Victorian period was, roughly, to have two ships to every commission in the current rival navy. This was not seriously challenged until Imperial Germany, bursting with energy from its own industrial revolution, developed colonial aspirations, inevitably seeing Britain's sea power as an obstacle. From 1897 Germany used her technological skill to become a major naval power in five years. Worried by what was happening, Britain increased her naval strength and France, Russia, Italy, America and Japan all joined in the naval armament race. This resulted in Britain's Naval supremacy being in doubt.

HMS Dreadnought, *launched in 1905, opened the era of the 'all-big-gun' battleships*
(Science Museum)

HMS Vengeance *at Portsmouth Naval Dockyard in about 1901. Shells are probably being put aboard from the sailing barge alongside* (National Maritime Museum)

Between 1904–10 Admiral Sir 'Jackie' Fisher was First Sea Lord, and this dynamic man shook off the peace-time role of simply going round foreign ports 'showing the flag' and put the Navy on a war footing. To meet the mounting German challenge, Fisher ordered the HMS *Dreadnought*, the world's first all big gun ship. Previously battleships had carried four big guns and many lighter ones. *Dreadnought* carried ten 12in guns and her top speed of $21\frac{1}{2}$ knots enabled her to outrun any

34

battleship in the world. For three years Britain had an unquestionable lead, but both Germany and the United States had started a building programme of capital ships capable of meeting the dreadnought battle-ships on equal terms. However, Germany had still not managed to equal Britain's battleship strength by the outbreak of war in 1914.

The opening phase of World War I saw naval engagements such as the Battle of Heligoland Bight in 1914 and the battles of Dogger Bank and the Falkland Islands in 1915, but these were not decisive big ship 'Trafalgar' actions. The main German High Seas Fleet spent most of its time in port, safely protected by minefields. The Kaiser was reluctant to allow his fleet to go to sea at all, although Admiral von Tirpitz was anxious to challenge

British sea power with the battle fleet he had created. Finally, in May 1916, Admiral Scheer was allowed to take the High Seas Fleet out into the North Sea, largely because there was a stalemate in the trench warfare on land.

For some two years the Royal Navy's Grand Fleet had been waiting at its base in Scapa Flow for a chance to meet the High Seas Fleet. British intelligence was picking up the German radio signals, enabling Admiral Jellicoe, commander of the British fleet in HMS *Iron Duke*, to intercept the High Seas Fleet off the coast of Jutland. When the two fleets met, it was late in the day and both Scheer and Jellicoe were very aware that to lose this battle meant literally to lose the war. With darkness approaching events overtook both Admirals and neither was able to score a decisive victory.

In all some 250 warships were involved in the action which lit up the whole horizon with gun flashes. The German gunnery proved more accurate, the British armour piercing shells were defective and the British fleet suffered higher losses because their magazines were not so well protected against fire. Also the German ships were more manoeuvrable. Admiral Beatty, in command of the cruisers based at Rosyth, summed up the situation while standing on the bridge of the battle-cruiser HMS *Lion* when he said 'there seems to be something wrong with our bloody ships today'.

Jellicoe tried to place the Grand Fleet between the Germans and their home ports, but by dawn Scheer had slipped through and returned to port. Both sides claimed a great victory. The Germans had done better in that they had lost only eleven ships and 2,500 men while the British had lost fourteen ships, including three battle-cruisers, and 6,000 men, but it can be seen as a British victory because the German fleet never went to sea again in force during the war.

The Battle of Jutland marked the end of the era of the battleships being the invincible warship although it took World War II and the use of a fleet air arm to prove this. With the failure of Jutland to give them supremacy at sea, the Germans switched from surface ships to submarines. The German U-boat campaign, which proved so successful against allied shipping that it almost starved Britain and France into collapse, reached a peak in August 1917 when 1,349 British and Allied ships were sunk. This situation was the first major naval crisis since Trafalgar, and made the anti-submarine campaign of 1917–18 the Royal Navy's most difficult challenge of the war. By November 1917 no fewer than 2,932 warships were employed to combat 170 German U-boats. The introduction of the convoy system meant that in the last eighteen months of the war only 102 ships were torpedoed and sunk during ocean voyages.

In spite of the obvious success of the original U-boat campaign, naval thinking on both sides remained in 'big ship' terms. In the closing months of the war, battle cruisers of 43,500 tons and capable of 30 knots were under construction. However, the steady crumbling of Germany's land offensive meant that she had to negotiate an armistice to prevent social collapse. In a last desperate bid to gain sea power the German Naval High Command ordered their High Seas Fleet to put to sea, but the sailors, suspicious that this was nothing more than a senseless effort to regain honour after the humiliation of Jutland, mutinied and refused to go to sea. A week later Germany signed the Armistice and the High Seas Fleet was ordered to steam across the North Sea and surrender to the British Grand Fleet in Scapa Flow. After long negotiations the whole German Fleet was scuttled by its own officers to prevent it being handed over to the British.

The signing of the Treaty of Versailles in 1919 officially marked the end of the 'war to end all wars'. The League of Nations was formed to prevent a repetition of the conflict; Britain, France and Italy all demobilised and Germany was stripped of any military force. The Royal Navy had some eighteen capital ships under construction when World War I ended, but following a conference in Washington in 1922, the main naval powers agreed to restrict their fleets. Although the era of intended British colonial expansion had ended, the Empire in fact grew because Britain took over many of Germany's former overseas possessions, particularly in West Africa. This meant that Britain was responsible for controlling and policing about a third of the world's land surface but since several industrially developed nations now had sizeable navies, Britain was no longer overall lord of the seas.

Before World War I most political leaders and the public considered Britain had every right to use her naval power to dominate world affairs. In practice it is doubtful if the Royal Navy really did have complete naval supremacy since Japan, Russia, France, Austro-Hungary, Holland, Italy and Germany all had battleships, but most nations believed that Britain ruled the seas and treated her accordingly. After Germany had almost cut Britain and France off from American supplies with her submarine campaign in World War I, no one was quite so confident in the power of the Royal Navy. There were in Britain, in the interwar years, two sharply divided opinions as to the role of the Royal Navy.

(overleaf) HMS Orion *shortly before launching at Portsmouth on 20 August 1910. The foreman in the middle of the group rang the bell to beat the rhythm for the men to knock out the wedges in unison, ready for the actual launching* (National Maritime Museum)

One body of thinking wanted the Royal Navy to once more out-build every other nation with new capital ships. The other body of thinking was appalled by the carnage of World War I and wanted lasting peace, not imperial achievement. The actual naval policy was in effect somewhere in the middle of these two attitudes. Britain did build new ships because she wanted to protect the sea routes to her Empire, but at the same time the Admiralty was not given the financial resources to build on a scale that had been undertaken in the run up to World War I. Britain also adhered to the Washington and London treaties which limited the size of navies.

There were other policy decisions which affected the size and role of the Royal Navy between the two great World Wars. Firstly, for much of the time there was a serious world depression and there was no money available for maintaining a navy on the pre-World War I scale. Secondly the opinion within the Navy was rather divided as to which vessels were the capital ships. The submarines had left serious doubts about the effectiveness of a battleship. However, many British admirals who decided navy affairs remained firmly committed to the 'Big Gun' ships. Events proved that this was wrong. The aircraft carrier became the capital fighting ship of World War II.

Another influence on naval affairs in the interwar years were the various international conferences which were genuinely attempting to

HMS Ark Royal *was under construction as an oil tanker by Blyth Shipbuilding Co when the Admiralty bought her and had her completed as the first ship on which planes could land on the deck. At 7,080 tons displacement,* Ark Royal *soon proved too small for an aircraft carrier. The first purpose-built craft carrier was HMS* Hermes, *which was completed by 1917* (Science Museum)

The bridge on HMS Rodney *was placed well aft, although this view does not give the true impression of the long foredeck. When the* Rodney *was completed in 1928, the idea of a tall bridge structure was to offer better resistance to shell-blast than the bridges of the type seen astern* (Science Museum)

secure world peace by trying to limit the size of the world's naval forces. This did not stop the naval designers from trying to produce a battleship which could out-gun all possible opponents. In 1922 HMS *Nelson* was designed in the beginning of a new age of long range gunnery, but she had great emphasis laid on her bulkhead defence systems against torpedoes which indicated that the admirals were just as concerned about her being attacked by submarines as any other battleship. There was growing awareness of air attack because both *Nelson* and her sister ship *Rodney* were designed with high-velocity high-angle weapons. These two 35,000 ton Nelson class battleships, completed in 1927, were the first battleships built after World War I and were limited in size by international treaty. Britain's position as a leading naval power was still maintained in the interwar years. In 1932 Britain had sixty cruisers alone in her navy, spread around the world showing the flag to maintain good will amongst the colonial countries and friendly nations.

The Royal Navy remained committed to the 'Big Gun' ships because the submarine had not replaced the need for battleships in World War I. However, while the battleships could have defended themselves against submarines they were very vulnerable to air attack. Aircraft development had reached a point in the 1930s where it was becoming increasingly clear that seapower would in the future depend upon the air space above it. The Royal Air Force was responsible for air defence, but the navy had a small Fleet Air Arm. The effects of the depression and the public reluctance to have money spent on the armed forces meant that the size of the Navy was totally inadequate for the task it was required for during the opening stages of World War II.

By the late 1930s Hitler was overrunning neighbouring European countries. Britain attempted to stay out of another European conflict but it soon became clear that a joint effort would have to be made to control the insane ambitions of Nazi Germany. In the autumn of 1939 Britain and France declared war on Germany. In his rise to power Hitler had neither the time, money, nor patience to build up a fleet of battleships although he did bend the treaty rules by building three 'pocket battleships'. Britain's naval force, at the start of World War II, was less than in 1914, but she still had 22 'Big Gun' capital ships and about 80 cruisers as her main force.

Hitler's main objective was to overrun France as quickly as possible and this was achieved. Britain sent an Expeditionary Force to help the French, but this was driven back to the coast by the German army. The British army made for Dunkirk but bombing put the port out of action so that many weary troops had to be evacuated from the open sandy beaches. Because the sea off Dunkirk was shallow the Admiralty organised for dozens of small fishing boats, barges and yachts to help in May 1940. The 'little ships' ferried the troops out, under enemy fire, to the waiting ships but the greater part of approximately 330,000 men recovered in the Dunkirk evacuation were lifted in the destroyers. This provided enough of the expeditionary force to act as a backbone for founding a new British army.

The Royal Navy was more prepared for a major European war than the other services. Typical of the cruisers which Britain had started to build again was HMS *Belfast*, built by Harland & Wolff in 1937. She was a 'town' 9,000 ton, 32 knot cruiser with nine 6in guns and was chiefly in operation in the North Atlantic. The opening months of the war went very well for the Royal Navy because it managed to track down and put out of action the German 'pocket' battleships and other surface raiders, but the lack of proper air cover soon led to heavy British losses. The importance of air power linked to sea power was brought out when

Swordfish torpedo bombers, flying from an aircraft carrier, crippled three of Italy's battleships in one raid in the Mediterranean.

Hitler expanded his U-boat campaign to prevent Britain receiving vital war supplies from North America. Germany's Admiral Doenitz proclaimed in 1940 that the 'U-boat alone can win this war', and he was nearly proved right. The British quickly adopted the convoy system for merchant ships on coastal, North Atlantic and Mediterranean routes. Perhaps the most difficult of these convoys were those sailing to Russian ports which entailed going into the appalling conditions of the Arctic Circle. To begin with the Germans caused havoc with the convoy system and the U-boat commanders spoke of this period as being a 'happy time'. At the beginning of 1942 the Americans were losing ships at a rate of 400,000 tons a month and the British around 240,000 tons. However most of the American losses were in coastal waters with ships not in convoys and silhouetted against shore lights. British losses were mostly in the 'gap' in the middle of the Atlantic where there was no air cover.

The Battle of the Atlantic cost the allies 6·2 million tons of shipping in 1942, a total of some 3,000 merchant ships; the Royal Navy lost 100 ships in a year keeping the convoys sailing. Rarely did the Germans have more than 60 U-boats at sea at any one time, and only an average of 25 of these were in the North Atlantic. The British 'backroom boys' fought back with inventions such as asdic for tracing submarines under water and the tide was turned against the U-boat 'wolf packs'. The Royal Navy used cruisers, destroyers and frigates for convoy protection and the small corvettes, which were built at great speed in small commercial shipping yards, were most successful. However, the most important fact in making the convoy system safe was the building of small carriers which provided air cover all the time the convoys were at sea. The Royal Navy's strength at the end of World War II was about 14 battleships, 52 aircraft carriers, 62 cruisers, 257 destroyers, 131 submarines and 9,000 other ships ranging from frigates to landing craft. The last battleship to be built was the 42,000-ton HMS *Vanguard* in 1944. She was commissioned too late for service in World War II and was the last battleship afloat when broken up in 1960.

The Royal Navy had by then moved into another age of even more terrible destruction. Typical of the Royal Navy's new capital fighting ships was HMS *Resolution*, a 7,000-ton ballistic nuclear submarine launched by Vickers at Barrow in 1966. Her main armament was Polaris missiles with a range of 2,500 miles. With the nuclear submarine, Holy Loch on the Clyde had become an important naval base.

As Britain's place in world affairs changed, so did the role of the Royal Navy. The duty of defending what was the Empire has been left largely to the new nations of the British Commonwealth. The creation of separate national navies started with the Indian Navy: the first force responsible for the defence of India was four ships belonging to the East India Company, in 1612. This fleet moved through six different name changes to finally become the Royal Indian Navy in 1934. The Indian ships were mainly gunboats with British officers and Indian crews, and were controlled by Britain until India's independence in 1947. Difficulties over the granting of independence to former colonies gave the Royal Navy and the Marines a new post-war role.

The British Dominions, in which the bulk of the population were descended from immigrants from the British Isles were encouraged to organise their own defence. Most Dominion navies were formed after the Imperial Conference of 1909. The burden of the arms race with Imperial Germany prompted Britain to ask the Dominions for help. Australia was the first to set up her own navy, between 1911–13, and had a battle-cruiser in World War I. Canadian politicians at first believed that they could defend their huge new land mass with an army moved by train, but public pressure caused a Navy to be formed between 1911–15. New Zealand at first paid to maintain ships of the Royal Navy, but later set up her own force. The South African Naval Forces were started in 1923. The Royal Navy was responsible for training and usually provided the first ships.

World War II created a more realistic approach to world peace. The United Nations was formed to start the very long process of persuading all nations to live in peace, but at the same period the United States and her democratic allies in western Europe established a united armed force to combat any attempt on any individual nation's sovereignty. This force, the North Atlantic Treaty Organisation, was formed in 1949 so that small nations would not be overrun through lack of co-operation as they had been in Hitler's war. Britain's fellow members of NATO are the USA, France, Belgium, Luxembourg, Canada, Denmark, Iceland, Norway, Italy and Portugal. Greece and Turkey became members although at one stage they went to war over Cyprus.

The awareness of the importance of aircraft in previous confrontations has encouraged the Navy to develop sophisticated ship-based helicopters for anti-submarine duties. Furthering the policy of counteracting the threat of submarines with aircraft has led to the creation of a class of 16,000 ton anti-submarine carriers. The first of these, HMS *Invincible*, was the largest and most expensive surface warship built for the Royal Navy since World War II when launched at Vicker's yard, Barrow-in-Furness, in 1977. She was followed by HMS *Illustrious*, built on the Tyne at Swan Hunter's Wallsend yard in 1978, which was followed by the *Ark*

Royal from the same yard in 1981. This means that Britain has three carriers out of a total world force of about twenty.

Britain's position as a world naval power ranks her third in size and her ships are amongst the most technically advanced. The *Invincible*, for instance, has the British 'ski-jump' idea for easier take off by Sea Harrier aircraft. NATO carriers have adopted the angled deck, to allow more aircraft to be carried, and the mirrored landing sights which were invented by the Royal Navy.

Many of the Navy's new ships in recent decades have been frigates with radar controlled guns, ship-to-air missiles and anti-submarine equipment. These ships, with their mass of technical equipment, allowed fewer ships to have far higher striking power than ever before. The new technical age necessitated clear thinking and to this end the daily 'rum rations' for sailors have been abolished.

Another long chapter of naval history closed in 1964 when all Britain's forces were placed under the control of the Ministry of Defence. Since Pepys' time, the Royal Navy had been controlled by the Lords of the Admiralty.

The basic role of the Royal Navy has not changed since the first ships followed King Alfred the Great to beat off attacks from the Vikings—to defend the shores and ships of Britain against any attackers. In Alfred's time this meant in effect southern England, while this role now means England, Wales, Scotland, Northern Ireland, the Isle of Man and the Channel Islands. In order to strengthen our position, the Royal Navy has strong links with some of the navies in the British Commonwealth. The Standing Naval Force Atlantic, NATO's multi-national fleet of warships, has destroyers and frigates from six nations. Some of these nations have at some time in the past centuries been our enemies. The presence of a multi-national force at least gives hope for the future, that one day nations will be able to co-exist in peace with some form of international force policing the seas.

2

Exploration of the Sea

The majority of people living in medieval Britain naturally had a limited knowledge of the world. Most knew only their village and nearest market town, and beyond that it was speculation and heresay. The existence of some foreign kings and the Holy Land was common knowledge, but the exact location of such places was indistinct until first-hand accounts of the Holy Land were brought home by those who had been on the Crusades. Men of learning and merchants knew of the existence of the East and that it was a source of luxury goods and wealth, but it was too far away to reach.

The various groups of people living in the British Isles were really on the edge of the civilised world, which revolved around the Mediterranean. The Vikings had made voyages to North America, but it was the Portuguese who had started making regular voyages of discovery which led to western European nations discovering and linking up the entire world's surface.

Because of trade links a great deal of knowledge about the East was known in the Italian city states. It was the Italian dreamer and adventurer Christopher Columbus who managed to talk King Ferdinand and Queen Isabella of Spain into financing a voyage in 1492 which resulted in the discovery of the West Indies. The news of Columbus' discovery excited thinking men all over western Europe. It was another Italian, John Cabot, who, when living in England, saw that if Columbus had failed to reach China and India because of some islands, then he might make a voyage to the fabulous East by sailing farther to the north.

Before he undertook his voyage of exploration, Cabot is believed to have travelled from Venice to the eastern Mediterranean in search of a trade route to Asia. Of course this route to India was barred by Muslims who would not allow Christians into their lands. Cabot had been in London as a merchant and then moved to Bristol where he managed to persuade the merchants to back a voyage of discovery in search of trade routes to the East. He also needed permission for such a voyage from King Henry VII and agreed to pay a share of trade profits.

Columbus had sailed with a fleet provided by Spain but John Cabot left Bristol on 2 May 1497 in only one small ship, the *Matthew*, with his son Sebastian and seventeen local men as crew. The men of Bristol and their ships were used to trading with Spain, Bordeaux and Ireland so they understood deepwater sailing and had the adventurous spirit needed for a voyage of exploration. The King had forbidden them to sail in southern trade wind routes because Spain or Portugal would seize the *Matthew* for venturing into what was considered to be their seas. Instead Cabot had to sail straight out into the open Atlantic in his bid to reach the great spice and silk markets of the East.

Fifty-four days after leaving Bristol, land was sighted and the *Matthew* coasted around in the hope of finding a wealthy city but being unsuccessful they returned back to England. It is generally believed that the land Cabot actually found and claimed was Cape Breton Island in the Canadian Province of Nova Scotia. Of course, centuries before the Vikings had been this way, but that had been forgotten. Cabot, the Italian adventurer, was the first to rediscover the North American continent. He thought that this was Asia and returned a hero to London. The following May, Cabot sailed again with five ships and 300 men, carrying goods for trade. They headed a little further north this time, hoping like European men for centuries to come, to find a North-West sea route to India but were not heard of again. Because these voyages were an obvious commercial flop, the exploration of new lands stopped.

It was over a quarter of a century before another English captain, John Rut, made another attempt to discover the North-West passage in 1527.

The Valkyrja, *built in North Devon in 1975 as a replica of the Gokstad Viking ship, shows how exposed were the Dark Age and medieval ships. The crews camped ashore as much as possible* (Author)

Over this century the quest to discover such a passage fired the imagination of countless explorers. The Breton explorer, Jacques Cartier, sailed in 1535 in search of the North-West route to Japan and instead was the first European to sail up the St Lawrence River. This was the beginning of France's colonies in North America and eventually the cause of colonial competition with England.

Early adventurers were usually in search of quick wealth, although they mostly claimed new lands in the name of their sovereigns as a gesture to gain political favour when they returned home. The next stage, colonisation, was seen as an extension of the sovereign's territory. England's statesmen were aware that Spain and Portugal were deriving wealth and advantage as a result of their explorations. Spain in particular jealously guarded her trade routes to the New World and the gold which came from the West Indies and central and southern America.

Queen Elizabeth I clearly wanted to make profitable discoveries but she had to be careful not to offend the Spanish. Few English expeditions openly received Royal backing, but Elizabeth I and her court were deeply concerned with them. It was against this background of political intrigue that Sir Martin Frobisher made three voyages between 1576–8 to try to find the North-West passage to Cathay (China). None were successful and Frobisher and the shareholders lost a great deal of money.

The exact part Elizabeth I played in organising these voyages has never quite been determined, but it is fairly certain they would not have taken place if she had disapproved. It is typical of the shrewd queen that while one adventurer was trying to reach the Pacific via the North-West passage, she allowed another ship to try to sail round the southern end of the American continent. It was known that there was a sea route round the South Atlantic and the Pacific because Ferdinand Magellan had sailed that way half a century before. However, Spain used the overland route in central America to reach the Pacific and had already developed trade in this great ocean. Most of this trade came from working the Peruvian gold mines, and this source of wealth proved a great attraction to the Elizabethan adventurer, Francis Drake.

In 1577 Francis Drake sailed from Plymouth with five ships bound, everyone was told, for Turkey, but once clear of land, the seamen were told that they were really going on a voyage to the Pacific to raid the Spanish treasure fleets. Although England was at peace with Spain, the destination of Turkey had been given to mislead the Spaniards so that they did not trouble the expedition at an early stage. The seamen seemed to accept the change of plan fairly readily; it represented more gold, although the danger from the sea and the Spanish were greater. There was tension at an early stage between Drake and Thomas Doughty, his

48

On the replica **Golden Hinde,** *the Elizabethan practice has been followed of decorating the hull with bright paint work and leaving the rest of the wooden hull treated with fish oils. The square spritsail under the bowsprit is a very powerful pulling sail, but difficult to handle. These sails dropped out of general use in the late eighteenth century when the fore-and-aft headsails were found much easier to handle* (Golden Hinde Project)

second-in-command. Drake was an extremely demanding man, a seaman by profession, half pirate and half Protestant crusader by inclination. Doughty was a gentleman who undoubtedly thought of the ship's captain as being inferior. However, Lord Burleigh, who was opposed to the expedition because of the damage it would cause to Anglo-Spanish relations, apparently instructed Doughty to sabotage the expedition.

Just over six months after leaving Plymouth, Drake's fleet, which had already captured a Portuguese ship and was using her captain as a pilot, arrived at the remote Port St Julian on the South American coast. Here Drake tried Doughty, and having found him guilty of disloyalty and attempting to incite a mutiny, had him beheaded. Later in the voyage, after seizing several Spanish ships loaded with treasure, Drake calmly put the helpful Portuguese captain ashore to whatever fate the enraged Spanish chose to give him.

Drake found a safe way through the Straits of Magellan leading to the Pacific, but here he was driven south so he discovered that there was a sea passage south of Cape Horn leading to the Pacific. By then the other ships in his fleet had been lost or returned home. Drake alone went on, renaming his *Pelican* the *Golden Hind* when she was loaded with loot from the Spanish galleons.

As a man Drake was absolutely ruthless, but he was a superb seaman and navigator and succeeded in taking his little ship right the way round the world. He returned to England almost three years after leaving, by which time everyone believed that he had long been drowned. Since the *Golden Hind* was loaded with gold and precious objects, Elizabeth I welcomed the great sea captain.

Drake was the first English captain to sail round the world and his voyages set everyone talking about the possibilities to be gained from ocean voyages. In 1586 Thomas Cavendish sailed with three ships for a round the world voyage which entailed piracy. When he returned two years later, there was much talk about his ship *Desire* having a gold coated topmast and a crew dressed in silk. What was more useful was that Cavendish returned with charts and information about eastern waters. This helped to develop trade to the East which led to the founding of the East India Company.

While some Elizabethans financed their voyages by piracy, others looked to founding overseas plantations as a form of generating wealth. Sir Humphrey Gilbert was active in the search for the North-West passage and established a base for England in North America, but he was lost at sea in his ship *Squirrel* when returning from Newfoundland in 1583. Of all the great Elizabethans it was Sir Walter Raleigh who dreamed of an overseas empire for England. He was very active in organising the colonisation of North America and in 1587 was organising the Virginia colony in what is now the eastern United States. In 1587 Raleigh had built at Deptford the galleon *Ark Raleigh* which he sold to Queen Elizabeth; the ship became Howard's *Ark Royal* which led the fleet in the defeat of the Spanish Armada.

Drake died at sea in 1595 while on another expedition raiding the West Indies, but Raleigh was one Elizabethan on whom Spain was able to reap her revenge. The Navy was run down under James I and peace was made with Spain. In 1618 the Spanish Ambassador was able to put pressure on the King to the extent of having Raleigh beheaded. Discovery and adventure received Royal discouragement. Fortunately accounts of Elizabethan voyages had been recorded by the gentleman and lawyer Richard Hakluyt. He came from a landowning family at Eyton, Herefordshire, and was entrusted to the care of a cousin, who was a lawyer of the Middle Temple. Hakluyt also mixed with powerful and wealthy merchants in the London livery companies, so he was able to hear of the latest discoveries which were made in searches to develop overseas trade.

Hakluyt was also active in helping to promote exploration. For instance, he went to Bristol to raise financial support for Sir Humphrey Gilbert's voyage. He had also persuaded Drake to give aid after the highly successful piracy of the 1577–80 world voyage, for a School of Navigation in London. This was not established until Hakluyt's life was nearly at an end. However, it was Hakluyt's books, starting with *Divers Voyages touching upon the Discovery of America* in 1582, which inspired young men to consider the possibilities of discovery and colonisation.

In 1591 Sir James Lancaster voyaged round the Cape of Good Hope to India and then on to Sumatra and Java. This voyage to the East Indies, lucrative though it was, took several years, but merchants and gentlemen bankers wanted that elusive quicker route to the East. In 1607 the Muscovy Company sponsored Henry Hudson to find a route to China via the North-West passage. In a tiny craft with only ten men, he went right to the Arctic ice barrier; it was nearly two hundred years before anyone went that far north again. Later, in the pay of the Dutch East India Company, Hudson discovered the river upon which New York now stands. In 1610, under English pay, he was sent out again to discover the North-West passage. After a terrible voyage he reached Hudson's Bay, but his crew refused to go any further and turned him, his young son and his followers adrift. They were never seen again.

To secure financial backing for these voyages, explorers generally had to promise courtiers and merchants rewards from piracy or gold finds. An explorer who returned empty handed was not very welcome. The value of the new discoveries was not, of course, in bags of gold but, as Raleigh,

The square-rigged ketch Nonsuch, *a replica built to commemorate the 300th anniversary of the founding of the Hudson's Bay Company, has a lateen on the mizzen mast. The lateen mizzen remained in common use in both naval and merchant vessels until the second half of the eighteenth century when it was replaced by a gaff sail*
(Hudson's Bay Company)

Hakluyt and others believed, in the potential of the new lands they found to form colonies and trading stations. After each voyage of discovery, there was often a long interval before the worth of the find was fully realised. Over the centuries the financial and human cost of finding the North-West passage was considerable, yet the actual passage has been of little practical use to anyone; the discovery of the rich fishing grounds off Newfoundland and Nova Scotia in the early 1500s was very much more valuable than a route to the East. Fishermen from the West Country and Brittany started to work the fishing grounds off Newfoundland but, although they established bases ashore, they usually returned home for the winter.

In 1620 a group of Puritans sailed in the *Mayflower* and established a colony in Massachusetts. Captain Christopher James of the *Mayflower* made his landfall on Cape Cod. This was easily recognised because he had a copy of the detailed map of New England's coast which had been made by Captain John Smith in 1614. In the twenty years after *Mayflower*'s arrival, around 25,000 left the counties of south-east England to settle in the colonies along the eastern seaboard of America. Later the Welsh and Scottish and much later the Irish joined in this settlement of new lands. They also settled in the West Indian islands and later, because of the sugar plantations, these became much more prized to western European nations than the American colonies. In the late eighteenth century the original white settlers in the West Indies left so that the majority of the population were descended from the negro slaves.

While the British and French were busy exploring and settling in North America, the Dutch were sending ships to explore more areas in the East and across the Pacific. However, many of the first European ships to reach new lands were pirates and buccaneers who looted everything they found and left no records of their voyages. But at least one man recorded his travels, a Somerset man named William Dampier (1651–1715) who, at eighteen, sailed from Weymouth to the Newfoundland Fisheries. He so hated the cold that the rest of his voyages were to the tropics, first as a sailor before the mast on an East Indiaman to Java, then to a sugar plantation in Jamaica, and after that went logwood cutting in Honduras.

Dampier was a typical adventurer: he was determined to be free of all land-based ambitions and responsibilities, wanting to sail the seas and always seeking what lay just over the horizon. After years of wandering and a fair share of privateering, he published *A New Voyage Round the World* in 1699 and this was followed by three other books which became popular. Dampier was taken up by London society and as a result, he was given command of the first exploration the British Admiralty ever organised. However, the ships he was allotted were old and rotten and, although he reached Australia, the fact that he returned without discovering obvious wealth lost him official favour. Dampier went back to privateering but he has another place in history for rescuing, in 1709, Alexander Selkirk who had been marooned on the Pacific island of Juan Fernandez for five years. It was Selkirk's adventures which were embroidered into the novel *Robinson Crusoe*.

The war with Spain prompted the 1740–4 round the world voyage of the English naval captain George Anson in the 60-gun *Centurion*. Anson was supposed to take a squadron into the Pacific to harass the Spanish. However, the squadron was held up for months at Portsmouth because sailors refused to sail in the appalling conditions of naval ships. In the end, the authorities drafted in 500 Chelsea pensioners to make up the numbers. These were men of over sixty and the more agile ones promptly deserted. In the hard voyage out round Cape Horn, none of these pensioners survived. Scurvy broke out and some of Anson's ships had to be scuttled because they were in such an unseaworthy condition. However, the remainder of the squadron took several Spanish ships and returned home with a vast quantity of gold and silver. The real benefit of the voyage was that, when Anson became First Lord of the Admiralty, he started the reforms and organisation which resulted in the much better equipped Navy of Nelson's day.

During his voyage, Anson had headed north to raid ships in the Philippine Islands and had gone on to the Chinese port of Canton. Several Dutchmen had reported a land south of the East Indies (now Indonesia) and there was a great deal of speculation about the existence of a continent called 'Terra Incognita Australis'. The Scottish seagoing merchant Alexander Dalrymple, who had had experience in the East India trade, compiled a survey of all the land discovered in the Pacific before 1764.

The British Government and Admiralty had now realised that exploration to discover new lands contained more long-term benefits than schemes to find gold mines. They were particularly worried about what might lie in the South Pacific and even more worried that the French would find a new continent first.

The Admiralty sought a suitable captain to lead a Pacific exploration and found James Cook (1728–79). He was a Yorkshireman who had learnt his seamanship in colliers sailing from Whitby. Cook joined the Navy as an able seaman but rose quickly to be 'master' of the *Solebay*. Later the term master was used to describe the ship's captain, but Cook was warrant officer in charge of navigation. It was in this field that he excelled and, after taking part in the war against the French in Canadian waters, he surveyed and charted the coasts of Labrador and Newfoundland.

When the Royal Society decided to send a party to Tahiti to observe the transit of the planet Venus across the face of the sun, they persuaded the Admiralty to provide a ship. In contrast to the wretched way that Anson had been sent off, this voyage was thoroughly prepared and Cook, as leader, was a most able navigator and leader of men. Joseph Banks, a wealthy botanist, led the scientific party on the first voyage between 1768–9, but for the second voyage between 1772–4 he was left behind, Cook being full leader.

A thoroughly practical approach to the choice of ship for this expedition was the 98ft Whitby collier *Earl of Pembroke*, which was renamed the *Endeavour*, rather than one of the Navy's small vessels. The voyage to Tahiti and the observing of Venus took place as planned, and

Cook then sailed in search of the mysterious continent. He landed in New Zealand and the sight of fully dressed white men caused the Maori to flee in terror, thinking that the gods had landed. Cook established that New Zealand was not joined to Australia.

The *Endeavour* then sailed on to Australia, and in true methodical Cook fashion he surveyed some 1,300 miles of coast. In the course of the survey, he discovered Botany Bay and hoisted the Union Jack, formally claiming the whole land for the British Crown. He continued sailing north inside the Great Barrier Reef, travelling nearly a thousand miles and constantly taking soundings. This did not save the *Endeavour* from accident because she ran on to a reef in the night. To lighten the ship, six of the *Endeavour*'s guns were thrown overboard and the ship was refloated. Cook sailed back to the Australian mainland, found the Endeavour River, where the ship was repaired, and made the long voyage back to England.

The continual choice of north country ships for Cook's voyages of discovery was largely because they were strongly built and able to take the ground, fully loaded, without damage, essential characteristics if the expedition is out of touch with civilisation for long periods on a strange coast. For his second voyage to the Antarctic in search of a continent in the southern ocean between 1772–5, Cook advised the Admiralty to buy the Whitby colliers *Resolution* and *Adventure*. In incredibly brutal conditions of ice and gales, he beat these little ships right round the world. He was the first man to take a ship across the Antarctic Circle but although he went into the pack ice and saw what he believed to be a ridge of mountains, he did not confirm the existence of a continent.

When he finally brought the *Resolution* back to Spithead, Britain was at war with her American colonies. However, the Admiralty soon dispatched Cook on yet another exploration. While the war was raging on the east coast of America, Cook was sent to explore the west coast, where remarkably few Europeans had been since Drake had sailed there 200 years earlier. At the same time Cook was to try to discover the Pacific end of the North-West passage. This was a fresh approach, but even Cook could not find a usable channel leading to the Atlantic. There is a North-West passage but it is closed by ice virtually all year.

Cook sailed again on the *Resolution* with yet another former Whitby collier, the *Discovery*, as a support ship. The actual voyage lasted from 1776–80, but Cook was killed before the voyage ended. The voyage out was round the Cape of Good Hope to New Zealand and out into the Pacific to the Friendly and Cook islands. The two ships went on to the American west coast, Drake's 'New Albion', in search of the North-West passage. Cook went north through the Bering Sea until the Polar Ice barred his way. For a refit Cook sailed south and discovered the Pacific island of Hawaii. The natives were friendly at first but friction developed when they stole from Cook's ship. Tension mounted and finally, in an angry confrontation on the beach, fighting broke out in which Cook was killed.

Although he had contributed a great deal towards discovering and charting the Pacific, it was his landing on the Australian coast which had the greatest impact. Eighteen years after Cook had landed in Australia, the British Government, which had just lost the American colonies with the formation of the United States, decided to use Botany Bay as a penal colony. The ships which took out the founders of the modern nation of Australia, now referred to as the First Fleet, took eight months to sail the 15,000 miles from Portsmouth to Botany Bay. The Royal Navy ships *Sirius* and *Supply* and nine transport ships had about 1,200 people on board, of which 780 were male and female convicts. The First Fleet anchored in Botany Bay on 8 January 1787 but could not find a supply of drinking water ashore on which to site a settlement. Instead they sailed some 9 miles up the New South Wales coast to Port Jackson and here found a cove with a freshwater stream which they named Sydney, after Lord Sydney who had directed the deportation of convicts and settlers to this new country. It was the voyages of Cook which had made this kind of organised settlement and colonial expansion possible.

Much of the waters around both the North and South poles were first visited by whalers, and indeed many small islands were first visited by these hardy sea captains and their tough crews. The Royal Navy had officers who were virtually professional explorers. George Vancouver sailed as a young midshipman on Cook's voyages and went on to command surveying voyages to Australia and New Zealand, although he was best known for his survey around Vancouver Island on the Canadian Pacific coast. John Franklin sailed as a 'middy' on Captain Matthew Flinders' expeditions and surveying voyages round the Australian coast, but he later turned his attentions to finding the North-West passage. With HMS *Erebus* and HMS *Terror*, he sailed in 1845 to the frozen north and none of the 129 officers and men were ever seen again. Franklin's fate became a mystery which no fewer than thirty-two vessels from Britain and three from the United States tried to unravel by sailing to the North-West passage.

Sir Robert McClure was sent out to try and solve the mystery of Franklin's disappearance and find the North-West passage and he finally located a sea channel through the frozen isles to complete the North-West route to the Pacific in 1850. This ended the centuries long search. After this Lady Franklin used her influence and wealth to continue the hunt for her husband's fate. One of these searching parties led to the loss of the transport barque *Breadalbane* in the Arctic in 1853, although the crew returned safely. This ship was located in 1980, with her mast still standing, on the seabed near Queen Elizabeth Island. In 1859 the Franklin mystery ended when a cairn containing the log of *Erebus* was found. The log recorded that the ship's crew and expedition abandoned their ships in the ice. The Eskimos told a search party they had seen Franklin's men dying of exposure.

The *Erebus* and *Terror* had previously been under the command of James Clarke Ross when he surveyed Victoria Land in the Antarctic in 1842. James Cook had believed he had sighted land in the Antarctic in 1774 and land was again sighted in the far south by Captain William Smith on the brig *William* in 1819. The Admiralty sent the frigate *Andromache* out and she located the South Shetlands. In 1822 Captain James Weddell discovered the South Orkneys while searching for fur seals and gave his name to the Weddell Sea. The first definite sighting of the Antarctic continent was made by Captain Balleny in 1839.

It was the need for accurate charts as a basis for safe navigation which caused the Admiralty to set up a Hydrographic Department in 1795, and by 1820 it had seven survey vessels. The first catalogue of Admiralty charts was issued in 1825 and they became sought after as the only reliable source of information for navigation. There were many gaps in the charts' information in the early days, and there was a continuous need to update the material. One of the ships sent out on survey was the 10-gun, 90ft, 235 ton HMS *Beagle* which, between 1825–41, was employed surveying in South America and Australia. On the voyage between 1831–6 under Captain Fitzroy, the *Beagle* sailed along the South American coast and to the Galapagos Islands. On board was the young naturalist Charles Darwin who, as a result of his observations on this voyage, later wrote the books *A Naturalist's Voyage* and *Origin of Species*. The latter first put forward the whole theory of natural selection for all living creatures.

Between 1860–70 the Admiralty sent out several survey expeditions to chart and survey the oceans which led to the commissioning of the HMS *Challenger*, a 2,306-ton wooden, full-rigged ship with a steam auxiliary, to make a very thorough survey. The *Challenger* sailed in 1872 and over the next three and a half years covered some 70,000 miles, crossing and re-crossing the Atlantic and Pacific several times taking soundings all the way. The *Challenger*'s crew rescued two brothers who had been marooned for two years on an isolated island after they had gone there in 1871 to make a fortune seal hunting. The *Challenger* expedition discovered for the first time many features of great importance to the scientific world. Depths of over 5 miles were recorded in the Pacific; also the 12,000ft high mountain range was discovered on the ocean floor near Hawaii. The official reports on the voyage took fifteen years to edit and were issued in fifty volumes.

After the North-West passage had been finally located in 1850, the only remaining part of the world not mapped, at least in outline, was the Antarctic. Because commercial and naval activities were virtually non-existent in Polar waters, the Admiralty was reluctant to send their survey vessels south. However, the naval officer Captain Robert Falcon Scott commanded the Polar research vessel *Discovery* on the British Royal Antarctic Expedition, which surveyed the Great Ice Barrier during a voyage between 1901–4. The 171ft 1,620-ton *Discovery* was specially built at Dundee for the expedition. Dundee and Peterhead were then the last British ports to send whalers into the Arctic, but the *Discovery* was larger and probably not as good as the real Dundee whalers. On the return of this expedition, the *Discovery* was sold to the Hudson's Bay Company. When Scott sailed south again in 1910, he went on the ex-Dundee whaler *Terra Nova*, Scott's advance party losing their lives after being the second group after the Norwegian party, to reach the South Pole.

Sir Ernest Shackleton also became fascinated with exploration of the frozen south. He went south in the *Nimrod* in 1907 and returned again in 1915, but died at the start of another expedition in 1922 in South Georgia. The *Discovery* returned to the South Pole between 1928–31 when Sir Douglas Mawson used her on his expedition.

These occasional expeditions to the Antarctic eventually led to the permanent British Antarctic Survey. This Survey is responsible for continual scientific activities and exploration of the British Antarctic Territory. The Survey's origins go back to 1925 when whaling interests required better information on the Antarctic Peninsula region. In 1934–7 the British Graham Land Expedition did much work along the west coast of the Antarctic Peninsula and discovered that this was part of the Antarctic mainland and not an island as previously thought.

In 1944 two bases were established to investigate the scientific potential of the Antarctic. After World War II a permanent Survey was started. This Survey has its headquarters in Cambridge and its research vessels are based at Port Stanley, Falkland Islands. The early years of the permanent survey were largely taken up with exploring and mapping the Antarctic to assess its potential. This approach changed in 1959 when Britain became one of twelve nations signing the Antarctic Treaty in which it was agreed only to use the continent for peaceful purposes.

The name British Antarctic Survey was given to this research and exploration organisation in 1962. By this time the research programmes had been developed to cover all major areas of environmental research.

The Terra Nova, *built as a whaler at Dundee in 1884, leaving Cardiff on 15 June 1910 on Captain Scott's Antarctic Expedition. The* Discovery, *which Scott used on a previous expedition to the Antarctic in 1901, was sold to the Hudson's Bay Company in 1904 as a cargo ship* (Welsh Industrial & Maritime Museum)

To gather information the Survey maintains permanent bases in the Antarctic. These bases are at South Georgia, Signy Island, Argentine Islands, Rothera Point, Damoy Point and Halley Bay. To link up these bases on the islands and mainland the Survey has two ice-strengthened ocean-going vessels. These are the 1,584-ton gross RRS *John Biscoe*, built in 1956, and the larger and more modern 4,816-ton gross RRS *Bransfield*. The latter vessel is regarded as being amongst the finest research vessels in the southern Hemisphere. Both the *Bransfield* and the *John Biscoe* are classed '100 A1* ice strengthened' at Lloyds. These ships return to British ports for dry docking and refitting, but the Falkland Islands are their normal operational base.

The severe climatic conditions and great isolation of Antarctic waters can make navigation very hazardous. Much of the time is spent in pack ice and a helicopter is used to locate the best way through to clear water. The ships are painted bright red as this is the colour which shows up best in snow and ice.

In the nineteenth and early twentieth centuries, exploration was largely aimed at finding natural resources, while in recent decades the emphasis has been on scientific exploration of the environment. To actually explore and discover anything new is a personal adventure. It was to keep alive the spirit of adventure that 'Operation Drake' was planned and carried out. In 1979, approximately 400 years after Sir Francis Drake sailed in the *Golden Hind*, the British brigantine *Eye of the Wind* sailed from Plymouth Sound for a round the world voyage. The *Eye of the Wind* had been refitted at Faversham a few years before, and had already made one round the world voyage, but in 'Operation Drake' young people joined the brigantine on different sections of the voyage. Not every member of the expedition actually sailed on the brigantine, but 414 young people from twenty-seven countries joined the scientists, archaeologists and explorers in the world's little or unknown jungles, deserts and mountains. Each section of the voyage had some thirty-four regular crew and young explorers on the *Eye of the Wind*. After over two years of visiting isolated islands and remote places, the brigantine came up the Thames and passed under Tower Bridge as a signal that the voyage was over.

In 1979 the Transglobe Expedition left Greenwich in their motor vessel *Benjamin Bowring* at the start of the first longitudinal circumnavigation of the world by land, sea and ice. The main object was to cross the Antarctic icecap via the South Pole, and then the Arctic Ocean via the North Pole. These extremely difficult journeys were to be made on sledges, ski-doos and skis. To reach Polarbjorn Buchte, the unloading place for the expedition on the Antarctic Continent, the *Benjamin Bowring* had to push through pack ice and discharge quickly after arrival, so that the stores could be moved inland away from the fragile sea ice in the bay.

The whole expedition was planned to take three years and by January 1981 the ice team had crossed Antarctica to Scott Base on McMurdo Sound, where they waited for the *Benjamin Bowring*. The expedition had visited the lonely hut from which Scott had made his last journey seventy years earlier. In the hut, preserved by sub-zero temperatures, were magazines, clothing and even a seal carcass left by Scott's expedition. This visit was a link between two major expeditions.

3

Sail Supreme

In the nineteenth century, behind the protection provided by the Royal Navy, Britain built up the largest merchant fleet in the world. Around 1870, over half the world's ocean-going tonnage sailed under the red ensign. The United States had built some superb wooden clipper ships which were admired and even copied by British shipbuilders, but Britain's merchant navy was still four times larger than that of America, which by then already had a larger population. France, Italy and particularly Germany were all striving to create an empire and expand their share of the world trade, but the British merchant tonnage was larger than the combined tonnage of the three major European maritime nations.

This was the era of small ships carrying small cargoes to isolated places around the globe. The typical mid-Victorian ocean-going ships were still quite small, but there were hundreds of them moving slowly round the world's trade wind systems with small consignments of cargo. Speed was not very important because the running costs of these ships were so low. In the case of a voyage from the Australian Colonies to a British port, it did not matter too much whether a ship took 100 days or 120 days. The important thing from the shipowner's point of view was that the vessel arrived with the ship intact and the cargo undamaged.

The typical British deep sea sailing ship of the late Victorian period was the four-masted barque. They replaced the full-rigged ship which had square sails on each mast, while the after mast on a barque had a fore-and-aft spanker. Because of the extra square sail on the mizzen, the full-rigged ship required more crew, but did not guarantee extra speed.

The first four-masted barque was built in 1878 and this rig quickly proved to be more economical than the full-rigged ship. Mild steel in quantity was available for shipbuilding from about 1884, and for the next fifteen years, sailing ships were constructed more or less as fast as the yards could turn them out. The idea of standardisation had not taken root so every ship was slightly different. At first, the huge 'sailing warehouse', four-masted barques were not popular with the seafaring community, for they replaced the beautiful little clippers like the *Cutty Sark* and some attractive iron, three-masted, full-rigged ships.

These square-rigged ships and barques were at sea for months on end,

The four-masted barque Olivebank *was built in 1892 by Mackie & Thomson of Glasgow. She was typical of the last generation of cargo sailing ships that competed on the ocean routes until steamers became economic over long distances. The* Olivebank *was built for Andrew Weir's Bank Line, which at that time was running a fleet of four-masted barques from Glasgow* (Russ Lownds)

wandering from London, Liverpool or Bristol to some open anchorage in South America to load fertilizer in bags or grain from tiny riverside wharves on the west coast of America. Strangely enough, it was the spread of steam locomotives which gave a great boost to the number of British sailing ships. Once railways started to be constructed in almost every part of the world, the demand for steam coal escalated. Steam coal from mines in South Wales was particularly sought after, but coal was also exported from the ports of north-east England and the Clyde. The sale of coal created the capital to build more ships, and at the same time coal provided a source of energy to produce iron and steel so steel works and shipbuilding expanded in the proximity of the coal mines.

While the Industrial Revolution spread grime across the face of Britain near the coal pits, it also resulted in a continual stream of sailing ships being built to carry coal to foreign markets. It is customary now to decry the horrors of the Industrial Revolution and the many social problems it created in Britain, but the building of more factories and ships generated employment and livelihood, however basic. The Industrial Revolution improved the financial state of the average working man, although it did not produce a very pleasant environment in which to live and overcrowding in factory towns inevitably produced social and health problems.

Most sailors knew or cared very little about the effect of the Industrial Revolution. To them, the only thing that mattered was that every port was crowded with ships in need of a crew. The surplus male population from fishing communities and little country trading ports travelled to the large ports in search of berths in sailing ships. In the mid-Victorian period, most of the ships were still manned largely by British nationals. Although most of the sailing ships operated from large ports, many still had strong connections with the little rural ports. A captain from, say, the western isles of Scotland probably saw very little of his native village during his working life, but the movements of his ship were known there, so whenever he needed a fresh crew, young men wanting to go 'deep sea' set off to join a ship in which some of their relations and neighbours already served.

Shipownership was generally on a small scale: few ships were owned outright by one man, but by a group of shareholders. The ownership of any British vessel is divided up into sixty-four shares, and in the sailing ship era these shares were sold to individuals. Usually the man holding the largest number of shares was registered as being the owner, but the seamen spoke of a ship 'belonging to' Liverpool or Belfast, meaning that that was where the owners lived and the sailors were domiciled.

As the size of ships grew with the Industrial Revolution, a system of docks was needed to accommodate them, and this caused the centralisation of shipping into the larger ports, but many shipping interests still had their roots in the smaller ports. For instance, in around 1900, there were two fine steel barques sailing out of Liverpool with unmistakably Welsh river names, the *Afon Alaw* and the *Afon Cefni*. These were the last of a long line of ships owned by the Davies family of Anglesey between 1843–1905.

Richard Davies began with a timber yard at Menai Straits in 1828 and by 1843 was sending ships across the North Atlantic with emigrants, returning with timber. The voyages across the Atlantic in leaky wooden barques of about 600 tons were appalling for the emigrants who were crowded into the hold. Aled Eames, Anglesey's maritime historian, has unearthed a report of a voyage of the *Courtenay* in 1846, during which the sails were blown away when returning from New Brunswick in Canada. She drifted for forty-one days before being taken in tow and hauled to Menai Bridge. Davies was building up his shipping interests during the peak years of emigration to North America. This reached its height in 1847 when 30,000 people from England and Wales and a further 54,000 from Ireland landed in Quebec. In 1851 the discovery of gold in Australia caused emigration to switch to this new land, but this did not fit in with Davies' timber business.

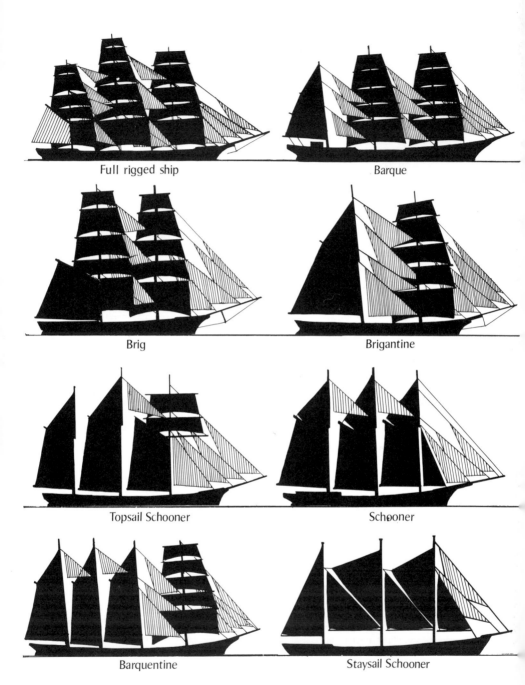

Full rigged ship

Barque

Brig

Brigantine

Topsail Schooner

Schooner

Barquentine

Staysail Schooner

Gradually the Davies bought larger vessels which went into general ocean trades, and this meant moving to Liverpool. This move also saw the change from wooden ships built in the Canadian Maritimes by emigrants from Britain to iron ships and then steel ships built in the yards of the United Kingdom. The first of Davies' iron ships was the 1,297-ton ship *Anglesey* in 1875, six further sailing ships being built at Liverpool by T. Royden & Sons and named after Welsh counties. The Davies switched to a Clyde yard for the 2,052-ton, four-masted barque *Afon Alaw* in 1891 and the 2,066-ton four-masted barque *Afon Cefni* in 1892.

Although the Davies' ships spent much of their time on long world voyages which kept the square-riggers away from their home ports for two or three years, they were still the centre of tremendous local pride in North Wales. When the Davies' ships began to discharge at larger ports like Liverpool, London, Cardiff, Swansea and Hamburg, the crews became more international, but virtually all the captains and officers remained Welsh. However, for their loyalty the Davies certainly did not spoil their countrymen with unnecessary comfort. Men from Caernarvonshire and Anglesey called the Davies fleet 'one gull ships', because it was said that food was so short on them that there were only enough scraps thrown overboard to feed one following gull.

The Davies' Welsh county ships were engaged in general trade and were little known outside Liverpool shipping circles, but the Davies family, basically a father and then two sons, owned ships for a period of around sixty years and created a sizeable fortune as well as owning large estates in Anglesey and Ireland. They naturally lived in comfort, but in spite of their wealth, the Davies lived quite modestly. They were like many Victorian business people in that they ploughed back profits into new ventures rather than spend it on themselves.

The Davies were primarily businessmen who developed shipping interests, while another self-made Victorian shipowner, Captain James Nourse, was a sailor who went ashore to concentrate on managing his ships. Nourse specialised in trade with India, which was then the 'Jewel' of the British Empire. He was born in Ireland in the 1830s, and in 1861 was first registered as the master and owner of the 839-ton iron ship *Ganges*. James Nourse was typical of the ambitious Victorians who, by sheer hard work and good judgement, built up a shipping line. Men like Nourse drove themselves hard and expected every one of their employees to make the maximum effort all the time. It was said that when Nourse took delivery of a new ship, the riggers were still working on her while the first cargo was being loaded.

Nourse took a great aversion to having to pay for a tug to tow his ships some 90 miles up the River Hooghly to Calcutta. The *Lena* once sailed

The four-masted ship Liverpool *wrecked on the rocks of Alderney, Channel Islands, in February 1902. She was bound from Antwerp to San Francisco when she ran ashore in a dense fog. Built in 1889, she was the only four-masted ship built for Leyland's of Liverpool; the rest of their fifteen vessels were three-masted, full-rigged ships* (National Maritime Museum)

right up to the Garden Reach mooring at Calcutta in only six and a half hours while the *Bruce* was also able to sail up river on one occasion, but normally a tug had to be hired. As his ships had gone half way round the world powered only by free wind, Nourse was not inclined to let the tug owners make a profit out of the last few miles, so in the end he bought his own tug.

The Nourse Line operated coolie ships which loaded general cargo in a British port and went out to Calcutta. There seems to have been constant emigration from the over-populated Indian sub-continent, and in the latter part of the nineteenth century, the coolie ships were taking people from Calcutta, Bombay and Madras to wherever labour was needed. This was mostly to the West Indies, Demerara and Mauritius for work on the sugar industry. From these places they usually loaded sugar back to Europe. A typical voyage was made by Nourse's *Rhine* in 1887 when she sailed with 700 coolies from Calcutta to Surinam and then north to Philadelphia to load case-oil.

There was great exploitation of the Chinese coolies being shipped from Macao to Cuba, but the British-run Indian Government were very strict about their emigration ships and the way the coolies were contracted. A passage for an Indian labourer and his family on a coolie ship was certainly not a pleasure trip, but their ships were well organised with a doctor and hospital provided on board. The ships called at the Cape of Good Hope and St Helena to buy fresh vegetables to minimise the likelihood of beri-beri or scurvy. By the standards of the day, the coolies were well treated on Nourse's British ships.

There is little doubt that James Nourse was a hard man, but he thoroughly understood the trade of his ships. If one of his masters made a slow passage, the log book would be examined to discover the reason. A common mistake was for a master, when beating up the Bay of Bengal to Calcutta, to stand on a tack too long, find himself eastward of the Andaman Islands and be becalmed there. Because the coolie trade was very lucrative, competition was severe, but at the height of the emigration from eastern India, the Nourse Line was the leader. Nourse demanded and received a high standard of work from his masters and men, but at the same time he ploughed back some of the profit into his ships and there was no skimping with new sails and paint. The pilots on board their brig off the River Hooghly could always tell a Nourse coolie ship when it appeared on the horizon by its smart appearance. With their painted gun-ports and cloud of sail, which included main skysail, they were an impressive sight. The Hooghly pilots, who were all men trained in sail and not used to giving out compliments, watched in admiration as the ships came on a fresh tack and the yards were smartly swung round.

The Nourse ships seem to have attracted good seamen, but they were probably, in that prosperous era, rather over-manned. They could carry up to fifty seamen and they were not very large. The full-rigged ships built for the line at Sunderland in the 1870s were only of around 1,000 tons, while the *Foyle* was 1,528 tons and the *Bann*, which sailed under the Nourse flag for thirty years, was just over 1,600 tons. Nourse remained stubbornly loyal to sail while other shipowners went over to steam. The *Mersey*, built in 1894, was one of his last ships launched, and later she became well known as a cadet ship for the White Star Line.

The last of the Nourse sailers was sold in 1909, by which time the economics of operating a sailing ship under the British flag had become increasingly difficult. The position had been very different in 1875 when the Clyde-built iron coolie ship *Jura* sailed on her maiden voyage from Liverpool to Calcutta. There were twenty-one seamen on her and every one was British. When she arrived at Calcutta after a long passage of 120 days, most of the fo'c'sle hands asked to be discharged. The captain was happy to pay them off and they departed for the dubious pleasures of the sailor town. When the *Jura* was ready to go to sea again, an Indian coolie crew was taken on for a voyage to Mauritius and back. With another

European crew she ended her nineteen-month voyage back in Liverpool. At this stage shipmasters discharged a crew in the larger ports because they could always find replacements, but from about 1895 British seamen were drawn to the better conditions in steamers. After this, men were often deliberately kept aboard in port so that they should not jump ship and desert. Also boarding house masters often made the seamen drunk and placed them aboard outward-bound sailing ships, taking part of their wages as a fee. Where seamen were in short supply, as on the west coast of America, the 'crimps' and their henchmen were busy drugging and selling as many men as they could find to fill the sailing ships which were waiting to go to sea. These criminal practices and the low wages made sailing ships even less attractive to British sailors and navigation officers. The final years of British sail were not a glorious era, with worn out ships sailed by elderly officers who were too old to start in steamers. Naturally other lines specialised in trade with other colonies, such as the Liverpool firm of Thompson, Anderson & Co whose Sierra Line traded mostly to Rangoon, the Burmese rice port. They operated the full-rigged ship *Sierra Miranda* for twenty-two years in this trade. These sailers made many 'flying fish voyages', mostly in latitudes where they had good weather. The *Sierra Miranda* went out from Liverpool to Rangoon in 105 days in 1885 and delighted her crew by running east for twelve days at an average speed of 10 knots.

The tropical climates had their drawbacks: ships could either spend lengthy periods at sea becalmed, and the crews were liable to pick up diseases in eastern ports. Three weeks after one of the 'Sierras' sailed from Chittagong, smallpox broke out on board. The four men who had contracted the disease were housed in the midship house and nursed by Captain Lyons who, as a younger man, had had smallpox himself. One seaman died, but the other three recovered.

Life under sail was too uncertain for anyone to plan for the future: a great many ships were 'lost at sea' and simply never arrived at their destination. Typical of these tragedies was the way the coolie ship *Jura* lost a man in 1875. The crew were busy aloft, taking in the stunsails (extra sails outside the normal square sails), and the bo'sun was busy hauling in the sheet on deck. Suddenly the stunsail flapped wildly and threw the bo'sun right over the high topgallant rail into the sea. The sailmaker working aft on the poop saw what had happened and threw the bo'sun a lifebuoy which he caught. A lifeboat was launched and several hours were spent searching in vain.

Most sailors began their life at sea at a very early age, such as F. H. Curtis who was only twelve when he joined the full-rigger *Merope* in 1873. This ship was one of Shaw Savill's clippers which was running

Sailmaker at work on the Loch Tay, *an iron, full-rigged ship owned by the Loch Line of Glasgow. In the background, rope halliards are made fast to the belaying pins in the fife rails. It is believed that the fife rail was given its name because, before the nineteenth century, the man playing a fife sat on it while the seamen hauled in time to his tune* (National Maritime Museum)

passengers, mostly emigrants, from Britain out to New Zealand. The *Merope* was towed out of West India Docks, London, on 15 April and a month later she had reached the tropics. Here the sailors, after a great deal of singing and ceremony, buried the 'dead horse' which was thrown into the sea, the dead horse being made up of old sacks with a tail of manila rope teased out. The point of the custom was that before sailing the seamen had all drawn a months wages in advance, which was all spent before they went to sea, so the sailors considered that they had worked for the first month for nothing or just a 'dead horse'. This custom lasted into the twentieth century, although by then the crimps ashore were often taking the advance from the master for supplying the seamen.

The *Merope* went first to New Zealand and then back to Melbourne, Australia. Here the crew all promptly left to go up country after gold. The captain managed to get together a new, but sadly inexperienced crew. When the time came to sail, the new crew refused to go because they said that there were not enough able seamen aboard. The authorities felt inclined to back up the seamen but the *Merope*'s master just handed out bottles of spirits. The next day, when the crew were all too drunk to leave their fo'c'sle, the officers and boys hove up the anchor and the *Merope* was towed out to sea.

When the *Merope* reached Cape Horn, a series of gales pushed her south into the ice regions. On Christmas Day 1873, young twelve-year-old Curtis sat alone in the fo'c'sle listening to the gale outside. Huge seas swept right over the ship, washing away everything movable including the lifeboats. Many of the bulwark's planks were gone, allowing the sea to wash right over the deeply laden vessel. At a time when most children were at home with their families, Curtis was alone, wondering if the ship was going to be overwhelmed at any moment.

In fact the *Merope* survived and eventually made landfall at The Lizard, but of three other ships which had left Melbourne at the same time, only one reached England. The life of a sailor was so uncertain that one wonders why men went to sea willingly. Some became trapped in the system whereby they stayed in boarding houses until their money ran out and they then had to find a berth on a ship found by the boarding house master to repay their debts. However, it is fair to say that most sailors enjoyed this roving life, and wages for the sailor were higher than those of a labouring man ashore. Many sailors were also deeply attracted by their ships. The sight of these beautiful square-riggers with their great clipper bows ploughing through the seas gave a sense of excitement which touched the hearts of the roughest men.

The true clippers were a rare breed of ship. The smugglers, privateers and slavers all had fast ships to avoid capture by the authorities, but speed was not developed in merchant vessels until around the middle of the nineteenth century. The American *Rainbow*, built in 1845, is regarded as being the first true clipper. By the 1850s the two Aberdeen builders, Hall and Hood, were leading the field in building British clippers for the lucrative China tea trade.

Fortunately, two ships from the clipper ship era have survived. One is the medium clipper *City of Adelaide* which was built for the Australian passenger trade in 1864 at Sunderland. Just before World War I, she became the stationary naval training vessel HMS *Carrick* and is still at Glasgow as a clubhouse. The other survivor, the *Cutty Sark*, is a true clipper and lies, beautifully restored, at Greenwich overlooking the River Thames. She used to race to the Thames with cargoes of fresh tea.

The *Cutty Sark* was launched at Dumbarton on the Clyde in November 1869. She was superbly constructed; indeed, at a contract price of £21 a ton, it proved to be ruinous for the young firm of Scott & Linton. There could have been few who saw that sleek hull slide into the waters of the Clyde who imagined that she would still be in existence a hundred years later; there would have been far more speculation over whether she could equal the *Thermopylae* and the others of that élite band of sailing ships which raced home from China each year for the profitable privilege of delivering the first consignment of tea to the London markets.

The design of the *Cutty Sark* is accredited to the genius of Hercules Linton. Since W. D. Scott-Moncrieff, the other partner in the shipbuilding firm, was then in his early twenties, his contribution must have been small. It was Linton's talent that undoubtedly persuaded the astute John Willis, a Scottish sea captain turned shipowner, to place the order for his ship with the new firm. Willis wanted the fastest ship in the world; it had to beat not only its rivals, but the hated steamers. The *Cutty Sark*'s entrusted duty was to prove that sail was supreme to the 'steam kettles'. This was a tall order.

All the clippers had fine hull shapes, but this alone did not guarantee speed under all conditions. Many had hull shapes that were too slim to carry sail in strong winds, when they began shipping water in a terrifying manner. Some literally sailed themselves under the water for good. But the *Cutty Sark* had a superior hull design and probably her greatest advantage was her powerful stern. She could carry sail in conditions that forced other ships to reduce sail, but to stand up to the punishment that relentless sail carrying entailed, every part of her mast and rigging had to be of the best quality and workmanship. No clipper owners could stay in business if their ships spent too long at sea.

What target had the *Cutty Sark* to beat? The *Thermopylae* had made shipping history on her maiden voyage the previous year when she had gone from The Lizard in Cornwall to Melbourne in a record breaking time of sixty days. From there she went to Shanghai in twenty-eight days and then back to England in ninety-two days, which included facing a monsoon in the Indian Ocean. The first master of the *Cutty Sark* was Captain George Moodie, a Scotsman who had already commanded two tea clippers, the *Laurel* and the *Lauderdale*, and thoroughly understood the business of commanding a deep sea sailing ship. But he had trouble with his new ship's rigging and his time out to China was only average. The first return voyage with tea from Shanghai took 110 days, but the *Thermopylae* had done it in only 105 days.

This was to be the pattern over the next ten years: every season the *Thermopylae*'s time back from China was just a few days shorter than that of the *Cutty Sark*. Once, when both ships left a Chinese port on the same tide, this was to have been the race to end all dispute over which was the fastest sailer. The general public took an interest in these annual tea races and the newspapers hailed Captain Kemball of the *Thermopylae* as being a great master in the art of obtaining the best out of a clipper. This he undoubtedly was, but it was not the end of the story. When the *Cutty Sark* arrived, it was found that she had lost her rudder during a gale in the Indian Ocean. Captain Moodie had not only performed the difficult task of fitting a jury rudder at sea, but had sailed 8,000 miles home without putting into port.

Captain Kemball was asked to show his log book to determine which ship was ahead at the time of the *Cutty Sark*'s misfortune, but Kemball maintained that his ship was home first and that was all that mattered. The tea from the *Thermopylae* was first on the market and his owners were satisfied, but the general public were not so convinced. The Victorians had a tremendous sense of fair play; all they wanted to know was the position of the *Thermopylae* at the time the *Cutty Sark* was lying helpless in the Indian Ocean. Kemball remained strangely silent, so there is no doubt that he was well behind at that stage. He only had to show his log book to a few reporters to regain the prestige that had originally been his, but he refused. The result was that *Cutty Sark*, the underdog, the one that made it against great difficulties, became a favourite with the British public.

However, the tea races in the 1870s were not being won by sailing ships at all, but by the steamers. They came back from China through the Suez Canal far faster and more reliably than could any clipper. The clippers had to take what tea the steamers left, which was a sad blow to their pride. Captain Moodie had a disagreement with Willis and left the *Cutty Sark* to take over a steamer. Kemball too left his ship to sail the iron clipper *Aristides*, and he continued his success in the Australian wool trade. All the clippers soon turned their attention to the Australian wool trade. This was in many ways similar to the China coast trade, in that they carried general cargoes out and raced back with wool for the London markets. This, however, was not such a lucrative trade and the owners could not afford lavish extras as they had done for the tea clippers.

The *Cutty Sark* was, compared to many sailing ships of that time, remarkably fast, but in comparison with other clippers her passages were only a good average. When Willis appointed Captain Richard Woodget to command his beloved ship in 1885, this situation changed. Son of a Norfolk farmer, Woodget had gone to sea in east coast colliers and had worked his way up to being master of Willis' *Coldstream*. In this he had surprised his fellow shipmasters by making some fast passages.

Woodget possessed not only the necessary knowledge of sail control and trimming but was also a first-rate leader of men. In *Cutty Sark* he proved this from the start, sailing from the English Channel to Sydney in sixty-seven days, only seven days longer than the *Thermopylae* had taken on her maiden voyage nearly twenty years before. Woodget brought the

Cutty Sark home in seventy-three days and then due to bad weather took five days to cover the last 305 miles to The Downs. Willis was delighted— his ship had at last proved herself and in a burst of enthusiasm he sent her to Shanghai to load tea in 1886. It was a forlorn hope: the merchants had lost interest in sail and there was no cargo for Willis' ship.

Woodget spent four idle months in China and then sailed in ballast for Sydney. He arrived there in January and had to wait until March before a wool cargo was ready. Then came the compensation—home in seventy-one days. It was the fastest voyage of the year; the *Thermopylae* came second in seventy-nine days while the average clippers took about ninety days. The *Cutty Sark* had at last had her revenge on her old rival, for the average length of time for homeward voyages while in the wool trade was eighty-two days, while *Thermopylae*'s was eighty-eight days.

It was during the ten years that Woodget commanded her that the *Cutty Sark* became a legend. But was she the fastest clipper? Old sailors used to say that she was best in a gale and the *Thermopylae* in light airs. Both ships are known to have sailed at over 17 knots for short periods. On a voyage the *Cutty Sark* could average 8 knots while her contemporaries managed only 6 knots. But as steamers were becoming larger and more efficient, there was no longer a place in the shipping world for a fine clipper of only 900 tons. Even Willis could not make her pay and sold her to the Portuguese. Woodget made only one more voyage in a ship called the *Coldingham*, but she was no compensation for the *Cutty Sark*. He left the sea and returned to his home at Burnham Overy in Norfolk, where he farmed and reared thoroughbred horses and hackneys.

The *Thermopylae* and the *Cutty Sark* appear to have been almost inseparable for both were sold to the Portuguese in 1895. The *Thermopylae* was sunk off the River Tagus in 1907 while being used as a gunnery target, but the *Cutty Sark* was carrying cargoes on long ocean voyages when she was over fifty years old, a credit to the Scottish craftsmen who built her. In the Scottish dialect 'cutty sark' means 'a short shirt' (as in Burn's Tam O'Shanter poem). Her time under the Portuguese flag cut out her finery. On 7 May 1916 she was dismasted off the South African coast and was towed into Cape Town. The cost, to say nothing of the shortage of spars, made re-rigging her as a full-rigged ship impossible and she spent her last years in trade as a barquentine.

In the shipping depression of the early 1920s, the Portuguese had no more use for her. She was too small for ocean voyages and too large for coastal trades. There was no alternative but to sell her for breaking up. It was then that Captain Dowman came to her rescue. He had been an apprentice in a sailing ship which had once been overtaken by the *Cutty Sark* in the days when Woodget sailed her. He felt that the British should not stand by and see this fine ship broken up for firewood. Dowman was determined that she would not have this fate, so he bought her in 1922 and had her towed to Falmouth. The following year he re-rigged her in full clipper style. Actually Dowman's version was not quite correct in that the mizzen mast was too small, hopelessly out of proportion and there were other mistakes which were eventually rectified, but the main point was that she had been saved.

After Dowman's death, his widow presented the ship to the Thames Nautical Training College. With Woodget aboard, she was towed to the Thames in 1938 and moored close to HMS *Worcester* for use as a training ship. In 1952 the *Cutty Sark* Preservation Society took over the responsibility of preserving her as a tribute to the Merchant Navy. It took time to arrange for her final berth at Greenwich, and it was not until December 1954 that she was towed up the Thames on her last voyage. At her mainmast flew the original flag of John Willis and at the mizzen her international code number J.K.W.S. This short tow up the Thames was the 'last passage' ever made by a true clipper. This beautiful vessel is now permanently docked at Greenwich and is the only survivor of her breed, except for the *City of Adelaide* at Glasgow.

Not only was *Cutty Sark* a good clipper, she has also been highly successful as a museum ship. Since being opened to the public by Queen Elizabeth II in 1957, she has been financially self-supporting for all the continual repairs and rebuilding needed. In the next twenty-two years, over eight million visitors paid to visit the ship and in her centenary year of 1969, well over 370,000 people visited her.

Not every ship has such success as a preserved ship. For over a decade the Liverpool ship *Wavertree* has been at the South Street Seaport Museum in New York and is being steadily restored, but lacks a sponsor to complete the work. *Wavertree* was actually towed there after spending a long period as a hulk in the Falkland Islands and then as a barge in Buenos Aires. This ship was originally owned by the Leyland brothers, Ralph and George, who, in the early 1870s, decided that they wanted to become shipowners. Their first ship was the *Doxford*, in 1878, and after that they steadily acquired a fleet. They were rather old fashioned in their approach as all their ships were full-rigged ships, which meant that they required large crews to handle the cumbersome sails. Although their ships were certainly not clippers, they earned modest dividends.

The height of the Leyland brothers' achievements was in 1885 when they had four large ships built. One of these, the *Southgate*, was sold to Chadwick & Pritchard before she was completed, but four years later Leylands bought her back, and following their policy of naming ships after areas of their home port of Liverpool, renamed her the *Wavertree*.

The hull of the full-rigged ship Wavertree *in a dry dock at Hoboken, New Jersey, in 1978. This great square-rigger loaded 2,500 tons of cargo. Sold to become a lighter in 1911, she was bought at Buenos Aires by the South Street Seaport Museum, who have since been restoring her at New York* (Norman Brouwer)

An iron ship, the *Wavertree* was 2,170 tons gross and was built at Southampton by Oswald, Mordaunt & Co. For the next twenty-five years, she was sailed wherever her owners could find cargoes for her to carry. Most of her voyages took her on the hard road round Cape Horn. She was an ocean wanderer and her voyages often kept her away from British ports for two or three years, but in the end she always seemed to turn up in British waters with a load of grain from San Francisco. Her officers were British but her crew, in the usual square-rigger tradition, were an international mixture and once they had brought the *Wavertree* back to its home port, they were paid off. After a short spell of nights on the town, they would be outward bound again on some other sailing ship. For these men, the sea was their only home and one port was very much like another.

While the sailors swung aloft handling the vast sails of this over-canvased ship, the owners in Liverpool struggled to find a profitable way of keeping her employed. The appeal of sailing ships had always been strong and the Leyland brothers did not give up sail easily, but as their fleet grew older three of their ships, *Grassendale*, *Woolton* and *Toxteth*, all 'went missing' at sea and they were replaced with grimy steamers. The economics of decline proved a vicious circle: the less money left after the expenses for each voyage, the less there was to spend on maintenance; with badly maintained rigging, the *Wavertree* made slower passages which, because she was at sea longer, cut down the returns even further. Worse still, because of the low profit, wages were poor and she had to be content with some inexperienced officers.

The *Wavertree*'s last round voyage began on 9 February 1904 when she cleared from Newcastle bound for San Francisco. She arrived there on 15 July, went on to Sydney, across to Peru and back to Australian ports before returning to South America and on up to British Columbia. After several passages on the west coast, she left Astoria with grain for Runcorn on 16 December 1907. A first-hand account of this passage round the Horn to Britain is recorded by Captain Spier in the book *The Ocean Wanderer*. He tells of the drudgery and brutality of sailing ship life in a very readable way.

Wavertree reached Liverpool after being at sea for 175 days, and the crew were literally starving, having only just managed to keep alive by grinding up the corn from the cargo. After three months in port, the *Wavertree* sailed again, this time for Vancouver for a charter of grain, but

The three-masted barque Glenbervie, *wrecked on the Manacles on the Cornish coast in December 1901* (F. E. Gibson)

her luck was running out, for off Ellesmere Port she was rammed by a steamer and had to turn back. Leyland had had enough. She was sold to Ernest Harry Neal and, after a year of idleness, he sent her off on her final voyage.

Her iron hull was still in good shape, but it was aloft where the real trouble lay—her rigging was worn out. Commanded by sixty-one-year-old Captain William Irving, she set out. Irving must have coaxed her along as best he could. Progress was bad enough in the Atlantic, but it was futile trying to round Cape Horn. To do this she had to beat continually against gale force winds. Going to windward was the worst point of sailing for any square-rigger and it put the utmost strain on their gear. The *Wavertree* did not make it: three months and ten days after leaving England, she turned up in Montevideo. The rigging was badly damaged and six of her crew were down with frostbite.

The owner's agent ordered repairs to be made, and after these were completed she sailed again with a largely fresh crew to make another attempt on rounding the Horn. It was no good; she ran into bad weather right away. First, the mainmast went, then the foretopmast and finally the mizzen was carried away. The helpless ship sighted a barque but could not attract attention. Finally *Wavertree* limped back to the Falkland Islands, virtually a wreck.

There were few places for a square-rigged ship to go after being driven away from Cape Horn, damaged and in need of repair to its complex rigging and huge spars. If the damage was not too great, then ships were often able to make a port on the South American mainland, but for many all they could do was run downwind to the Falkland Islands. Even these low-lying islands spread over this windswept area of the South Atlantic had only one real place of shelter, Port Stanley.

Many ships were actually wrecked in the Falklands and even those that made Port Stanley had little hope of leaving. The islands were inhabited by people who had gone out from Britain to develop sheep farming. There were no facilities for repairing the huge, steel, square-riggers or wooden ships which had come before them. If a ship could not be repaired by her own people, she had to stay there.

This is exactly what happened to numerous British, American and French lame ducks which limped into the Falklands. Usually they were stripped of their gear and used as storage hulks—most of the warehouse facilities at the tiny port of Port Stanley were hulks moored along the foreshore. The islanders knew how to make use of the boats, doors and numerous other fittings from the sailers, but there were no scrap dealers in the South Atlantic so there was little point in breaking up the hulks.

In the years between the two world wars, many ports had hulks of sailing ships broken up for scrap but no one took any notice of the Falkland Islands' hulks. But in 1943, war duty took G. L. Garratt to the Falklands, and his interest in sail lead him to start going through the local archives to identify the hulks. After the war, Garratt completed his notes and they were published in *Sea Breezes* in 1948. In the years that followed, sailing ship enthusiasts began visiting the Falklands to look at the hulks. Largely because of the cold climate, they had not rotted away. Of course they had deteriorated over the decades, but some ships are very old and of great historic interest. These include the wooden East Indiaman *Jhelum*, built in 1849, and the *Capricorn*, built at Swansea in 1829. Plans have been put forward to try to return the hulks of some of these back to Europe or North America for preservation. Only Isambard Kingdom Brunel's great iron steamer, the *Great Britain*, has actually been saved.

When the *Great Britain* was launched at Bristol in 1843, she revolutionised sea travel, but the great liner arrived in the Falklands in 1886 when her engines had been removed and she was a humble trader tramping the world's oceans. On her last cargo voyage, coal had been loaded at Cardiff for Panama. The voyage was straightforward enough until she got down towards Cape Horn. She was hit by a tremendous south-westerly gale which sent the seas crashing right over the forty-three-year-old iron vessel. When the wind reached hurricane force, the crew came aft and asked the master to put back for the Falklands as they considered that the hull could not stand the strain. The master, Captain Henry Stap, refused but fortunately the wind started to die away.

The coal cargo on *Great Britain* had shifted in the hurricane, but in the few days of fine weather that followed, the crew made a superhuman effort shovelling the 'black diamonds' to get the ship on an even keel. Then came another howling gale blasting across the Southern Ocean. This time her fore and mizzen topgallant masts came down, and the master had no alternative but to turn back and try to make the Falklands. Even when she did reach them, her troubles were far from over. She went aground near Williams Isle, refloated and then went aground again. Finally, she was towed into Port Stanley by the steamer *Rance*.

The *Great Britain* joined the storage hulks until she was no longer required when the Falkland Island Company thought of giving her a 'Viking Burial'. In the end her fame saved her and the hulk was beached in Sparrow Cove. Certainly when G. L. Garratt was in the Falklands, there seemed not the slightest chance that she would be saved, but in 1970 she was towed back to Bristol on a raft. Here she was berthed in the very dock where she had been built 127 years before. Although *Great Britain*'s return caught the public's imagination, the city fathers were not impressed. They had planned a motorway over the dock, but in the end they were persuaded to give a home to the *Great Britain*.

The *Great Britain* and the *Cutty Sark* were both ships of national importance so the case for preservation was very strong. However, it is a great deal more difficult to persuade people to give money to save ships which are just typical of a particular type. In the museum world, curators have to decide whether to spend the money at their disposal on maintaining a museum building to house exhibits, or whether to try to preserve actual ships. In the 1930s, the Science Museum organised the taking of lines from existing craft and made models from them. In this way the models housed in a museum could show many different types of craft in a very small area. However, another school of thought developed, arguing that the actual vessels should be preserved. Preservation of the actual vessel was shown to be possible when Nelson's HMS *Victory* was eventually restored at Portsmouth between 1922–8, although it was about another thirty years before it was generally accepted that the same principle should be applied to ordinary working craft.

Steering the course between financing museum premises and restoring actual craft remains a considerable problem for the museum world. The two functions are separate. The Maritime Trust, set up in 1969, was intended to be a preservation organisation freed of the responsibility of maintaining a building. The Maritime Trust has been successful in saving many craft which would otherwise have been scrapped. Their first success was the schooner *Kathleen & May* and they have had considerable success in saving many other vessels since then.

In Britain vessels tend to be scrapped shortly after their working life is over and they stand a better chance of survival in remote corners of the world. The four-masted ship *County of Roxburgh* sits on a reef in the middle of the Pacific. This 2,900-ton full-rigged ship was built on the Clyde in 1886 for the India–Scotland jute trade, but in 1905, while on passage across the Pacific, a hurricane drove her ashore in the Tuamotus Archipelago. Seventy years later, the *County of Roxburgh* was still sitting on Takaroa. Like all wrecks she had long since been looted of everything useful to people in the islands, yet her masts stood for forty years after she was abandoned. Eventually even these fell down, although in 1976 the bowsprit was still standing and the whole ship was basically intact. In spite of the tropical sun, it was still possible for the crew of the visiting brigantine *Romance* to trace the original colour scheme.

It is remarkable that a ship could have lasted so long, but what are the practical possibilities of preserving her? She is a long way from any British museum and she was a representative of a rare and rather awkward breed of ship, the four-masted, full-rigged ship. At least one British four-

The wreck of the four-masted, full-rigged ship County of Roxburgh *is still on the Pacific atoll of Takaroa where she was driven ashore in 1905. All the four-masted iron and steel full-rigged ships were built in Britain. The first one built, the* County of Peebles *at Glasgow in 1875, still exists at Punt Arenas on the Straits of Magellan as a breakwater. The third remaining four-masted, full-rigged ship is the* Falls of Clyde *at Hawaii* (Captain Arthur Kimberly)

masted, full-rigged ship has already been preserved, but not in Britain. This is the huge 323ft *Falls of Clyde* which has been carefully restored in Honolulu. The *Falls of Clyde* was built on the Clyde in 1878 and was one of six similar ships operated by the Glasgow Falls Line. However, in 1900 she was sold to an American and traded to Honolulu under the Hawaiian flag before finishing up as an oil barge. When her usefulness had finished, there was a great effort in Hawaii to raise the money to save her.

Sailing ships grew in size from 1875–1900 because of improved technology. Wire replaced rope so that much larger sails could be set. Also the yards and sails were controlled by winches and capstans, whereas in the early nineteenth century ships had blocks and tackles. In 1873 the Glasgow shipowner Thomas Dunlop had a new iron barque built for him in Sunderland. This was the 173ft *Clan Macleod* which loaded just over 500 tons and had a crew of twenty. The *Clan Mackenzie*, built nine years later, must have loaded three times as much yet only carried about five more hands, while Dunlop's four-masted barque *Clan Buchanan*, built in 1887, must have loaded yet another 1,000 tons, but only carried the same number of crew.

The little iron barques, such as *Clan Macleod*, with their large crews were like yachts compared to the great four-masters with their huge steel masts and spars and acres of heavy canvas, all handled by men's sweat and muscle. The iron hulls may have been out-priced by steel, but they were very strong. The *Clan Macleod* stood up to the punishing life of an ocean-going sailing ship for nearly fifty years, although in the end the sea nearly claimed her while on passage across the Bass Strait.

Thomas Dunlop moved on to larger sailing ships and then, like every progressive shipowner competing for freight markets, into steamers. The little iron barque was sold and in 1905 had her name changed to *James Craig*. She then had 'gun-ports' painted on her sides which greatly improved her appearance. Like many small sailers, she was sold to owners in Australasia and became one of the Craig of Auckland fleet.

The *James Craig*'s final years in trade were difficult with the economic slump of the early 1920s. She was finally abandoned in Recherche Bay in the very south of Tasmania, on the edge of the great Southern Ocean around Antarctica. In these cold waters, she rusted away for forty years. Sailing ships have a tremendously strong grip on the minds of men and she was not forgotten, but it was not until a letter in the ship magazine *Sea Breezes* that a move was made to save her. In 1972 an enthusiastic team

Hands caulking the fo'c's'le of the Clyde-built, three-masted barque Inverclyde. *They are hammering rolled oakum into the space between the planks after which they were 'paid' (covered) with pitch to make a watertight bond* (National Maritime Museum)

refloated her and it was found that she was intact where the hull was underwater but rust had damaged her sides above the water-line. Her ultimate resting place is at Sydney where she is to be the centre piece of the Maritime Museum. The *James Craig* is there as a reminder of the early period of a young country because most of the early settlers went there in ships of this size.

The most famous sailing ship built on the banks of the River Wear at Sunderland was the 221ft full-rigged passenger clipper *Torrens*, launched in 1875 with the figurehead of the likeness of the daughter of her first master, Captain Henry Angel. She was very fast in light airs and in the gale-lashed regions of the 'roaring forties' used to average 300–350 miles a day without taking any sea on the decks. The four-masted barques which later sailed these regions deeply laden, used to be like 'half tide rocks' with the sea sweeping right across their decks.

The *Torrens* took passengers out from Britain to Australia and back for twenty-eight years. She had a very good working record, but this alone did not single out *Torrens* for fame. She is largely remembered now because the novelist Joseph Conrad served in her as mate. Conrad joined the *Torrens* in 1891, and during the long passages home from Australia, he wrote part of *Almayer's Folly*. At the same time he became friendly with the novelist John Galsworthy who was a passenger aboard the clipper. It was Galsworthy who encouraged Conrad to try to have his work published and the two remained on friendly terms for life.

Joseph Conrad was born in Poland in 1857 into an aristocratic family, but his father was opposed to Russian domination and died prematurely through harsh treatment in prison. At seventeen, Conrad left his native land and went to Marseilles, where he shipped as a seaman in a French vessel. In spite of his fluent French, Conrad did not seek a career under the tricolour and when he was twenty-one he landed in Lowestoft. He spoke virtually no English but found a berth on the barquentine *Skimmer of the Sea*. She was already an old ship and was in the coal trade between Newcastle-upon-Tyne and Lowestoft. Conrad made only a couple of voyages in this collier before he shipped on the wool clipper *Duke of Sunderland* as an ordinary seaman.

Conrad had now learnt enough English to follow the promotion ladder needed to qualify for a second mate's 'ticket'. After more time at sea, he qualified as first mate and became a naturalised British subject in 1886. He also obtained his masters 'ticket' the following year, although for a long time he did not attempt to seek a berth as master. Instead he moved restlessly from ship to ship wandering the world, mostly to eastern countries, but nearly always in sail.

In 1888 Conrad was persuaded to become master of the 370-ton, iron barque *Otago*, which was owned in Australia, although she had been built on the Clyde. Conrad seems to have been very fond of the *Otago* as she was a beautiful and easily handled ship, but Conrad's period as a master lasted only eighteen months. It consisted of a single voyage from Bangkok to Singapore, on to Australia, Mauritius and back to Singapore. In this voyage he went 'north about' through the Torres Straits, a dangerous place to sail, where many a ship had been driven ashore by the currents and lost.

At the end of this voyage the owner of the tiny *Otago* was in debt and Conrad left this, his only real command. The *Otago* was cut down to a store hulk and was later taken to Hobart where she was broken up. However, some of the strong iron plates and frame were left on the foreshore, and in about 1975 the San Francisco Maritime Museum had these remains taken to the United States. It seems that the wheel of *Otago* found its way to London and was installed in the Honourable Company of Master Mariners' headquarters, the sloop *Wellington*, berthed at the Embankment in London.

Conrad kept no souvenirs, only memories which he used later with such effect in his stories. The next appointment of this withdrawn and lonely man was as first mate on the clipper *Torrens*. On his first voyage, in 1891, the clipper went out to Adelaide from Plymouth in ninety-five days with passengers and cargo. Including the amount of time needed in dock when discharging by hand, a round voyage to Australia and back took about nine months. After a further long period in London Docks, the *Torrens* was only averaging one complete voyage a year. With sailing ships the whole tempo of business life was so much slower, and for this reason steamers were constantly taking over more routes. At one time passenger clippers like the *Torrens* took the best men in the merchant navy. A decade before, Conrad would not have stood a chance of becoming first mate on such a ship. However, even after Conrad left her in 1893, the *Torrens* continued in the Australia run for another ten years.

An outstanding writer both reflects and shapes his generation's attitude to any subject, and Joseph Conrad coloured many people's views of sailing ships at the beginning of this century. Like most good story tellers, Conrad heightened the facts to make many of them more exciting but his stories were founded on experience. In *Lord Jim* he tells of a pilgrim steamer abandoned by her European captain and officers who reported the ship lost after reaching land safely. The ship, however, was found later and towed into Aden with the pilgrims still sitting aboard. This actually happened, although the steamer was actually called the *Patna*, not the *Jeddah*. No doubt Conrad had heard of this incident out east.

Most of Conrad's sea stories were based on his own experiences. He was second mate on the ship *Narcissus*, although the 'nigger' in *Nigger of the Narcissus* was actually a shipmate on the *Duke of Sunderland*, and there were similar parallels throughout his work. Conrad has given an outstanding portrait of life in small British square-riggers of the later Victorian period. Like all seamen, he was suspicious of harbour officials and his regret at having to leave the beautiful *Torrens* in the dirty London Docks at the end of a voyage comes over in published memories *Mirror of the Sea* and *A Personal Record*.

It seems that Conrad's last voyage in a square-rigger was in the brigantine *Ready* when she made a North Sea passage in 1916. The *Ready* was a 'Q' or decoy ship armed for sinking German submarines. In World War I German submarines did not waste expensive torpedoes on little coastal schooners and allowed the crews to row away before placing a bomb aboard. The Admiralty had a number of sailing vessels fitted out as decoy ships which met with some success by waiting for the submarine to surface and then opening fire.

Conrad joined the elderly brigantine *Ready* at Dundee in the hope of experiencing the excitement of action. He was then sixty-nine and had been ashore for over twenty years. Few men of his years would have gone off in winter during war time on such an adventure. However, nothing happened while Conrad was aboard, although a few months later, when the *Ready* was under sail in the English Channel, two German submarines surfaced. They approached, thinking that another piece of Britain's merchant navy was to be sent to the bottom, but the *Ready* threw off her disguise and opened fire, sinking one of the submarines.

World War I saw the destruction of many fine sailing ships which were never replaced. Before the war, deepwater sailing ships, although no longer being built, were still a common sight in most British ports. Within a few years of the Great War ending, nearly all had gone. Conrad had portrayed the human side of sailing ships, but many of the facts about them were gathered together by Basil Lubbock. A man with a minor aristocratic background who had gone out to the Klondyke Gold Rush in search of adventure, he went to San Francisco in 1899 and signed on as an ordinary seaman on the Glasgow four-masted barque *Commonwealth* bound round Cape Horn and back to Britain with wheat.

Lubbock later wrote *Round the Horn Before the Mast* which ran to many reprints and described the life of an ordinary seaman in sail. Even at that time, the majority of sailing ships only managed to get cargoes for the west coast of America because steamers used too much coal trying to round Cape Horn. All this ended when the Panama Canal opened in 1914, but for the previous twenty years owners had had to economise by cutting crew numbers and other costs to the bare minimum.

When Lubbock sailed from San Francisco, the barque which he called *Royalshire* in the book was undermanned and there was not enough food on board for a long voyage. He was young and strong and able to stand up to the hardships of the voyage. In spite of the obvious difficulties, the master was determined to achieve a reasonable passage out of the barque. With her steel hull, masts and spars, the barque stood up to the really hard driving in heavy weather, but as they approached Cape Horn, life aboard became miserable and dangerous. Huge seas crashed aboard, sweeping right along the open main deck. Everyone lived in wet clothes and slept in wet bedding. They could not light the galley fire so it was even impossible to make any hot food or drinks. The wet, cold and continually heavy work pushed some of the men to total exhaustion, but the captain drove his ship on. As soon as the wind dropped, more sail was set. Usually in a few hours the wind rose again to a screaming gale and the hands had to go aloft to take in the heavy, wildly flapping canvas sails. Once, near the Horn, most of the crew were down on the open deck

Looking aft on the full-rigged ship William Mitchell *running in a big sea. She was one of five sailing ships built between 1890–2 by W. J. Bigger in Londonderry for William Mitchell. He named most of his ships after Derry merchants and was the last owner of deep sea sail in that Northern Ireland port. After Mitchell was accidently drowned in Carlingford Lough in 1902, the* William Mitchell *was sold to London owners and twenty years later was the last British full-rigged ship in trade* (National Maritime Museum)

hauling on a brace (which controls the yards) when a monster sea broke right over the side and engulfed them all. The captain saw only a boiling mass of white water with his men floating about in it, as he looked down from the poop. It was not unknown in this situation for a whole watch to be simply swept overboard for ever, but in this case the only casualty was Lubbock. He hit his knee badly and the injury troubled him, not just for the rest of the voyage, but for the rest of his life. After the barque had rounded 'Cape Stiff' the captain told Lubbock:

This is my thirtieth passage round the Horn as master, and outward bound I've never been more than a couple of weeks beating off the pitch of the Horn; and what's more, I never will be. Why is it that some ships spend months beating off the Horn? Simply because, directly he gets off the Horn, the captain puts his ship under lower-topsails, and just beats backwards and forwards, waiting for a slant to get him round. That's not the way to get round the Horn; why, I've come round under royals and passed ships under lower topsails. Whenever you get a chance, you must take advantage of it, and cram on sail and force your way against the Westerlies. No, don't tell me that it's not the master's fault when his ship spends a month or six weeks off the Horn, for I know it is. Look at that foreigner under lower-topsails; if we were outward bound now I'd have the *Royalshire* under six topsails and whole foresail;—though, mind you, I'm not saying that if I was captain of that dagoman I'd have all that canvas set, for the *Royalshire* has got seven backstays, whilst that old tub's only got three.

The barque was four months at sea before she finally reached the British Isles, but even then Lubbock states that she was the first of the San Francisco grain fleet home. When she had sailed from San Francisco, the grain had not been sold to a miller so as the ship closed with the land, the captain had to find out at which port he was to unload. Most masters made for Falmouth to receive their orders. However, the wind had pushed the barque on to the southern coast of Ireland and the master hove-to off Queenstown (Cobh) and ran up his ship's number in flags. He received a signal in reply saying that they were due at Birkenhead on the Mersey.

During the long voyage, the crew had had no contact with the outside world. The fact that Britain had been at war with the Boers in South Africa for two months came as a complete surprise to them. Once the barque was in her discharging berth, her crew were paid off. Lubbock never saw the ship again. Nor did he see many of her crew again. He became an army officer and gained distinction for bravery in battle. After the Boer War, he married and settled on the south coast of England, using a small private income on which to live while he began to gather facts about sailing ships.

Some of the crew of the three-masted ship Zealandia *have managed to catch a shark and haul it on deck. One of the seamen is holding a belaying pin in the shark's mouth, presumably to stop it biting* (National Maritime Museum)

Lubbock's books are full of tales of fast passages and record-breaking clippers, as if he was trying to prove that sailing ships really should not have been abandoned. A great many men who went to sea in sail genuinely disliked having to seek a career in steam. Such a man was Captain B. A. Hardinge who, after training on the *Worcester* anchored in the Thames, joined the four-masted steel barque *Crown of India* in 1907. He was in this ship for nearly four years, until she arrived at Belfast, by which time he had enough sea time to sit for a ticket. Hardinge described his parting from the *Crown of India*: 'That was the last I had to do with sailing ships. A very good friend advised me to leave them alone, which was only too true. I had regrets,—though—as was ever the case, the last ship was always the best ship.'

Far away in Australia, another young man, Alan Villiers, had an ambition to go to sea in some of the glorious British sailing ships. He managed a limited time in a British square-rigger, but by the early 1920s all the glory had gone. Later Villiers sailed in Finnish square-riggers, most of them ex-British, and he began writing about his time in them. With the proceeds, he bought a small Danish full-rigged ship, renamed her *Joseph Conrad* and sailed round the world. He then returned to writing about square-riggers.

The best-known works on sailing ships are by Conrad, Lubbock and Villiers. The first two saw Britain's merchant fleet at its height and Villiers saw it in considerable decline. This decline started in the late 1890s and ended in the 1920s. Most of the British ships were scrapped when their commercial life finished. The only ones to survive, apart from a few in museums, were those which finished up in remote corners of the world. The Falkland Islands acquired a great collection which were used as warehouses. There are still the remains of some mid-nineteenth century wooden ships there such as the *William Shand*, built in 1839, the *Jhelum* of 1849 and the wooden barque *Vicar of Bray* built at Whitehaven in 1841 which is the only ship left of the fleet which went out to the 1849 California Gold Rush and for this reason San Francisco museum would like to save her.

The lower part of the brig *Fleetwing*, built at Porthmadog in North Wales in 1874 is also in the Falklands, but the best preserved are the iron barque *Garland* and the best of them all the iron barque *Lady Elizabeth*, built at Sunderland in 1879 and still, a century later, with her lower masts standing. It was also even possible to see sailor's pin-ups on the fo'c'sle walls.

In New Zealand is the *Edwin Fox* which was built of teak at Calcutta in 1853 for a London merchant and was later in the immigration trade being run by Shaw, Savill & Company of London. She is now a hulk in a cove

The Saxonia, *built in 1935, is fairly typical of the beamy, carvel-built Thames estuary bawleys which evolved after about 1875* (Caroline Simper)

'Stiff Breeze off Ramsgate', a painting on canvas by John Wilson Carmichael signed
and dated 1837 (N. R. Omell)

Queen of the South *in the Pool of London in 1966. Built on the Clyde in 1931 as* Jeannie Deans, *she only had one final season on the Thames because driftwood kept breaking her wooden paddles* (E. H. Cole)

The Humber keel Annie Maud, *built at Thorne in 1893, at York in 1976 when she was practically the only surviving wooden keel* (Author)

near Picton, but in 1981 much of the timber was still very strong. Like most wooden ships trading in tropical waters she was sheathed in copper below the waterline as a protection against the boring worm.

In Australia the *Polly Woodside*, built by Workman, Clark & Company of Belfast in 1885 is restored at Melbourne and the Sunderland-built *James Craig* is being restored at Sydney. There are others such as the iron barque *City of Foochow*, built by Barclay, Curle & Company on the Clyde in 1864 and wrecked on Flinders Island in Bass Strait in 1877. Miraculously one mast was still standing in the surf over a century later. The sailing ship hull which is perhaps in the best condition in Australia, outside a museum, is the steel Sunderland-built barque *Caradog* of 1891 which was wrecked on Vansittart Shoal off the SE point of Flinders Island.

Also in the Bass Strait on Phillip Island are the remains of the steel Liverpool ship *Speke*, which was wrecked there in 1906. She was built, like the *Wavertree*, for Leylands as a full-rigged ship. The *Speke* came from T. R. Oswald & Co of Milford Haven in 1891, a successor to Oswald, Mordaunt & Co of Southampton. In an attempt to rival the tramp steamers, Leylands had produced these huge full-rigged ships which had a reputation for being very heavy to work.

Some of the sailing ships which were abandoned in lonely coves have been restored. The Clyde-built *Balclutha* is fully restored at San Francisco, while the iron *Euterpe*, built at Ramsey, Isle of Man, in 1863, is restored at San Diego and has even been taken out for a sail. Another American museum ship is *Elissa*, built by Alexander Hall & Son at Aberdeen in 1877. Much later she was converted to a motor vessel and finished her trading career being operated by Greek cigarette smugglers in the late 1960s. The *Elissa* was actually at a shipbreakers in Greece waiting to be scrapped when an American bought her to prevent this happening. The Liverpool Museum tried to raise the money to save her, but in 1975 a group from Galveston, Texas, bought her and had her towed across the Atlantic for restoration. This does not end the list of former British square-riggers still in existence. At Stockholm, as a hostel, is the *Af Chapman* which was originally the full-rigged ship *Dunboyne*, built at Whitehaven in 1888.

In the age of sail, Britain's merchant fleet was the envy of the world. In the late nineteenth century, every commercial harbour had some ships flying the red ensign. Many of these smaller sailing ships were away from the home country for years. In fact most British shipowners must only have seen their ships very occasionally so it is perhaps appropriate that they have been restored and preserved in ports all over the world.

4

The Coastal Trade

While great admirals won decisive battles and places in history and explorers risked life and limb to reach distant corners of the globe, the coastal traders of Britain plodded on year in year out virtually unnoticed, but vitally important. Since bulk goods were easier to move on water than by land, the sea became a commercial highway. The movement of coal provided the largest coastal trade. After the Great Fire of London in 1666, the government brought in laws to encourage coal to be burnt to reduce the risk of wood fire sparks. Also wood was becoming scarcer and the state wished to preserve timber for ship and house building. There was already a considerable trade between the North of England and the Thames when the Industrial Revolution triggered off an even greater demand for coal.

The seventeenth-century colliers seem to have confined their voyages to the summer months, and by 1755 the average Whitby collier was still only making about nine round voyages between the Tyne and the Thames every year. This leisurely pace had disappeared well before the end of the eighteenth century and it seems that London and Yarmouth merchants dominated the trade until around 1800 when the North of England started to take control. The ports of Blyth, The Shields, Newcastle, Sunderland and Hartlepool were the homes of the famous Geordie collier brigs and by 1843 some 585 of them were taking coal south. The collier brigs required less hands than their predecessors and were designed for maximum carrying capacity, not speed. The passage south was mainly a matter of dashing from each anchorage every time they got a fair wind. The brig's ample bluff bows were said to push a fathom and a half of white water before them and their wide counter sterns to drag half the North Sea behind them.

A head wind caused the colliers to lay windbound in the Tyne in their hundreds. When the wind dropped the whole fleet streamed out to sea and headed south. At that stage, before dredging, there was only a fathom of water on Shields bar and many old colliers bumped their way over which resulted in them leaking all the way to the Thames. Many of the Geordie brigs made summer voyages to the Baltic and even further afield, but many old ships of every description were put into the North Sea trade hauling 'black diamonds' for the fires and furnaces of the south.

94

Collier brigs in the inner harbour at Whitby (Frank Sutcliffe)

Every gale saw good men, often in their hundreds, drowned after their ships foundered or were thrown ashore. At this time Britain had the greatest merchant fleet in the world, but between 1850 and 1865 no fewer than 20,000 vessels were lost. Some of these were perfectly good ships lost through the rigours of the sea, but many more were 'coffin ships', sent to sea in an unseaworthy condition and overloaded by unscrupulous owners. In 1868 the coal merchant Samuel Plimsoll became a Liberal Member of Parliament and began to become concerned about the coffin ship scandal. Plimsoll was dubbed 'the sailor's friend' because he devoted the rest of his life to reforms within the merchant navy. In 1872 he published a book *Our Seamen* which caused a sensation when it revealed the conditions of merchant ships. Plimsoll advocated the fixing of a line the side of a ship below which she should not be loaded. This simple safety measure was fought ruthlessly by some merchant interests while the enlightened shipowners, the press and some other Victorian social reformers rallied to make sure that the fixing of a load line became law. In the Merchant Shipping Act of 1876 it was still left to the owners to fix where this line was painted. One shipmaster showed his contempt for any form of regulation by painting a circular disc 'Plimsoll Line' on the funnel! It was not until 1890 that another Act made the Board of Trade responsible for fixing the line.

Plimsoll also saw that to win better conditions seamen needed a trade union and he helped to found one. He became the first President of the newly founded Seaman & Fireman's Union in 1890. By this time he was battling for better conditions on the cattle ships in the Atlantic trade. After his death at seventy-four in 1898, the city fathers of his birthplace, Bristol, erected a bust at the City Docks, while in 1929 the National Union of Seamen had a bronze statue of the Sailor's Friend placed on the Victoria Embankment, London, in gratitude for the service he had done for seamen of all nations.

The casual way that the shipping community viewed the state of a ship has been recorded best by Walter Runciman. He left his home at Cresswell on the Northumbrian coast in about 1859 when he was twelve years old and went to Blyth. Here he joined the brig *Harperley* which was bound with coal for Mozambique. Runciman became a master in sail and then went on to become a millionaire owning a shipping line. In later life he wrote informatively about the collier brigs and gave a realistic insight into them and the rough and honest men who sailed them. There was Captain 'Barley' Readford of the brig *Honour* of Blyth, a deeply religious man who once saw a Dutch galliot sailing in the Swin clear of the Thames Estuary sandbanks while he was having difficulties and he swore, 'That's a fine thing for God Almighty to give a leading wind to a Dutchman and let his own countryman be left on a lee shore!'

Because these sailors went to sea as young boys, the Geordie skippers had little or no education and were quite unable to make use of navigational instruments. They claimed to be able to smell their way around the North Sea and Baltic, but really it was simple pilotage backed up by hard experience. They were stoutly, independent men who stood by their brig's huge wooden tiller wearing a stove pipe hat, velvet-collared pea-jacket and regardless of weather, a woollen muffler. A story goes that one such skipper was driven so far off his course, first by a gale and then by fog, that he completely lost his bearings. In almost apologetic terms he enquired from the mate if there was such a thing as a chart aboard. In these early Victorian days it was considered an indication that he did not know his job if a shipmaster relied on anything which smelt of 'book learning'. The mate snorted with disgust that he thought that there was an old chart in the chain locker and he would go and get it. Down in the after cabin, the collier's skipper pored over the crumpled chart and discovered that he was heading for some islands in the middle of the North Sea. This was strange because he had never heard of any offshore islands; besides, these marks looked very much like fly marks on the chart.

Suddenly he realised that he could not take the risk and leapt up the steps on to the deck shouting 'wear ship' and came on a fresh course just in case there were islands out there.

The North Country wooden sailing ships traded to any port in the world, but the North Sea coal trade employed by far the largest numbers. Runciman states that in 1851 Blyth had 118 wooden ships, mostly brigs of around 350 tons. By 1874 this fleet had increased to 201. However, the impact of steam ships meant that most of them were sold or not replaced when wrecked so that by the late 1880s they were nearly all gone.

Owners in southern England continued to operate sailing colliers right up to 1919. After about 1870 most of the trading vessels from places like Littlehampton, Shoreham, Newhaven, Folkestone, Dover and Whitstable were built cheaply in the Canadian maritime provinces. Much of the forest in this part of Canada has still not recovered from the mid-Victorian era when shipwrights built vast numbers of traders from virgin timber. Prince Edward Island was the centre of this activity and turned out traders with very little metal in their construction. They were often intended to be little more than sailing lighters which made perhaps a couple of voyages across the Atlantic with timber and were then sold to owners in South Wales. They operated them for a few deepwater voyages with coal and then sold them to owners in ports like Whitstable from where they worked for the next forty years in the North Sea coal trade.

The only survivor in 1980 of all the hundreds of Prince Edward Island vessels was part of the hulk of the Whitstable *Sela* in Milford Haven. She was built in 1859 and during her many decades at Whitstable she must have had consistent reconstruction work on her hull. As the planking went soft they simply 'doubled' her with another skin of planks and metal fastenings were driven in as the original wooden 'tren'al' fastenings gave out so that after some seventy years her sides were about 18in thick.

John Bull of Newhaven ran the local Sussex-built traders and Canadian vessels right up until 1906. One of the Bull Line ships sold by his executors was the 260-ton Shoreham brig *Commerce*. Many of the brigs had had a long deep sea career in general cargo before they were relegated to the coal trade. The Lowestoft brig *Celerity* was driven ashore and wrecked near her home port in 1908. The brig *Utopia* was driven ashore at Whitstable in 1911. No ship was ever too old for the Whitstable owners to try and get a few more freights and the *Utopia* was dragged off and sent back to the North only to be finally wrecked a few months later.

As the Industrial Revolution gathered momentum and the population of Britain increased, so the coastal trade expanded. Although the railway system was steadily pushing its way across the face of Britain, it never reached every village. Steam and sailing coasters usually undercut the

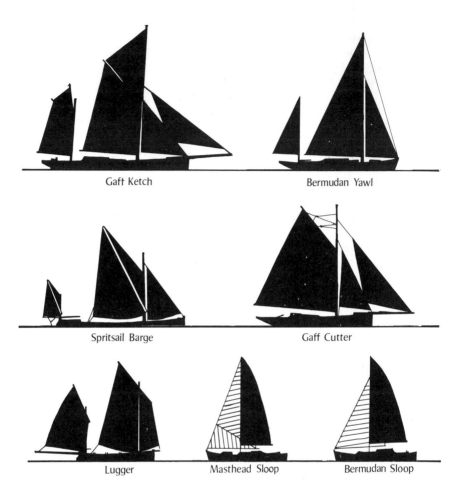

Gaft Ketch

Bermudan Yawl

Spritsail Barge

Gaff Cutter

Lugger

Masthead Sloop

Bermudan Sloop

railway freight rates on bulk cargoes so that most coastal districts received their coal by sea at least up until World War I.

In order for sail to remain practical, a more flexible rig than the brig had to be found and this resulted in the appearance of barquentines, brigantines and above all the schooner rig. The favourite rig of the British coastal seamen in the late nineteenth century was the topsail schooner. This combined the ease of handling of the fore-and-aft rig with the tremendous pulling power of the square sails by having gaff lower sails with two or three square sails on the foremast, which were powerful when sailing off the wind. The square topsails on the foremast were greatly liked by the Victorian seamen because they were an 'insurance policy' against getting caught in 'irons'. In other words these slow moving traders were rather prone to fail to come round on to a fresh tack in a

98

Thames Spritsail Barge

Lowestoft Drifter

Brixham Trawler

Humber Keel

Zulu

Fifie

Bawley

Norfolk Wherry

Itchen Ferry Boat

Bristol Channel Pilot Cutter

Tenby Lugger

Hastings Beach Boat

Coble

Morecambe Bay Prawner

TRADITIONAL
BOAT TYPES

Steam Drifter

Clyde Puffer

seaway when beating against the wind. However, with square topsails which could be backed so that the head of the vessel was pushed through the eye of the wind, the schooner would fall off on a fresh tack. The two-masted ketch was increasingly popular after 1900 because it required fewer hands, but they were not generally as fast.

In the latter part of the nineteenth century, apart from stretches of the coast where local conditions gave birth to a seagoing version of the local barges, the majority of coastal trades were handled by topsail schooners. The early topsail schooner 'fruiters' went out to the Azores and the Mediterranean after fresh oranges and other citrus fruits. Naturally the speed in which their destination was reached was absolutely vital or the valuable cargoes went rotten under the crew's feet. Leading builders all over Britain constructed very fine lined schooners for the fruit trade, but this trade seems to have been centred in the West Country.

It was not unknown for a fruit schooner to leave the Thames, sail through a huge fleet of coasters lying windbound in The Downs (the Straits of Dover anchorage sheltered by the Goodwin Sands) and beat out to the Azores against the south-westerly gales. On roaring back 'up channel' three weeks later, they often found The Downs still full of windbound shipping. Basil Lubbock has recorded some of the outstanding fruit schooner passages. The *Elinor* sailed from London Bridge to the Azores, where she was loaded by a small boat bringing the cargo out to the schooner at anchor in the open sea, and then returned back to London in seventeen days. The Salcombe schooner *Bezaleel* probably created something of a record for this trade when she sailed from St Michaels to Liverpool in only five and a half days.

The fruit schooners had curved clipper bows and usually had masts raking aft which gave them a very fast appearance, although by 1860 it was customary to step the mast straight upwards. But the clipper-bowed fruit schooners set as much sail as possible. The price they paid for obtaining the maximum speed was that they were intolerably wet at sea. Seamen used to say that fruit schooners took a dive off St Michaels and surfaced again in the Thames.

It was still quite common in the 1880s for small vessels to be built to take part in the ocean trades. The 95ft three-masted topsail schooner *Mount Blairy* was built to take part in the ocean trades in 1874. She was one of a whole fleet of small wooden sailing traders built in the Moray Firth by Geddie of Kingston.

Strictly speaking, the schooners and smaller square-riggers, such as barquentines and brigantines which made ocean voyages, could not be called coasters, but they were owned in small ports and often carried coastal freights between deepwater voyages. Steamers conquered the fruit trades in the 1870s and gradually took over the other deepwater freights. Only the Newfoundland fish trade, which dated from the earliest settlement of North America, remained in the hands of schooners. This was because steamers, which were expensive to operate, could not afford the delays in loading a small cargo in a remote creek for an ocean voyage.

In the mid-nineteenth century, once the orange season was over, the fruit schooners loaded salt in a British port and sailed across the Atlantic to load cod which had been preserved by drying and then salting. They then sailed back to the Latin countries where the cod was eaten on days of fast. The salted cod or stock fish was loaded in any of the hundreds of creeks or 'out port' settlements around the coast of Newfoundland.

Businesses were built up at certain ports in this specialised work of moving small freights from tiny communities across the ocean. Some Clyde owners and James Fisher & Sons of Barrow sent small schooners on long voyages. In 1884 Fisher's had some forty sailing ships in the short sea ore and coastal trades. They were one of a few owners to build up a fleet of schooners. Usually one schooner had her sixty-four shares of ownership divided between several owners as business people seldom had the capital to own a vessel outright. Fisher's must have found schooners very suitable for their trades as between 1880–92 they had twelve new three-masted topsail schooners built for them by the renowned builder Paul Rodgers of Carrickfergus on Belfast Lough.

The slate quarries of North Wales brought a boom in schooner building to the little port of Porthmadog. The harbour was created by William Madock and opened in 1824 with the name 'Portmadoc', by which it was known throughout the schooner era. Between 1824–1913 at least 263 ships were built at Porthmadog of which not one survives. The 76ft trading ketch *Garlandstone* is preserved at the once important port, but she was not strictly speaking even a local vessel although it is appropriate that she should have ended up at this famous sailing ship port.

The slate traders built at Porthmadog at the head of the tiny River Glaslyn were wooden. Being deep draught they could load more on a shorter hull length than the pure coastal vessels and barges. For instance, the 81ft topsail schooner *Cadwalader Jones*, built of oak by Morris Owen in 1878 could load 220 tons. She was in the deepwater trades for many years and is reputed to have crossed the Atlantic forty-two times. As well as the North Atlantic trades, many schooners were in the slate trade. The 89ft three-masted topsail schooner *M. A. James* created a record in 1906 when, deeply loaded with Ffestiniog slate, she covered the thousand miles between Porthmadog and Hamburg in only four and a half days. The roofing slate trade to German North Sea ports was a long standing one by the time the 102ft three-masted topsail schooner *Frau Minna Petersen* was launched in 1878, named after the daughter of a German merchant, with whom the owners hoped to do business. Long afterwards, in World War I this name was changed to *Jane Banks*. It was unusual for any sailing vessel to have her name changed. Indeed it was considered very bad luck to alter a name. Sailing men were rigidly superstitious and very careful not to offend whatever Gods of fortune governed the moods of the seas.

Another reason that coasting traders spent their whole career under one name was that they were seldom part of a big fleet, but were owned by individual shareholders. Seamen used to say that a schooner 'belonged' to Porthmadog, Barmouth or any other port and this meant that the shareholders lived in that port. One man was registered as being the owner, but usually he was a chief shareholder who fixed freights and undertook the general management. It was quite normal for the master to be offered shares in a vessel, and in some cases he managed the business side as well as commanding her. Every British ship was and still is legally divided into an ownership of sixty-four shares so that in small ports virtually everybody had some connection with shipping. In a little town like Porthmadog the welfare of the town's shipping affected everybody.

Life aboard the Welsh schooners which sailed from Barmouth, Aberdovey, Aberystwyth and many other places round Cardigan Bay was quite different from working conditions aboard the big steel, four-masted barques which sailed from Liverpool or the South Wales coal ports. Life on a coastal schooner was certainly not easy, in fact it was probably harder. There were no breaks with long peaceful days in tropical conditions, but the endless grind of working round the coast, usually in cold weather, and arrival in port simply meant that the crew had to turn to and discharge the freight by their own labour. However, the difference was that men sailed with friends and neighbours and the master, although usually respected and obeyed, seldom used the brutality that sometimes passed for discipline in the deepwater ships. The crews often knew the owners of the vessels personally and there was a strong sense of loyalty which bound the whole community together. Porthmadog was one of the most outstanding examples in Britain of a community which banded together to keep expanding the local fleet. There would have been some pretty cutting remarks spread about in basic Welsh if any shareholder had reinvested his capital outside the town. It was not just England which was foreign land, they were not too keen on Barmouth or Criccieth creating a schooner fleet. This rather inward looking policy proved, in the end, to be ruinous. When the slate trade collapsed so did the shiping of Porthmadog. From the mid-1920s–'50s Porthmadog harbour was virtually abandoned until yachts moved into the empty wharves by the slate warehouses. Partly because the nineteenth-century schooner port survived intact, it is well known, but there were other similar places.

Perhaps the most forgotten of the other schooner ports were those on the waterways leading in to the River Humber. Some of these were far from the open sea. The largest of these inland ports was Goole, some sixty miles inland from Spurn Head. However, Knottingley, another twenty miles further inland up the River Aire was also home port to a considerable number of sailing ships in the mid-nineteenth century. Knottingley lies on the edge of the West Yorkshire industrial area, and it was the town's potteries, glass and tar works which created the basic trade. Although Knottingley still has commercial traffic on the inland

A Humber keel on the River Trent in about 1910. The keel was an ancient type of craft dating back to medieval ships, but it was mechanised in the nineteenth century by adding nine winches for handling the sails, so it was very handy in confined waters. The Humber Keel and Sloop Preservation Society have restored the steel keel Comrade, *and in 1981 their steel sloop* Amy Howson *also began sailing* (H. E. R. Hallgarth)

A Humber sloop ghosting along in light airs. The Humber sloop had the same hull-shape as a keel, but the gaff sail was used so that it could sail against the wind better in open estuaries. The local barges relied on the tide to do much of the work and were anchored between favourable tides (H. E. R. Hallgarth)

waterways, it is difficult to think of this little inland town as ever being a home of ocean-going sailing ships, but it once had four yards building ships for local owners.

Although Goole on the tidal River Ouse was the main coal shipping port for Yorkshire coal pits and a considerable ship-owning and ship-building centre, many of the new ships came from yards in surrounding villages, notably Howden Dyke a little further up the Ouse and Burton-upon-Stather which is on the River Trent. There was also a yard which built topsail schooners right up the Ouse at Selby. Again rural places like this seem totally removed from the cruel North Sea. Many of the men who worked all their lives in the local shipyards probably never saw the open sea.

The barquentine *Golden Wedding* built by William Caisley at Howden Dyke in 1893 was the pride of Goole. While most of the British sailing vessels had black tar on their hull topsides, the *Golden Wedding* was painted a handsome white above the waterline. Captain Lee, who as a young man joined the barquentine as an apprentice, later recalled how hard life was in her. It was almost continual hard work at sea and in port, all on a simple diet of hard biscuit, salt beef, pea soup, rice and curry. She traded to the West Indies and South America and was lost on the Mexican coast when only fourteen years old.

Another man who went to sea under much the same conditions as Captain Lee was my old mentor Arthur Hunt. He ran away to sea from his parents' home in rural Suffolk in about 1908 and joined a boomie (or ketch) barge when it was discharging coal at Ramsholt Dock (all the little farm wharves were called docks in Suffolk) and spent a few years toughening up in the coastal trade. The boomies, although they could sail without ballast, used to follow the old schooner practice of going on the beach at Bawdsey Ferry or Landguard Point and filling the hold full of shingle. This was sold in the North of England to help construct the new docks which were being built. Shingle was a poor freight, but the crew were still paid on a share basis so that it brought in enough to 'fill the grub locker'.

The boomies' real trade was bringing coal south from either the Tyne or later the Humber ports. The passage north to the Tyne was often made in forty-eight hours on the prevailing south-westerly winds, but the passage back against the winds, deeply laden with coal, sometimes lasted for weeks. Basically it was a dash from one sheltered anchorage to the next whenever the wind gave them a 'slant', which meant that they stayed at anchor for days in open roadsteads, like the famous Yarmouth Roads, rolling about until the wind was not dead ahead, but just enough on the beam so that they did not have to beat.

Some of the boomies stuck to the coal trade right to the end of their careers. The lovely *Sussex Belle*, a boomie built of Sussex oak at Rye, like many other fine barges, spent many days lying in Yarmouth Roads riding out the worst possible weather on her anchor. She was trading from the Humber with coal to Suffolk for over thirty years, until in 1927 her luck ran out. While bound from Keadby on the River Trent to Orford she was driven ashore in an ESE gale at Yarmouth and broke up on the beach.

Arthur Hunt had left the barges many years before this and had been skipper of the *Dover Castle* until he left after a row with her Bradwell

owner and signed on the three-masted topsail schooner *Alert*. This fine
schooner had been built at Runcorn, a port built up on exporting coal
from the Lancashire coalfields, but when Arthur joined her she was
owned in Fowey. In later years, Arthur was one of the last professional
yacht skippers on the River Deben, and in the winter made fishing nets by
hand. His yarns conveyed the whole atmosphere of the age of sail as it had
been in the opening years of this century. Arthur had finally left sail after
the mate of a steamer went down into the *Alert*'s fo'c'sle one night and
talked all the young crew into leaving and joining his steamer. Arthur and
the other young sailors were amazed at life in steam. They got regular
meals and stood regular watches and were never called out to shorten sail
when they were asleep. For this they were actually paid far more than on
the barges or schooners. Arthur had a little twinkle in his eye when he
ended his story with the comment that it was the time he 'left the sea and
went into steam'.

The whole coastal sailing ship era about which Arthur so loved to
reminisce had vanished and the only tangible evidence he had was a
portrait of the *Alert*. This was in watercolour by an artist from Gravesend
and was typical of the pier head ships' portraits that were undertaken for
sailors. These portraits had plenty of primitive colour, but were usually
accurate down to the last block. The most famous of these ship painters
was Reuben Chappell (1870–1940). He was born at Goole and as a young
man set out to earn a living painting ship portraits and taking
photographs. His sailor customers soon took a liking to his bright, fresh
portraits so that the photography side faded out and he supported himself
modestly on commissions. Chappell had no real art training and no
connection with the art world. He was a quiet man who went down to the
waterfront every day to take orders from the crews. Usually the paintings
had to be finished very quickly before the ship sailed and he sold them for
only a few shillings. He worked mainly in watercolours because it was
quicker and within the means of most seamen.

Reuben Chappell had a bronchial weakness and was advised to leave
the Humber area with its bitterly cold east winds. He had once made a
voyage on the Humber billyboy *Daisy* down to Cornwall and knew that
many Danish schooners went there to load clay, so he decided to move his
family south to Par. The move appears to have been a wise one as he lived
to be seventy and was always able to secure enough orders. Because
Chappell's sailor customers demanded absolute accuracy, his portraits
grew in popularity because they were such a perfect record of the small
coastal sailers and steamers. Many people thought that he must have been
a sailor to have painted them so correctly, but he was simply the master of
the art of absolute detail. In fact he only ever made two sea trips, once to

Par and another time to Hamburg. However, his paintings appeared in the homes of sailors all round Britain, but probably the best collections now on display are in Denmark at the little maritime museum at Marstal and at Holm–Petersen's museum at Troense, while in Britain, Reuben Chappell is well represented in Goole Museum.

Chappell's move to Cornwall in 1904 also coincided with the decline of coastal sail in the Humber, while in his new beat along the china clay quays of Fowey, Par and Charlestown, schooners and ketches were common visitors until World War II. Indeed, most of the better schooners and ketches from Wales, Lancashire, the Humberside and many other little coastal ports all the way round Britain had gravitated down to ownership in the West Country about the time of World War I. The social conditions which created the great British fleets of coastal sailers lasted in the West of England long after lorries or company owned motor coasters had replaced sail in some other stretches of the coast. The men in the small rural ports thoroughly understood the low investment, low return management of the schooners. The comparatively small amount of capital needed to buy a schooner was probably raised by two or three families clubbing together. The skill needed to maintain these vessels was still found in West Country shipyards and sailmakers, while the steamers required much more capital and the necessary engineering skills were only to be found in the industrial centres. Besides the freight rates for small cargoes to rural ports, where long delays were often met, did not attract steamers which required a quick turn round in port to make them profitable.

It was quite common for coastal trading smacks, ketches and even sizeable schooners to discharge on the open beach. This was usually done only in the summer when they were run ashore at high tide, and at low tide, horses and carts were taken out and the cargo, usually coal, was discharged by hand. The schooners required no sophisticated cranes or grain suckers to discharge, and most of the places they visited had only a short length of quay. Just about every sheltered bay or creek in Britain was a 'port' in the age of sail. Even a tiny place like Porlock Weir on the coast of West Somerset once had a little fleet of locally owned schooners.

The railway never penetrated down to this stretch of the Bristol Channel so that Porlock served as an outlet for this agricultural area until lorries arrived. Since trading conditions were more or less static, some of the craft had an incredibly long trading career. The Porlock trading smack *Looe* was built in 1787 and was later lengthened and altered to a ketch. Finally she was broken up at Minehead in 1905 when she was 118 years old. Another Somerset old timer was the ketch *Good Intent* which was built in 1790. When she was 135 years old, this ketch was trading

Stone being discharged by hand from sailing barges on the open beach at Clacton, Essex, in about 1912. It was the normal practice for barges to be discharged on the beach and from creek wharves until the early 1920s. After this they worked only to ports which had cranes, grabs and grain sucking equipment (Author's Collection)

from Bridgwater to Cardiff with tiles and back with coal. The *Good Intent* had also been lengthened and no doubt been considerably rebuilt over the years, but basic trading conditions could not have altered much for her to have lasted that long.

In 1893 some Porlock Weir shipping people combined resources to buy the topsail schooner *Florence Muspratt* from Connah's Quay owners. There was great excitement when this schooner sailed into Porlock Bay and into the tiny Weir (dock) under the shadow of the Exmoor hills. However, this schooner had a deep draught and her fine, lined hull made her unsuitable for the local stone and timber trade. Instead, she traded from Bristol and the South Wales ports of Swansea, Barry, Cardiff and Newport across to Ireland, usually with crews drawn from Porlock and Minehead.

The pattern of trading was considerably altered when lucrative freight rates attracted just about every sizeable British schooner, ketch, boomie and spritsail barge to trade to France in World War I with the materials desperately needed in the trench war against Germany. The German navy counteracted Britain's shipping effort by using small submarines to destroy as many British coasters and fishing boats as possible. In the autumn of 1917 the *Florence Muspratt* left Paimpol, Brittany, for another freight of coal. For the return voyage the schooner had had orders to meet up with other coasters off Brittany and form a convoy back across the English Channel.

Suddenly, in the early hours of the morning, a German submarine on the surface fired a shell across the bow of *Florence Muspratt* as a sign for her to stop. Without any further warning the submarine continued to shell the schooner so the captain and crew hurriedly started to get the boat over the side. None of the schooners were fitted with davits—the boats were kept on the forehatch and put over the side with a block and tackle from aloft. However, they managed to do this quickly, but an exploding shell killed the mate before he could join them.

The Captain and crew saw the *Florence Muspratt* sink within a few minutes. The German submarine then came over and questioned them about shipping movements and told them in which direction to go to find the crew of another vessel that had been sunk recently. They were then about fourteen miles offshore and were passed by a French schooner bound for the same convoy. The French offered to take them aboard, but the Somerset crew decided that as the German submarine was still about it was safer to head for land. Eventually they were picked up by a French

The Bristol Channel pilot cutter Frolic, *built by J. Westacott in Bideford in 1905, on the Glamorganshire Canal, Cardiff, in 1912* (Welsh Industrial & Maritime Museum)

patrol and landed at Paimpol. They returned to West Somerset and it was a great blow to local people that their best schooner had been sunk. Their misfortune had not ended, for when her captain and most of the same crew took over the three-masted schooner *Crystalite*, and sailed out of Swansea, they were missing within a few weeks, presumed run down and sunk by a steamer in the Bristol Channel.

The schooners and ketches which the German submarine campaign did not sink were finally made uneconomic by the shipping depression of the early 1920s. Even after this, some owners managed to keep a few wooden vessels sailing and some of the best known were in the schooner fleet owned by Stephens of Fowey. In the golden age of schooners at the end of the Victorian era, the Stephens family had a fleet of schooners in the Newfoundland trade which were noted for their fast North Atlantic crossings. Most of these Newfoundland traders were called 'Little . . .' such as *Little Secret* and *Little Pet*. However, the rigours of the sea and German submarines took most of these so that by the early 1920s, Stephens only had a handful left. Edward Stephens exercised considerable management skill and ran his fleet on a shoe-string with a very small profit margin. On his death in 1935, he left the 88ft two-masted topsail schooner *Katie*, the 102ft three-masted topsail schooner *Jane Banks* and even more amazingly, the 112ft barquentine *Waterwitch*, still trading under sail. To maintain every group of sailing vessels which survived, there had to be shipyards where the specialist skills connected with sailing vessels survived. The Stephens of Fowey fleet, although it diminished, was able to survive under sail virtually until World War II because the yard and dry dock of Benjamin Tregaskis at Par survived. It was to this yard that the *Waterwitch* was brought in 1918 after lying sunk in Newlyn harbour for several years. She had been built at Poole as a brig in 1871, and in her forty-seven-year career had built up a reputation for speed; she was totally rebuilt at Tregaskis yard and went back to sea to become the last British square-rigger trading under sail.

Stephens put the *Waterwitch* into the coal trade between the Tyne or Humber to the Cornish ports. Sometimes she had to lay for weeks between freights, but Stephens managed to keep her going. The man who commanded her became as famous in the inter-war years as the barquentine herself. This was Captain Charles Deacon who had previously commanded Stephens' barquentine *Ocean Swell* and the schooner *Bessie Stephens*, both of which had been sunk by German submarines. He was master of the *Waterwitch* for a further eighteen years and finally retired when he was seventy-three. This quiet, loyal man never went before a Board of Trade examiner and the only sextant he ever owned went down in the *Ocean Swell*—he never troubled to replace it.

Yet he was at sea for fifty-five years and of these was master for forty-five; he never had a serious accident or lost a vessel through his own error of judgement. He navigated on long passages to the Mersey or Tyne with little more equipment than a few battered charts and a liquid compass slung in gimbals in the cabin skylight. With these limited aids, he stood aft in the *Waterwitch*, protected in the worst weather by a battered oilskin suit and huge leather thigh-boots conning his ship in the same way as Sir Francis Drake and the medieval seamen had done.

Even the *Waterwitch* only managed to average about six knots so the master had time to work out where he was. Men like Captain Deacon and Captain Will Cort of Par, who had the *Katie*, developed a second sense for gauging whereabouts they were on the coast. They carried most of this information of tide sets and movements in their heads and only a few of them made very rough charts of the channels or creeks they visited. Most of the coasting schooner masters and barge skippers spent a great deal of time at the wheel of their vessels, unlike the Royal Navy in which the master purely commanded and never touched the wheel. The long hours spent at the wheel watching out for headlands as they bashed their way along the coast gave them tremendous experience in how to gauge speeds and distances sailed. Also a master had to be fairly philosophical about his vessel's performance: long periods were spent at anchor windbound when a master could seldom relax but was constantly watching for a break in the weather so that they could make a few miles along the coast before another head gale stopped them. Often a gale could drive them back over many hard fought miles so that they had to start again.

By the end of the 1930s, Captain Will Cort (he liked to be known as 'Cort of the *Katie*' just as the proud masters of deepwater square-riggers had been named after their ships) was the most photographed man in the British merchant navy. The little *Katie* which plodded between the Cornish clay ports and the Thames seemed a very romantic sight compared to the endless line of black British steamers and little grey Dutch motor coasters which filled every port. But being in a sailing vessel in a sea full of powered coasters had its own hazards. Helen Bruce remembers being totally becalmed in the fog on her Porthmadog-built schooner *Sarah Evans* in the Bristol Channel and how terrifying it was to have huge steamers which were outward bound from the coal ports suddenly loom out of the white mist and pass only a few feet away from the helpless schooner.

Helen Bruce's reason for owning a schooner was romantic. She had gone on holiday to the West Country in the late 1920s and seen 'the little ships that went to Newfoundland' lying up for sale at Fowey. Mrs Bruce could not bear to see these lovely vessels rotting away so she bought one and put her back into trade under sail. However, it was not paying its way so her Captain, Ben Harris of Bideford, asked if he could have one fitted with an engine. The result was that Mrs Bruce purchased the *Mayals*, an ex-Swedish three-masted iron schooner which had a low-powered oil engine. The *Mayals*' end came in 1931 when she was sheltering in Milford Haven while on passage from the Mersey to Cornwall. She was anchored there waiting for a favourable 'slant' of wind when a steam trawler ran into the schooner and she sank. At the enquiry it was shown that the trawler's skipper was so drunk that he had had to be carried on to the bridge. So ended this attempt to keep a sailing ship going.

There were others, such as the syndicate which bought the 93ft auxiliary three-masted schooner *Mary Jones* and intended trading her between the Firth of Forth and the Thames with coal. The *Mary Jones* had been built by Jones of Flint and had been in the Newfoundland stock-fish trade in her youth, but when her final owners bought her she was sixty-eight years old and had been laid up for a long period. Captain Waddell was appointed master. He had been an officer in the great Shire Line, but taking an ageing coastal schooner up the North Sea in the dead of winter was a very different proposition to his youth in deep sea square-riggers. The schooner cleared London on the first trip and spent seven days beating about trying to get out of the Thames Estuary. Captain Waddell turned back in disgust and ran for Southend anchorage but he grounded on Tongue Sands. The crew of four were rescued but the schooner was smashed to pieces.

Once ashore, no wooden hull lasts in a gale for long. Even the strongest wooden hull goes to pieces under the relentless pounding of the sea. In October 1980 the British-owned former Baltic trader *Luna* made an unsuccessful attempt to cross the North Sea. She put back to Great Yarmouth and anchored in an easterly gale in the North Roads but the anchors dragged and she went ashore in the early hours of the morning. The ebb receded and protected the wooden hull for a while, but on the flood tide the sea just knocked the hull to pieces. Twelve hours after she was beached all that was left of the brigantine was part of the stern and a mass of broken timber and spars strewn along a mile of the beach.

Beautiful though sailing ships are, 'romance' alone is not enough reason to keep a vessel at sea. They have to have a purpose and be sailed by men who understand and are in sympathy with them. In the inter-war years there were several romantic ventures connected with trading schooners, but the only people who managed to keep them going were some hard-headed coastal seamen in North Devon. In the little town of Appledore and across the River Taw in the village of Braunton, they found that by buying old schooners and ketches cheaply and running them as motor sailers on low overheads they could just make them pay.

Other shipowners in Arklow near Dublin did the same with mostly ex-British sailers and traded them from the Mersey. The Appledore motor sailers also traded across to Ireland, mostly with coal from the Forest of Dean which they shipped at Lydney, up the River Severn. The Appledore schooners and ketches were also kept busy distributing to Devon and Cornish ports the animal foods which had been brought into the South Wales ports on the coal export ships.

Some of the larger motor schooners such as the *Kathleen & May* and the *Result* stayed in the general coastal trade. The author remembers seeing the *Result* coming up the London River in 1956. She was loaded deep, almost down to her decks, and only had two stumpy masts but her fine clipper bow and lovely rounded counter stern gave away at once that she had begun life as a thoroughbred sailer. In fact she had started life as one of the fine three-masted topsail schooners which were built in Northern Ireland. While most schooner builders turned out only wooden hulls at a rather leisurely rate of production, Paul Rodgers at Carrickfergus on Belfast Lough switched to steel hulls. The *Result* (the 'result' of much planning) was completed for Thomas Ashburner & Co of Barrow-in-Furness in 1892. When this company was wound up in 1909, a group of sailor businessmen from Braunton bought her. By continually altering the *Result* until she was eventually a power vessel, she became the last of the North Devon traders working until 1967 and only gave up then because of the death of her skipper-owner Peter Welch.

There is no doubt that the North Devon sailors thought highly of the little fleet they had got together, but they worked them until they earned the last penny out of them. Many were finally put up on the mud above Appledore and sawn up for fencing posts so they owed nothing to anyone to their very end. The real tragedy was that the central government never encouraged the North Devon community of shipowners in the way the Dutch did so successfully with their Groningen motor coasters which dominated the medium tonnage of British coastal traders in the 1950s.

The North Devon schooner community was something special. The shortage of tonnage after World War II even caused old vessels to be refitted again. In 1947 there were nearly fifty schooners and ketches afloat, mostly owned in Appledore and Arklow. Motor ketches were still trading into little places like Portreath, Bude and Porlock which were not big enough for motor coasters, even the shoal-draught Dutch ones. The little ketch *Agnes* had just about been able to hold her own in the 1930s against the railways by running 100-ton cargoes from Avonmouth down to Bude. In the mid-1950s, when *Agnes* was skippered by Peter Herbert of Bude, she again held her own in a trade competing against lorries. By that time she was mainly trading in the Bristol Channel with grain, with only the occasional freights down the land to Padstow and Wadebridge.

In 1955 the *Agnes* put into Bude for shelter behind the breakwater for the night and was the first trader to visit this port for several years. Her connection with this North Cornish town was a very long one. Officially *Agnes* was built at Bude in 1904, but in fact she was a much older vessel called *Lady Acland* which had been built at Bude in 1835. Henry Stapleton's yard at Bude had hauled the bluff-bowed nineteenth-century trader *Lady Acland* ashore, cut her in half and added 13ft to her length amidships. They fitted a new mainmast from the Bude ketch *Wild Pigeon* which had been wrecked earlier that year and she was relaunched as the new *Agnes*. This type of rebuilding was very much a part of a sailing trader's life. The *Agnes* received another major repair in the 1930s after being driven on the rocks at St Davids. At that time she had been trading to Solva in Dyfed. While waiting for the weather to moderate so that she could go on the beach to discharge, her anchor chains parted and she was driven ashore. Her final end also came in this way, but not in her old trading routes in the West Country or Wales. A group of adventure seekers had sailed the old ketch across the Atlantic to the West Indies in 1957 and then traded her there for a while. When she was eventually lost south of Barbados, she was owned by local merchants.

Captain Richard England saw the shortage of shipping just after World War II as his chance to fulfil his dream of owning a sailing vessel. He bought the *Nellie Bywater*, which had been the last Northern Ireland-owned schooner to trade from Belfast across the Channel to English ports. At first the demand for tonnage was so high that Captain England was able to afford to steadily re-rig the schooner. Later she was given some film work and he even managed to refit a square topsail. Most square sails had vanished from British schooners when engines were fitted in the 1920s. However, even with an auxiliary engine, Captain England could see no future for sail in British waters and decided to go out to the West Indies. The ship cleared Falmouth in December 1951 with Captain and Mrs England, their daughters and seven crew on board.

Out in the Atlantic the schooner was hit by gales and started to leak badly. Captain England turned back and called for help. A tug took her in tow, but the weather was still bad and the *Nellie Bywater* sank about four miles off Bolt Tail near Salcombe. Most of her crew were picked up but sadly Captain England's eldest daughter and a crew member drowned.

The last schooner carrying freight under sail only was the 99ft three-masted topsail schooner *Brooklands*. She was built as the *Susan Vittery* at Dartmouth in 1859 for the Azores fruit trade. Under Arklow ownership she actually sailed until 1946 when Captain C. C. Halliday bought her to seek an idyllic life in the West Indies. She sailed from Liverpool in 1947 bound for Jamaica and all the romance of the Caribbean. In the Irish Sea a September gale battered the eighty-eight-year-old *Brooklands* so that with most of her sails in shreds and her crew down with sea sickness, Captain Halliday had to give up his dream of sailing to the tropics and put back into the Mersey. The *Brooklands* was sold back into trade and received a great deal of publicity as the 'last sailing schooner' when she sank off the Irish coast in 1953, although by that time she had been cut down to a motor vessel.

Many fine sailing vessels had a pitiful end, like the handsome ketch *Sunshine* of Bridgwater which was used for smuggling in the Mediterranean and finished up rotting away in a backwater in Genoa. Some didn't even leave their home port like the fine ketch *Clara May* which was broken up at Braunton Pill because her owners had abandoned her. The ketch *C.F.H.* spent a long time working at Braunton but ended by being abandoned up the River Severn. However, her sister ship, the *Garlandstone*, went on trading, one of nine motor schooners and ketches left by the end of 1956.

The Mersey coal trade from Garston across to Wicklow, Arklow and Youghal was still finding work for the *De Wadden, Invermore, J.T. & S.* and *Windermere*, but the increasing use of oil for energy began to kill the coal trade everywhere. In the Bristol Channel ketches like the *Emily Barratt* and *Irene* lost their cattle food work to lorries which could deliver to their final destination, not just to a quayside. In 1956 the little *Agnes* made five trips to Lundy Island with supplies for the owner. It was a difficult task because the island did not have a pier and everything had to be landed by boat on a small shingle beach under the high cliff. But even these few freights were lost because the owner of Lundy Island bought the motor fishing vessel *Pride of Bridlington*, renamed her *Lundy Gannet* and used her as a supply vessel.

Although in the mid-1950s there was still the constant activity of the Appledore motor sailers going out of the Taw and Torridge estuaries, their owners were finding it very difficult to compete in the general coasting trade. Most of them only loaded a small tonnage and their masts and rigging impeded the new cargo handling machines. Also their hatches were too small for this machinery. The motor sailers had their rigging reduced and their hatches enlarged but were still not as flexible as the motor coasters. One by one the North Devon owners gave up the struggle and offered their vessels for sale.

The *Eilian*, a steel three-masted schooner built at Amlwch, Anglesey, in 1908 with a small engine installed, was sold to Danish owners in 1957. She was actually still trading in the West Indies in 1980 which says a lot

A wooden hull requires more maintenance than an iron or steel hull. Here the Whitby brig Margaret Nixon *is having new planks fitted in her side* (Frank Sutcliffe)

for the quality of the hull. The *Garlandstone* dropped out of trade in 1956; the last wooden ketch trading was the *Irene* while the last wooden schooner was *Kathleen & May* which carried cargoes until 1960. By then she had been skipper-owned for some thirty years by Captain Tom Jewell. He had always sailed with a mixture of good seamanship and a down to earth business approach which had been typical of the North Devon seafarers. This style of shipping had more in common with the first Elizabethan era and medieval England than the big companies and union dominated operations of modern shipping.

Captain Jewell had grown up in coastal sail and had gone to sea in 1910 with his father who had been master of the Appledore ketch *Dolphin* which traded from Swansea down to the little harbour in St Bride's Bay and Milford Haven. Although the *Kathleen & May* was fitted with progressively larger engines, Captain Jewell was not one to waste free wind power and always set some sail. Even this tradition was eventually rendered impracticable by changing technology and the *Kathleen & May* lay for years on the mud above Appledore. Eventually she was restored by the Maritime Trust and is now in St Katharine's Dock, London.

The *Kathleen & May* had a long and useful career and was altered very little. The engine of course took up cargo space so that while she was able to load 226 tons when built at Connah's Quay in 1900, in later years as a motor schooner she carried about 190 tons. The *Kathleen & May* was a particularly good example of the British sailing trader which had a deep, round-bottomed hull. It is a great tragedy that no more have survived. They dropped out of trade just before it became acceptable to restore former working craft. Most of them were sold for 'one way' ocean voyage schemes which usually collapsed at some stage through lack of proper financing or organization. By the time museums became interested in preserving actual vessels, most of the schooners had gone. Although there were four schooners and four ketches still in existence when the National Museum of Wales wanted to buy a sailing trading vessel, none seemed to be available. The *Isabel*, which was built in Milford Haven, was suggested by the author but attempts to find her took a long while, and eventually it was revealed that she was sunk as a yacht off the coast of Brazil in 1976. Much the same happened when the author tried to trace the steel billyboy (Humber ketch barge) *Mavis* for a local group. We discovered that she had been scrapped a short time before. The moral of these tales is that time never stands still and old ships just fade away so preservation should never be delayed.

Even after the *Kathleen & May* and the *Result* had stopped trading, the Dutch-built, steel, three-masted motor schooner *De Wadden* of Arklow was still trading and was then sold to owners on the Clyde. The *De*

Wadden continued to carry ballast on the Clyde. She used to be run ashore at the head of the Kyles of Bute and loaded 230 tons of sand (before the engine was fitted she loaded 320 tons). This sand was sold at Dunoon, but in 1977 the authorities stopped the *De Wadden* from trading and she continued doing film work and angling trips.

Most of the large schooners which have come under the British flag since the early 1960s have been Danish, Swedish and Spanish. These have been quite a common sight around the coast and even better known to the public because of the BBC television series 'Onedin Line'. From 1970 to 1980 the 'Onedin Line' was filmed fairly regularly and the work it created helped more vessels to return to sail.

Some vessels connected with the 'Onedin Line' became very well known, especially the ex-Danish *Charlotte Rhodes* until she was burnt out at Amsterdam in 1979. The smart ketch *I. P. Thorsoe* of Dartmouth appeared fairly frequently in the series in between charter work, while the Davies brothers have actually built up a small fleet of traditional sailing vessels for use in film work. Robin 'Rob' Davies approached the business of operating sailing vessels in the second half of the twentieth century in the same down to earth way that the North Devon community had done in the first half. However, the Davies line on the east coast of England have never attempted to revive cargo carrying.

Rob Davies' first ketch was the *Clausens Minde* which he brought over from Denmark to Hythe Quay, Colchester, in 1967. After some seasons of charter work he was able to sell her and buy the larger 76ft *Nora Av Ven*. His younger brother Anthony was now sailing with him, and in 1973 the *Nora Av Ven* was sold; they returned to Denmark and purchased the motor ketch *Esther Lohse* which they brought back to Brightlingsea and converted to a beautiful three-masted topsail schooner. The pattern after this was for Rob to stay ashore at Colchester and look after the business side, while Anthony became skipper and shipwright. The success of the Davies Line has been largely based on the principle of buying sound ships cheaply and then undertaking the restoration themselves, except for the specialised work like sail making, which was done by Jim Lawrence of Brightlingsea. The hulls had to be sound to start with because it would have been prohibitive for them to have had to be hauled up on a slip for a long time. However, the *Esther Lohse* was completely redecked before she made her first passage under sail in 1975.

Two years later the *Esther Lohse* was sold and Rob and Anthony bought an even larger wooden-hulled vessel. This time it was the 105ft cruiser-sterned *Søren Larsen* which was built as a motor ketch at Nykøbing Mors in 1949 to trade between Lim Fjord and Copenhagen with 220 tons. The sail plan for the *Søren Larsen* was based on a plan from a Norwegian brigantine *Leon* which was then adapted, and Anthony put 60 tons of shingle into the hull as ballast to counteract the weight of the masts and spars. In one winter they turned her into a brigantine; it was not just any winter, because in the early part of 1979 England was gripped in ice and snow and had its worst winter for seventeen years. Yet in the spring, the *Søren Larsen* sailed completely rigged as a brigantine round to Gloucester Docks and was used for film work.

This is the kind of tenacity which, in the previous century, had built up many a small port's coastal fleet. Although unlike many of the nineteenth-century traders which often went to sea in highly doubtful conditions the Davies' ships kept up a high standard in hull, engine and rigging, they almost totally disregarded accommodation. In the *Søren Larsen*'s first season, which included a trip to Portugal, the crew lived on the floor of the open hold. At the end of that summer, Fleur and Anthony Davies purchased the 107ft Swedish, wooden, three-masted motor schooner *Tullan* and brought her back to Essex for conversion to a square-rigger under her original name of *Orion*.

The other sailing vessels that are still seen off the British coast are the sail training vessels. Although Britain had in the age of sail the largest and finest fleet of sailing merchant vessels, the whole idea of training under sail was totally abandoned when steam came in. Other nations maintained sailing ships to train young men for careers at sea. But in Britain it was argued, quite rightly, that there was little point in spending several years training men to handle sail if they were going to spend the rest of their career in power ships which were totally different. However, there was always a strong body of opinion which said that sail was useful as 'character training' for young people, whether they made a career at sea or ashore. Coupled with this was the belief that sail could be a way of bringing together young people from all nations.

The promoters of these beliefs started the Sail Training Association and in 1956 held the first of what have become known as the Tall Ships Races. These races, held every other year, are international events, but in 1964 the Sail Training Association built their own three-masted topsail schooner, the *Sir Winston Churchill*, and in 1967 a sistership, the *Malcolm Miller*. These two schooners, which are based in design on large yachts, have done superb work in giving young people a taste of the reality of life under sail. Another of the modern sail trainers is the Sea Cadet brig *Royalist*. When she was built at Cowes in 1971, she was the first square-rigger launched in Britain since the four-masted barque *Archibald Russell* was launched on the Clyde in 1905. Again she is more like a yacht than being traditional, but this is a new concept in seafaring. There have been other sail training vessels right back to the Victorian naval brigs, but although Britain still does not have a large prestige square-rigger, she has led the world in the development of the 'character training' concept.

To continue our study of coastal craft, we must return to the nineteenth century when London was an important centre of trade. Not only was London the largest concentration of population in the British Isles, but it was also the trading centre of a huge empire which embraced a third of the world's land surface. To cater for this everlasting flow of goods from all over the world, London's dockland spread out in a seemingly endless complex of docks, wharves and warehouses along the banks of the Thames.

The tremendous movement of goods within the Port of London and the coastal ports in south-east England triggered off the development of the Thames sailing barges which must be classified as being the most successful British sailing cargo carriers. The origins of the sailing barges were the flat-bottomed lighters used for ferrying goods ashore from ships anchored out in the Thames tideway. The early barges used on the Thames were rowed when the tide 'served' (flowed in the direction the barges moved) or carried a simple square sail to aid the progress. The spritsail rig was widely used in northern Europe so it is not in the least surprising that it was adopted on the Thames in the eighteenth century. However, the spritsail rig gradually dropped out of use in most places, while the Thames bargemen developed the sprit by the use of winches into a highly effective rig controlling a large sail area with only two men.

The Thames barges probably reached such a high standard of development because so many were built and this allowed for a great deal of trial and error. Other similar local barge types, such as the Mersey flats and the Severn trows were not built in very large numbers so that their design altered little. Also, although there was a huge amount of freight to be moved to and from the London docklands, the competition was very fierce. Bargemen literally raced to be the first to get the next freight, and after 1863 there were annual races on the Thames, Medway and at a few local regattas; owners even started ordering new barges just to win these highly prestigious events. From the awkward sailing lighters of the early 1800s, the barges had become highly sophisticated seagoing craft by the 1890s. The Thames barges were an economic rather than a practical success. Going on long passages down the English Channel or across the North Sea in a flat-bottomed hull, which was loaded down almost to the deck and having virtually no bulwarks with only a low rail, could be extremely wet, but the sailing barges could cope with these conditions and deliver their cargoes at a relatively low cost.

The great winning points of the barges were that they could sail up narrow creeks or into docks without having to hire a tug, and they could make sea passages light and not have the cost of ballasting. Other local

The Crescent Shipping barge coaster Pepita *and the sailing barge* Mirosa *seen from Southend Pier. The wooden* Mirosa *was the type of trading craft built on the east coast until 1930. The sailing barges were replaced by vessels like the steel* Pepita
(Hugh Pcrks)

barge types were able to sail without ballast but were not really up to long sea passages, while brigs, brigantines and schooners could make sea passages in reasonable comfort but were unmanageable sailing in confined waters. The Thames barges were a compromise and this allowed them to go on trading long after other sailing barges and coasters were driven off the narrow seas by hard maritime economics.

Although they were usually described collectively as Thames barges, there were several different types and most of them were built and owned outside the River Thames. The common factors were the flat bottoms, flat sides and leeboards which, when lowered, allowed them to grip the water when beating against the wind. The use of leeboards was an idea probably borrowed from numerous Dutch craft which traded into the Thames. Most of these Dutch craft were, by the time that Thames barges were evolving, round bottomed and gaff rigged so the Thames barges were uniquely English.

Until around 1840 most of the Thames barges were swim-heads; that is, they had a flat sloping bow and were only suitable for short trips within the sheltered river. The London lighters continued to be built with swim-heads and one lighter has been re-rigged like an old swim-head sailing barge. This is the *Montreal* which was built of wood at Sittingbourne in 1916 but was never intended to sail. However, in the early 1970s she was fitted out with a spritsail rig to take part in the annual barge races. The *Montreal* has too much beam for sailing, but seen at a distance on the Thames she gives a fair impression of the long extinct swim-head barges.

Most of the early round-bowed barges were 'stumpies' which were not fitted with topmasts. This type of barge later proved very popular for short hauls with bricks and cement from North Kent up the Thames and into the numerous small waterways so that they could supply building materials to the fast-growing suburbs. The stumpies were all replaced by lorries in the early 1920s and the only one still sailing is the *Lady of the Lea*. However, she is not a true stumpie as she was built solely to carry ammunition from a factory down the tiny River Lea through London's suburbs to the huge government arsenal at Woolwich.

An extinct type of barge is the big wooden gaff-sail 'boomie' barges which were built in 1880–1900 for long coastal passages. However, these boom-sailed barges required more hands than the spritsail barges so owners began to ask why the skippers needed gaff sails. Most skippers were worried about the spritsail for long passages because in a really big sea the sprit jerked about aloft and could break. Because of this another rig was evolved—the mulie—which was a compromise between the boomie and the river spritsail barge. The mulie had the huge sprit mainsail, but a gaff mizzen, the idea being that if the sprit did break at sea then a mulie could make a harbour unaided under just headsails and gaff mizzen. In practice it was found that the large gaff mizzen right aft tended to make the barge's sail plan unbalanced. The mulie barges like the barge *Cambria* have a most handsome appearance but in practice the rig was never very popular with skippers, because the sprit very rarely broke at sea and the ordinary 'spritty' mizzen was much more handy.

It is estimated that in around 1885 there were some 2,000 sailing barges owned and trading from the east coast of England. These were not all brilliant sailing craft; some sailing barges were badly built and sailed indifferently, but the 'spritty' barge reached the limit of its development in the early years of the twentieth century, and was the most effective all round craft of the British sailing coasters.

The Thames barges reached their peak at the same period as the virgin North American forests were being exploited so that there was plenty of very good timber available to back up the native supply of oak. Some of the wooden barges, although built for purely functional purposes were exceptionally handsome. At Maldon, a salty little town at the head of the Essex Blackwater estuary, John Howard built some very attractive 'stackie' barges which sailed with hay and straw piled in stacks half way up the mast. These went to the London wharves as 'fuel' for the street horses. The stackies required a wide beam to keep stability when the straw stack was above the deck, and a shallow draft which allowed them to creep up to farm wharves at the head of tidal creeks.

Most of Howard's barges were built with the London stackie trade in mind, but they were still very fast. The *Mirosa*, which Howard built in 1892, is still one of the fastest barges left afloat. The *Salcote Belle*, built by Howard in 1895 to trade with malted barley from Salcote Creek maltings to London, was another fast barge. She won the local race cup outright with wins in 1925, 1926 and 1927. In the 1960s she was still taking part in the Maldon barge races but by then her ageing hull had hogged and lost much of its fine shape.

At a distance, it is very difficult to tell barges apart. Indeed, most of them are around 79–88ft long and have a beam of from 18–20ft, but within this basic design there was a tremendous difference in the hull shape and size. For instance, Howard's barges were noted for their fine lines, but in James Cook's yard only at the other end of Maldon's Hythe Quay, barges with virtually no deck sheer and very full bluff bows were built. Cook's *Dawn* won the Maldon race in 1924, but his barges were aimed at maximum carrying capacity, not speed. Who is to say which were the best barges; Howard's fine bowed barges could be very wet and uncomfortable in heavy seas, while Cook's *Lord Roberts* and *British King* were like trusted old work horses usually delivering their freights dry.

The Essex and Ipswich builders were not striving to produce barges to win races. They endeavoured to turn out barges which could make passages from the Thames to the Humber in a reasonable time while deeply loaded with freight. Perhaps the most perfect spritty barges were launched by J. & H. Cann from their yard at Gas House Creek, Harwich. There are more Cann barges left afloat than from any other builder. The *May* (1891), *Kitty* (1895), *Beric* (1896), *Gladys* (1901) and *Edith May* (1906), to mention the best survivors, seem to represent the perfect wooden spritties. In their working days, none of these ever took part in the classic races; they were simply well built and good all rounders so that they outlasted most of their contemporaries. The Cann barges were always highly thought of by skippers when they were trading, but these barges did not become so well known for speed until the revival races started after 1962. In 1965 the *Edith May*, skippered by Jack Spitty, became the first barge to win all the season's races. However, her success was greatly aided by having a larger sail area than most of her rivals. After this the *May*, mostly skippered by the legendary 'Chubb' Horlock of Mistley, won the Challenge Trophy for several years.

In the Thames Estuary there was a tremendous rivalry between Kent barges and those owned in Essex and Suffolk. No one quite knows how this rivalry grew up, but if a Kent and an Essex barge met on the tideway they at once started to race. They also played a war of nerves when tacking up the Thames and would not give way even on the port tack to a barge from the opposite shore of the estuary. This rivalry reached its peak in the classic Thames and Medway races, held most years, when the Medway and Thames barges fought to take the prize from the Essex barges sent by Clem Parker of Bradwell and later by Fred Horlock of Mistley.

In the Thames and Medway races, only about a dozen barges took part in several different classes. That does not sound many when one considers that between 1885–1910 there remained around 2,000 barges. However, the impact of racing made itself felt right through the barge world because builders began competing to turn out the fastest craft. The owners on the Thames and Medway ordered new barges to try to beat the established champions. Goldsmith of Grays had four barges built just to try to win the Queen Victoria Jubilee Races in 1897. They chose builders with the reputation for producing fast barges. Horace Shrubsall was asked for two barges and he produced the *Castanet* at the Dock End Yard, Ipswich, and the *Her Majesty* at a yard in Limehouse. The *Satanita* came from White's yard at the head of Conyer Creek in Kent while *Giralda* came from J. R. Piper's at East Greenwich. When Goldsmith's skippers saw the 86ft *Giralda* no one was very keen to take her because she was rather plain above the water-line. In fact *Giralda* won the highly publicised Thames Race and went on to dominate the races for the next decade. At 49 tons she was too small for much more than river work, but she was usually held to be the fastest barge ever built. Like so many flyers, part of the success of *Giralda* lay in her lightness which meant that she was not constructed very strongly and her trading career was quite short.

In the series of races held after both World War I and World War II, the *Sara*, built by White at Conyer in 1902, was top prize winner with the Shrubsall-built *Veronica* equalling her in speed. Racing and trading took barges to the peak of their development by about 1910. Barges were built of wood and steel until 1930, but the basic design did not go much further after about 1910. Skippers and owners with bright ideas have tried all sorts of improvements since then—bermudian mizzen, drop plate rudders, synthetic sails—and many more ideas have been tried but really made little difference. Of all the ideas tried by yacht barge owners, perhaps the main if slight improvement was discovered by Everards who fitted leeboard winches up on higher blocks, making them a little less back-breaking to work, and had motor engines to operate the hand windlass. However, most barges still sailing have not even had these slight improvements fitted.

The sailing barge was evolved to provide cheap but effective transport to serve the rapidly expanding industrial centres. Apart from taking goods from London's Docks out to coastal ports, the largest single trade was carrying cement from the Medway works. By the 1890s, there was probably an average of a hundred barges leaving and entering the Medway every twenty-four hours. In the end the small cement firms amalgamated into the huge Associated Portland Cement Manufacturers which at one time had a fleet of 128 barges with the 'Blue Circle' emblem in their topsails. In the 1920s the APCM sold off their fleet and went over to road and rail transport. This was during the great trade slump between the two world wars and most of the cement barges were sold off very cheaply. One of the few survivors is the wooden 80ft *George Smeed* which was built at Sittingbourne Creek for the owner of a large cement works at Murston.

George W. Smeed was one of those vigorous individuals who was the backbone of Victorian industrial Britain. Born in 1812, the youngest of eighteen children, he began life by selling coal from a handcart through the streets of the little Kentish country town of Sittingbourne. By the time he died in 1881, Sittingbourne Creek was dotted with cement works and barge building yards which either emulated Smeed's cement works at Murston or were owned directly by him.

As a young man, Smeed created a thriving coal merchant's business, progressed on to owning and building colliers and barges and then went

The Rochester auxiliary sailing barge Thyra *passing Long Sutton Bridge on the River Nene, bound for Hull with her last grain cargo from Peterborough in about 1965. In the 1960s the* Thyra, Varuna, Beatrice Maud *and* Will Everard *were all trading with motors, but still used sails. The* Cambria *traded under sail only until 1970, and the auxiliary* May *still occasionally carries small freights* (Peterborough Evening Telegraph)

on to build a gas works, cement works and what was claimed to be the largest brickfields in the world. After Smeed's death he was summed up as being a man 'of strong purpose and strong language, and the traits of character and habits of life became more accentuated in the later years of his life'. That was the local paper's polite way of saying that he had been a difficult man if he did not get his own way. For Smeed, the sky was the limit and nothing was too difficult to attempt. Since he operated both schooners and barges, he attempted to combine the better qualities of both by building huge schooner-barges for the coal trade.

The Smeed 119ft schooner-barge *Seven Sisters* was about twice the size of the average barge when she was launched in 1862. The next, the 140ft *Eliza Smeed*, loaded 750 tons while the average spritty of that time was loading 100 tons. Still Smeed thought that he could push the flat bottomed barge with leeboards to an even larger size, because in 1868 he built the *Esther Smeed* at Murston which was rigged as a barque, no less, and loaded 800 tons. She was the largest barge ever built and it seems that all these really big barges were very poor tools at beating to windward in a seaway. Their flat bottoms gave no grip on the water. In sixty-five years George Smeed and the company which he created, Smeed, Dean & Co, built at least eighty craft at Murston. The last spritty was the *Youngarth*, in 1913, but they continued to rebuild their barges until 1928.

The number of sailing barges in trade had dropped to 1,100 by 1930 and over the next twenty years it fell to 80 in 1950 so that it looked as if they would shortly follow all the other barge types into extinction. Every time bargemen met in docks or were lying waiting between freights, there was news of yet another barge dropping out of trade. Some sank dramatically at sea, but generally the owners were finding the ageing hulls too expensive to maintain and were having difficulty in finding crews, too, so they were selling them off for yachts and houseboats. Nearly every creek had its little colony of decaying barges. Only the larger barges escaped, ending up as floating homes, but they had all their majestic gear cut down and were turned into motor barges. A barge without its sailing gear is little more than a long box which attracts little attention.

In the 1950s sailing barges were still a common sight in the Thames Estuary ports. For instance ICI had a fleet which was used for carrying explosives, but these 'powder barges' were towed around the Thames so that by 1956 only nine were left really trading under sail with a regular crew. Most of these were owned in Ipswich by R. & W. Paul and Cranfield Bros. Both were millers who loaded imported grain from ships in London's Royal group of docks and then took it 'down and along' the coast to Ipswich. Cranfield's barges mostly loaded between 120–140 tons of wheat and really the company was using them as warehouses since grain for immediate use went by road and the barges turned up some time later. The barges then loaded flour back, which was usually discharged at wharves above the London bridges. However, even the Ipswich owners slowly sold off their barges; the last to go was the *Spinaway C* in 1967. The *Cambria* was still carrying freights under sail until 1970.

From the great depression of the 1930s until about 1960, a great many barges were sold as yachts. Generally a hull which had been too old for carrying cargoes could still be sailed as a yacht for a few more years in safety. After that they were left to rot quietly in some creek and the owners bought another or moved on to a fresh interest. However, the slow decline of barge numbers made an enormous impression on people, and in the early 1960s the idea sprang up that instead of just scrapping ageing barges, they should be preserved by keeping the hulls in good repair and actually still sailing them.

It was apparent that if barges were to survive, they had to find a new role to serve society. They were too expensive to have much of a future just as yachts, but in the early 1960s 'chartering' barges out to parties for holiday trips proved to be a way to raise the finance to pay for maintenance. Formerly all the races had been for trading barges only, but in 1962 new annual races were started at Maldon and Pin Mill which were open to every remaining barge, although they had to be sailed by trading skippers. Still the barges hovered on the edge of extinction, and in 1967 there were only thirty left capable of making a passage under their own sails, but interest in barges increased and dedicated young men started buying hulls and completely restoring and re-rigging them. The *Kitty* and the *Dawn* were brought back under sail for chartering at Maldon in 1964, and after this every season saw a few more barges sailing again.

It was part of the tremendous versatility of the flat-bottomed spritty barge that they could be adapted to totally different roles from those for which they were built. In the early 1930s, barges were used as yachts by individuals who were keen on having a barge, but in 1964 a subsidiary of the huge Tate & Lyle sugar company bought the Cann-built *May* from Cranfields. This was really the first 'company' barge, bought by a concern with little previous association with trading barges. The nimble *May*, which had been popular with Ipswich men because her small gear made her light to work, was fitted out to take part in the increasing number of races. Although like many barges the *May* tended to be fitted out like a yacht after leaving the grain trade, her new owners still used her for transporting small and very occasional freights of sugar. Although fitted with an auxiliary engine she went on trading after the *Cambria*.

The new style of company ownership has been very beneficial to the preservation of barges because only these firms have the financial resources needed to completely rebuild and maintain them. The continual use of barges for chartering and promotion cruises has given them a new sense of purpose. Barges on promotion work visit ports all round the coast of Britain and go over to the Netherlands just as regularly as they did when trading until World War II. The *Northdown* even visited Oslo in 1973 and 1975, while the *May* and the *Ethel* were shipped out to North America and the *Ethel* remained there.

The main difference from the trading days is that most of the surviving barges have engines which are extensively used. The charter and company promotion barges now often sail round the coast to a definite schedule, something that the pure sailing barges could not have attempted. When a sailing barge left a wharf loaded almost down to the deck, her skipper never knew whether it would take hours, days or weeks before she reached her destination. In 1956 the *Portlight* had a couple of freights to deliver from Tilbury to Ipswich. The first round trip took three days, but the second, due to having to lie at anchor windbound because of a gale, took two weeks.

The *Portlight* was one of the last barges relying on 'seeking' work from merchants and brokers, and sail had only lasted that long because the barges had been able to actually sail right into the docks to load while the schooners and ketches often had to be towed. The spritty's topsail was particularly useful because it could catch a breeze coming over the tops of warehouses and roofs. A barge had to be able to beat to windward up the Thames when it was alive with every type of shipping from the huge liners to the groups of lighters drifting on the tide.

The author has sailed with one of the older generation of barge skippers who cut fearlessly across the tideway right under the bows of huge cargo ships. The ships bows, towering walls of steel, passed within a matter of feet and the skipper totally disregarded them. One was never sure whether it was all brilliant judgement or familiarity breeding reckless contempt. Barges were evolved to sail in crowded waters, but at the turn of the century shipping moved slower than it does today. Even when the last Ipswich sailers were trading up the Orwell in the late 1950s, the river was wide and comparatively uncongested. Now much of that river is lined with yacht moorings and there are three marinas. Also the upper reaches are narrower because of the saltings at Ipswich being turned into more wharves and the construction of the Orwell road bridge. Sailing barges could have coped with these conditions—they are no worse than the crowded Thames or Medway in the early 1900s. However, in the neighbouring River Deben, the yacht moorings have become so thick that it is impossible to turn a barge to windward through them, so charter barges on holiday trips have to use their engines.

The revival series of races which have been held since trading days are particularly important because they force skippers not to rely on their engines and this helps to keep alive the actual skill of handling barges under sail. Most of the eight races are day events, but in 1978 a 60 mile passage race from Gravesend to Pin Mill was started in which only sail could be used. In the 1960s, after the re-rigging of barges had started, the one factor that looked like preventing their revival was the shortage of skippers. It was not possible to train a skipper in trade after about 1960 so that most of the sailing barges were skippered for the next fifteen years by men around retirement age who were happy to return to the skills of their youth. However, it gradually became the case that the majority of skippers had never even seen a barge carrying a freight under sail, let alone sailed on them. This new generation of bargemen have to cope with a different type of sailing and are often as skilful as the thinning ranks of former trading skippers, although handling the spritsail rig is a complex art that requires years of practice to reach perfection.

In the 1980 series of races, the most outstanding barge was the Faversham based *Ironsides,* which in her trading days was never considered to be a racer. The *Ironsides* was built of iron at West Thurrock in 1900 and is the only barge left sailing which was once part of the massive APCM cement fleet. When they sold up their barges, *Ironsides* joined the London & Rochester Trading Company (now Crescent Shipping) which had the largest fleet of 'seeking' barges. They cut her down to a motor barge in 1938 and finally sold her in 1968 to the ex-lighterman Alan Reekie. He spent two years getting her back under sail for charter work. Later he considerably enlarged the barge's sail area and concentrated hard on improving his own skill in the races. Although the *Ironsides* sail area had been increased, the stemhead staysail rig was kept, but she still managed to overhaul bowsprit barges in the races. In the trading days, the coasting barges always had bowsprits which could be lifted up in dock, while barges making short passages, such as from the Swale and Medway to the Thames, only had five sails in a stemhead rig 'inboard'.

So the spritty barges are still alive and well in a very successful form of preservation. Although there seem to be quite a number left, this is still only a fraction of the number which were trading before World War I. When one visits St Katharine's Dock, London, and sees a dozen barges, it seems a lot, but in their trading days they were seen like this throughout the whole of London's dockland. In 1980 at least sixty-three barges still had sailing gear and of these forty-nine were capable of making passages under their own sails. Barges will go on sailing as long as people are able and willing to dedicate their time and money to them.

5

Passenger Travel and International Trade

Britain was amongst the forerunners in developing steam-powered ships. Early experiments were very low powered and usually confined to canals. These early attempts at creating a self-powered craft included Mr Smith's steamer which propelled itself along the Sankey Canal near Liverpool in 1793 by a paddle of seven oars. This invention seems to have faded into oblivion, but in 1801 the steam paddle wheel tug *Charlotte Dundas* began work towing two 70-ton barges on the now filled-in Forth–Clyde Canal. The *Charlotte Dundas* is credited with a towing speed of 3½mph which suggests that she was a technical success. However, there was much opposition to this newfangled invention which belched out black smoke all over the canal, and it was claimed that her wash was damaging the banks so she was stopped.

These early efforts proved that steam engines could move craft on water, but they were full of engineering defects and used a great deal of coal to produce a relatively small amount of power. It took almost a century of work on steam power to finally produce more effective power than sail in every type of vessel. Since steamers were expensive to build and operate, for a long time they could only be used on high return and low volume trades which in effect meant carrying passengers.

The world's first passenger steamer started service in America in 1807, but its engines were supplied by the British firm of Boulton & Watt. In 1811 Henry Bell commissioned John Wood & Co of Glasgow to build the 42ft steamer *Comet* which was used to carry passengers between Glasgow and her owner's hotel at Helensburgh, further down the Clyde. The paddle driven *Comet* was Britain's first passenger steamer and established the Clyde's long association with steam power and merchant shipping. Lowland Scotland became the birthplace of many new steam inventions, and it was said, later in the steam age, that if you shouted 'Jock' into the engine room of any British merchantman it would almost certainly have been answered by the chief engineer and probably half the engine room staff.

In 1821 Wood & Co of Port Glasgow built the 140ft paddle steamer *James Watt* for passenger trade between Leith and London. This was long before the railways, and at that time the best way to travel from

Edinburgh to London was by sailing packet. These were huge gaff cutters and the arrival of the *James Watt* cut sharply into their lucrative trade. The *James Watt* was the first steamer entered at Lloyds and soon the shipping world saw that steamers, because of their speed, could reap rich rewards on passenger routes. However, there were serious technical handicaps. The steam boilers and engines only developed low power and were often far from reliable. Then there was the question of coal. The ship had to carry enough for its entire voyage, but to start with, early steamer engines were so inefficient that they could not make long ocean passages. Steam driven engines were progressively improved, but right up to the end of the steam era, coal supply and the availability of good quality coal was a problem. Steamers on a long voyage generally had to call into several ports for bunkering, while naval ships often took on supplies at sea.

The competition between western nations, which had arisen with sailing ships, quickly extended to the development of the world's passenger routes with steamers. The ferries between Britain and her Continental neighbours were gradually taken over by steamers from about 1830. Several steamers using paddle and sail crossed the Atlantic before a race developed to establish a regular passenger route. The first British steamer to cross was the 703-ton *Sirius* in 1838. She arrived at New York nineteen days after leaving Queenstown (Cobh) on the southern coast of Ireland. The engines had used 24 tons of coal a day, to maintain $8\frac{1}{2}$ knots. However her crew had seriously doubted the steamer's ability to make the crossing and at one stage had mutinied. Her master, Lieutenant Roberts, acted quickly and forced the men back to work at gunpoint.

The honour given to *Sirius* was only brief because, shortly afterwards, the 1,340-ton *Great Western* arrived in New York after crossing the Atlantic three days faster and using a quarter of the *Sirius*'s fuel consumption. The *Great Western* was the product of the steam age genius Isambard Kingdom Brunel. She was built as an extension of the railway from London to Bristol; the Great Western Railway Company's idea was that they should carry passengers from London to New York. The *Great Western* showed that size and speed were going to be of vital importance in the domination of the North Atlantic routes. However, her record crossing only lasted a few months because later in the same year the Transatlantic Steamship Company's 464hp paddle steamer *Liverpool* crossed from Queenstown to New York in seventeen days at an average speed of 10 knots.

All the early passenger ships were paddle steamers but, although they were very easy to manoeuvre in confined waters, they lost power when they rolled heavily at sea. The idea was put forward that some kind of screw or worm which revolved in the water might be developed to power a ship. Experiments were going on when Brunel was designing the huge new iron-hulled ship to be built at Bristol. After seeing an experimental screw ship which visited Bristol, Brunel became convinced that his new 3,270-ton *Great Britain* should be propelled in this way. She sailed in 1843 and could really be called the first of the new breed. This was the birth of the 'liner', a vessel which ran on a regular 'line' between two ports. Brilliant though the *Great Britain* undoubtedly was, she had only a short Atlantic career, but other steamship companies were quick to learn from her.

The most successful period for the *Great Britain* was on the Australian passenger and cargo run between 1852–76. She served as a troopship in the Crimean War and the Indian Mutiny, and ended up as a dismasted sailing ship in the Falkland Islands. After a letter to *The Times* by a naval architect in 1967, a campaign was launched and her iron hulk was brought back to Bristol in 1970 on a raft. She was warped back into the Great Western Dock at Bristol for preservation 127 years to the day after she had left this actual dock as a new ship.

Brunel developed his ideas after the *Great Britain* to try to produce a ship which could travel to India and Australia without the need to stop for fresh supplies of coal. For this ship, the huge 692ft *Great Eastern*, he used screw as well as paddles with engines designed by the great engineer John Scott Russell. She was launched sideways at Napier Yard, Millwall, on the Thames, in 1858 after innumerable problems which drove her designer to an early death. The *Great Eastern* dwarfed everything else afloat and it was over forty years before a larger ship was built.

Although the port of Bristol had played an important part in opening up trading and passenger links with North America, it received a major set back when the British Government awarded the American mail contract to the Liverpool-based Cunard company. This new company had been created in 1840 by Samuel Cunard, a native of Halifax, Nova Scotia, who had left the Canadian Maritimes to establish business interests in England. Cunard's ships had gained a reputation for reliability in the North Atlantic service which won them the contract over the more spectacular Bristol ships. The mail contract carried with it an annual subsidy so that Cunard was able to start building new ships and operate a regular service. There was nothing outstanding about Cunard's *Britannia*, *Arcadia*, *Columbia* and *Caledonia*. They were wooden paddle steamers of about 205ft long capable of around 9 knots and consuming about 40 tons of coal a day. By 1850 the Cunard Line had virtually gained a monopoly over the passenger trade in the western ocean. Already a pattern was emerging, for these liners were built at Port Glasgow, and during the next eighty years close links were seen between the shipping interests of Liverpool and the engineers and shipbuilding promoters on the Clyde. The early Cunard Line ships were not particularly comfortable, but they kept up a regular schedule and the company kept the mail contract, although it was not until 1862 that they took delivery of their first screw steamer, the 2,638-ton *China*.

After establishing the North Atlantic routes, British interests concerned themselves mainly with linking up the Empire, particularly regular steamer routes with India and Australia. In 1834 the Peninsular Company was formed to operate a London–Lisbon–Gibraltar run. Their first ship was the paddle steamer *William Fawcett*, but the company soon realised that with larger ships they could reach India, 'the Jewel of the British Empire'. Of course the Suez Canal was not built until 1869 so that for the first decade of the P & O's Indian Service one ship took passengers to Egypt from where they went over land to join another steamer for the final leg to India. The company was awarded the all-important mail contract to India, and with the general expansion east of Suez they changed the name to the Peninsular & Oriental Steam Navigation Company, which is now more generally known as P & O.

Most of the early paddle steamers used by individual companies to develop the regular lines to America, the West Indies, India, the Far East and Australia had wooden hulls and were propelled by simple low-powered, side lever machinery, ideally suited to paddle vessels. The average speed was around 8 knots, and sails were used in conjunction with the engines to make use of the favourable winds and during the frequent mechanical breakdowns. The sailors hated these sail carrying steamers because the soot and general grime from the smoke made handling the sails an incredibly filthy job. For the stokers who worked below in the murk, feeding the ever hungry fires, the heat, coal dust and motion of the ship made their existence plain drudgery. The officers and deck sailors looked down with lordly disgust on the 'black gang' who toiled away endlessly below to keep up steam pressure and at the same time produce so much grime which they had to work equally industriously to remove from the ship's paint work.

The Americans and the French were soon competing fiercely on the North American route so that it was on these services that most of the new developments were tried in order to stay ahead. This early era was one of prosperity and optimism which ended with the Crimean War in 1854. The effort of taking an army to the shores of the Black Sea and supplying it took up a major part of Britain's merchant fleet, including the fast steamers. In the late 1850s the steamship companies were re-establishing their routes and ordering new ships. The new ships were iron screw vessels which still relied quite heavily on sails, but their size and speed were increased. They were all over 1,000 tons and could average between 10–13 knots.

While Cunard's Liverpool liners fought to hold the 'Blue Riband' for the fastest Atlantic crossing, another Liverpool line, the White Star, concentrated on the emigrant trade. The man behind this line was William Inman who had started as a clerk in the Liverpool merchants' house of Richardson Bros. The Richardsons had operated sailing packets which offered cheap fares and had then moved into steam by buying the barque-rigged iron screw ship *City of Glasgow*, built on the Clyde by Tod & McGregor in 1850. The *City of Glasgow* was not backed up by a mail contract and concentrated on moving as many people as possible as cheaply as possible. As well as some first- and second-class passengers, the White Star Line carried emigrants who wanted to seek a new life in Australia and later America.

In the Crimean War, the Richardsons' two steamers were chartered by the Government for troop carrying. This proved to be more than the Richardsons' religious conscience would allow because they were, like many successful merchants, Quakers and dedicated to peace and non-violence. The ships were transferred to the ownership of young William Inman who gradually gave up his interests in the Australian trade and concentrated on the North Atlantic routes. In 1866 Inman's *City of Paris* crossed the Atlantic at a speed of 13½ knots and took the Blue Riband. The Belfast builders Harland & Wolff convinced Inman that they could build liners which would give him control over the North Atlantic. In 1871 Inman expanded the White Star Line, and their first fast liner, the 470ft *Oceanic* (I) was built by Harland & Wolff. This liner was very much a new concept in ocean travel. Firstly, she was powered by a compound engine which made her cheaper to operate, but she also had a long narrow hull which made her fast. This hull shape was the idea of Edward Harland and had previously been tried out in smaller ships for the Liverpool shipowner J. Bibby. When the first long, lean, flat-bottomed Belfast steamers appeared in the River Mersey, they caused a sensation and were nicknamed Bibby's Coffins. She also set a new standard for accommodation which was arranged across the full width of the ship, a pattern which was to become the norm. There were technical problems with the *Oceanic*, but lessons learnt from the Bibby ships allowed her to be a success. The White Star Line and Harland & Wolff went on to build *Oceanic* (II) in 1899 which was the first ship to be larger than the *Great Eastern*.

With so much competition on the North Atlantic route, speed alone was not enough to attract passengers. Comfort and splendour were being introduced to woo the wealthy passengers. New ideas were incorporated into the *Oceanic* when first-class cabins were placed amidships instead of being right aft as they had always been in the sailing ships. Moreover, the *Oceanic*, with a top speed of 14 knots, was the fastest ship afloat. A few years later the White Star Line built the *Britannic* and the *Germanic*, both 455ft long and capable of 16 knots. They crossed the Atlantic in 7½ days and consumed about 100 tons of coal a day. By this time the long, lean hull had been adopted by steamers everywhere.

When mail contracts were given, the Government insisted that the liners concerned should be capable of conversion to armed cruisers in the event of war. When Britain did eventually find herself embroiled in World War I, the use of liners as warships proved to be fairly useless and they were really only suitable as fast troop carriers. However, in the 1889 Naval Review at Spithead, the White Star Line's new *Teutonic*, the holder of the North Atlantic record of 5 days 16 hours, was there as a merchant cruiser. It was at a banquet on board her that Sir Edward Harland predicted that liners over 1,000ft in length would one day be built. In fact it was not until 1928 that the keel of a liner this size, the *Oceanic* (III), was actually laid. The White Star Line's attempt to keep its position in the North Atlantic after the *Teutonic* and the *Majestic* was the

The promenade deck on board the 7,558-ton P&O liner Caledonia, *built in 1894 by Caird & Company, Greenock. This liner ran at 19½ knots on her trial run and was designed to be fast for the Indian mail service. Her usual route was from London to Bombay via Marseilles, often with a short call at Falmouth or Queenstown, now Cobh, Ireland.* Caledonia *was scrapped in 1925* (P&O)

building of the 800ft *Titan* and the 883ft *Titanic*. Both ships were described as being unsinkable, but both sank after hitting icebergs. The *Titanic* did so with an unnecessary high loss of life on her maiden voyage, taking down with her the chairman of the White Star, J. Bruce Inman, son of the founder, and most of her passengers.

The short-lived *Titanic* was one of the 4-funnel liners which dominated the North Atlantic. Actually there was a need for only 3 funnels, the other was there as a dummy to improve the appearance. The emigrants were particularly impressed with the drawings of the 4-funnel ships on the posters as it made them look faster. The North Atlantic liners had become more than a form of transport by the 1890s, they were a symbol of national prestige. In order to attract wealthy passengers, particularly Americans on the way to view the cultural centres of Europe, liners had to provide increased luxury and opulence. The result was that the cost of operating a liner mounted so that the profit margin was almost eliminated. America began to buy British lines and Germany was financing smaller liners which captured the Blue Riband and some of the publicity.

To meet this challenge, Cunard ordered two new express liners which were little short of floating palaces. These were the Clyde-built *Lusitania* in 1907, which won the Blue Riband back for Cunard after thirteen years, and her sister ship, the Tyne-built 790ft *Mauretania* which carried 2,145 passengers and, with her crew, had a floating population of a small country town. Not only were these Cunard liners the largest afloat, they also had the new turbine engines driving four screws to make them the first 25-knot liners. It had taken ten years for turbines to be developed to a point where they could be fitted to an express liner, and even then it took great courage for Cunard to commit themselves to turbines. The turbine was first brought forcefully before the public's attention at Queen Victoria's Diamond Jubilee Review at Spithead in 1897, when the yacht *Turbinia*, at a speed of 34 knots, out ran all the naval vessels that tried to intercept her.

The *Lusitania* and the *Mauretania* were great favourites with the travelling public and held the Blue Riband for Cunard for twenty-two years. The *Mauretania* started as a coal burner with the huge 'black gang' of 250 stokers labouring away in the depth of the hull feeding the fires with 1,000 tons of coal a day, but after World War I, like most liners, she was converted to an oil burner. The *Mauretania* was scrapped in 1935 and Cunard ordered a second *Mauretania* which was built by Cammell Laird at Birkenhead in 1938. This second *Mauretania* was slightly larger than her famous predecessor, but not quite so fast. However, she had a career of twenty-seven years sailing from English ports to New York as a troopship and cruise liner. (Liners were sent on holiday cruises, usually

The express liner Mauretania *of 1907 with the steam launch* Turbinia *under her bows. She carried around 2,200 passengers in three classes. The first-class passengers were surrounded by Edwardian splendour in the dining rooms and saloon lounges. The* Turbinia *is now in the care of the Science Museum, Newcastle-upon-Tyne* (Cunard)

in the Mediterranean, as early as 1904, but it was not until after World War II that this became popular.)

The first *Mauretania* was taken over by the Royal Navy as an auxiliary cruiser in World War I, but they found that she ate up a vast quantity of coal and was of little practical value as a warship. The Royal Navy left the *Lusitania* with Cunard who kept her on the New York run. However, Germany realised that if she was going to stand a chance of winning the war, the link between Britain and France and North America had to be snapped. Since the United States was neutral and many of her nationals continued to travel on British liners, many people considered that the Germans would never dare to attack them. The liners relied mainly on their speed for safety in both wars but in May 1915 the *Lusitania* was torpedoed by a German submarine off the south coast of Ireland. The great ship took down with her many American passengers and this loss was a major factor in bringing the United States into the war against Germany.

Although the Thames, the Mersey and Glasgow still remained bases for liners on international routes from the 1890s onwards, Southampton increasingly became the passenger port of Britain. Liners originally came here because they could cross over to Cherbourg and collect the European passengers before sailing on to New York and the St Lawrence. Southampton had 35ft of water at low tide at the head of sheltered Southampton Water which made it a natural harbour. The town had been important as a port until the end of the reign of Elizabeth I, but after this it had declined until two brilliant Victorian engineers, Francis Giles and his son Alfred, began to lay out its docks. The Outer Dock was built in 1842, the Inner Dock in 1851 and in 1890 the Empress Dock was constructed. With an increasing number of liners arriving, the White Star (later Ocean) Dock was opened in 1912 as a terminal for Atlantic liners.

By the inter-war years Southampton was handling one-third of all the passengers leaving and arriving in Britain. There were occasions when eleven large liners, with a combined gross tonnage of 403,859 arrived or left in one day. To cater for all the maintenance work a floating dry dock was brought to Southampton in 1924, and in 1933 the King George V Graving Dock was opened, then the largest dry dock in the world.

By the late 1920s, Cunard were operating the express liners *Mauretania* of 1907, the *Aquitania* of 1914 and the 885ft *Berengaria* which had been built as the German *Imperator* in 1913, but this ageing

The bridge on the express liner Aquitania. *The open bridge must have been a very unpleasant place during bad weather in the North Atlantic* (National Maritime Museum)

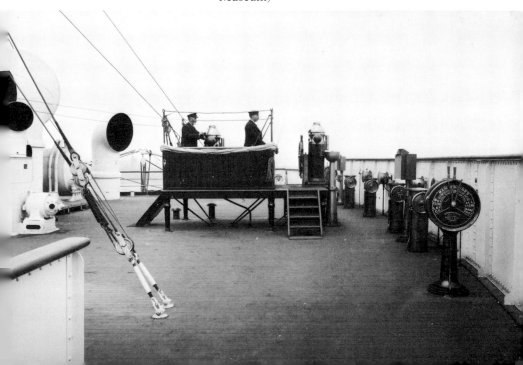

ORIENT LINE

Dinner.

CONSOMMÉ VERT-PRÉ
POTAGE CRÈME D'ARGENTEUIL

BARBUE, SAUCE AUX CREVETTES

CÔTELETTES DE CHEVREUIL À LA MILANAISE
CHOUX-FLEURS EN BRANCHES AU FROMAGE

ROAST FILLET OF VEAL
BRAISED SHOULDER OF MUTTON

Melon Sorbet

POACHED CHICKEN

BLACK-CURRANT PUDDING
BAKED VANILLA CUSTARDS
ARCTIC CHOCOLATES

SARDINE AND TOMATO CROÛTES

COLD SIDEBOARD:
CUMBERLAND HAM   ROAST SIRLOIN OF BEEF
SALAD

S.S. "OTRANTO."
MONDAY, 1ST AUGUST, 1927.
MOLDE.
Breakfast will be served to-morrow from 7.30 a.m.

The menu card on the Orient Line's Otranto *while on a cruise to the Norwegian fjords in 1927. Cruise liners began trips to the Mediterranean early in this century, but this work did not replace their regular passenger service until the late 1950s* (Author's Collection) trio were being overshadowed by the new German liners so again Cunard set out to update their main passenger liners to regain their status as world leaders. The first new liner was the 1,019ft *Queen Mary*, completed in 1936 after six years under construction by John Brown & Company of Clydebank. The long delay had been caused by the uncertainty of the future of the North Atlantic trade. Basically the *Queen Mary* was simply a larger, up-dated version of the *Aquitania*, a splendid old ship which went on working over another decade.

The *Queen Mary*'s best crossing was from the Ambrose Lightship to the Bishop Rock in 3 days 20 hours in 1938; at one stage she had achieved 32 knots. The crossing generally took about 4–5 days but of course much depended on the weather. In order to stay ahead, Cunard ordered John Brown & Company to build the largest liner ever built, the *Queen Elizabeth*. By the time she was completed in 1940, World War II was already developing into a very bitter struggle. When the *Queen Elizabeth* sailed for New York on her secret maiden voyage, her speed, because of the war, was not made public, but she was capable of averaging 31 knots.

There were no trials before this voyage. The *Queen Elizabeth* just steamed from her builder's yard to New York—later claimed to be the first occasion on which this was attempted. The first master of the 83,673 ton *Queen Elizabeth* was Captain John Townley who, like many of the men who commanded liners, had begun his career as an apprentice in sailing ships. Cumberland born, Townley had joined Cunard in 1904 and his first command was the cargo ship *Thracia* in 1915. He worked his way up to commanding large liners, and after Cunard and the White Star Line merged in 1934, he became the relief commander of the new line.

Both the *Queen Mary* and the *Queen Elizabeth* became war time troopships. The numbers of men they could carry and their speed made them a tremendous asset. Winston Churchill said that the effort of these two ships shortened the war by a year. However, with the mid-Atlantic full of submarines which were wreaking havoc with allied convoys, every crossing was a gamble. For all the dangers the only real disaster was when the *Queen Mary*, going at 24 knots, ran down and sank the escorting Royal Navy light cruiser *Curacao* off the Clyde.

After the war, these two Cunard liners took up the Southampton–New York route and the commercial future looked secure. The record number of people to cross the Atlantic by sea in a single year was not reached until 1958 when 1,200,000 passengers were carried in liners of several nations. In the same year, the first jet planes began flying the Atlantic routes and the demand for sea travel quickly fell. Cunard started to make massive losses. The *Queen Mary* made her last Atlantic crossing in 1967 and went off, via Cape Horn, to become a major tourist attraction at Long Beach,

A dining-room scene posed by professional models with stewards on the Pacific Steam Navigation Company's liner Reina del Mar. *This 19,320-ton liner was built by Harland & Wolff, Belfast, in 1955 for the Liverpool–South American service*
(Stewart Bale)

California. The *Queen Elizabeth* made her last Cunard cruise in 1968 and went into American ownership, but she never made another commercial voyage. Under the name *Seawise University*, she was burnt out and sank in Hong Kong harbour in 1972.

The 'Queens' had been not just a comfortable way to cross the North Atlantic, but a symbol of Britain's merchant navy. For Cunard to have lost a flagship which was a household name seemed unthinkable. Besides, the leisure cruising trade seemed to be offering liners employment after most passengers had changed to air travel. Cunard had met this challenge before and with government help they had the *Queen Elizabeth II* built at John Brown's yard on the Clyde in 1968. This liner, usually known as the 'QE II' is a beautiful ship which achieved over 32 knots on the measured mile in the Firth of Clyde. She had the dubious distinction of being the last great liner built. As for the old style liner routes, they did not quite die out with the 'Queens'. The Union Castle Line was running a service from Southampton to Cape Town until 1977, but the age of long-distance passenger sea travel had finished. However, the rapid rise in living conditions and long, paid holidays increased the demand for travel to Europe from the mid-1960s so that by 1980, Britain had virtually the largest fleet of ferry ships in the world.

The great ocean-going express liners which many companies operated to every part of the world attracted publicity and prestige. But most shipping lines also ran much less glamorous cargo liners which relied on cargoes for their main income but had cabin space for passengers on less popular routes. Then there were the ferries to every part of the British Isles and across to European ports run by numerous companies which sprang up as soon as reliable steamships were available. Much has been written about how the railways ended the isolation of many small rural communities on land, but it is often forgotten that the steamship drew the whole of the British Isles closer together. The link between the Isle of Man and the River Mersey area was already centuries old, but when the Isle of Man Steam Packet Company started a steamship service in 1830, it became even closer. The original paddle steamer on this route, the *Mona's Isle* (I) was only 116ft long, but she covered the distance between Douglas and Liverpool in only 8 hours. She lasted for twenty-one years, but all the time ships were getting faster. The 188ft 17½-knot steamer *Douglas* reduced the crossing time to 4 hours in the 1860s and was reputed to be the fastest ferry afloat.

Because of their obvious link with passenger travel on land, the expanding railway companies tended to either buy up ferry companies or start rival services. By the late Victorian era, independent companies were being formed to run coastal excursion steamers. One of these was the Liverpool & North Wales Steamship Company, formed in January 1891, for services from Liverpool to the coast of North Wales and from resorts there across to the Isle of Man. This company was running about three steamers for the summer holiday period only, after which they were laid up. These steamers could not compete with the already established railway lines, but they and many others like them all round Britain were very popular. They carried holiday-makers from the industrial areas to the seaside resorts in a few hours and gave a great sense of adventure and escape to the whole outing which rail travel alone sometimes lacked.

The Liverpool & North Wales Steamship Company was helped by the fact that the two great rivers, the Mersey and the Dee, cut into the coast. Anyone who wished to reach the resorts in North Wales had to go round or cross these rivers, which took time, while the steamers which left Liverpool went straight down the coast and reached Llandudno in just over a couple of hours. These excursion steamers had to be very versatile. The Liverpool & North Wales steamer *St Seiriol* had been designed to stand up to the heavy weather that was often encountered on the

Llandudno to Douglas crossing, but she was still shoal draught and handled well enough to be navigated and turned round in the tortuous Menai Straits.

One of the companies that operated excursion steamers on the south coast of England was Cosens of Weymouth which began in 1852 with the *Prince*. This steamer was built by Scott Russell at Millwall inshore of the great hull of the famous *Great Eastern* and was actually launched through the framework of the 'monster'. As the excursion trade expanded, Cosens bought more steamers and at least four of their paddle steamers were specially designed to land on the beaches of Devon and Dorset. It was a common sight to see a Cosens steamer collecting passengers off the beaches at West Bay near Bridport, Lyme Regis, Seaton, Sidmouth and Torquay. They also landed in Lulworth Cove and even, if the tide and weather were right, on Chesil Beach and Church Ope on the Isle of Portland. The first Cosens steamer to have a cross-channel certificate was the *Empress*. She did trips to Alderney and Cherbourg, and in 1881 was the first steamer to run between Bournemouth and Torquay, taking 13½ hours on passage.

There was keen competition with the Bournemouth Steam Packet Company, and on one occasion their *Bournemouth* and Cosens' *Empress* met at sea and started to race each other when bound from the resorts of Hampshire to Torquay. Off Portland a fog came down but Captain Perrin in the *Bournemouth* was convinced that he had rounded the Bill and pressed on, only to plough up on the land. Another steamer called the *Empress* was one of three paddle steamers owned by the Goole & Hull Steam Packet Company who charged one shilling (five pence) for a return 'voyage' between Goole and Hull at the turn of the century. This inland trip caused many a brief bout of seasickness as the steamers buffeted their way down the open River Humber.

There were many of these small companies operating steamers all round Britain, but they were most numerous and, indeed, the most useful on the Clyde. The geographical make up of the area made steamer travel quicker and easier than road travel in the Clyde and the western isles. Competition between the companies in the 1860s resulted in the steamers racing whenever they met. The fiercest competition was between the three steamers on Broomielaw–Rothesay runs. The captain of the *Ruby* offered in the *Glasgow Herald* to race the other two for a £100 wager. The *Neptune* actually won and set up the record of 2 hours 28 minutes which was never equalled again. However, the authorities took a dim view of the steamers thrashing down the Clyde with their machinery running at maximum speed. Also passengers were sometimes left standing on piers as steamers went hammering past trying to prove their speed.

The 300ft, 18-knot Clyde excursion paddle steamer Columba *at Ardrishaig Quay near the entrance to the Crinan Canal. The boats in the foreground are Loch Fyne herring skiffs* (Author's Collection)

Racing flared up again on the Clyde about 1900. The North British Railway Company's *Waverley*, a 19-knot paddle steamer, usually managed to beat the Glasgow & South Western Railway's paddler *Jupiter* when racing down the Clyde to Dunoon. On one occasion they were racing virtually alongside with sirens wailing when they all but collided in trying to reach Innellan Pier first. In 1907 the *Waverley* actually did hit the *Neptune*.

After World War I the Clyde steamers had a hard time and most of them came under the management of the new London & North Eastern Railway Company in 1923. The LNER based their six steamers at Craigendoran and ran regular Clyde services. In the late 1930s these services were losing money and most of the steamers were over thirty years old. In 1939 only the paddle steamers *Talisman*, *Jeannie Deans* and the *Marmion* were in service with the *Waverley* and *Lucy Ashton* laid up.

In the Thames estuary, as in the Clyde, steamers had been operated on a regular passenger service before the railways had made travel faster and easier. The General Steam Navigation Company turned to operating a fleet of paddle steamers which ran summer excursions from the Thames. These routes were all to resorts with piers. The Belle steamers also ran from the Thames and collected passengers from pier heads at Southend, Clacton, Walton and Felixstowe before terminating at Yarmouth. Many

One of the Victoria Steamboat Company's excursion steamers on the Thames at Blackwall in about 1900 (Graham Jensen)

One of the most popular Thames tideway excursion steamers was the New Medway Steam Packet Company's Medway Queen *of 316 tons, built at Troon in 1924* (Hugh Perks)

of the Victorian piers were badly damaged in World War II, but in spite of this the General Steam Navigation Company resumed their schedule from Tower Pier, London, in 1948 with five ships. Once more, steamers called at Clacton and Herne Bay but mines off the Kent coast still prevented stops at Margate. The company took delivery of the new 20-knot screw steamer *Royal Sovereign* from the Dumbarton builders William Denny & Brothers and all seemed set for the continuation of the pre-war pattern of trade.

The wealthy and adventurous were able to travel on ocean liners, the career men sailed on naval ships and merchant vessels, but to the vast majority of British people the summer excursion steamer was their only link with the sea. For Londoners a fascinating trip down the Thames, through what was then still the world's greatest port with miles of dockland, was part of the holiday. There were stops at Gravesend, Southend, Chatham and Margate. The 21-knot paddle steamer *Royal Daffodil*, which rescued 8,000 soldiers in the 1940 Dunkirk evacuation, was based in 1948 at Gravesend. Her route in the 1950s was from Gravesend to Southend and across to Boulogne and back all in one day. In the Bristol Channel, a smart fleet of paddle steamers, such as the *Bristol Queen* and the *Cardiff Queen*, was run by P. & A. Campbell of Bristol and they gave thousands of people a taste of the sea that they would otherwise never have experienced.

The excursion steamers belonged to a particular social era of British development. Many historical writers stress the poverty and grime of the industrial towns of Victorian Britain and there can be no doubt that there were many people who really were poor. However, the vast majority of people did have a wage which allowed some form of holiday every year. That holiday still had to be cheap and stay within a day's railway travel of their homes. The excursion steamer companies existed to provide a day out for the industrial workers and office staff from Glasgow, Liverpool, Bristol, London and many other centres of population. In the late 1950s standards of living and car ownership rose sharply. More and more people went abroad on package holidays and the old steamers at the end of the pier lost their appeal and glamour.

One of the last of her generation of excursion paddle steamers was the *Waverley*, built for the LNER in 1946 to replace the famous Clyde *Waverley* which was lost at the Dunkirk Evacuation. The second *Waverley* and the Caledonian Steam Packet Company's 17-knot *Caledonian* operated on many Clyde routes until October 1969. She was sold and became a Thames pub until a serious fire in 1980 which led to her being scrapped. The *Waverley* was lucky in being a newer steamer and managed to avoid the scrap yard or degeneration into a waterside attraction. In 1974 she was handed over to the Paddle Steamer Preservation Society for a nominal sum and they formed a new company, the Waverley Steam Navigation Company, to operate her. A small group of people have put a tremendous amount of work into keeping the *Waverley* going, not only on the Clyde, as she has been right round Britain doing traditional excursion work. On the Clyde the *Waverley*'s status as Europe's last seagoing paddler helped to attract day trippers when competing with Caledonian-MacBrayne's turbine steamer *Queen Mary*.

The pleasure steamers of P. & A. Campbell at the Pierhead, Cardiff, with the coal-loading docks in the background. Campbells were based at Underfall Yard, Bristol, but their ships ran excursions from Ilfracombe to Lundy and Cardiff (Welsh Industrial & Maritime Museum)

The present 240ft oil-fired *Waverley* is actually the fourth steamer to have that name. At 693 tons she is one of the largest paddle excursion steamers ever built and came from the yard of A. & J. Inglis Ltd, Pointhouse, Glasgow, who built her predecessor in 1890 and many other fine paddlers. Paddle steamers remained popular in the excursion trade because they were much easier to control when coming alongside a pierhead than a screw vessel, at least until bow thrusters were introduced in the 1960s. In 1953 Inglis built the 14-knot, 208ft excursion paddle steamer *Maid of the Loch* which was then taken to pieces and transported over land and re-erected on Loch Lomond. The *Maid of the Loch* is oil fired, but the last operational coal-fired paddle steamer in Britain was the *Lincoln Castle*, a Humber ferry which ran between Hull and New Holland.

With the decline and eventual extinction of the English excursion paddle steamers in the 1960s, the three paddle ferries on the River Humber became the focus of a great deal of attention. The oldest ferries were the *Tattershall Castle* and the *Wingfield Castle* built for the LNER in 1934. Paddlers were kept on this run because they could turn so easily and were of shallow draught. In 1940 A. & J. Inglis launched the 12-knot, 200ft *Lincoln Castle* which made the delivery voyage the following year from the north of Scotland to the Humber and she began her long, reliable career as a car and passenger ferry. In 1972 the *Tattershall Castle* was withdrawn by British Rail and sold to become a picture gallery on the Thames. The *Wingfield Castle* was retired next, in 1974, and was laid up in the Thames. British Rail continued to operate the *Lincoln Castle* because with the Humber Bridge under construction, it was hardly worth replacing her. The Humberside steam enthusiasts made a considerable effort to keep the *Lincoln Castle* at Hull for preservation after she had to be withdrawn from service in 1978, but she was later towed to Hessle for use as a restaurant.

Steamships have been such a deep-rooted part of Britain's maritime and industrial past that it is desirable to save some for future generations to see. Some steamers that would have been ideal for preservation were the passenger steamers that ran on the East Anglian broadland waterways. The Veteran Steamship Society bought the $9\frac{1}{2}$-knot, 73ft *Resolute*, a steel double-ender built at Millwall in 1903, which spent most of her career running pleasure cruises in Breydon Water in the summer. The 74ft steamer *Yarmouth*, now on display at St Katharine's Dock in London, belongs to the same era. She was built in 1895 by Thomas Bradley at Great Yarmouth as one of the 'Lily-boats' which, with the *Resolute* and the *Southtown*, ran the 3-mile ferry service between Yarmouth Town Hall and Gorleston. They were double-ended with screw and rudder at each end so that they did not have to turn round in narrow waterways.

The last steam ferry Lincoln Castle *on her Hull to New Holland run across the River Humber. The New Holland ferry was started early in the nineteenth century, and the first steamer was introduced in 1832. The last of the Humber's once numerous network of ferries finished in June 1981, when the paddle vessel* Farringford *made her last New Holland to Hull run* (Author)

The steamer Yarmouth *was built as a Great Yarmouth–Gorleston ferry in 1895. After 1946, she ran pleasure cruises on the Broads until being sold for preservation in 1969. She is now on display at St Katharine's Dock, London* (Author)

The VIC 56 *was based at Rosyth on the Firth of Forth until the Ministry of Defence sold her to Mr Cleary in 1979; he converted her from oil burning to coal and wood burning. Now based at Rotherhithe on the Thames, he hopes to keep her steaming as long as possible. The MOD's last VIC, the* VIC 65, *was sold for breaking up at Inverkeithing in 1979* (Author)

Of about 190 steam-powered vessels in existence in Britain in the late 1970s, eight were paddle steamers, but most were small river launches kept by enthusiasts. The Broads' steamers with passenger carrying potential seemed ideal, but they were just too large for the individual enthusiast, but not large enough, like the *Waverley* or the *Lincoln Castle*, to attract national attention. Most of the surviving steamers were originally everyday working craft such as the 9-knot, 52ft Admiralty Harbour Launch *Puffin*. This was built in 1919 but was restored in the early 1970s by Bob Partis, and since then has cruised widely on the English coast from her base at Holbrook on the River Stour. Steam is not quite as convenient as petrol or diesel, because it takes three hours of stoking the Ruston & Hornsby boiler to build up a head of steam to power the engine built by Plenty of Newbury. When the *Puffin* is under way, she has to be stoked with just under 1 cwt of coal an hour. Before this steamer can go off on a trip, $2\frac{1}{2}$ tons of coal have to be manually put into her bunkers.

One of the most popular types of steamer to be preserved are the World War II VIC (Victualling Inshore Craft) lighters. These were quickly assembled cargo craft produced for the government to relieve the shortage of general purpose small tonnage during World War II. The design of these self-propelled lighters came from the Clyde puffers. These were small steamers built for use on the Clyde and west coast of Scotland. They were called puffers because in the early days, steam escaped directly into the sky up the funnel in short puffs. Later, Clyde-built steam lighters or coal boats were fitted with condensers, but the name puffer was retained. To pass through the Forth & Clyde Canal, the puffers could not be more than 66ft long so they tended to be rather stubby craft with pointed sterns which were derived from the old sailing gabbards, the round bottomed trading sloops of the Clyde.

Puffers loaded around 100–120 tons and often discharged on the open beaches of the west coast, the Hebrides or at the coastal towns of the Clyde and the Forth. The puffers were usually rather grimy, except the *Pibroch*, owned by the White Horse Distillery, which was spotless. She traded to Islay and distilleries on the west coast.

J. Hay & Sons of Glasgow operated the largest fleet of puffers, and their boats were mostly built at Kirkintilloch. When the Ministry of War Transport wanted to build a reliable, well-tried design, they turned to the puffer. The war time VIC had higher sides and better accommodation than the Clyde puffer, but in the smaller 6-knot, 66ft VIC the funnel was still in front of the wheel-house. This dated back to the puffer's origin as a simple canal lighter. The 66ft *Basuto*, built at Port Dundas in 1902 and still operated by the Manchester Dry Dock Ltd in the late 1970s, was one of the early steam lighter types, her funnel above the engine room and the wheel-house aft, as in the old sailing days.

The Ministry of War also had an 80ft VIC type with the funnel aft of the wheel-house which was more like a coaster. One of these to survive is the *VIC 77*, built at Rowhedge Ironworks, Essex, in 1945, which was used by the Admiralty at Portsmouth and was then bought from the scrap yard by a steam enthusiast. Renamed the *Vic* and then *Victual*, her excursions under steam were often fuelled by driftwood. The main hatch top was lined with willing helpers sawing up assorted lengths of timber.

The fine 100ft seagoing tug *Challenge* which is to be seen as part of the Maritime Trust's wonderful collection of vessels in St Katharine's Dock was built at Aberdeen in 1931 and represents the craftsmanship which went into the last steam tugs. Some preservationists have saved TID tugs which were the product of World War II. These tugs have never been called beautiful but represent the ingenuity of men faced with appalling difficulties in the dark days of the early 1940s. Through enemy bombings and mines, ships were lost much faster than conventional ship-building methods could replace them. Then Richard Dunston of Thorne near Doncaster came up with a revolutionary prefabricated TID tug. The official explanation for TID is usually that they were 'Towing in Dock' tugs; however, Dunston's explanation is that it was simply an abbreviation of 'Tiddler'.

These 'utility' single-screw steel 8½-knot tugs proved to be very useful and Dunstons built about 158 while most of the remaining 183 were built by William Pickersgill at Southwick, Sunderland. The majority of these were coal fired. The idea of returning to coal in World War II was because it was a more reliable source of power than oil which had to be brought through submarine infested seas to reach this country. The TIDs were made in sections by different contractors and then welded together. The first TID was completed in 1943 and towed down to Hessle on the Humber to be engined. She was completed and finished her trials in time to go up river to collect the next TID hull to be launched. Dunston continued to increase production and at their peak they were able to complete a hull in 4½ days. Even though they were constructed for an emergency, many TIDs continued working for thirty years. The *Brent* *(TID 159)* which worked in London Docks until 1969 was then sold for scrap, but was rescued by Ron Hall and kept in steam. Another tug with a long working life was the *Biddick (TID 54)* which was owned by the Port of Sunderland Authority until 1973.

The question of deciding which ships are worthy of preservation is a difficult one. It is quite right that the *Great Britain* should take prime place as the most important steamer left, but she always had been

The Cardiff tramp steamer Pontypridd *was owned by the Morel Brothers. They first came to Cardiff to sell potatoes from their Jersey farm. Cardiff, as 'the coal metropolis of the world', attracted enterprising people from all over Britain. The well-known shipowners William Reardon Smith and W. J. Tatem both came from Devon* (Welsh Industrial & Maritime Museum)

amongst the élite. The bulk of Britain's deepwater merchant fleet were not liners, but humble tramp steamers which, as the name implies, tramped anywhere carrying anything. The 143ft steamer *Robin*, on open display in St Katharine's Dock, is typical of hundreds of simple merchant steamers which ploughed the seas under the red ensign right into the 1950s. The 336-ton *Robin* was really only a coaster, but the ocean-going tramp steamer was little more than an enlarged version of this ship.

Every sizeable port in Britain had small shipping companies operating tramp steamers. It was a cut-throat business in which every economy was made in order to keep buying new ships and expanding the fleet. The large companies whose liners were household names were often assisted in difficult times by government aid, but the State was not so worried about the tramp steamer companies. In their part of the shipping world, it was a case of the survival of the fittest. If the small tramp companies made the wrong decisions, experienced falling markets, wrecks or strikes then they went out of business.

One of these now long-forgotten fleets of tramp steamship owners was the Scholefield Steamship Company of Newcastle. The firm had its roots in the Durham shipowners, H. Scholefield, which had two brigs. It seems that a Scholefield went into partnership in 1879 with Tully of Newcastle and bought a single small steamer, *Peninsula*. So successful was this ship that Scholefield senior sold his ship and they joined forces to create a new H. Scholefield & Son which concentrated on steam tramps, starting with the *Andalusia* in 1881. Before the company ceased trading thirty-five years later, they had owned about fourteen steamers which traded more or less anywhere they could find a freight, although generally owners stuck to a particular trade in which they built up contracts and their crews achieved some experience.

This expertise in building and operating ships was particularly important. A man who saved many lives was Robert Stevens of Plymouth who wrote a weighty volume familiarly known as 'Stevens on Stowage'. This was first published in 1858 and for the next half century was the standard reference book used by ships' officers. Stevens was a printer, but he lived in the atmosphere of ships and his father had been a coal factor (merchant) on the New Quay (now the Parade) at Plymouth. In the age of sail and small paddle steamers, many ships called at Plymouth for fresh supplies before and after long voyages. In 1849 no less than 130 emigrant ships carrying nearly 16,000 passengers visited Plymouth Sound outward bound. The actual material in 'Stevens on Stowage' was gathered by Robert Stevens from personal contact with owners, masters and agents. In this way, the Plymouth printer was able to give advice not just on the best way to stow cargoes safely so that the ship did not capsize, but also on such matters as the tea market conditions in the Chinese ports or the best natives to hire in the South Sea (Pacific) Islands. So important was Stevens' work that the Admiralty ordered a copy to be available at all their dockyards. An Aberdeen shipowner gave a copy to each of his masters too, a rare event in an age when shipowners were not above forgetting to pay their masters, let alone give them anything. The Liverpool Black Ball Line, which before the coming of steamers operated a packet line of crack sailing ships in the North Atlantic passenger trade, once referred to Stevens' book as being an 'invaluable work on stowage which we always keep by us'.

Two of Britain's leading shipping assets are Lloyd's of London, a famous corporation dealing with insurance, and a quite separate body, Lloyd's Register of Shipping. It is believed that Italian merchants who settled in Lombard Street established marine insurance, but the first surviving English insurance policy dates from 1555. The Great Fire of London in 1666 destroyed the old streets of the insurance underwriters and they tended to meet in a coffee house in Tower Street. The ambitious coffee house keeper Edward Lloyd, a Welshman, made great efforts to make his establishment the centre for shipping interests. Insurance underwriters, shipowners and agents gathered in Lloyd's coffee house to discuss business. Lloyd was never involved in insurance, merely in encouraging shipping people to use his establishment. In 1696 he started a news-sheet *Lloyd's News* in which he provided information of interest to his customers. However, the last issue contained references to the House of Lords' proceedings which broke confidence and it was demanded that he should print an apology. Rather than do this Lloyd stopped his publication.

Nearly forty years later, in 1734, *Lloyd's List*, which included the movements of ships and general information, was started. It was this list that has grown into Lloyd's Register of Shipping which is the oldest and largest organization to supply information to the international shipping world. Lloyd's Register of Shipping provided information on the condition of every ship, which was of obvious interest to anyone buying, insuring or chartering a ship. Lloyd's classification 100A1 which denotes a first-class ship, came into being in 1775, although their first published register of ships had begun eleven years earlier.

By 1834 Lloyd's Register had sixty-four surveyors appointed to cover every British port. This increased to around four hundred surveyors just after World War II, but by 1980 Lloyd's Register had some three thousand surveyors spread all over the world who classified ships and sent in information to their headquarters in Fenchurch Street, London. Lloyd's Register is a data collecting agency which publishes statistics on the world's shipping and supplies information to shipping companies and governments to help them with their planning.

Lloyd's of London is a totally separate organization situated in a nearby building. This corporation now covers every type of insurance, but still deals primarily with shipping. Until around 1950, Lloyd's of London maintained some 150 signal stations and 1,500 agents who reported hourly movements of ships. A vessel overdue on a voyage is posted missing at Lloyd's until there is definite evidence of her loss, or a decision is made to declare her loss, when the Lutine bell is rung and the owners can then claim against the underwriters. The *Lutine* was a Royal Navy ship which was wrecked off the coast of Holland in 1799 when carrying gold. Part of this bullion was successfully salvaged from the wreck between 1854–61.

Britain's economy has been greatly boosted by her part in international trade; not just through the earnings of the merchant fleet, but also hidden assets like insurance. There are also the Baltic Exchange and other meeting places where merchants arrange freights. The liners and cargo ships of the old days and container vessels of today tend to run on regular schedules, while the old style tramp ships went anywhere that a freight could be fixed for them. The freight was actually arranged between brokers on exchanges which were set up in most ports. London was and still is an international centre for trading and fixing freights.

At the time of the South African War (1899–1902), Britain's ships carried over half the world's trade. Most of these ships were plain steam tramp ships which made long voyages at little more than 6 knots. By 1914 Britain's share of world trade had dropped to 38 per cent. War time losses soon sent up freight rates, but this was followed with a slump in the 1920s which put many smaller shipping companies out of business. When business transactions on the New York Stock Exchange collapsed, there was comparatively little freight moving anywhere in the world and the tramp companies had to lay up their steamers. One of the places where these idle steamers were laid up was in the Fal River off the Cornish village of Old Kea. Around fifty ocean-going ships were packed in here. There were ships belonging to the Canadian Pacific, Federal, British India lines, British Tanker Company, Chellews, Chapmans, Goulds of Cardiff and many more left idle. Many firms such as the Leyland Line and Thomas of Anglesey's 'Cambrian' ships collapsed in the slump.

Also among the ships packed in the Fal were many belonging to the Hain Steamship Company which was originally a Cornish based company. The Hain family of St Ives had started with sailing ships, but Sir Edward Hain had turned to steam and most of the sixty-eight steamships built for his company came from the Tyneside firm of John Readhead & Sons, South Shields. Sir Edward's only son had been killed fighting in World War I so he sold the line to P & O in 1917. In spite of this the Hains' ships retained Cornish names and had a high proportion of Cornishmen serving on them. There remained a strong sense of 'family' loyalty to the company which dated back to the days of individual ownership.

In Britain the high safety requirement forced every shipowner to keep updating his vessels in order to be allowed to go on trading. Owners in other countries with little or no inspection of their ships bought up the old British sailers and steamers and ran them in competition with even lower paid crews. In a few years the new maritime nations were able to buy new ships and Britain's share of the world trade diminished. The rise and fall of individual companies is hard to trace, but the Lamport & Holt Line which traded to Brazil and the Argentine had thirty-six steamers totalling 198,992 gross tons in 1914. In the depression between 1929 and the early 1930s part of this shipping empire went bankrupt, but later in the 1930s the Line's fortunes began to recover: Harland & Wolff built the cargo

The anti-submarine cruiser HMS Invincible *carries Sea King helicopters and Sea Harrier aircraft. The Royal Navy is the strongest navy in Western Europe* (Royal Navy)

'*View on the Avon at Hotwells*' showing the Clifton Suspension Bridge, a painting
c1831 by Samuel Jackson (*1794–1869*) (Bristol City Museum & Art Gallery)

The Cunard liner Queen Elizabeth 2 *fitting out at John Brown's Clyde yard in 1968*
(Keith Byass)

Sir Winston Churchill *at the start of the 1976 Tall Ships Race from Plymouth to Santa Cruz de Tenerife* (Tony Griffiths)

ship *Delius*, the first of the 'D' class 10,000-ton motor ships with the speed of 15 knots and accommodation for twelve passengers.

The Lamport & Holt Line had twenty-one ships just before World War II, but enemy action sent 70 per cent of the fleet to the bottom. Nine Lamport & Holt masters were awarded the OBE, and many other officers and crew received awards for devotion and gallantry in helping to keep both the army and the civilian population supplied. Like many other smaller lines, Lamport & Holt came under the control of a larger group, in this case the Vestey Group and their Blue Star Line which also traded to South America. However, Lamport & Holt retained its identity with its own office and personnel, and in 1976 had four ships comprising 30,471 gross tons.

Most of the deepwater merchant ships lost in World War II were torpedoed by submarine, some were bombed and a few mined, while with coasters the highest losses were from mines. Every company lost ships and men. The Houlder Line lost fifteen vessels totalling 120,028 tons, and with them 3 masters, 3 chief engineers and 105 seamen, while many others were seriously injured or taken prisoner. The Prince Line lost fourteen ships but even in the war they managed to get eleven new ships as replacements. It was their *Malayan Prince* which led the first convoy into Tobruk, North Africa, after it was recaptured. The crew also managed to shoot down a German bomber and General Montgomery went aboard and congratulated the ship's company. The *Malayan Prince* was one of those lucky ships which seemed to have a charmed existence while every other ship in the company in the same class was lost. She traded all over the world during the war and even took supplies to Normandy beach-head operations. Nearly all the ships sent on this were single screw to lessen the chance of their vibration setting off acoustic mines. However, the *Malayan Prince* was a twin-screw motorship, but survived.

By 1949 the Prince Line with its subsidiary, the Rio Cape Line, was operating seventeen ships. Many companies had of course replaced wartime losses with Liberty and Empire ships, but in the following decade they replaced these with general purpose motorships. The pattern of trade was still fairly stable. Trade connections, often going back to Victorian times, favoured ships which were British built, owned and manned, enabling them to continue to handle the vast majority of goods arriving in the United Kingdom ports and much of the world's trade, particularly in the Far East. With the breakdown of the empire, the new nations wanted their own fleets but there was more to the decline of Britain's merchant fleet than this. In the 1960s, with the rise of the 'flag of convenience', shipping became international in ownership.

The General Steam Navigation Company's 1,316-ton steamer Falcon, *built in Troon in 1927, in the upper Pool of London. The* Falcon *was one of eighteen cargo vessels with limited passenger accommodation which the company operated. They also had sixteen cargo vessels and five excursion steamers. In the foreground is a Thames waterman in his skiff* (Hugh Perks)

Then came the container revolution which virtually ended the need for the tramp steamers. Many small tramp companies in the Bristol Channel, north-east England and the Clyde were obliged to give up the struggle and go out of business. Companies such as W. H. Seager & Company and Morel Brothers (both of Cardiff), Connell & Grace Ltd of Newcastle, Andrew Crawford & Company Ltd and Maclay & MacIntyre (both of Glasgow) faded from the shipping scene. It was not because they had to renew their tonnage that these small lines vanished. When the Albyn Line of Sunderland finished in 1966, their three 11,000-ton motorships were little more than ten years old. It was just that there was no further demand for this type of ship, largely due to handling costs in the docks.

It obviously cost less to run ships under the new 'flags of convenience', but most British owners seemed to prefer to retain their ships under the Red Ensign. However, there was a major switch to buying vessels from foreign yards, which had become cheaper and often quicker than the old established British yards.

As the new generation of container ships were far larger and more sophisticated than the old tramp steamers they naturally cost more and raising the huge capital sums to purchase container ships strained many companies. To overcome this some companies linked up to form an international consortium. The Bristol City Line did this with Canadian and Belgian companies to form Dart Containerline which in 1971 operated under the British flag one of the world's largest cellular container ships, the 759ft 22,500-ton deadweight *Dart America*, on a service between Antwerp, Southampton and North American ports.

The arrival of container ships pushed small companies out of the shipping world and forced huge consortiums to change their policies. The Furness Withy Group did this abruptly in 1971 when they announced that twenty-three ships would be withdrawn because they were uneconomical. Some of these were passenger-cargo liners such as the Shaw Savill's *Akaroa*, *Aranda* and *Arawa*, but most were the conventional dry cargo ships on general charter or on regular services in the North Pacific or the Caribbean. This bout of reorganisation by Furness Withy showed how rapidly ship sizes had grown. The twenty-three ships sold equalled 218,000 tons deadweight, but they had just ordered from Swan Hunter and Tyne Shipbuilders one ship which was virtually three-quarters of this size! This was the 'obo' (ore/bulk/oil) carrier of 166,700 tons deadweight, 957ft long with a speed of $16\frac{1}{2}$ knots.

These huge bulk carriers had suddenly mushroomed in size from the early 1950s, and so did tankers. Although British designers were the first to tackle seriously the problem of carrying liquid in bulk, it was the Americans who started moving oil in sailing ships, a few of which had small tanks that had to be emptied with hand pumps. Usually oil was moved in barrels or tin cases and just loaded into the hold normally. Because of the danger of leakage, the Anglo-American Oil Company changed over to tanks but kept with sailing ships, presumably because they were cheaper to operate. The last oil sailers were the 351ft 3,698-ton, four-masted barques *Brilliant* and *Daylight* built by Russell & Co, Port Glasgow, in 1902. These were the largest four-masted barques ever built so even then, oil transport encouraged large vessels.

Twenty years before this, shipbuilders on the north-east coast of England were fitting steamers with tanks to cut down the time taken in unloading. The next step was the world's first purpose-built oil tanker, the 270ft 2,307-ton *Gluckauf* in 1885, by W. G. Armstrong, Mitchell & Co. This tanker was ordered by a German company, but the first British-owned tanker was the 260ft *Bakuim* launched in 1886 by William Gray at West Hartlepool. She was a steamer loading 1,950 tons of oil and was ordered by William Suart. Owners and shipbuilders now pushed ahead with the development of steamer tankers. Suart alone was operating seventeen tankers by 1895, but there were many problems connected with handling such highly inflammable liquid. Perhaps the worst problem was the control of dangerous gases which caused several tankers to explode. The obvious danger of coal-fired tankers encouraged Palmer of Newcastle to build two diesel-powered tankers before 1914.

America was also pioneering the development of tankers, but since it was realised in Britain that her future supply of oil was going to come mostly from the Arabian Gulf, special efforts were made to create a tanker fleet. Since the work was constant and the oil refining companies made high profits, they started creating their own subsidiary tanker companies and chartered tankers from other owners in periods of high demand. British Petroleum started their British Tanker Company in 1915 by building the 5,500-ton *British Emperor*. Over the next fifty years their fleet increased to 170 tankers.

The real increase in the world tanker fleet was not in the number of ships, but in their size. Tankers such as the *Brunswick*, built in the late 1920s, was 15,740 tons and in this case the first diesel-electric powered tanker. In 1949 the 24,900-ton *C. J. Hambro* was the largest tanker built in Britain up to that time, but in the next ten years tankers virtually doubled in size, partly because oil companies had long realised that the larger the cargo the cheaper the transport cost. But the trend was also accelerated by the unstable political situation in many oil producing countries. Initially, oil companies built refineries near the Middle East oilfields, but they tended to become pawns in revolutions and international confrontations. Instead oil refineries were built in western Europe and the crude oil was shipped in from the Arabian Gulf and other sources. Esso already owned a small refinery at Fawley on Southampton Water and this was greatly expanded to come on stream in 1951. It cost £40m and is the largest refinery in Britain and the second largest in Europe.

All the oil companies began to order tankers to carry increasing quantities of crude oil. In 1953 Esso took delivery of the *Esso Oxford*, the first of six 16-knot 26,000-ton tankers designed to bring crude oil from the Arabian Gulf and the eastern Mediterranean. Shell had already taken delivery of the motor tanker *Velutina*, 28,330 tons, 16 knots, which was launched by Princess Margaret in 1952. After World War II, Vickers Armstrong of Barrow in Furness started to build a series of tankers for Stavros Niarchos. With the 757ft 47,750-ton *Spyros Niarchos* in 1955, they launched the largest merchant ship built in Britain after World War II. In fact British yards had then only built three larger vessels and these were all passenger liners, the *Mauretania*, *Queen Mary* and the *Queen Elizabeth*.

The supertanker was born and in most cases they were ten times the size of the average merchantman on international routes and they continued to grow in size. In 1961 the 81,000-ton *Esso Pembrokeshire* joined the Esso fleet. For the six Esso 'County' class supertankers, the channel from Nab, Brambles and Calshot had to be dredged for them to reach Fawley. In 1967 Shell had the 103,490-ton *British Admiral* built, which, like their 102,368-ton *British Argosy*, had bulbous bows to improve her speed and fuel consumption. The Arab–Israeli Seven Day War closed the Suez Canal in 1967 so that all tankers had to go round the Cape of Good Hope. With Suez firmly closed, oil companies wanted vast shipments of crude oil moved at speed so they doubled the size of the supertankers to produce the VLCC (Very Large Crude Carrier). In 1973 Esso added the 1,117ft 252,000-ton, 16-knot VLCC sister ships *Esso Dalriada* and *Esso Demetia*. Like most companies Esso had a definite naming policy. The 26,000-ton tankers had been named after cathedral cities, the 47,000-ton tankers after capital cities and then they had the counties series for tankers of around 100,000 tons. For the VLCCs they used the names of the ancient tribes and kingdoms of England. By 1977, Esso's tanker fleet was one of the largest tonnage groups under the British flag with eleven ocean-going ships and twenty coastal craft. It is a great credit to the established shipping companies that they have kept their fleets under the British flag, for they could have made higher profits by placing them under flags of convenience.

One of the great maritime achievements in recent decades has been the exploration, discovery and exploitation of natural resources under the North Sea. The first commercial oil produced in Britain came from a

The 249,952-ton deadweight tanker Esso Cambria *has a service speed of 16 knots when loaded and is 1,141ft long* (Esso)

British Petroleum well at Eakring, Nottinghamshire, in 1939; oil discoveries continued until by 1964 some 130,000 tons of oil was being produced in Britain. However, it was the finding of natural gas off the north coast of the Netherlands which prompted the North Sea drilling. Most of the international companies which bought licences to drill in the British sector already had a great deal of expertise in offshore drilling in other parts of the world, but the wild gales of the North Sea soon proved this to be a difficult undertaking, as shown by the loss of the BP exploration drilling barge *Sea Gem* with thirteen men in 1965.

The first rig to drill was the *Mr Cap* on the Dogger Bank on Boxing Day, 1964. Geologists were convinced that the North Sea gas belt extended from Holland, across the North Sea to North Yorkshire, so that most of the early drilling was in search of gas deposits. The first strike of natural gas was made in October 1965 when BP discovered the West Sole field off the Humber. The following year there were more strikes when Phillips, the Gas Council and Shell/Esso all found gas further east and nearer the Norfolk coast. The gas from these fields was brought ashore by underwater pipe line to Bacton, Norfolk, and by 1970 most of Britain was using North Sea gas.

Most of the West Sole gas field drilling was undertaken by BP on the 9,300-ton drilling platform *Sea Quest* which was built by Harland & Wolff in 1966. The *Sea Quest* was later moved north and in 1970 discovered the Forties oil field some 140 miles off Aberdeen. Although the ports of Great Yarmouth and West Hartlepool had been major bases for the offshore drilling industry, the hunt tended to move further north to the deep water east of the Shetland Islands, and it was there that the richest oil fields were discovered under great difficulty during the next five years despite the severe weather conditions. On the mainland, the main centres were Ardersier, Aberdeen and Montrose, where P & O opened the Sea Oil Support base in 1975. In the Shetland Islands, Lerwick was obviously the best harbour to use as a base for exploration, but later the oil was brought ashore through the Brent and Ninian pipelines to a new terminal at Sullom Voe.

By 1980 Britain was producing about half her oil requirement, although one field, the Auk, had already been closed down. However, as they say in the drilling business, 'oil is where you find it', so that more oilfields were being developed. In all, the British sector of the North Sea had more than eighty platforms and installations spread over thirteen oil and seven gas fields. To the general public, the offshore industry is largely unseen except for news reports and perhaps a glimpse of the drilling rigs from the North Sea ferries, so it is difficult to recognise the daunting engineering feats being achieved. The early strikes like the BP West Sole

The first loading of crude oil from the Shell/Esso Brent oilfield in December 1976. The tanker Esso Warwickshire *is loading at a floating 'spar' and the cargo was bound for Fawley on Southampton Water* (Author's Collection)

gas field were found from a steel platform of several hundred tons which worked in about 100ft of water. This caused enough problems in a North Sea gale when the waves hammered against it. However, the Ninian central plant in the wild sea to the east of the Shetland Islands stands in 530ft of water and displaces around 10,000 tons. From the sea-bed to the highest point of this plant is 968ft which means that on land it would dwarf many of London's tallest buildings.

6

Luck at the Fishing

The seas around Britain must once have been absolutely alive with edible
fish. At every centre of population men evolved simple methods of
harvesting this rich source of protein food. Until at least the end of the
Saxon period, fishing was open to anyone who liked to try his luck, but the
Norman Conquest brought England firmly under the grip of the
manorial system. Since the Crown had no reliable method of collecting
revenue, fishing rights belonged to the Lord of the Manor, and the holder
of this title was obliged to pay a percentage of their fee to the Crown.

The *Magna Carta*, signed in 1215, took away the Crown's right to all
the fisheries, but certain fishing rights, especially those connected with
oysters and salmon, continued. Most of these medieval fisheries seem to
have been land based and did not involve the use of boats. Fish were taken
simply by placing stop nets across creeks, or wicker traps were set up on
the foreshore in which the fish were left by the falling tide. Individual
fishermen were given the right to set up these traps or 'kettles' by the
Lord of the Manor who in turn took what amounted to a rent. In
Scotland, where rivers and stretches of the coast belonged to the
landowner, a similar system lasted longer than in England.

This control of fisheries had its advantages in that it prevented over-
exploitation. For instance salmon are still caught in Gloucestershire on
the River Severn near Lydney in the centuries-old wicker traps. These
conical wicker baskets or 'putts' have a 2ft mouth and are left facing
upstream so that unsuspecting salmon swim gently down on the ebb tide
and go straight into the baskets and cannot get out. Local men claimed a
right or charter to put out these 'putts', but in the early nineteenth
century thousands of them lined the bank and threatened to wipe out the
fish so an Act of Parliament was needed to resolve the problem.

Now all the commercial salmon fishing on the Severn is licensed and
worked by boats, putts or lave-nets. The lave-net is a hand-held scoop
which men use when wading out into the Severn on the ebb tide to whip
the fish out of the water as they come down the channel over the vast
sandbanks. In the nineteenth century, hundreds of men just about made a
livelihood by lave-netting, but by the mid-1970s only about a dozen men
from Gatcombe and Purton still fished in this way.

After the collapse of Crown control over coastal fishing, many large seaports claimed rights over their estuaries. The City of London was particularly possessive over its right to control the Thames. This right had been purchased from Richard I in 1197 when he was raising money for a crusade to the Holy Land. To make sure that everyone knew the extent of his rights, the City of London placed the Crow Stone on the foreshore near Southend and another over on the Kent shore to mark their limits in 1285. About every six years the Lord Mayor of London was rowed or carried to the stone limits to make sure they were still in place and to remind everyone of the city's authority over the Thames. This was done with a cheerful ceremony which reinstated the city's indisputable right over the Thames. At the Crow Stone any alderman who was not a freeman of the water (not a freeman of the Watermen's Company) was politely and respectfully bumped, after which the Lord Mayor tipped the free watermen two guineas for providing transport and then threw silver coins amongst the spectators.

This ceremony stopped in 1857 when the Port of London Authority took over control of the Thames. Another custom which lasted until World War II and was revived again in 1974 was the sending of a consignment of the first of the season's sprat catch from Aldeburgh to London for the Lord Mayor's Banquet. This may have originally been a fee, but the Aldeburgh merchants no doubt saw it as a good way of keeping the tiny Suffolk port's name to the fore in the days before modern advertising was invented. The Colchester Oyster Feast in September is another instance of an old form of advertisement; in medieval times the town burgesses would have been most anxious to keep reminding everyone that they owned the rights to the river. The first charter granted to Colchester was in 1189 and that made reference to their control 'from time immemorial'.

Once a year the city fathers of Colchester go down to Pyfleet at the entrance of the River Colne to go out with the dredgermen to see the first of the season's dredges and read out the proclamation stating their rights over the river. It is then traditional to consume gin and gingerbread. The Colne Oyster Fishery was at its height around 1908 when some eighty smacks and one steam dredger worked the beds. In fact to keep the oysters on the river bed healthy almost continual work was required. Between 1889 and 1928, with the exception of only five years, the Colne Fishery Board sold over a million local oysters every year but after this a decline set in. In 1963, during severe freezing conditions, the salt water froze and killed most of the oysters.

However, a new company was started and the fishery gradually nursed back into an economic state, enabling the custom of the official opening by the Mayor to be revived. To add further colour, some old sailing smacks which have been restored make the dredge under sail. The smacks *Hyacinth* and *Iris*, built in 1900 and 1903 respectively by the great smack builder Aldous of Brightlingsea, have made the ceremonial first dredge on different occasions since the custom was revived in 1970. During the rest of the season, three modern power craft work in this long-established fishery.

The old rights of restricted fisheries only continue where salmon and oyster fisheries exist. It is a practical arrangement because it prevents over-exploitation. It would be easy to work out the oysters in one glorious bonanza rather than leave some for the next year. However, one of the old medieval guild 'free' fisheries still survives. This is the Rochester Oyster & Float Fishery on the River Medway in Kent, which was created by an Act of Parliament in 1727 but has account books going back to 1571. The Chamberlain of the Fishery acts as a water bailiff and every year anyone who has broken the fishery rules has to appear before the 'Admiralty Court'. The Mayor of Rochester presides over the court in the capacity of Admiral.

In 1865 a very hard winter killed off all the oysters in the River Medway. To make matters worse, the fishermen had purchased £30,000 worth of oysters the previous year and laid them in Curel's Bite off Frinsbury. The loss of these oysters was a major disaster to the fishermen of Strood because they were liable to have their boats seized for debt and without them their families would have starved. However, an Act of Parliament was devised to enable the Fishery to lease parts of the river bed. Even with this help it took the Medway fishermen fifty years to pay off the debt.

The Act of 1865 left the medieval guild structure more or less intact. Only a freeman who had served a seven year apprenticeship could 'take a fish' from the twenty miles of tidal Medway between City Stone and Sheerness. The freemen did a little trawling and shrimping and went after smelt above Rochester Bridge in their dobles, but oysters provided their main income. In the early 1920s the freemen dredged two million oysters over a period of four years from under Cockham Woods. Standing on the deck of his bawley *Minion*, Fishery Chamberlain Len Wadhams recalled the windfall of nearly half a century ago and ended by saying 'the tax man did not know we were alive in those days!'

Perhaps such memories of that far-off bonanza caused the fishermen to battle on, and they kept the Fishery traditions alive long after industrial pollution had hit the Medway. In 1968 there were still sixty freemen and six apprentices, but only four old bawleys were at Strood while there had once been eighteen, and more down at Chatham. The bawley was a true fishing boat of the Thames Estuary. Her enormous beam was developed to provide a stable hull which was comfortable to work on and did not spill the hot water from the shrimp cooking boiler while sailing home at the end of the day. Some say the name 'bawley' came from the corruption of 'boiler boat'. Certainly the Medway fishermen corrupted the Peter Boat into the name Doble. These double-ended Peter Boats had wet fish wells amidships, making them two halves or double boats which when said quickly became 'doble'.

The longshore fishermen in the age of sail were notoriously conservative in their outlook on boat design. In theory their local boat types were evolved to suit local conditions. However, in the Thames Estuary there were two totally different types of fishing boats. At Gravesend, Southend, Leigh, Harwich and on the Medway the fishermen would have nothing but a bawley. These bawleys usually came from yards which also built spritsail barges and, although they have round bottoms, the bawleys with their loose-footed mainsails sailed more or less like a loaded spritsail barge. Their huge mainsails and topsails made them fast down wind but poor going to windward.

The other type of fishing boat was the smack. The fishermen from villages along the Colne and at Tollesbury went away in the summer crewing in the huge gaff yachts as paid hands. Many of the Essex

The Medway bawley Thistle *was built in 1887 and rebuilt between 1976 and 1981. A development of the bawley was the cockle boat which went out on to the sandbanks where cockles were gathered by hand. A remaining sailing cockle boat is the* Mary Amelia, *built in 1914 with a centreboard* (Author)

smackmen were crack racing skippers and acquired a taste for speed. They ordered new smacks from yards which also built yachts. In fact the Essex smack and the Victorian yacht developed hand in hand. The yacht-like Essex 'long boom' smacks, with their straight stems and beautiful low counter sterns, were very fast to windward but often wet at sea. Both sets of fishermen were entrenched in their belief that a bawley or smack was superior. However, because they spent much of their time working in narrow channels both the bawley and the smack had to be much more manoeuvrable than the average cruising yacht of the period.

The Essex fishermen of West Mersea and Maldon were still working, mainly on the River Blackwater, in the inter-war years so the sailing smacks lingered on. A group of young men from the Colchester area realised that a whole way of life would vanish with the smacks, so they set out to buy some in the late 1930s and work them just at weekends in the traditional manner. Following World War II this local enthusiasm for the smacks remained and some have been kept in their working state. Naturally a wooden hull has a limited life so many of these smacks have had to be rebuilt. One of these is the transom-sterned *Boadicea* which was originally built at Maldon in 1808. The present hull is a new one completed in 1970, but it has the shape of the original. The Maldon smacks retained the transom stern long after other Essex smacks had gone over to a counter stern. The *Mayflower*, built in around 1903, was still trawling under sail for pleasure in 1980 while most of the other smacks were taking part in the annual races. Most of the West Mersea smacks have been rebuilt in wood, while at Maldon in the 1970s, they preferred to sheath the old hulls in ferro-cement. One of these, the *Maud*, was sheathed at Howard's Yard where she had been built in about 1889.

Most of the sailing bawleys finished working under sail in the 1930s, but some have been restored. The first traditional east coast bawley to be restored was the *Vivida* in 1958. She had been built in about 1860 and was one of the little clinker bawleys which worked in the Thames from Bawley Bay, Gravesend. Another restored clinker bawley is the *Lilian*, built in 1864, which has been rebuilt at Maldon, and in 1980 a new bawley based on the same lines, the *Marigold*, was nearing completion. The later carvel bawleys which have been restored include the 39ft *Doris*, built by the barge builders, Canns at Harwich, and the 36ft *Helen & Violet* which Cann built in 1906. These are kept at Brightlingsea where the Colne Smack Preservation Society have leased a small dock so that one area is reserved for local traditional craft. Of course this has nothing to do with modern commercial fishing, but these craft are every bit as important as the local architecture and customs, and it is desirable to keep them in their home environment.

The bawley hull did not die out with the age of sail. The fishermen who worked from Leigh-on-Sea progressed on to shoal draught cockle boats with a raised foredeck for ploughing under power through the seas, but they retained a transom stern. When motors came in at Harwich, Fred Good was one of the many fishermen to realise that the deep keel of the sailing bawley was no longer needed so he asked Harry King of Pin Mill to build a shoal draught motor bawley. Charlie Brinkley, a Felixstowe Ferry fisherman, saw Fred Good's boat and went to King's in 1927 to have a slightly larger vessel, the *Silver Cloud* built. After World War II he went back to King's and had the *Silver Surf* built. This helps to explain why local working boats become part of any coast's culture. King's went on to build the motor bawleys *Why Not*, *Girl Elsie*, *Endeavour* and in 1954 the 40ft *Molly Lass* as a replacement for the motorised bawley *Molly* built in about 1900.

All the sailing smacks and bawleys that are still to be seen in Essex are just the inshore craft, the Class I smacks from Brightlingsea which went all round Britain searching for oysters have all gone. It was on one of these powerful cutter smacks that 'Shad' Sparling joined as an apprentice in 1879 at the age of thirteen. It was quite normal for a boy to go away to sea full time at this very early age. The indenture of John Death of Brightlingsea to the Colne Fishery Company in 1851 shows that he was only twelve when his working career started.

Shad Sparling later recorded something of the life when he went to sea in smacks in the mid-Victorian period. The smackmen were, he tells us:

Men with no real learning, these skippers, yet they were real smart, nimble and ready for anything. The smack I first went round Land's End in only had one chart of the English Channel and Irish Sea. No parallels, [for drawing straight lines on a chart] instead the skipper used two match boxes to prick off his course. His chart room was the locker top. With the chart laid flat the skipper would manipulate the match boxes into the compass rose on the chart.

Any sailing craft has great difficulty in maintaining a steady course because of the changes in wind strength, but the smacks were further encumbered by fairly primitive compasses which swung sluggishly; to improve this the smackmen sharpened the spindle with a cinder.

In 1886 there were about forty-three smacks at Brightlingsea and this fleet had long out-grown the local fish and oyster stocks. These smacks were noted for their speed so they found extra employment ferrying fish from trawlers out in the North Sea, carrying fresh salmon to London or collecting new potatoes from the Channel Islands. Their most regular

An oyster skiff alongside Brightlingsea hard, Essex. The Pyefleet oysters are about to be unloaded in the baskets (Author's Collection)

employment was deepwater oystering, and throughout the nineteenth century the Essex smacks and others from Emsworth in Sussex worked out most of the natural offshore oysters in Britain. The Essex smackmen were virtually pirates when it came to oysters. If they discovered a good ground, they kept dredging without mercy until they got the very last oyster. The French patrol vessels had to put in a lot of effort to keep the English smacks from raiding their coastal waters, while once in the Firth of Forth ports, troops had to be called in to protect the Essex smacks from the rioting locals who were furious at seeing their oysters going south. Even the neighbouring east coast rivers were usually raided by bands of smacks arriving in force. The River Deben and Walton Backwater were amongst the places where the native sources were exhausted by visiting smacks.

Certainly life aboard these smacks, working off the Channel Islands or in shoals off the Solway Firth in all weathers, cannot have been very pleasant. To make it worse, their heavy iron dredges were hauled by hand on a single barrelled winch. The large trawlers and drifters from Lowestoft, Yarmouth and the Humber all had steam capstans which cut down the drudgery of hand-hauling, but the Essex men reckoned that investment in steam capstans could not be justified. Right at the end, in the late 1920s, the deepwater oyster fishery at Brightlingsea bought old Lowestoft steam drifters with capstans and converted them for scallop dredging in the English Channel.

During the winter, the Essex smacks went after sprat with stow nets. Before World War I, the landlord of the Anchor Hotel at the top of Brightlingsea Hard used to order five gallons of milk so that he could serve it with rum to the skippers and crews of over fifty smacks as they came down at five in the morning to get aboard. The smacks stayed out until they had found sprat which the skippers usually detected by seeing the gulls feeding on the shoals. The smacks either filled up in a day or were away most of the week, but the crews liked to be home for drinking in the pubs on a Saturday night, old scores and rivals being settled with street fights.

Out on the water they were just as tough. The river police, who patrolled the oyster layings in the River Colne in smart little sloops, were warned never to hold the rail when running alongside a smack suspected of poaching in case the dredgermen stamped on their hands. Nor were the police allowed to board a smack single-handed. The initiation into this hard world of fishing was just as tough on the young apprentices, for at the end of their indentures they had to go through a 'shoeing'. The young

A Lowestoft trawling smack leaving her home port. The steam coming out of the side is from the steam-driven capstan. This capstan was for hauling in the trawl, but it was also used to do all the heavy work of handling the sails. The fire in the boiler was kept alight even in port so that the capstan could be used to raise the heavy mainsail which is being done here (Author's Collection)

teenagers were taken by force, if necessary, to a pub where their feet were held up, just as a horse's hoof was when shod. The boys were kept in this position until they agreed to buy 'beer all round'.

Oystering and fishing were usually separate winter occupations. Most of the Brightlingsea and Tollesbury smacks were layed up in the summer or went trawling or shrimping. The Tollesbury smack *Sallie* is remembered shrimping under sail off the Suffolk coast out of Harwich in the summers during the 1920s. By then most of the Essex smacks had engines but still used sail if there was a fair wind. The fishermen originally fitted very low-powered engines, and even in 1950 a 40ft Tollesbury smack with a 30hp engine was considered ridiculously overpowered. The fishermen were content with low-powered engines for a time because they went on using the fishing techniques used in the age of sail. In the Thames Estuary the narrow channels prevented boats from drifting with nets; instead they anchored and lowered the huge 'stowboat' nets down below the hulls. The stowboat gear was used for sprat for five hundred years between Elizabeth I and the jet age, but then the Danish Larsen trawl was introduced for herring. Larsen fishing was basically a mid-water method of trawling with otter-boards. The old style smacks and bawleys with their low-powered engines simply could not pull such nets so the fishermen of Brightlingsea and West Mersea went out and bought boats with really powerful engines.

The men of Tollesbury and West Mersea clubbed together to hire a jetty at Brightlingsea where the sprat could be landed during the winter. In 1963 they landed 200 tons in two days and then had difficulty in selling them. The revival was partly due to the government subsidy paid to small longshore boats, but men also wanted the hard, but independent life of fishing. Bill Read was still using sails on his smack *Iris* for part-time trawling in the early 1960s, but when he took it up full-time he bought the 36ft Danish *Nightjar*, fitted with a 60hp diesel. At that time there were only two boats winter longshore fishing from West Mersea apart from the small boats which worked the oyster layings. By 1980 this had risen to eight full-time boats. These varied in size between 30–55ft and generally speaking the Dutch and Danish boats were considered to be most suitable for the short seas of the southern North Sea.

In the days of sail, the fishermen who worked off the beaches of Suffolk used open transom-sterned clinker boats which were known as punts because they were almost flat-bottomed. A variety of punts which set a dipping lug mainsail and a standing lug mizzen were used at the beach landings between Bawdsey and Pakefield. Because Lowestoft and Yarmouth had harbours, the longshore boats based there were deeper in draught. Continuing north along the Norfolk coast, beach landing was again necessary so they used open boats, but with pointed sterns. It is probable that the Suffolk punts originally had the pointed Norse stern, but by at least 1860 the present hull shape was adopted. All these beach boats were rather poor to windward. However, in about 1910, a Southwold fisherman started using a plank as a lee-board, an idea possibly inspired by a passing barge, and these were adopted for the few remaining years of sail on this coast.

Thorpeness was a typical Suffolk beach landing where, before World War I, fourteen fishermen worked six punts and a similar number of beach skiffs which used to go after lobster and crab on the rocks (Suffolk crag) off the hamlet. In 1976 the author heard some reminiscences from ninety-two-year-old Henry Harling who had lived all his life in the house where his father and grandfather, born in 1795, had lived. With his mate, Harling used a different boat for each type of fishing. The 21ft *Gypsy Queen* IH 29, built in 1884, was for trawling, the 18ft *Industry* IH 62 was handy for rowing along the shore following the herring drift nets at night, while the 14ft 'beach skiff' was just right for rowing round the lobster pots.

The Suffolk beach punt Pet *of Thorpeness has the two-masted lug-rig which was used in a variety of forms all round Britain from the eighteenth century to the coming of the diesel engine. Although the forelug sail should be lowered and shifted round the mast on each tack, it was a simple and effective rig for longshore fishermen. The small mizzen made luggers more manoeuvrable under sail. Bawdsey Manor, where radar was developed in the late 1930s, may be seen in the background (Author)*

Because of the limitations of sail and oar, they seldom went further than three miles off Thorpeness. However, during a lull in fishing they once went about twelve miles down the coast in the *Gypsy Queen* to try their luck trawling in the Hollesley Bay ground. At the end of the day the wind dropped suddenly and they had to spend seven hours rowing with heavy wooden sweeps to get back to Thorpeness. They arrived home in the early hours of the morning to find their families waiting on the beach with lanterns.

In 1912 Stuart Ogilvie started to turn Thorpeness into a fascinating holiday village of mock-Tudor architecture. The building continued until 1937 and most of the fishermen took on work in the new resort but continued to fish part-time. Fishermen's gear stores are an attractive part of any longshore fishing community, but Thorpeness has a particularly attractive group of tarred huts with pantiled roofs nestling behind the sand dunes. Down on the shingle beach are not only the usual collection of motor winches for hauling up the boats but also the last usable hand capstan on this coast. Actually three men on a capstan could haul a boat up the beach just as quickly as a motor winch, but it was very hard work at the end of a long working day.

Southwold harbour has another attractive group of fishermen's huts. The beauty of this type of place is that although there is a total lack of planning the end result is attractive. Because of the bad entrance at the mouth of the River Blyth, the sailing boats used to work off the beach in front of Southwold. The now deserted beach once had a fleet of nearly eighty beach punts. The fishing went on throughout the year, but the brief autumn sprat fishing was their 'harvest' and a good sprat season would give them enough money to carry them through the year.

The fishermen seldom went further than three miles off the beach because of the difficulty of beating back if a gale sprung up. The 'Southwoldies' trawled south from Dunwich Bay with the flood tide for over twenty miles round Orford Ness into Hollesley Bay and then returned with the ebb. A retired fisherman once told me how, when he was a young man in about 1900, the beach punts were caught south off Southwold in a gale. They ran round Orford Ness, into the River Ore and up to Orford. Here the boats were pulled up on the beach and they lived in them under the sails for ten days until the weather moderated and they could return home.

In the old days the only real hope of a longshore man making a fortune was from salvaging ships in distress. All round the East Anglian coast the 'beach companies' which had special beach yawls thrived while the coal trade was handled by a motley collection of collier brigs. The last time the Shingle Street fishermen went off salvaging was in about 1905 when they spotted a schooner ashore on the Shipwash Sands. Their 40ft lugger the *Jane* was already well past her prime but she was hastily launched and a large anchor was put aboard to kedge (haul) off the schooner. The twelve miles out to the Shipwash took several hours and the *Jane* was leaking badly all the time. When they arrived alongside the schooner they found the skipper standing on deck, belaying pin in hand, barring their way. He refused all help and swore at the fishermen for wanting to prey on his misfortune. The fishermen said they had come away in a hurry without provisions and could they have a drink of water, but the skipper refused and laughed at them, saying that they had enough water in the bottom of their boat. Bailing furiously, they just managed to get the *Jane* back to the beach but the men were exhausted and disheartened at having earned nothing.

The longshore fishermen lived at only slightly above subsistence level, but they were very independent of all authority. Hollesley Bay had two good trawling grounds but there was no real way of transporting the fish to market. The Shingle Street fishermen made a precarious living from fishing, salvaging, piloting, wildfowling and poaching and lived on a shingle ridge between the sea and the marshes in single storied houses built mainly of driftwood picked up on the beach. After the road across the marsh was built, most of the fishermen looked for employment ashore. In about 1928, Robertson of Woodbridge built the motor beach boat *Lassie* to fish from Shingle Street, but shortly after this the men gave up the struggle to earn a living from longshore fishing. In World War II most of the hamlet was flattened when it became a practice bombing area but the Government later rebuilt some houses.

Most of the Suffolk beach punts were fitted with engines in the 1920s. However, the 15ft *Pet* IH 45, built in about 1902, was too small to justify the expense and remained probably the last unconverted boat at work. George Wilson of Thorpeness used to row or sail her out to the lobster and crab 'rocks' until 1959, carrying the dipping lug so beloved by the British longshore fishermen. She still had the amidship section divided up with boards into 'rooms' for storing the fish. Her bow is very fine and the lines much more shapely than those of the later motor boats, to allow her to sail. In 1981 she was bought by the author to be restored to her former working state with dipping lug sail.

Building motor beach boats began after World War I. At Southwold, Palmer used his £50 gratuity for serving in World War I to have the *Arthur & Phyllis* built in 1919. Sails were used for the first eighteen months until her owner could afford a petrol engine. In 1981 Palmer's grandson was still working the rebuilt *Arthur & Phyllis* from Southwold. After World War II, most of the motorised punts were worn out and

The Eastbourne beach boat Seeker *has the form of elliptical stern favoured by many south coast beach boats* (Author)

fishermen ordered new boats. However, when Frank Fuller of North Beach, Lowestoft, built the 18ft *Valsand* LT 311 in 1948 for long lining off Kessingland Beach, she was powered by a petrol engine, but still had sails for safety.

With the increasing use of powerful diesel engines and the convenience of motor-driven winches for hauling the boats up on greased skids, it was possible to have slightly larger craft. The beach boats were now given a little more length, higher sides and wide 'bulldog' bows so that the fishermen had more working space for standing in the bow to operate their long-lines. In the 1950s and 1960s, Woodbridge builders were producing beach boats, and it was boatbuilders at Knights yard who started the bulldog bow for Billy Burrell of Aldeburgh. About twenty two-man boats worked off the beach, and in the winter they caught sprat which they used to bait their long-lines for cod. They still used their huts for storage and for a deep freeze in which they stored baited long-lines. Since the mid-1960s, an increasing number of fishermen at Southwold, Aldeburgh and Felixstowe Ferry have used their huts to retail fresh fish to the public.

Between Southwold and Aldeburgh lies the little village of Dunwich where three beach boats were still going out long-lining for cod in the winter of 1980. Under the water off the shingle beach lies the medieval town of Dunwich, once, before erosion, the capital of East Anglia and the

Longshore fishermen at Southwold in about 1900. At the end of every day's fishing, their Suffolk beach boats had to be hauled up the beach by hand capstans which can be seen in the background. This scene vanished in the 1920s (Suffolk Photo Survey)

largest fishing port on the east coast. The harbour was formed by the Dunwich River and in 1000 the town was sending fifteen ships annually to fish cod off Iceland and had twenty-four in the home fishery. Other East Anglian ports sent ships to Icelandic waters throughout the medieval period, and after the sea had eaten away the sandy shore and finally closed the Dunwich River in 1700, her ships moved to other ports. Aldeburgh then became the centre for the declining cod fishery and the last smack to go after cod was the *Gypsy* in 1913.

Apart from cod which was salted into what they called stockfish, the other main fish which was available to ordinary people in medieval and Tudor periods was the herring. Yarmouth's association with the humble herring was a very long and really a very prosperous one. In 1270 a large 'Free Fair' was begun as a means of selling the herring while its annual migration brought it near the East Anglian coast. For the following two centuries, the forty day Yarmouth Herring Fair was a major trade event in eastern England. From the second half of the sixteenth century, the Dutch dominated the North Sea fishery but they used Yarmouth as one of their bases. The last Dutch boats came in about 1830, by which time the Yarmouth luggers were rapidly taking over the fishery. In about 1860, the first Scottish luggers started to find their way south in order to prolong their working season. The real success of the fishery was due to the fact that merchants built up contacts in Russia and eastern Europe and vast numbers of cured herring were exported in barrels.

The great North Sea fishing bonanza was in full swing by 1880 when local yards were building luggers and trawling smacks as fast as they could. No one became really wealthy from herring, but it brought a living to hundreds of fishermen. The second reason for the growth of the fishery was the attitude of the men: the East Anglians were mostly chapel men, and the Scots also were predominantly Protestant. These men believed in hard work and that money should be saved and made to work. To these nonconformists thrift was a virtue. Any man with a few pounds saved and a good reputation for finding fish was able to get a lugger built on credit. Many built up a little fleet of two or three drifters, although a bad season or bad luck sometimes wiped them out financially. These self-made skipper-owners demanded a great deal from their boats and their crews.

The fifie Reliance *with her deck piled high with herring drift nets. The* Reliance *is seen here at Great Yarmouth having come south from the Firth of Forth in the autumn season. The clothes and leather thigh boots worn by the crew were typical fishermen's clothing of the east coast of Scotland in around 1900* (Scottish Fisheries Museum)

The construction of railways meant a great market for fish in the industrial towns. Yarmouth, as the old established centre, continued to build boats, while Lowestoft, its new rival a few miles to the south, was being vigorously expanded by the railway company who did everything in its power to increase the number of drifters using the port.

Until the late 1860s, all the trawling smacks were powerful cutters, but the single mainsail made them rather difficult to handle. At the North Sea ports and Brixham, the smackmen went over to the two-masted ketch smacks. This meant a slight loss of speed, but with the mizzen and jib sails at either end of the hull, the smacks could be steered as they slowly dragged their heavy trawl down wind. These ketches, or as the fishermen called them 'dandies', were greatly sought by Scandinavian owners when Britain went over to steam trawlers. They were such superb vessels that a few have survived and are still sailing. The Göteborg Sea Scouts have the *Leader* and the *Gratitude* which take part in some of the Tall Ships Races, and another, which has been completely restored to the original tiller-steered state, is the 84ft *Westward Ho*, built by Leaver & Co of Grimsby in 1884 and sold only eleven years later to the Faroe Islands.

Fishing ports far away from the coal-mines kept sail longer, and a few Brixham and Lowestoft trawling smacks worked right up to World War II. Top prices were paid for their catch because the fish were not bashed about like those from steam trawlers. Four Lowestoft smacks were still in England in 1980, but some Brixham trawling smacks were still sailing: the *Provident*, owned by The Maritime Trust, is sailed by the Island Cruising Club while the *Vigilance* was doing charter work on the south coast.

With the increase in the number of fishing craft in the 1870s, the large ports were able to support a fleet of paddle tugs to tow the luggers and smacks out to sea. The next step was to tow the trawlers in calms and then some of the tugs started carrying their own nets. The obvious next development was to build steam trawlers, and it was probable that the *Zodiac* launched at Hull in 1881 with a 35hp engine and sails was the first of the new breed. Astonishingly, in the following ten years, some 2,000 steam trawlers were built. All of the 450 sailing smacks from Hull had gone by 1900 and the new port of Grimsby abandoned sail for steam with similar haste. In fact these two ports alone had more steam trawlers than the rest of northern Europe put together.

The chief reason for the rise of the English trawler companies was the adoption of the fleet system. The boats stayed at sea trawling while the carriers collected their catch and raced back to the markets. This idea started with smacks and was perfected with steam trawlers, but in human terms it was sheer misery because the fishermen were condemned to

The paddle tug Meteor *towing drifter luggers into Great Yarmouth in 1875. In the days of sail, most harbours had tugs for towing in sailing craft* (P. A. Vicary)

spend endless weeks pitching around in the depth of winter out in the cruel North Sea. The loss of life was high: good though the smacks were, every gale took some, while fishermen were drowned when they ferried the trunks of fish across to the carrier.

Being near coal-mines, the Humber ports enjoyed cheaper coal than the East Anglian ports where consequently the change over to steam was not quite so rapid. However, in 1897 Chambers of Lowestoft launched the *Consolation*, the first steam drifter. She was fitted with a low-powered Elliot & Garrood compound engine, but the impact was tremendous. There was then a headlong race to build steam drifters, first with wooden hulls but this quickly changed to steel. In Scotland the story was the same. Early attempts at trawling under sail were not very successful; then, when the railways arrived they were closely followed by the steam trawler. The first successful Aberdeen steam trawler was the *Toiler*, a Tyne built paddle tug, in 1882. Ten years later Aberdeen had thirty-eight iron screw trawlers, all over 100ft long, which covered the whole of the North Sea in search of prime flat fish.

In 1890 there were 20,000 men working on the North Sea, and often as many as 800 smacks were working the Dogger Bank at the same time. The powerful steam trawlers were working new, deeper grounds and landing incredible quantities of fish. In fact the markets were constantly flooded with huge quantities of fish. Cheap fish created Britain's new 'take-away' food—fish and chips. However, there were bound to be some financial disasters in this competitive fishing and the most spectacular was the collapse of Hewett's Yarmouth based 'Short Blue' fleet in 1901.

The Hewett family had begun as smack owners on the River Thames, based at Barking Creek. The fishermen of Barking were London's main suppliers from the medieval period until the railways were built. The Hewetts moved their trawling smacks to Yarmouth and then in 1890 combined with the diminishing Columbia fleet. These were the smacks that Baroness Burdett Coutts had operated to supply the poor of East London with cheap protein food through her Columbia Market. At its peak the Short Blue fleet had some 220 smacks and carriers working in the North Sea, but the fleet kept in sail due to the lack of cheap coal while the Hull and Grimsby fleets went over to steam. The bankruptcy of the Short Blue fleet caused the smacks to lie rotting in rows off their base at Gorleston and created tremendous unemployment problems in the area. In fact, Yarmouth never regained its position as a trawling centre.

In spite of the trawling set back, Yarmouth still retained a fleet of steam drifters and in the autumn the Scottish boats came south in force. Before World War I, there were often 1,000 drifters using Yarmouth as a base and perhaps another 700 at Lowestoft. In around 1906, the congestion and expense at the two major East Anglian ports prompted a company to try to develop Southwold as a herring port. In 1909, 761 boats used Southwold and the Scottish fisher lassies arrived to pack the herring in barrels for curing, but the little port was too far south and the boats lost time getting to the grounds. With so many drifters laying out miles of nets around the Smith's Knoll, it is surprising that any herring escaped.

It was not just off East Anglia that herring were caught as the fleets moved round the coast following the shoals. In the 1880s the Cornish luggers from St Ives were joining the local keel boats of Berwick upon Tweed. In most of the ports the majority of the herring landed were cured. The curing process which was used at Robert Boston's Yard, Spittal, until 1947 was as follows. Herring were brought ashore and sprinkled with salt while being tipped into the gutting trough, or 'farlan'. The women worked in crews of three, two gutters and one packer. The gutters cut the throat of the fish, removed the gut and gills and selected the fish for size and quality in an instant. They were then soused with more salt in a large tub and the packer lifted them into the barrel and packed them belly up across the barrel. The tiers were crossed and liberally sprinkled with salt all the way up the barrel. After eight days the herring was fully cured. During the eight days the blood from the fish dissolved most of the salt and became pickle. Enough coarse salt was left to keep the fish apart and allow the pickle to circulate.

World War I saw most of the steam drifters being taken up for Admiralty work, but after 1918 the fishermen returned with even more determination and skill. The new steam drifters were highly effective and left very few fish. The golden years were from the late 1920s to 1936. In 1930 the combined English and Scottish fleets amounted to about 1,500 drifters and Yarmouth was the largest and busiest fishing port in the world. There was a continual stream of drifters pouring out black smoke as they raced towards the harbour. There were so many drifters that Yarmouth was one of the first places to introduce traffic control. Drifters had to wait until the 'all clear' sign flag was dropped and then they all made a dash up the harbour to make contact with the waiting buyers. The incoming drifters were so keen to get in before the flag went up again that they steamed full ahead for the harbour. Sometimes they had to turn an abrupt circle if the flag went up to allow the empty drifters to get out to sea.

For forty years experts had been trying to tell the fishermen that some kind of restraint was needed to prevent the decline of the herring. Suddenly, in 1937, the catch dropped dramatically, but no one could really believe that after centuries the herring were really being depleted. In 1938, 725 drifters, employing 6,000 men sailed from Yarmouth. No authority dared to restrict fishing at this stage because every fisherman afloat supported the jobs of four men ashore. In the late 1930s Britain was just starting to recover from the trade depression and the loss of any jobs was political suicide to any government.

The Scottish herring lassies followed the drifter fleet round the coast working in curing yards. These young women are at Blyth in about 1910. The girls started at Lerwick in early summer and moved south to arrive in East Anglia for the autumn. In the 1930s, about 4,000 fisher lassies were following the drifters (Scottish Fisheries Museum)

A group outside the yard of a Lowestoft herring merchant. It was said that for every fisherman afloat, there were at least four men ashore deriving employment from his work (Scottish Fisheries Museum)

As the herring became scarce, better techniques were developed for hunting them down which kept up the boats' earning power while fish stocks declined. There was great rivalry to win the 'Prunier Trophy' which was given by a London fish restaurant every year between 1936–66 (except during the war years) for the skipper who landed the largest night's catch. The winning drifter proudly wore a special weather-vane on the mizzen, but by this time the real battle had been to find any herring shoals, let alone large ones. By 1953 the number of drifters using Yarmouth had dropped to 331. This was still a considerable fleet, but although the end of the fishing was clearly in sight, no one wanted government control.

In the early 1960s the traditional pattern of catching herring in drifters off the Norfolk coast finally came to an end. Yarmouth's last steam drifter, the *Wydale* YH 105 made her last herring voyage in 1960 and the following summer the *Lizzie West* LT 495, Lowestoft's last steam drifter, also gave up. The steam drifter had once been so common that few people looked at them twice, but strangely by 1970 the only survivor was the *Lydia Eva* YN 89 and the Maritime Trust wisely preserved her.

With the East Anglian herring fishery fading away, Yarmouth virtually finished as a fishing port. Lowestoft had emerged as the main East Anglian fishing port and herring continued to be landed there. Some came from the small longshore boats, and one motor drifter, the *Wisemen*, was still going in 1968. At the same time, herring caught on grounds off Yorkshire and the Northumbrian coast were falling steadily. However, the Scottish boats using drift, ring, and purser nets and trawls were catching great quantities of herring in the Minch between the Highland coast and the Outer Hebrides.

British trawler owners never lacked enterprise in finding new grounds. In 1910 Dodds, a Yarmouth man who moved to Aberdeen and created a fleet of steam trawlers, sent some of his *Princess* trawlers to operate from Cadiz and they landed their catch in Lisbon. They then fished off South America and landed at Buenos Aires. World War I stopped such voyages and some 470 trawlers and drifters were bottled up in Aberdeen. Some of the Aberdeen 'scratchers', as the trawlers were called on the north-east coast, had very long careers because low fish prices did not give enough return to build replacements. In 1950 Aberdeen had 196 trawlers, most of which were over twenty-five years old. It was said that salt water and oil do not mix and this was never more true than on the scratchers between the engineroom and the fishermen. The difficulty came from friction over the loss of boiler pressure and speed, while trawling, which was usually due to poor coal, but usually resulted in sharp exchanges between skipper and engineer. The last steam trawler built for Aberdeen owners was the *Avon River* in 1950, but to remain progressive the Government had requested that owners should modernise their vessels by 1963. The diesel trawlers could tow at a steady speed and were cheaper to operate. One of the difficulties with trawlers was that the trawl nets had to be hauled over the side which in heavy seas was awkward and dangerous. A move away from the old 'side-winder' type was made in 1945 when a trawler was designed with a wide square stern so that the nets could actually be hauled up over the stern slip. These 'stern' trawlers were not immediately accepted. In 1955, amongst the huge middle and distant water trawlers in the docks at Hull, there was not a 'stern' trawler in sight. The first 'stern' trawler, *Universal*, did not enter into ownership at Lowestoft until 1961. In 1964 Britain had some 500 deepwater trawlers and the majority were still 'side-winders', even those going to the Arctic and Greenland. However, Grimsby and Hull progressed by building huge 300ft stern trawlers that bore no resemblance to the simple smacks of eighty years before.

In the course of the century after the arrival of the railways, the British fishing industry split up into roughly three groups. The longshore fishermen usually work with the boat types evolved to suit just a local set of conditions and traditions. Then there are the inshore boats which usually work from small communities and are usually skipper-owned. The term 'inshore' is a little misleading because the boats travel great distances. For instance, the Fife coast inshore boats go right over to Norway. Finally there are the 'industrial' fishing ports with huge stern trawlers. These expensive ships have had a particularly poor time since the three 'cod wars' when Iceland pushed British trawlers out of Icelandic waters. By 1980 Hull only had 27 of her 130 distant water trawlers still at sea. British United Trawlers (Aberdeen) Ltd, which had the largest fleet in Aberdeen, survived the loss of the Icelandic grounds well and in 1978 still had 19 trawlers, 2 long-line boats and 8 oil rig standby safety vessels. However, they could not survive a flood of cheap imported fish and by 1980 they were down to 1 trawler and 2 long-liners.

Lowestoft was hardly affected by the cod wars, but was hard hit by foreign dumping. Even the trawler *Suffolk Challenger*, top boat for several years, was converted to an oil rig safety standby vessel in 1980. By then Britain's active distant water fleet was down to 105 trawlers, but the history of fishing is a boom and bust situation. Iceland is not totally to blame for the change in emphasis. Even in 1973 the 1,000 inshore boats owned on the east coast of Scotland between Burnmouth and Shetland landed more weight of fish than the combined deepwater fleets of England, Wales and Scotland.

In the history of European fishing the Scots were not amongst the forerunners, but what was lacking in tradition has been made up for in modern vigour. There was very little fishing in Scotland before the early nineteenth century, but the railways enabled Scottish fish to reach new markets. In the age of sail the Scottish fishermen were often incredibly obstinate in resisting innovations, but by contrast the twentieth-century fishermen have been quick to accept and perfect new ideas. Indeed, the east coast of Scotland must be considered the leading fishing area in Britain.

Sailing craft in Scotland were almost entirely devoted to drift net fishing. A few fishermen used sloops, which would be called gaff cutters today, but most common were the open yawls which had a single dipping lug sail. When the yawls found the herring shoals, the masts were lowered to reduce the rolling motion, the nets put out and they drifted all night. They returned to port next morning with a catch. Although the Dutch used to preserve their herring by curing them in salt while at sea, the Scottish and English drifters always brought their catch back to port.

Two trawlers owned by W. H. Kerr Ltd which were operating from Milford Haven in 1964. The Welsh Prince *M137 has a square stern, while the trawler on the right has a pre-World War II counter-stern. On the* Welsh Prince, *the gallows can be seen for hauling aboard the 'trawler doors' at either end of the otter trawl* (Scottish Fisheries Museum)

The seas around the north and east coast of Scotland yielded a harvest which was the only means of livelihood for many families. Many crofters left the virtual starvation level of the small-scale hill farm and went down to the coastal villages to look for work in the herring fishery. Although herring brought in a wage by which men could just about support their families, the loss of life was appalling. If a severe gale sprung up when the boats were at sea, a high percentage of the working men from a village were often drowned in a single night. Even though the half-decked boats did not go far out to sea, they were either swamped by the sea or lost trying to come in on to the open beach. Hundreds of fishermen were drowned within sight of their own homes.

The needs were very obvious—safe harbours and better boats. The fishermen were all in favour of safe harbours but most stubbornly resisted any change to their boats. During the nineteenth century, dozens of tiny harbours were created, often on the most incredibly rocky foreshore. Many of these, like Pittenweem on the Firth of Forth and many more, dried out at low water but at least they offered shelter in a storm and the fishermen and their families did not have to haul their boats over the long foreshores to safety above the waves.

Fishermen resisted decking over their boats for a long time as it was easier to work and row an open boat than one decked over. However, they did eventually see the wisdom of this safety measure. Four main types of craft emerged. Firstly, the 'fifie', a two-masted lugger which usually worked from ports between Berwick and the Moray Firth. North of there on the mainland of Scotland was the 'scaffie', a powerful, highly seaworthy, single-masted lugger with a low-raked pointed stern. In 1879 a Lossiemouth builder, William Campbell, hit on the idea of combining both good points in the fifie and the scaffie and produced a craft which, because of a colonial war in South Africa at that time, quickly became known as a 'zulu'. These retained the characteristics of a small, open, beach boat in a vessel which was around 75ft long. The two-masted zulus still had dipping lugs which had to be shifted on to different sides of the mast every time they came on to a fresh tack. Hauling up the heavy sail was either done with a steam net-hauling capstan or it took the tremendous effort of the whole crew. The zulu was entirely open with no rail, but in spite of the difficulty of handling these huge craft they were very fast. A zulu, given the right breeze, could make over 14 knots.

The Firth of Clyde and the Ayrshire coast were slightly protected by the Kintyre peninsula so that an open, half-deck boat remained a practical proposition. Here a single-masted lugger with a slightly raked stern, known as a 'Loch Fyne skiff' was evolved. These were the result of mixing features of the east coast zulus and fifies with the techniques learnt in yachts. The Clyde fishermen, like those from the Solent and Essex, went away as yacht hands in the summer so they enjoyed speed and raced

The steam herring drifter Noontide *leaving the Inner Harbour, Anstruther. The steam drifters were almost a standard design throughout Britain. In 1913 there were about 1,500 steam drifters. The only survivor of this type, the 95ft* Lydia Eva, *was taken over by the Admiralty in World War II and was not scrapped when drift-net fishing became unprofitable* (Scottish Fisheries Museum)

their fishing boats. As a result, the Loch Fyne skiffs were probably the fastest and most manoeuvrable of the Scottish boats. However, in the quest for speed, the skiffs were often built very lightly and had a short career. The Loch Fyne skiffs were very fast off the wind, but like most luggers were rather poor at beating against the wind. In common with the zulus, they set a jib, but appear to have sailed better without them. The Loch Fyne skiffs were light enough to be rowed home when the wind fell away.

While all the small ports stuck to sailing drifters and long-lining for cod, Aberdeen, Scotland's largest fish landing centre, turned to using steam trawlers. By 1881 there were already in English ports about 2,000 trawling smacks. Most Scottish fishermen were opposed to trawling, probably quite correctly, because the trawl, bumping along the sea bed, destroyed many young fish and the feeding grounds. However, by 1880 steam trawlers were landing their catch at Aberdeen and there were fifteen owned here by 1883. Aberdeen developed into an industrial fishing port and by 1902 was the third largest landing market after Hull and Grimsby. The Aberdeen trawlers were ranging all over the North Sea, to Faroe, Iceland and into the western grounds. These were 115ft long, coal-burning screw boats and by 1913 it was common to trawl for herring.

The sailing smacks used beam trawls because they could not maintain a fixed speed and keep the net mouth open, but by the 1880s the steam trawlers were more powerful and the new otter trawls were used but these could not be used on a rocky bottom so that many grounds were left clear for surface drift netting and long-liners.

Aberdeen also had a sizeable fleet of drifters and long-liners, and pressure was brought to close several grounds to the trawlers since by the 1920s it was already noticeable that the herring were disappearing. Something of a peak in boat numbers was reached in 1937 when Aberdeen had 277 steam trawlers, most of which were working in the North Sea, but their average catch landed seems to have been dropping.

Sail vanished early from the fishing ports of eastern Scotland because of the difficulty encountered when entering the small stone harbours in bad weather. Some owners solved the problem by buying steam vessels, but most tried to become more competitive by fitting petrol engines. The straight-sterned fifies took a propeller quite well, but the zulus of the Moray Firth, with their raking stern posts, were not so successful and so were fitted mostly with twin engines and propeller shafts through the quarter.

The pre-1914 combustion engines seem to have been something of a mixed blessing and fishermen still relied on sail to a great extent.

However, the problem may not have been all the fault of the manufacturer, as this anecdote from Essex indicates. In 1910 the *Alberta*, an Aldous-built smack of 1885, was the first Tollesbury boat to be fitted with an engine. After the engine seized up, a manufacturer's mechanic was summoned to put it right. Again the engine seized up, but this time the mechanic spotted the trouble and explained to the smackman that it was not only the petrol tank that had to be filled, the oil had to be checked too. All these early engines cannot have been bad because in 1980 the Falmouth oyster dredger *Caterina* was still relying on her 1912 engine.

The zulus and fifies were at their height in about 1900 and the last fifies were built in around 1906. The *Sunbeam* was the first Anstruther fifie to be fitted with an engine. This particular engine was a failure, and it was not until Kelvin and Gardner engines were brought into use that fishermen had reliable engines. The men from the east coast had a strong preference for Kelvin, but it was perhaps a touch of patriotism that caused them to favour these Glasgow-built engines. After World War I the sight of the great black lug sails of the zulus and the fifies had already become an unusual sight. However, although she was fitted with a reliable Kelvin, the St Monance fifie *Emblem* sailed the whole way back from Lowestoft at the end of the 1921 East Anglian herring season since it was faster under sail. The last pure sailing zulu was the *Muirneag*, built at Buckie in 1903 and broken up in 1947, while the 78ft *Radium*, built at Findochty in 1904, still had her lug sails and masts when she finally finished working as a motor fishing vessel in 1964. But both were instances of elderly fishermen preferring to end their working lives in a craft that they understood.

The Scottish Fisheries Museum at Anstruther held the official renaming ceremony of their restored 70ft fifie *Reaper* in 1980, but the first fifie back under sail was the 43ft *Isabella Fortuna* AH 153. She had been built at Arbroath in 1890 for long-line and drift net fishing. She had a crew of five and five oars for them to use in a calm. In 1908 she was sold for £65 and, following the Scottish custom, the seller had to give a bonus or 'good luck piece', which in this case was the fore lug sail. Her new skipper-owner, William Smith, used her for local fishing around Arbroath, but in the herring season he used his 70ft fifie *Ocean Queen* AH 64. An engine was fitted in the *Isabella Fortuna* in 1919, but Hobson Rankin restored her to sail sixty-one years later with advice from a ninety-year-old fisherman from East Neuk.

Between Lossiemouth in the Moray Firth and Fraserburgh, there were some particularly progressive fishermen. In the early part of the nineteenth century, the women of Lossiemouth followed the traditional pattern of fishwives throughout Scotland and walked inland to sell the fish caught by their men. When the herring fishery started in the Moray Firth in about 1819, the catch was cured and sold later. Because the herring did not have to be sold daily, the whole of the industry was able to expand and it became a major form of employment in Scotland. By 1881 Lossiemouth had 149 boats and later on steam drifters were used, but a miners' strike and the resulting unavailability of coal in 1921 caused a ruinous season. After the strike, the expense and inconvenience of coal encouraged fishermen to turn more to oil for a source of power.

The Lossiemouth fisherfolk looked for some alternative to herring drifting and were the first in Scotland to adopt the Danish seine-net method of fishing. The seine net is basically a type of trawl, but whereas the trawler drags a kind of net bag over the bottom, the seiner pays the net out over about a mile, and then stays stationary under power and drags the net back to the boat on a powerful winch.

There was another miners' strike in 1926 and the small English trawlers became tired of delays through lack of a coal supply, so they were quick to follow the Scots' example of adopting petrol and hot-bulb oil engines for their boats. The first diesel drifter in Britain was the steel cruiser-sterned *Veracity* LT 311, which was built by Richards of Lowestoft in 1926.

The seiner Strathyre *arriving at Lossiemouth with white fish. The pointed cruiser-stern was virtually standard on Scottish inshore boats between 1930–65* (Author)

The introduction of engines and a new method of fishing put the Scots in the market for a new type of boat. They no longer needed deep keels for sailing, but the general appearance of the forward end of the zulus and fifies remained and the cruiser stern now became general. The cruiser stern was started in 1921 by Robert Robertson of Campbeltown who had the *Falcon* and other boats built for ring netting by Miller of St Monance. By around 1930 various forms of the cruiser stern had become general. This stern was used on Scottish fishing boats until about 1970 and is still regarded by fishermen as being the most seaworthy hull form.

The fitting of engines meant that boats started to go round and open up new grounds on the wild west coast. Since the 1860s drifters had been following the herring south, on the east coast every year, indeed the zulus, fifies and steam drifters could never have paid their way unless they had moved to the English ports for part of their campaign. The inter-war years also saw a tendency for fishing to be centred at a few harbours while many of the small Victorian harbours which had been the homes of zulus and fifies suffered from silting. Aberdeen built up a fleet of steam trawlers while the drifters from smaller harbours declined. Some of the small harbours silted up, and Lossiemouth, Buckie, Macduff and Fraserburgh remained the main centres, although many of the Moray Firth boats worked full-time out of Peterhead because of its proximity to the North

Between 1908–14, over a hundred Scottish inshore fishing boats were fitted with internal combustion engines which were cheaper than steam engines, largely because they did not require a stoker. Here, in about 1950, a Fraserburgh diesel drifter puts to sea. The steam and motor drifters all carried the mizzen sail because, when drifting with nets, it kept the bow up into the sea and made life more bearable (Author's Collection)

Sea grounds. However, many Moray Firth fishermen went off and found new grounds off the west coast and based their boats for long periods in Highland ports such as Ullapool, Mallaig, Oban, Lochinver and Kinlochbervie.

Before the mid-1950s, it was believed that a wooden hull of over 80ft could not stand either the kind of pounding the boats had to take out in the Atlantic around the Faeroe Isles and St Kilda, or the strain imposed on a boat while towing a trawl. However, since wood had become cheaper than steel, some owners decided to experiment. First came the wooden 108ft *Faithlie*, a trawler built at Montrose in 1956, and then the 97ft long-liner *Radiation* built at Anstruther. J. & G. Forbes of Sandhaven built two 112ft trawlers but in spite of these really large hulls it seems that the average Scottish inshore fishing vessel has remained about 80ft in length because it was more economical to operate.

Many cruiser-sterned boats were built for herring drifting. These, like the steam drifters, were always recognisable at sea because a tiny mizzen was kept permanently set. When the boats were drifting with about $1\frac{1}{2}$ miles of net stretched out just below the surface, this sail pushed the bows of the boat up into the wind and made the motion aboard the boat slightly more comfortable. The Scottish skippers kept loyally to herring drifting but the last year that they went south to Great Yarmouth was 1961. Probably the last boat built at Buckie for herring drifting by Herd & Mackenzie was the *Estrolita* BCK 6 in 1954. In Macduff boats were built for drift netting until 1960 after which they built herring trawlers of 70–75ft. By the mid-1960s over half the fish landed in Scottish ports were caught in seine nets. The Scottish and Northern Ireland seiners had their own version of the original Danish method. Boats were either 'day boats' which returned home nightly or 'trippers' which went to sea for several days. Minor repairs were often carried out by boatyards on Saturday mornings. For new boats most of the skipper owners preferred wooden hulls, while the companies had gone over to steel as far back as the 1890s.

The mid-1960s saw great changes in the amount of equipment carried by fishing boats. The old herring drifters had just a motor and capstan for hauling the nets. However, the wooden trawlers and seiners had to have very powerful winches, and there were new innovations to make handling the nets easier. The use of hydraulic 'power blocks' on the stern to cut out hand-hauling became universal in seiners. Some skippers sought to remove the discomfort of working on an open deck by fitting a 'whaleback' over the bows and a later idea was to extend these to 'shelter decks' which covered most of the deck space forward of the wheelhouse. The actual wheelhouse became larger to accommodate the mass of electronic equipment carried to help the skipper in his search for fish.

The Silver Crest *entering Arbroath in 1981. The drifters had only a steam capstan, but the modern inshore fishing vessels carry electrical equipment for hunting fish. The obvious piece of recent technology is the windlass and the 'power block' on the stern, which lifts the net aboard* (Author)

The old style cruiser-sterned boats became very cramped with the extra equipment, and the skipper who came up with a solution to this problem was Joe Buchan of Fraserburgh. He had seen a boat in Shields which had a forward wheelhouse, and another time he had been aboard a minesweeper and admired the amount of space aft given by a square transom stern. The two ideas were combined in the first Scottish square-sterned, 65ft *Constellation*, built in 1965 by J. & G. Forbes at Sandhaven. Skipper Buchan admitted that this was not really a new idea because the old Lowestoft sailing smacks had square counter sterns to allow more deck space.

In 1978 Joe Buchan had the 74ft *Constellation II* built which incorporated more new ideas. In spite of all these changes, the skippers have still remained very loyal to wood. There are exceptions though, like the new Lossiemouth seiner *Emma Thomson II* INS 277 which was built of steel in Denmark in 1980. This vessel is probably the result of the Moray Firth tendency to look to Norway and Denmark for new ideas rather than the rest of Britain. While yards in southern Britain were lured by the propaganda of fibreglass manufacturers into believing that there

The launching of the Constellation *at Sandhaven in 1965: the beginning of a new generation of square-sterned Scottish inshore boats* (J. R. Buchan)

was a shortage of wood in the 1960s, Scotland and north-east England remained loyal to wood and never seemed to have had any difficulty in obtaining it. Right from the early days of the first highly successful steam drifters, the companies in the larger ports went for steel hulls. A steel hull requires virtually no maintenance for a long time, but if a steel hull is to last it requires more painting than a wooden hull to keep out the rust. The policy of the big trawling companies was to replace their steel-hulled ships about every fifteen years if finance allowed.

For a skipper to survive in the highly competitive business of fishing, his boat and gear have to be reliable, and this constant repair work keeps the yards viable and busy between building new hulls. In 1980 on the east coast there were building and repairing yards at Eyemouth, Port Seton, St Monance, Arbroath, Johnshaven (open boats), Fraserburgh, Sandhaven, Macduff, Buckie and Lossiemouth, while on the south-west coast Girvan remained a repair and building centre. Most of the wood used was locally grown—oak for the frames, larch for planking and Oregon pine for decking. Some steel is now used: for instance, Gerrard Bros of Arbroath have used steel frames to build a composite hull, while the Macduff Boatbuilding & Engineering Co have used steel deck beams. The skills exist at Macduff to build steel hulls, but wood is preferred. Macduff has the typical walled harbour which was created for the herring fishery in the nineteenth century. Both fifies and zulus were built here, and in 1881 109 boats were owned here. The introduction of steam drifters and then motor seiners saw the size of vessels increase so the 64 boats which operated from there in 1928 employed a larger number of crew than those in Victorian times. The port also had ten herring curing houses at one time, but the inter-war years and the depression saw the steady collapse of the century-old herring fishery. The depression saw the four family boatyards in the Macduff/Banff area forced to amalgamate to form the Macduff Boatbuilding & Engineering Co in order to survive.

After World War II there was a great boom in building new boats which came to an abrupt end in the early 1950s. The government then introduced grants, largely through the White Fish Authority, to stimulate employment in the fishing industry. Interests in the smaller ports on the east coast of Scotland were particularly active in obtaining these grants which became the basis of the modern industry. However, as the failure of many state-owned industries has repeatedly shown, the injection of capital is no guarantee of success. The real success of Scottish inshore fishing is largely due to the individual enterprise which runs through the whole industry.

The obvious danger is over-fishing and wiping out the stocks of fish so restrictions are essential. For instance, the boats from Campbeltown which work in pairs can only land their quota of herring and then go on to some other form of fishing. However, in spite of all the difficulties the inshore boats have had to face, these are not as great as the problems of the distant water trawlers from Aberdeen, Hull, Grimsby and Fleetwood who had their traditional grounds closed by Iceland in the mid-1970s.

The prosperity of the Scottish east coast depends on the ability of each skipper and crew continually to find saleable fish. In 1979 there was great consternation in Cornwall because Scottish boats were selling mackerel to the huge Russian factory ships at low prices and were emptying the waters around Land's End and the Isles of Scilly. However, inshore fishing is very much a case of survival of the fittest so every boat has to sell its fish where the best prices can be obtained. This also means working where the fish are so that of Macduff's thirty boats working in 1980 many fished continually on the west coast. Many only returned home for an annual refit.

The top skippers at many ports change their boats about every ten years. In that period new developments and fishing gear will necessitate a different hull layout. The old boats are often sold south—many fishing ports in Britain and Ireland are filled with former vessels of the Scottish inshore fleet. Usually the skipper returns to the same yard for a new boat and spends a great deal of time discussing his requirements. It is this close involvement which makes for a successful industry. George Watt, manager of the Macduff Boatbuilding & Engineering Co, used to cut all the timber for a new boat personally so that he knows just how every job on the yard should be done. In 1980 this yard employed over seventy people and averages about four new boats a year, built under cover and not out in the open as they had previously done. Macduff, like many little coastal towns, is almost as dependent on the harvest of the seas as it was a century ago.

In 1980 the Macduff yard was building *Quiet Waters III* which incorporated yet another innovation—the Norwegian idea of water tanks so that the mackerel could be kept fresh in chilled water. If the boat returned to port and found that the price was low, the catch would not have to be sold straight away. The *Quiet Waters III* replaced another boat of the same name and was ordered by three families from Inverallochy, near Fraserburgh. Another hull under construction was a 75ft seiner for two brothers in the Shetland Islands. It is very difficult for anyone new to start in fishing, but a reputation for finding fish will encourage the banks to lend surprisingly large sums of capital. This says much for the reputation of Scottish skippers and the amount of money that a boat can earn. The White Fish Authority grants have also been backed up by the European Economic Community.

The Northumbrian cobles Brothers *and* Admiral, *built in 1943, show the typical shape of this traditional boat type. The* Brothers *has a deep forefoot, while the* Admiral's *sloping transom stern leads down to a flat bottom right aft. They are seen here at Amble* (Author)

In Scotland the word 'coble' is applied to the open boat used for salmon fishing. The Scottish coble has an up-turned bow and wide transom in which the nets are stowed, but from Berwick south to Spurn Head the longshore fishermen (and in the old days the pilots) used the English coble which is a totally different craft.

Many writers have made hazardous guesses at the origins of the coble and it is usually referred to as being a Viking ship or even less likely of Dutch origin. Coble has many pronunciations and has been used for at least a thousand years. The earliest record is of a Lindisfarne monk referring to a 'cuople' in 950. However, this is no indication that he was referring to a coble as we know it. The only really hard fact is that by the early nineteenth century, cobles were established on the north-east coast of England and the fishermen of this coast still prefer them to any other hull shape.

The oldest coble in existence is the *Grace Darling* which is in the little museum at Bamburgh. This is said to be the coble that the Victorian heroine Grace Darling used when she went out in a gale with her father in 1838 to rescue survivors of a wrecked steamer off the Farne Islands. The only difference between later boats and the *Grace Darling* is that the top plank of this vessel is almost upright like the usual boat hulls while the later Northumbrian cobles all have tumblehomes with the top plank sloping inwards. The tumblehome, like everything else about the coble, has its practical use. It helps to force the water away when the coble is being sailed hard and also when the fishermen lean over the side working pots or lines, it is at the right height to support their legs and make the work less back-breaking. The reason for the *Grace Darling*'s lack of tumblehome could have been that she was built as a ferry boat for the Darling family and this extra refinement was not thought necessary. The only conclusion which can be drawn from this coble is that the type was already highly developed in 1838, and that lighthouse-keeper Darling would not have gone out with only his daughter in wild seas if he had not thoroughly trusted his boat. One can only assume that the coble was already a very old and well-tried design. Of all the traditional craft in Britain, the coble is the one which has survived in the largest numbers and is probably the oldest in origin.

Why had fishermen of this coast evolved such a complex hull shape? The reason must be the nature of the coast. There are very few harbours, and in the past most of these dried out at low water or had shallow bars across the entrance. The men had to have a craft which could be beached in any weather, but if the weather turned bad they had to be able to stay afloat out in the open sea. The fishermen also needed craft which were light enough to be rowed and pulled up the beach. The hull has a very deep forefoot and shoal draft stern so that the coble can be rowed in through the breakers stern first. In this way the bows face the breaking water and prevent the open hull from being swamped. As a daily occupation they went through surf which would have sunk many ordinary boats.

A disadvantage of the deep forefoot was that, when running before a strong breeze, it could grip the water making the coble swivel round and it could broach-to and roll over. For a modern racing dinghy to capsize is a frequent occurrence, but for a work boat to go over it is total disaster. The fishermen were heavily dressed and often could not swim. To avoid the possibility of a coble being overpowered, the mainsheet which controlled the sail was not made fast and the main halliard led aft so that the sail could be dropped instantly.

There was no such thing as a standard coble. Every fisherman and every builder has his own ideas of how a coble should be shaped. The men using them usually referred to their length as being from the ram—the main plank running the length of the bottom—and this is slightly shorter

The fishermen working off the north Norfolk beach kept to the beamy double-ended boats because they were the best at coming through the breaking water created by the shallow water off the beach. Here a hoveller, a boat with a cuddy forward, is coming ashore on Cromer beach in about 1905 (Poppyland Photographs)

than the overall length. A salmon coble would be about 24ft overall and a winter coble about 30ft. With their unique flared bow, they are a most intriguing craft and very suitable for their usual waters.

In Victorian times the Scottish fifies and East Anglian luggers were coming to the north-east coast after herring, and, since most of the cobles were really only small longshore boats, some fishermen asked the builders to create a larger coble to compete with the visitors. Like the local keel boats, they were given a pointed stern which possibly made them cheaper to build. Any coble with a pointed stern was called a 'mule' because it was a half-breed boat. The big herring drifting mules of about 35ft overall came from Staithes, Scarborough and Filey, and were known as 'sploshers', possibly because of the noise they made at sea. The big cobles from Bridlington were over 40ft long, had two masts and carried a 'calf' or small coble aboard when they were long-lining in the winter. However, these cobles were rather dangerous and it seems that the type is at its best between about 27ft and 35ft.

The keel boats were used all down the north-east coast, but have not survived like the cobles. The only place that they can be seen is at the harbour on Holy Island. Here, in the early part of this century, some were hauled up above the water line, turned upside-down and were converted into sheds. Some of them were from Eyemouth and they are now a unique collection of historic craft.

The cobles were the most numerous vessels on the north-east coast in the 1890s but they gradually dropped out of favour so that by the 1930s it looked as if they might become extinct like so many other traditional boats. When inshore fishing did revive, fishermen started experimenting with other hull types, usually in a bid to obtain more room and speed. However, they have returned to cobles, not out of force of habit, but because they are safe and comfortable to work in the conditions of the north-east coast. In 1970 motor cobles of up to 40ft were being built. At first glance they looked like larger versions of the old sailing winter cobles, but the bows are much fuller and the sides much higher. The Whitby builders seem to have added a foredeck and wheelhouse to their motor cobles, while the Northumbrian motor cobles mostly carry a cover over their bows. The high covers keep the spray off when motoring into a head sea, but in high winds when working pots or salmon nets these cause the bow to be blown off course so they are usually taken down. The custom of the bow cover probably originated with these fishermen who had carried their sail over the bow in this way when motors were first fitted.

In 1980 three half-decked cobles were still kept in the tiny harbour at Beadnell, but in Victorian times this harbour was only used by the schooners which came in to the lime kilns, groups of cobles working off three different beach landings. To avoid the daily task of pulling their boats up the beach the fishermen tended to move to the harbours to try and make life easier. One place they moved to was Amble which had been mainly an outlet for coal in sailing ships. The entrance to the River Coquet at Amble was too narrow for a coble to beat in against the wind, so fishermen used to tow them in by walking up the pier or they rowed in if the tide and wind were not too strong.

Before World War I, when some of the Northumbrian fishermen wanted a new coble, they used to write to Hartlepool builders to order their new boats. It was unheard of for fishermen to actually travel that far to see the builder and the new coble was eventually sent up the coast by rail. The yard of J. & J. Harrison started at Amble in 1870 and was then mainly concerned with collier brigs, but it has been concentrating on building cobles since 1920. The yard is now run by John Matthews, a descendant of the founders, and Hector Handyside, master builder, who started in 1948 and is the grandson of William Handyside, a Beadnell fisherman. When a new coble is built, no plans are made or necessary. The fishermen usually come into the shed and spend hours discussing what type of coble they require for the fishing that is lucrative at the time. The only measurements which are fixed are the length of the ram and the height of the sides. A short measuring stick is used to gauge the width of the flat bottom aft and a longer one for the mid-ship width. Every other measurement simply falls into the traditional pattern.

Victorian longshore fishing was so closely linked with continual poverty that after World War I many young men went off into other industries. In the 1960s there was a steady return to longshore fishing and the use of cobles. Harrison's yard has been building about 5 cobles a year and have produced well over 400 since 1870. Cobles are a common sight on the North Sea coast but the old sailing cobles are very rare. Hector Handyside has totally rebuilt the 30ft (overall) *Sweet Promise*, which was originally built in 1906 by William Cambridge whose cobles were regarded as being the best sailers. Handyside also built in 1976 the *Gratitude* WY 263 on the same lines and has restored the 27ft *Brothers* which was built in the early 1930s by Harrison, then named *Kindly Light* BH 122, as a motor coble for Jack Stewart of Alnmouth. She was on the lines of a sailing coble with a little more side height.

A few cobles have been built for pleasure sailing, but not many of the working sailing cobles are left. The Maritime Trust have the mule *Blossom* which was built at Berwick upon Tweed and was later sold from Burnmouth to Seahouses. The National Maritime Museum at Greenwich has the Sunderland foy coble *Sunshine*, built in 1890. Small cobles like the *Sunshine* were called 'half cobles' and used for foying. The *Anne Isabella* at Paddy's Hole, Cullercoats, was built in 1912 at Beadnell for William Handyside and was the last sailing coble to be built there. The *Fulmar* of Sunderland was built by Cambridge for Jack Brunton of Cullercoats; she became the *Lydia & May* and then *Hope On* when bought by a Sunderland man.

Cullercoats, just north of the River Tyne entrance, was one of the main sailing coble centres. Here, in around 1900, there were about 150 three-man cobles. The reason for this was that the men could get work during the winter in the Tyne shipyards and then go salmon fishing in the season. Cobles were used as pilot boats off both the Tyne and the Tees. The pilots of the Tees lived at Seaton Carew and Redcar on the opposite side of the river mouth. Their cobles were painted black to distinguish them from the brightly painted fishing cobles. Sailing pilots finished on the Tees during World War I, and after this they were no longer seen racing to be the first to reach an incoming ship. Back in the Victorian era, cobles had raced under oar and sail in Whitby Regatta, but there have been no races in modern times—a pity since it might have aided the return of the sailing winter coble.

Every landing place had its own version of the coble, and at Redcar the mules were very popular because the beach is shallow and the pointed stern proved better for coming through the surf. Redcar and Filey have become some of the many places where tractors are used to haul cobles up the beach. As an old Yorkshire fisherman put it, 'cobles is getting heavier and men's getting weaker'.

Whitby was the centre of longshore fishing on the rocky coast between the Tees and the Humber in the 1970s. As well as five-man MFV keel boats, there were around thirty full-time cobles and more part-timers working out of Whitby. It was also the main building centre with William Clarkson, Gordon Clarkson and J. N. Lowther working on the tiny Esk estuary, and C. A. Goodall just up the coast on the open beach at Sandsend. There is no harbour at Filey, but around sixteen cobles worked from the beach. These cobles were mainly using long-lines, some four miles long, with baited hooks attached. Before World War I, Filey had some forty-five cobles. The lack of a harbour prevented them from having larger boats although there were three yawls, *Contest, Albion* and *Susie*, owned by Filey men which operated from Scarborough, and about 240 men from the Filey area worked on Scarborough steam drifters. At that time Scarborough had around twenty-nine steam drifters supplemented by the Scottish and East Anglian drifters which went there in the late summer for the herring fishery.

The most unusual fleet of fishing boats in Britain and, indeed, in northern Europe, are the Cornish oyster boats which dredge under sail near Falmouth. This is not an out-of-date fishing method, but a perfectly practical way of preventing over-fishing of the natural oyster beds. The dredge licences issued by Truro City Council merely state that no mechanical power can be used in boats while they are fishing. Every week-day morning during the winter, about twenty sail boats put out from the sheltered moorings at Flushing, Mylor, Restronguet and Pill to spend the day dredging under sail in Carrick Roads, the mile-wide natural harbour by Falmouth. Small haul-tow punts, most operated by one man using a hand winch, also dredge, usually in the shallower waters.

The Truro River oyster boats are half-decked gaff cutters which have a good reputation for speed and handiness. The oldest boat dredging in 1979 was the 32ft *Morning Star* which local legend claims was originally built in about 1840. During one of the periodic rebuildings that most of these boats have experienced, the *Morning Star* was lengthened to become one of the larger dredgers. The older river boats were a very mixed bunch, often old sea-fishing boats which were converted for dredging. Since little was recorded about the Carrick Roads dredgers, the history of many boats comes down as part of the local folk lore. The counter-stern 32ft *Zinguench* was believed to have been built as a yacht at Restronguet in about 1840, but was still dredging a century later. The *Harriet* was almost as old when she was broken up in the 1950s and had a great reputation for speed, as did all the boats built by the Ferris family. The Ferris's were all said to have descended from a couple who built a boat between them, the husband building one side and the wife working

The Truro River oyster boats Ada *and* George Glasson, *a wooden boat dating from 1880, dredging oysters under sail in Carrick Roads, Cornwall, in 1979. There is barely enough wind for these boats to tow their dredges along the bottom and they were forced to give up for the day not long afterwards* (Author)

on the other. It seems likely that William Ferris, the master shipwright responsible for building the famous fruit schooner *Rhoda Mary* at Devoran in 1868, also built the dredgers *Florence* and *Harriet* which lasted for over a century. He is also thought to have built the dredger *Six Brothers* which was worked by George Vinnicombe until in 1968 she unfortunately broke loose in a gale from her mooring off Mylor Dockyard and was wrecked. The present *Six Brothers* is a wooden replacement.

After World War II it was assumed that the sail boats would die out with the older generation, but local young men continued to come into the business and by the early 1960s they started to build new boats. Most of these have been designed by Percy Dalton and built by Terry Heard at his Tregatreath yard at the head of Mylor Creek. The Victorian boats had a very straight deck line, but Terry Heard was keen to build boats with a little more style so his have a curved sheer deck line. The first of these were wooden, but in order to produce hulls that the oystermen could afford, the Tregatreath yard switched to glass-reinforced plastic in 1972. The first of this series was the 28ft *Meloris* named after the Cornish saint whose name was taken by the village. Several of these GRP 28-footers joined the work boats dredging, but some men thought they were a little too tender when driven really hard under sail. The original mould was altered to give a fuller bilge and the first of the second series to join the fleet was John Moore's *Orca* in 1979.

The 28-footers are worked by two men hand-hauling three dredges. Heard also started a class of Dalton-designed, one-man, 23-footers with the *Verona* in 1978. Not everyone had adopted GRP because in 1979 the wooden *Rhoda Mary* joined the dredging fleet. Her builder-owners, Rex and Roy Collins, had family connections with the famous clipper schooner of the same name. Ferro-cement has also been tried but, making the boats slightly heavier, it was not popular as the Cornishmen wanted speed for their summer races in the Falmouth area.

These races are very keenly fought affairs and work boats come out under a cloud of sail, including topsails and spinnakers which are not seen during winter dredging. In 1977 the new *Six Brothers* was carrying such a press of sail while racing that she sailed under in a sudden squall off Flushing. When she was raised with air bags, the boat came up, the sail filled and although full of water the boat sailed away!

Most of the sailing fishing boat centres used to have an annual race. The trawling smacks of Plymouth and Brixham raced annually and the race at Brixham was revived again in 1919. The 1927 Brixham race was sailed in a hard blow and the winning smack averaged 12 knots. This was particularly good because in these races, held during the Brixham Regatta, the smacks raced three times round a triangular course in Tor Bay. Smacks were fishing under sail out of Brixham until World War II. However, the presenter of the race cup, a Brixham man, who had emigrated to Canada, requested after the war that the races be revived, but by then the remaining smacks were sailed for pleasure.

Only three smack yachts took part in the 1953 race with *Provident*, built at Galmpton in 1924, the winner, followed by *Terminist* and the 25-ton *Rulewater* built at Brixham in 1917. The race lapsed until 1963 when the first Brixham International Trawler Race was held for power craft. Usually around forty commercial fishing vessels turn up in the third week of June for this race. The record number was seventy-two in 1979 which does not only include boats from Devon, but also from Leigh-on-Sea, the Channel Islands, France, Belgium, The Netherlands and Norway.

While the sailing smacks used to compete in one race for three cups, the motor fishing vessels have a staggered start on a handicap basis in two classes. In 1973 a third class was introduced for crabbers, while the major trophy remained the King George V Cup. These races make a pleasant interlude to the serious business of catching fish.

7

Changing Designs and Achievements

It is in the design of smaller craft that the native traditions of Britain have been the strongest. In the past, almost every waterside community had its own special type of working craft. These were evolved to suit local conditions and were as much a part of the regional heritage as local architecture or dialect. Some museums have made a determined effort to save local craft and record the background of their working lives. However, boats were a living tradition and there is a danger that once they become institutionalised the living culture becomes static and dies. An instance of this is the sailing barge *Cambria* which lies in St Katharine's Dock, London, which is lifeless compared to the usual environment of the working barge. This is not to belittle in any way the good work of the Maritime Trust which has saved her, but it is the other barges which are still sailing that keep the tradition alive. The same is true with square riggers. It is a wonderful achievement that so many people saved the clipper *Cutty Sark* at Greenwich, but the tradition of handling a square rigger at sea is being achieved by the dedicated owners of vessels such as the brigantines *Eye of the Wind* and *Søren Larsen* who still sail them and actually make them earn a living.

Fortunately the maritime traditions of the British coast are far from dead, although of course a tradition is rarely frozen but continually evolves. The introduction of power craft has meant greater standardisation of boats and working methods than before, but each region still manages to retain an identity. There are no hard and fast rules as to the way that local craft evolved and there is no set pattern to explain their survival. The fact is that all round Britain there are little groups of craft, very well known locally, which have been saved by the individual effort of local people.

Really good sailing craft were not developed until there was a tremendous burst of inventive genius in the second half of the nineteenth century. Before this most small craft had either limited sailing qualities or were rowed. In the days of large families and widespread poverty, there was never a shortage of strong men willing to pull on an oar. Nowhere was this more true than in the far West of England so that it is not surprising that the fast pulling gigs of Cornwall and the Isles of Scilly appeared long before the superb sailing boats of that area.

Richard Gillis, who worked hard and skilfully to save the gigs from extinction, states that the history of these craft began with a 30ft six-oar gig built by the Peter family at St Mawes in 1790. However, fast, narrow pulling boats under various names and with slightly different hull shapes appear to have been common all round southern England in the late eighteenth century, so the Peter's gig of 1790 was part of an already strong tradition, although there is only scanty documentary evidence. It is unquestionably true that Peters of St Mawes was the leading gig builder for virtually the whole of Cornish working gig history.

The Peter's gig of 1790 was built for a clergyman, probably from Padstow. In this wild and largely roadless country, travel by sea was faster and safer than by land. However, most early gigs were built for either smuggling or pilot work. The great advantage of the gigs was that if they were spotted by the sailing revenue cutters when smuggling, they could be rowed into the wind at speed and avoid being captured. To increase their speed, gigs to be pulled by seven and eight oars were built, but these were outlawed as the extra men made them uneconomic for anything but smuggling. The six-oared gigs were used for pilotage and passengers, but even then the Revenue Service burnt any suspected of smuggling in a vain attempt to stamp it out. In the early nineteenth century, the Customs tried to ban pulling boats with more than four oars,

The Scillonian gig Nornour *under sail. When the gigs were rowed they were open, but a temporary foredeck has been added for sailing* (F. E. Gibson)

but many honest Cornishmen (and no doubt several dishonest ones) protested that for fishing, carrying cargoes and other longshore work, they had to have larger open boats.

The smugglers certainly did not earn their money easily because to cross the mouth of the English Channel in an open boat involved hours of continual rowing. From Scilly to Roscoff in Brittany is 136 miles. The gigs were fitted with lug sails which were used whenever possible, but in a gale there could be no rest at all as they had to row continuously to keep the bow head to the sea. Although Cornish and Scillonian gigs frequently crossed to France, the most common method of smuggling was to meet incoming ships and barter fresh food for spirits and tobacco.

By the second half of the nineteenth century, smuggling had become a sideline and the chief work for the West Country gigs was pilotage and attending wrecks. There was tremendous growth in international trade and every day sailing ships came in from the Atlantic to pick up a pilot for European ports. In bad weather many were driven on to rocks and wrecked. The tiny, easily manoeuvrable gigs could be rowed into rocky outcrops where no other craft could go. The gigmen went out in almost any weather to try to save lives and they brought hundreds of people ashore, but after that they regarded the wreck as being theirs. The Scillonians were particularly adept at salvaging ships, but if it was impossible to refloat them then they stripped the hull of everything movable. Many of the gigs from Scilly such as the 30ft *Sussex* were named after the wrecks which originally financed their construction. Another gig built for the pilots on Bryher is called the *Golden Eagle* because the pilots were awarded the new American gold dollar pieces after saving the crew of an American ship which was ashore on Gweal Island. Sometimes the gigs were towed behind a sailing cutter, then when a ship was sighted the gigs set off to get there first with their pilots.

In Scilly in around 1880, pilotage was virtually the only regular employment. About a dozen cutters and forty gigs were competing to put their pilots aboard homeward bound ships. Gigs which always came second were of no use to the pilots. Since there was little work on the islands, their families starved if they could not find pilot work. In the days before reliable charts, Scilly pilots took ships to any port in Europe and then found other ships to take them back towards home. On approaching the Scillies pigeons were released which took messages from a pilot and hopefully a gig would collect them or they would board any other gig in the vicinity.

It was a hard life out in an open boat cruising in all weathers in search of ships needing a pilot. Above all they had to have fast, seaworthy craft and the pilot gigs came up to this standard, although a great many gigs were lost at sea, particularly during a depression in Scilly when many men with no real sea experience began to take gigs out. Others suffered the misfortune of being swamped.

The gigs had lug sails and used them extensively, but they were fastest under oar. Most crews averaged 8 knots while a good crew could pull at 12 knots for short distances. The gigs were about 28–30ft long with a 5ft beam and weighed only 7cwt which meant that they could be lifted by their seven-man crew. If left on the open beaches, these gigs were soon blown over and smashed in the high winds. Consequently the gigs were always kept in special gig houses which were low buildings built at the top of the beach. At Hugh Town, the little capital of Scilly, there were gig houses all along both foreshores. Sadly these have been pulled down, but some old gig houses exist on the other islands and a new, much larger house has been built for the gigs that are still at Hugh Town on St Mary's.

The gig houses were the reason for the very long careers of the gigs because they never lay in the open and many remained for decades after their use had finished, safely shut away and forgotten in their houses. In Victorian times gigs in Scilly and on the Cornish mainland used to race for cash prizes in local regattas. After the introduction of motor launches and the fading away of pilotage, only the Cornish port of Newquay kept its gigs to race as a club sport. The oldest gig is the 30ft *Newquay* built by Peters at St Mawes in 1812. In 1980 the other Peter's gigs, the 31ft *Dove* of 1820 and the 32ft *Treffry* of 1838, which was the longest and some believe the fastest of the surviving gigs, were still here.

In 1953 members of the Newquay Rowing Club went out to Scilly and bought some of the better gigs. One of these was the 28ft *Slippen* which was built by Peters for the pilots of St Martin's in 1830. Another gig bought by the Newquay club was the *Bonnet*, built in 1830 and said to have been named after a St Martin's woman who had magical powers which looked after the gig's safety and luck. These old gigs have been repaired and rebuilt over the years and in some cases their sides are now a different shape, although they are basically the same and remain clinker, six-oared craft.

Interest in the gigs in Scilly was restarted in 1962 when the 30ft St Agnes carrying gig *Campernell* and the 31ft Tresco pilot gig *Czar* were taken out of their houses and raced. This revived everyone's interest in the gigs and the Scillonians asked Newquay if they could borrow the *Bonnet*, which was a good sailing gig and the *Shah* to restart races the following year. Regular Friday night races were started in the summer, and by the late 1970s these had become more popular than football with Scillonians. It seems that every island now has its own gig and these gather at Hugh Town to race.

This reawakening of a tradition has resulted in the building of new gigs. Most of these are the work of Tom Chudleigh of St Mary's. The first one, the *Serica*, built in 1967, was based on the *Bonnet*, but they hoped to make her faster by making the bows slightly finer. However, the *Serica* tended to bury her bows which suggests that even in 1830 the Peters knew the limits to which a hull shape could be pushed. In fact the old working gigs have proved faster than the six new gigs (one of which is in California). In all, sixteen gigs were still in existence in 1980, and the *Slippen* was returned to St Mary's so that young people could use her to learn to row and the tradition of pulling a six-oar gig could be kept alive.

One of the most unusual rowing events in Britain is the Thames Barge Driving Race from Greenwich to Westminster. Moving goods in barges which drifted on the tide was a very old practice on the Thames and required a good knowledge of tidal currents. Every man had to serve as an apprentice waterman and lighterman before he could take charge of a lighter on the tideway. In 1937 there were some 6,000 working watermen on the Thames, although many companies had tugs, but there were still firms that only had lighters which drifted on the tide and were controlled by men with 30ft oars. A later practice was for a tug to tow a maximum of six lighters which had been loaded from ships in the docks. They dropped the individual lighters off near the wharves and the lightermen aboard then rowed them in.

The busiest time on the Thames was 'tide time' around high tide when the docks opened and large ships, barges and lighters poured out on to the tideway. The whole of the Thames was alive with shipping activity. The pattern of trade on the Thames made extensive use of lighters because they could be loaded over the ship's side and save the higher costs of putting cargoes over a wharf. The lighters were originally moved on the tideway by drifting with the tide; this was known as 'driving' but the term dates no further back than the 1950s when there was a fashion amongst lightermen to refer to their lighters as 'vehicles'. The old men spoke of controlled drifting as being 'rowing' or being 'under oar'. When driving on the tide, if they were drifting, the anchor was often 'drudged' (dredged) along the bottom to help to control the lighters. This method was used when bound 'up-through' the bridges. Lighters were often used for storage and lay moored to buoys in groups known as 'lighter roads'.

The art of controlling a barge on the tideway by oar is centuries old, and as part of the 1973 Greenwich Festival, Reg Coombes revived the practice and drove a 50-ton swimhead 'punt' lighter from Barking Creek to Greenwich. The tremendous interest aroused on the Upper Thames through so many people's association with the work resulted in an annual race being started.

The use of lighters declined with the fading away of general cargo tramp steamers. An agreement between the lightermen's employers and the Transport & General Workers Union resulted in many lightermen being transferred to other dock work, and between 1974–80 no new apprentices were started. However, although trade on the Thames has changed, there is still traffic. Lighters are now towed and the PLA ruling stipulates a maximum of six lighters to one tug.

Strangely the most overlooked type of craft is one which is common to the whole of the British Isles—the small, open, clinker, transom-sterned boat. They never even had a proper name to describe the type, yet the foreshore landing places of every harbour were lined with them, and every ship and yacht had them as tenders. With the coming of outboards and then GRP mass-produced hulls, the ordinary open boat has become a traditional wooden boat type which could totally vanish.

Variations of the British open boat were found everywhere, although they seem to have been strongest in the south-east of England and this could have been where the transom-stern boat evolved. They appear to have started with the open, clinker, double-ended hulls such as the Thames Peter boats and the Cromer crab boats. The great disadvantage of the pointed stern craft was the lack of working space aft, so the next stage was to add a small transom to make the stern wider. However, the double-ended boat could be rowed stern first so the original transom was kept above the waterline to avoid spoiling the underwater lines.

A good example of this first step is the Thames waterman's skiff which is on display in New Neptune Hall at The National Maritime Museum, Greenwich. It clearly shows that they were little more than double-ended boats with a tiny transom. This design reached its peak by the eighteenth century. Watermen wanted craft that were fast and easy to row for passenger work, a need which produced gigs and pulling skiffs with narrow and fine lines. An example of the Victorian pulling skiff which survived in Woodbridge is the skiff *Teddy* built in about 1875 for the river pilot to row down the River Deben and meet the sailing barges coming up river. This type had been built on the river at least as far back as 1830.

In most ports there was a builder who specialised in building small open boats. Such a man was Leslie W. Harris who worked until 1936 in a little yard near Coronation Hard at Burnham on Crouch which was then the main yachting centre of East Anglia. He built the 36ft yacht *Jorrocks II*, but mainly turned out open clinker transom boats. A 10ft boat that Harris built in about 1920 as a yacht tender to *Deva* has been fitted out again for sail by Jonathan Simper under the name *Wonder*. With dagger-plate and standing lug sail she handled very well and also rowed easily. She towed behind a yacht cleanly and with quarter benches round the

On the east coast the barge, smack and gaffer races, which have gained popularity since the early 1960s, triggered off a revival of interest in local work boats. Here are the class winners in the 1980 Colne Match, the spritsail barge Ironsides, *setting the stemhead staysail rig, and the Essex stowboat (spratt) smack* ADC. *These two were the champions of the coast at that time* (Author)

stern at least five people can be carried. Perhaps the only disadvantage is that by modern standards she is heavy to drag up a beach. The general impression from *Wonder* is that years of experience had gone into producing a thoroughly handy boat.

The transom-sterned boat type was used all round the coast in the late nineteenth century for fishing and general hack boats. The sailing beach boats used on the Suffolk coast were an enlargement of this hull design. In Essex the clinker-built 'winkle brigs' were used at West Mersea either for collecting winkles or for dredging oysters in creeks. They were a very deep beamy boat because they had to carry sacks of shellfish. At West Mersea the 18ft *MaNabs* was being used by Sam Carter to dredge oysters in Besom Fleet until 1953, by which time many of these winkle brigs had been bought for pleasure sailing. At Mersea, and further up the River Blackwater at Maldon, the 'brigs' were rigged as gaff sloops. Most of the Maldon brigs which had finer lines seem to have been built at Cook's barge yard. Here Alf Last worked mainly on building these 'brigs' and barge boats. The last one he produced was the 15ft cutter *Prudence* in 1973.

Every builder varied the open transom boat for local needs. For instance, the barge boat usually had rather full bows so that they were stable when the bargemen stepped down on to the bow deck. Also their full bow made them tow better from the high barge's transom, while the Essex smacks' boats were finer forward because they were towed from a low counter stern. Everything about these local traditional craft had been evolved for a particular reason. Usually these open boats were sculled with a single oar over the stern, seldom were they rowed because there was not enough room in the crowded docks. The use of open transom boats as tenders and lifeboats seems to have led to their fall in popularity. Most tramp steamers and steam tankers carried a transom 'jolly boat', but because they were officially the lifeboat on many commercial craft, a tubby hull shape was encouraged. This spoilt their rowing quality and coastal sailors were not so keen on them for rowing ashore. The terms 'jolly' and 'yawl' came from the Scandinavian word 'Jolle' meaning double-ended open boat.

Other types of boats in danger of being forgotten are the numerous yacht club one-design racing boats which were very popular between about 1920–60. Some of these local classes actually had their origins in the old work boats, such as the Salcombe yawl, a restricted class which grew out of the fishing and pilot boats. The Salcombe fishermen used to go out through the narrow river entrance on the ebb tide and then race back on the flood. The yachtsmen were so impressed with the performance of these yawls that they started to buy and race them, and in the 1920s a bermudian dinghy class based on them was begun. Being wooden hulled, these eventually became too expensive to build and in about 1968 David Quick of Salcombe started to produce GRP hulls. However, as so often happens, these were definitely not accepted for racing so they were called Devon yawls.

The 22ft Norfolk Punt class developed from the old duck punts which were raced for fun in the East Anglian broadland regattas. The punts from Hickling Broad were particularly fast so in 1926 a club was formed to preserve them. In 1949 the old design was more or less abandoned but the present high-speed Norfolk Punts still have flat sides and a hard chine bottom like a punt.

The oldest one-design class still raced in Britain is the 20ft Seabird Half Rater. The first Seabirds were built in 1899 for racing at Southport, Lancashire. This class spread in popularity so that within a decade they were racing under a variety of names at Gourock on the Clyde, at Donaghadee in Northern Ireland and on the Menai Straits. Ninety Seabirds were built, although only sixty-nine have survived. They still race under the original gunter rig at Trearddur Bay, Anglesey, at

The Edwardian yacht Bona *racing in the Clyde. The hands on the deck of this yacht are dwarfed by the towering press of the gaff cutter's huge sail plan* (Author's Collection)

Abersoch under the Caernarvonshire Yacht Club, and on the Mersey at the Wallasey Yacht Club. Almost as old as the Seabird class is the Thames A Rater, an Edwardian class which is still raced on the upper Thames at Surbiton. When the first Thames A Raters were built in about 1905, they were gunter rigged and had massive bronze centreplates. In the mid-1920s there was a great deal of experimentation and the boats were changed to a bermudian rig. Because they were only used for river sailing, their most striking feature is their very tall masts. Most have settled for 45ft masts on a hull of about 28ft overall, although some have even tried a 55ft mast.

The first organised, one-design class to race in Britain was the Solent One-Design in 1895, but these open gaff cutters have long since gone. The oldest class still racing on the south coast of England are the 20ft X One-Designs. The first X One-Design was built to Alfred Westmacott's design in 1909, and most of the 174 built still race. They were originally gaff-rigged, but this was changed to bermudian in 1928. The X One-Designs have a strong class in the annual Cowes Week. Another class designed by Alfred Westmacott is the 26ft Sunbeam class which was started in 1923. They also race in Cowes Week, but none have been built since before World War II.

Although the X One-Design had fleets which raced at Poole, Yar-mouth, Lymington, Cowes, Hamble and Itchen Ferry, many of the local classes were confined to just one club. Usually what happened was that a yacht club committee wrote to a well-known designer and asked for a design which would suit their local waters and their members' pockets. It seems that designers did not always visit the area so it is not surprising that some local classes never quite lived up to their promoters' dreams. However, when Linton Hope designed the 24ft Broads One-Design in 1900, he produced a keel racer which stood the test of time because they are still raced on the Broads and in the sea off Lowestoft.

Because the gaff sloop Broads One-Designs originally had varnished hulls, they were called the Brown Boats, while the small open sloop class which raced only in the Broads were painted white, so they were known as the White Boats. Just after World War I the Racing Association produced the first set of national rules for dinghy racing based on the rules of some West Country and Broads yacht clubs. The inter-war years saw national classes of racing dinghies being introduced while the Dragon replaced the old half-raters as the open, keeled boats. Good local classes produced strong pride and sailing men have in some cases gone to a great deal of effort to keep them going. The main difficulty with the remaining local classes is the cost of building new boats. To keep them going most of the Thames A Raters have had to be coated with glass fibre skins. Some Broads White Boats have been rebuilt, but in 1980 the *Herald Moth*, the first White Boat built in GRP took to the water.

A few months later the Broads River Cruiser Class organisation banned the introduction of GRP yachts into their races. It is perhaps surprising that this step was taken because Broadland racing had always been open to new ideas. Although classes of racing yachts were built specially for Lake Windermere, the East Anglian Broadland was the only area in Britain to develop a type of inland sailing yacht. The Norfolk gentlemen have been taking part in water frolics and presumably races since the late eighteenth century.

In the mid-nineteenth century there was a great craze for racing lateeners in the Broads. This was the only area north of Lake Geneva where lateen sails were used. There was great rivalry on the Broads between lateeners and gaff cutters. When the first Norfolk and Suffolk Yacht Club Challenge Cup was sailed in 1860, it was won at Cantley by the lateener *Enchantress* which had a 75ft lateen yard on a mast right forward in the bows. Another of the crack lateeners was the *Maria*, built in 1826, which followed the normal practice of having a lateen on a mast in the bow and a gaff sail on a mast stepped almost amidships. When straight-stemmed cutters finally dominated the Broads after about 1880, the *Maria* was left abandoned in a boat-house on the Broads and was discovered in a boatshed by John Perryman. He drew up a scaled set of lines from her, enabling the 16ft lateen *Britannia* to be built in 1968 by apprentices of the Lowestoft College of Further Education.

The Broads cutters were used to cruise at sea, but in 1892 a village carpenter realised that deep-keeled craft were pointless on the Broads and he built the *Castanet* which had a shallow 'skimming dish' hull. As a racer she swept the board, and soon everyone was building spoon-bowed gaff sloops with huge jackyard tops'ls cut flat to catch the wind over the tree tops. About the time of World War I, the most successful racers were built by Collins of Wroxham. Since the railway companies had promoted the Broads for tourists in the 1880s, the number of sailing hire/charter craft had been steadily growing. However, the next generation of racers were built by Herbert Woods, to his own imaginative design, at Potter Heigham. His 30ft *Moonraker*, built in 1930, was the first bermudian Broads yacht. The idea for the *Ladybird*'s double-ended hull, which was built in 1935, came from the Sharpie dinghies which were then regarded as being the fastest small boats. Woods followed her with the *Evening Flight* in 1939, which marked the end of that phase of Broads racing.

In 1937 a handicap system was created so that the mixed bunch of yachts could race as the Norfolk River Cruiser Class and compete

The Broads River Cruisers on the River Yare, Norfolk, at the start of the 1979 Yare Navigation Race. The Smuggler *in the foreground has some typical features, such as a cabin top which can be raised to increase cabin space, and the tiny cockpit aft for the mainsail trimmer to sit in* (Author)

The 'J' class yacht Endeavour II *racing at Harwich in 1936. Some of her professional crew of nineteen can be seen in white* (Author's Collection)

equally. Sadly many Broads yachts rotted away during the war and most of the remainder were sold into hire fleets. By the 1970s the hire companies were mainly concerned with powered craft and the old hire yachts were sold off cheaply to local people who started to restore and race them. The Yare Navigation Race was started in 1976 and soon around 130 cruisers were back under sail. The nimble Broads cruisers can turn virtually in their own length and have given many owners great satisfaction. With their unique jackyard sail plan, they have become a symbol of the Broads.

Speaking nationally, small yachts have survived, but the great yachts crewed with professional skippers and paid hands are no more. The great yachts belonged to a social era when there were extremely rich people who could afford such luxuries. One of the great yachts which has survived is the famous J class *Shamrock V*, which was built for Sir Thomas Lipton in 1930 for another of his attempts to win the America Cup. Also still afloat is the huge 133ft schooner *Heartsease*, built in 1903 as the *Adela* for Mr Claude Cayley. She originally set 16,000sq ft of sail

221

The main saloon of the Edwardian schooner yacht Heartsease. *The owners of such vessels used them as they would a country house, entertaining guests during the summer*
(Author)

which was made by Ratsey & Lapthorn. In her first season *Heartsease* took part in the Dover to Heligoland race which was a forerunner of regular, organised ocean racing. It is known that King Edward VII raced aboard her, and that Cayley crossed to Canada in her several times. In her racing period she had a master, mate and a paid crew of twenty-four who lived forward, most of them in the fo'c'sle which had bunks down either side, while the master, mate and stewards had tiny cabins. The owner and his guests lived in state rooms which occupied three-quarters of the space below decks.

Even in the 1920s the *Heartsease* dropped from the racing scene to be used for cruising. She made long voyages to the Mediterranean before she became a houseboat at Tollesbury, Essex. In 1971 Gordon and Caroline Waller bought this huge Edwardian yacht at Lowestoft and undertook the daunting task of completely restoring her. The incredible thing about this schooner is the craftsmanship that went into her construction at Fay & Company's yard, Itchen near Southampton. Even when launched she was described as 'one of the finest schooners afloat' and now, well over seventy years later, the hull and all the surviving fittings are in near-perfect condition. After ten years the Wallers have restored her accommodation and found a way of fixing a new keel since the original 62-ton lead keel was sold in 1952.

One of the attractions of sailing is that it has always drawn people of different backgrounds together in a spirit of fellowship. Of course the great age of yachting with its elite yacht clubs and large crews of paid hands could only have belonged to a bygone social background. However, behind the glamour of the huge yachts owned by the aristocracy and the kings of industry, there were always the small yachts owned by the less prosperous which were sailed or rowed purely for pleasure. Some of these men ordered one-designs or raced smacks, but there was a growing band of men who wanted nothing to do with yacht clubs or racing and only wanted to cruise on their own.

Many yachts designed around 1900 were scaled-down versions of the great yachts, but men like the Scarborough artist Albert Strange were trying to work out a design for a type of yacht suitable for single-handed or family cruising. The Humber Yawl Club, started in 1883, was vigorous in promoting small yacht sailing, and Albert Strange, who was very experienced in small boat sailing, achieved a great degree of balance in the small canoe-sterned yawls that he designed. The Strange designed 22ft gaff yawl *Sheila*, built at Port St Mary on the Isle of Man in 1905 for Robert Groves, was intended for cruising in the Hebrides. The tiny *Sheila* was also cruised round the Irish Sea by Groves, which was a totally different type of yachting to the main purpose of the great yachts, which spent the summer moving round the coast from one fashionable regatta to another. Of course none of these small early yachts had engines so they had to be rowed if the wind dropped. Many more yachts were built to the Albert Strange design in the 1920s and other designers, particularly Harrison Butler, adopted the idea of a canoe-sterned yacht for much larger craft.

In the inter-war years there were two opposing schools of thought in British yacht design. The cruise boat designers were still heavily influenced by the deep-keeled, heavy displacement hulls of pre-World War I work boats, particularly the pilot cutters from the Bristol Channel. When the 600-mile Fastnet Race was first sailed in 1925, the leading boats were all either converted work boats or boats based on their designs. After this first British ocean race, which was actually greatly disapproved of by most yachtsmen of that time, the yachts designed by other schools of thought steadily came to the fore. These were the narrow spoon-bowed yachts which evolved from the Edwardian racers like the *Heartsease*, but were considerably smaller. Most of the professional yacht skippers were used to taking part in day races and disliked the discomfort of the new sport of offshore racing. Although most cruising yachts still carried one paid hand who did the maintenance work, it became the custom for the owner to be the skipper and his friends to act as crew. Most British yachts went over to the bermudian rig, but they still tended to keep to the deep-keel design, and it was not until the 1950s that light, displacement hulls, often with bilge keels, were really accepted.

It was a reaction to the contemporary yachting scene which started the Old Gaffers Association in 1963. The idea of an Old Gaffers Race in which only gaff and lug sail craft could take part, proved surprisingly popular. The impact was far greater than the organisers of the informal one-day races had originally expected. Within about five years boating people were once again taking real pride in their gaff craft. Like most associations, the OGA had its growing pains. Many members thought that it should be devoted to just traditional wooden gaff and lug sailed craft. However, since the original intentions had been to encourage the use of the gaff rig, the races and rallies remained open to any gaff or lug sail craft regardless of age or hull material.

The revival of gaff craft led to designers starting to promote a whole generation of new gaff classes. The movement towards the class boat has grown stronger since World War II. The old practice was for a designer or master boatbuilder to produce individual 'one off' yachts for every owner. Of these, there were rarely two boats exactly the same. Builders turned towards class boats so that they could set up partial mass production methods to keep their costs down. However, many people have been drawn to gaffers because each craft is unique. Yachts such as Chris Waddington's handsome 42ft cutter *Moya* would be hard to replace in an age when wood and craftsmanship are expensive. Of course when *Moya* was built by Crossfield Brothers at Arnside in 1910 on the enlarged lines of a Morecambe Bay prawner or nobby, it was possible to produce a hull at a reasonable price.

The growth in numbers of restored and new generation gaff craft has meant that Old Gaffers races have grown in size. The 1980 East Coast Old Gaffers Race attracted an entry of 107 boats. Because of bad weather not all arrived, but it had become one of the largest traditional small boat events in the world. The gaffers which take part in these events are a wide mixture: sleek Edwardian racers, tubby cruising yachts from the inter-war years, small open racers and a host of others. In the 1970s East Coast Old Gaffers Races, the local-restored smacks usually led the fleet in every weather condition, while the previous decade had been dominated by the 22ft cutter *Fanny of Cowes*. It is worth noting that she was also a fishing craft. The *Fanny* was built at Cowes in 1872 for the Paskins family who used her mainly for taking sacks of oysters across the Solent, but she was also built to beat the 21ft *Star*, which she did, in the town regatta.

In some villages around the Solent, and on the east coast, the pattern of life up to World War II was for men to spend the summer away on yachts as professional crew and return home to spend the winter fishing. Since the Solent was fairly protected by the Isle of Wight, they only needed small boats, usually worked by one man. In the first half of the nineteenth century, small open lug or spritsail boats were used, but the contact with yachting led the Solent fishermen to look for a higher performance sailing boat. In such confined waters there was a great deal of beating to windward, so in about 1850 the fishermen switched to half-decked gaff cutters of 16–22ft long.

The River Itchen just outside Southampton was a leading yachting centre, and at Northam some of the early Itchen boats were built. The leading builder seems to have been Dan Hatcher and incredibly some of the boats he built are still afloat, notably the 19ft *Wonder* which he built in 1860, the 21ft *Nellie* of 1865 and the 16ft *Flutt* of around the same period. So handy were these fishing boats that in the 1870s the yachting writer and designer Dixon Kemp was taking a keen interest in them and suggested that their hull shape should be adopted for small yachts.

Because yachtsmen like Dixon Kemp used to see the group of cutters lying near the ferry across the Itchen, this type of fishing boat became known as the Itchen Ferry cutter, but the type was used throughout the area and were known to fishermen as the Solent smacks. There were fleets of these cutters working from the Itchen and Hamble rivers, Gosport, Portsmouth, Wootton Creek, Cowes and Hythe. In the 1902 Customs register Tanner's Lake and Pitts Deep near Lymington are also listed as anchorages of fishing boats. Another place was Weston, now like Northam engulfed by Southampton. The Weston boats lay in a 'lake' or creek which gradually silted up as the seaweed on the foreshore died. This allowed the tide to pick up mud and shingle which was swept along and silted up the creek. At the head of this creek stood the Seaweed Hut where the fishermen stored their gear and which was reputed to have been marked on an eighteenth-century chart. Whenever the Seaweed Hut's roof started to leak, the fishermen just threw on another layer of seaweed.

The typical Solent fishing boat was a gaff cutter with a long bowsprit and platform tray or 'sternsheet' in the after end of the open well (cockpit) on which the trawl or oyster dredge was sorted out. The normal hull colour was black or grey and they carried a topsail for racing but a pole mast for working. Many of these Solent boats were built by leading yacht yards and it is believed that they were constructed of left-over timber from the large yachts and given as a 'present' to the yacht skippers for co-operation in bringing business to the yard.

Certainly the yachtsmen/fishermen were very keen on racing their boats in the local regattas. For instance, there was Captain Charlie Bevis of Bursledon who was known as the 'Strawberry King' because of his expertise at growing them. In 1902 he had the 24ft *Morning Star* for racing and winter fishing, but his real employment was as skipper of the 75ft yacht *White Heather*. Since most of the Itchen boats belonged to yacht skippers, the later ones built by Payne in the 1890s were intended largely for racing, but at other places, like Portsmouth, they were still being built just for day fishing.

After World War I, longshore fishing declined in the Solent and the boats were mostly sold as yachts. Since yachting in the Solent was very progressive, the little Itchen Ferry cutters were soon forgotten, but in 1980 the Solent Smack Society was started and they managed to race six cutters at the Bursledon Regatta. At the same time the society had managed to trace about sixty-nine boats of the Itchen Ferry type. Two were even doing part time fishing under sail. The 24ft *Alice* SU 37, an exact replica in fibre glass of the original *Alice* built in 1872, was fishing from Lymington, while the 22ft *Nellie Dean* SU 21 was fishing from Titchfield Haven.

The Itchen Ferry type of day boats were gradually superseded by the lightweight dinghies for racing. Some local classes proved so popular that they spread along the coast. The 14ft WEC Redwing dinghy designed by Uffa Fox in 1946 grew to be more than a local class, and so did the 14ft Jewel designed by Robert Stone of Brightlingsea which was used in much of eastern England. Long before this, in 1927, the International 14-footers had become the first truly international class. Most of the local classes were quite happily left on moorings while the post-war breed of lightweight racing dinghy had to be kept out of the water, but they sailed up to 12 knots and were tremendously exhilarating to sail.

In the wider field of yacht construction, mass production methods brought down the cost of racing dinghies so that a high percentage of young people could afford them. The National 12 was introduced in 1936 by the Royal Yachting Association with the aim of bringing dinghy racing within the reach of more people. After World War II the new type of dinghy racing club mushroomed wherever there was sailing room, not just on the coast and in the rivers, but far inland on gravel pits and reservoirs. This new breed of highly competitive dinghy racers eagerly scan the yachting press and make the annual pilgrimage to the Boat Show at Earls Court to view the latest high-speed sailing machines.

The success of all the high-performance classes depended entirely on them remaining within the financial reach of as many people as possible. To try to promote a class which the young and less affluent could afford,

The 42ft gaff cutter yacht *Moya* was built by Crossfield Brothers at Arnside in 1910. Before 1939, the gaff cutter was the favourite rig of the British yachtsman. Often yachts were based on work boats, and the *Moya* was really a larger version of the Morecambe Bay prawner (Chris Waddington)

The Itchen Ferry boat *Wonder* setting an old mainsail which has been cut down in size. The Itchen Ferries carried a large topsail for racing, but normally they did not set one for oyster dredging, spratting or shrimping (E. F. Nicolay)

the RYA brought in the 12ft Firefly, designed by Uffa Fox just after World War II. This was a completely new innovation because the hull was a smooth skin of moulded multi-plywood exclusively produced by Fairey Marine. This material had been developed by the aircraft industry during World War II. The Firefly was very similar in cost and in speed to the National 12, and there was great rivalry between them until the newer Enterprise started to replace them both in the early 1960s. The Enterprise could be built by the amateur from kits and these naturally undercut the professionally built craft.

The Merlin class was introduced in January 1946 and after *Yachting World* published a set of Jack Holt's plans, they rapidly increased in number, particularly in the West Country. In 1950 the Rocket was started and finally this was merged with the Merlin to produce the Merlin-Rocket, an out-and-out racing machine.

By the time classes like the Fireball came on the dinghy racing scene in the late 1960s, there had been a complete break with the traditional local classes being produced by skilled boatbuilders. Uffa Fox again adapted aircraft technology to produce the cold-mould Atlanta class yachts. It is fair to say that the Atlanta, with its hull shaped rather like an aircraft's fuselage, never gained much popularity, but designers and public alike realised that lightweight yachts could be mass-produced successfully. Most of the modern yacht classes are really using the basic ideas which were developed from the high-performance racing dinghies.

With lighter and faster yachts, which had auxiliary power for leaving and entering harbour, sailing became a pleasurable family recreation. The bermudian rig required less handling than the beautiful gaff sails so it also became possible for more people to sail single-handed on long passages. Single-handed sailing was certainly not new. The staunch Victorian Richard McMullen became disillusioned with paid hands who did not have his stamina and he took to sailing single-handed in a lugger. McMullen's cruises were published in his book *Down Channel* in 1869, and in the same year Empson Edward Middleton was the first man to sail single-handed round the British Isles in his 23ft gaff yawl *Kate*. Empson was something of an eccentric; for instance, his diet for the voyage was sherry and raw egg. He called in at many ports and avoided the north of Scotland by passing through the canal which linked the Clyde and the Firth of Forth. His book *The Cruise of the Kate* and McMullen's book became widely read yachting classics, but the rigours of small boat sailing before the introduction of reasonably reliable marine engines kept many men and even more women away from cruising.

In the 1920s an increasing number of amateur yachtsmen were making long ocean passages, and round the world voyages became more frequent.

In the winter of 1933–4 W. B. Reese sailed the small double-ended ketch *May L* single handed from England across the Atlantic to Nassau. There is unconfirmed evidence to suggest that the first women to cross the Atlantic single-handed did so before World War I. However, the first confirmed lone crossing was Ann Davison in her 23ft bermudian sloop *Felicity Ann* which arrived in the West Indies early in 1953. This was a remarkable piece of personal courage because the previous attempt to sail the Atlantic with her husband Frank had ended in tragedy. Frank and Ann Davison had bought the 64ft Fleetwood smack *Reliance* which had been converted to power but was in a rough state. However, they returned her to seagoing order and set out to sail on a great circle passage across the Atlantic, going north from southern Ireland to the St Lawrence Gulf. Tragically the voyage did not get very far as the *Reliance* was driven ashore and wrecked on Portland Bill, Frank Davison being drowned.

It was really to complete this dream of an Atlantic voyage that Ann Davison sailed alone in the *Felicity Ann* from Plymouth in May 1952. On her voyage she called at a French port and ports in Spain before crossing to Las Palmas in the Canary Islands. She then set out to run before the trade winds across the Atlantic to English Harbour, Antigua. She was not in a particular hurry and from the West Indies she sailed north through the United States inter-coastal waterway to New York. About fifteen years later a German woman followed the same route single handed in a trimaran, and then, in 1971, Nicolette Milnes Walker sailed single handed from Dale in Milford Haven to Newport, Rhode Island, in the 30ft fibreglass sloop *Aziz*. Her crossing in 44 days made her the first woman to sail non-stop from Britain to North America.

After World War II it became quite common for British yachts to try to sail round the world. However, John Gusswell's circumnavigation between 1955–9 in the 20ft bermudian yawl *Trekka* was the first single-handed voyage by a British yacht. Although most of the early voyages were made in gaff sailed craft, it was really the advent of the bermudian rig and the increasing number of winches and gadgets to simplify yacht handling which made single-handed sailing feasible. The most important of the increasing number of gadgets was of course the self-steering gear which allowed the yacht to sail itself while the sole occupant either slept or was able to do other work. With a yacht there was always enough for one person to do, but being alone during a gale at night in the open Atlantic stretches any person to their physical and mental limits.

Single-handed ocean voyages had been proved possible, although the risks have always remained high and they had caught the public imagination. In 1960 *The Observer* joined with the Royal Western Yacht Club to promote and organise a race for single-handed yachts across the

Atlantic. The first Single-handed Transatlantic Race only attracted five entries, and the first to reach America forty days after leaving Plymouth was Francis Chichester in *Gypsy Moth III*. The STR has since been held every four years, but two years after the first, Francis Chichester sailed back again and managed to take nearly a week off his first record time of forty days.

Francis Chichester took to single-handed ocean sailing at an age when most men are preparing for retirement, but the sport might have been tailor-made for him. In the inter-war years Chichester had been a pioneer in solo flying and he had great personal determination which made him a natural loner. His greatest achievement was to be the first man to sail round the world, only making one port of call. In 1966 he sailed from Plymouth in the 53ft bermudian yawl *Gipsy Moth IV*, a yacht specially designed for the voyage by Illingworth & Primrose and built by Camper & Nicholsons at Gosport. Since there were no other yachts to compete against Chichester, he set himself the task of trying to beat the clipper record to Australia. He did not quite succeed in this, but after sailing with the trade winds he arrived at Sydney, via the Cape of Good Hope, and proved that one man alone could make very long ocean passages. Despite warnings from experienced sailors that it was impossible to sail single-handed across the great gale-lashed Southern Ocean and round Cape Horn, Chichester did so and returned to Plymouth nine months and one day after setting out. The sailing time on the voyage of 26,630 miles had been 226 days at an average speed of 5·71 knots.

Sir Francis Chichester's great courage and example attracted universal admiration, but Alec Rose sailed closely in his wake and became well-known as the second single-handed circumnavigator. While Chichester was seen as the tough professional adventurer, Rose was seen as the skilful amateur. At fifty-eight Rose had left his Portsmouth greengrocer's shop and set off in his yawl *Lively Lady* to sail round the world. However, he was already a very experienced small boat sailor who had been fourth in the 1964 Single-handed Transatlantic Race, to say nothing of having served in the Royal Navy during World War II in the tough Atlantic convoys. Rose called in at New Zealand and his sailing time was 318 days before he returned to Portsmouth and a knighthood.

While the voyages of Chichester and Rose and a growing band of single-handed sailors received wide publicity the cruises of Frank Dye remained largely unknown outside the yachting fraternity. He chose to make long sea trips in his annual holidays in his 16ft *Wanderer*, a Wayfarer class designed by Ian Proctor of Warsash, Hampshire, in 1958 as a safe family dinghy. Frank Dye's voyages in this open boat to northern waters surprised everyone. His most spectacular voyages included a passage from Kinlochbervie in the Highlands across to Iceland in 1963 and in the next year up the Norwegian coast almost into the Arctic Circle.

On ocean routes single-handed sailors were looking for new barriers to break, and in 1968 the *Sunday Times* newspaper promoted the Golden Globe Race which was a non-stop round the world race, returning to a British port. In this ambitious race only one entrant actually finished and this was Robin Knox-Johnston who arrived at Falmouth on 17 January 1969 after 313 days at sea in the 32ft ketch *Suhaili*. This was then the longest time that any lone yachtsman had been sailing and the first single-handed circumnavigation without touching land. Robin Knox-Johnston had been a merchant navy officer with the British India Line, but he had also had plenty of small boat experience when sailing the *Suhaili* back from Bombay before his world voyage. Another competitor in this race, Nigel Tetley, actually crossed his tracks in the 40ft trimaran *Victress* so that he was the first solo circumnavigator in a multi-hull, but his craft sank off the Azores.

All the voyages round the world had been made eastward with the trade winds, but perhaps the most remarkable was the first 'wrong way'

Chay Blyth and the property millionaire, Jack Hayward, who enabled the Great Britain *to be returned from the Falkland Islands, on the trimaran* Great Britain III *on the Solent* (Ajax News Photos)

The ocean racer Great Britain II *off Cape Horn in the 1973 Round the World Race with* Endeavour *in the background* (Chris Waddington)

circumnavigation, completed in December 1970 by Chay Blyth in the 59ft steel ketch *British Steel*. Blyth, who with John Ridgeway had in 1966 rowed the 20ft *English Rose III* across the Atlantic, sailed down to the South Atlantic and then for forty-eight days beat against the terrible winds of the great Southern Ocean past Cape Horn and the three other capes and back into the Atlantic. Chay Blyth had succeeded in making this remarkable voyage in the largest yacht to complete a circumnavigation, but while he was on passage the British Army radioed him and asked if they could have his ketch for the 1973 Whitbread/RNSA Round the World Race. For this race the *British Steel* became the *British Soldier*, while Chay Blyth and his crew of nine raced the 72ft *Great Britain II* over the different sections of the course from port to port.

This Round the World Race was in four legs, and the ketch *Great Britain II* was placed first in the finishing order, but was sixth on handicap. The *Great Britain II* was built of foam sandwich construction by Derek Kelsall of Sandwich, Kent, and financed by Jack Hayward, the patriotic Englishman who had paid for the steamer *Great Britain* to be brought back from the Falkland Islands. He also gave Lundy Island to the Nation.

Jack Hayward backed Chay Blyth in his attempt to set up an Atlantic east to west yacht crossing record in the trimaran *Great Britain III*. Chay Blyth and Rob James managed to achieve the record when they won the 1981 Observer-Europe Two-handed Transatlantic Race in the 66ft trimaran *Brittany Ferries* GB. They covered the 3,000 miles from Plymouth to Rhode Island in 14 days, 13 hours and 54 minutes.

Although not as long as the ocean races, *The Observer* Round Britain Single-Handed Race is an equally gruelling affair. The first race was won in eleven days in 1966 by Derek Kelsall sailing his trimaran *Toria*. At his yard at Sandwich, Derek Kelsall constructed the 56ft *Sir Thomas Lipton* in which Geoffrey Williams won the 1968 Single-handed Transatlantic Race against thirty-four competitors from nine different countries. These very large yachts for ocean races are now mostly built under sponsorship, but Geoffrey Williams joined the Ocean Youth Club after his win and helped them to replace their fleet of traditional yachts with the powerful 65ft sail training ketches based on the *Sir Thomas Lipton*.

The first woman to sail single-handed non-stop round the world was Naomi James. She left Dartmouth on 9 September 1977 in the sloop *Express Crusader* and returned 272 days later. Around the same time,

The Great Britain III, *the largest fibreglass trimaran built, was launched from Wicormarine, Portchester. She made an unsuccessful attempt to beat the North Atlantic crossing record* (Ajax News Photos)

Shane Acton was completing his round the world voyage in the smallest craft yet to get round. Acton left Cambridge in 1972 in his tiny 18ft sloop *Super Shrimp*, and made his way down to the sea at King's Lynn where this former Royal Marine had to learn how to sail. The eight-year voyage in the engineless *Super Shrimp* was a leisurely one. The route taken was via the Panama and Suez canals and finally back to a tremendous welcome at Cambridge.

Most of these outstanding ocean voyages made by British yachts have been made in conventional single-hulled craft. In spite of their incredible speed off the wind, multi-hulls have not yet proved very successful in ocean racing, but they usually put up a very good performance in the Round the Island (of Wight) Race. Also Britain has a gifted multi-hull designer in Rod Macalpine-Downie who has been closely connected with the International C Class catamaran trophy which has become known as the 'Little America's Cup' because it was chiefly contested against America and Australia. Rod Macalpine-Downie designed and sailed some cats, particularly *Lady Helmsman*, which won the Little America's Cup. Macalpine-Downie worked closely with multi-hull helmsman and builder Reg White of Brightlingsea, and it was White who won a gold medal sailing one of his catamarans at the 1976 Olympic Games.

In 1971 the RYA held some trials at Burnham-on-Crouch to find the fastest craft under sail. Following this, an annual speed week was organised at Portland Harbour, and Norwich newspaper-owner Timothy Colman commissioned Rod Macalpine-Downie to design the 60ft proa *Crossbow* especially for sailing at high speeds on just one tack. The *Crossbow*, which was little more than a couple of floats and a sail, astonished everyone when, in a 19-knot breeze, she reached 26·3 knots. It took a further ten years of work to increase this world speed record under sail by another 10 knots. First, in 1977, the 74ft *Crossbow II*, a catamaran with a single sail on each hull, pushed the world record up to 31·8 knots over a half kilometre. But to get better winds Colman, Macalpine-Downie and the three crew which made up the team went to Portland in November 1980 after the official speed week. They remained there with *Crossbow II* for nearly two weeks, waiting for the right conditions and then, in gathering darkness late on November 17, with a wind gusting Force 8 and putting up a nasty sea, they made their final attempt. At times on the run they reached 45 knots which created a new world record of 36·04 knots (41·5mph).

The sail speed records never attracted the glamour that the power speed record did in the 1930s. High-speed power craft were mainly developed from the Royal Navy coastal motor boats (CMBs) of World War I which averaged between 30–40 knots. The water speed record created by Sir Henry Segrave in 1930 of 95 knots (110mph) was broken in 1932 by Lord Wakefield's Thornycroft designed and built *Miss England II*, achieving 104 knots (119·81mph). Next, Sir Malcolm Campbell took the record at 113 knots (130mph) with his *Bluebird*. However, at that speed Sir Malcolm felt this power boat was becoming unstable so he asked Vosper Ltd of Portsmouth to produce a craft capable of higher speeds. Vosper were then closely involved with the Admiralty in developing a motor torpedo boat (MTB), and they produced a prototype capable of 44 knots fully loaded with armaments, which had been proved seaworthy in a Force 7 gale in the English Channel. The managing director of Vosper from 1931 had been Commander Peter Du Cane who led Vosper on to become one of the world's forerunners in high-speed craft. The production of *Bluebird II* was a special 'one-off' job, designed to plane at speed on three surfaces in tricycle plan. This proved successful because in August 1939 Sir Malcolm Campbell created a new record of 123 knots (141·7mph). The lessons learnt in developing this record breaker caused Vosper to move into a new hard-chine hull form for fighting and working craft. They developed the MTB into a particularly effective small fighting boat and some 350 were built for the Admiralty and allied navies.

Of all the achievements in small craft in Britain, none can surely equal those undertaken by the men of the lifeboat service. Britain had the first lifeboat and the first organised lifeboat service, which became the model for most services started round the world. The first lifeboat came into existence in 1789 as a result of a loss of the *Adventure* at the entrance of the River Tyne. At that time there was a Gentleman's Club at South Shields and some of the members witnessed the pitiful loss of the *Adventure*. Like many ships in the coal trade, she was driven ashore off the Tyne and thousands stood on shore in a gale and watched the crew drop one by one from the rigging and drown. So appalled by this event were the gentlemen that they raised money for a special boat to be built which could go out in any weather to rescue people from a vessel in distress.

The boat built for the Tyne Lifeboat Society was the *Original*, which took her station in 1790 and remained in service on the Tyne for forty-one years. This lifeboat was built by Henry Greathead and a few years later another group of public-spirited men asked him to build a boat on the same lines to be stationed at the entrance of the River Tees. This was the 30ft *Zetland* which was built in 1802 and made her last rescue in 1880. She is preserved and on show at Redcar and is the oldest lifeboat in the world.

After the introduction of the first few independently operated lifeboats, it soon became obvious that a much larger and better organised service was needed to cover the whole of the British coastline. The effort in bringing together public interest to create the Royal National Lifeboat Institute in 1824 was largely due to Sir William Hillary. He lived on the Isle of Man and was appalled at the terrible loss of life every time a ship was wrecked there. As well as campaigning to create a lifeboat service which would cover every part of the British Isles, Hillary was actively engaged in saving lives. In 1830 the Royal Mail steamer *St George* was anchored in Douglas Bay in a gale when her anchor cable parted and she was driven ashore on the rocks.

The new Douglas lifeboat was not quite ready so Sir William Hillary induced sixteen men to go out with him to the wrecked paddle steamer. In the first attempt to put to sea Sir William and three other men were washed out of the boat. It was found that Sir William's chest was badly crushed and he had broken six ribs. However, he would not allow rescue efforts to be halted until all twenty-two crew had been taken off the *St George*.

Sir William Hillary assisted in the rescue of no fewer than 305 people from wrecks in the Douglas Bay area. The actual rescues required seamanship and courage, but steering the lifeboat service through its first early years was equally difficult. Many of the independent societies that were formed round the coast to operate lifeboats were very reluctant to hand over authority to a central organisation. From the start the lifeboat service concerned itself solely with saving lives by voluntary lifeboat men and they did not charge any fee for their service. The institution could never have become established if it had not worked on these principles because many fishermen and beachmen relied on shipwrecks for a living. Salvage companies of beachmen existed wherever shipping tended to congregate in the days of sail.

Such a group of beachmen existed at Deal; they relied on supplying goods for a living and doing ferry work for the hundreds of sailing ships which used to shelter in The Downs, an anchorage between the Kent coast and the Goodwin Sands. The Deal men used the 'great galleys' for salvaging. These powerful luggers were kept ashore on beaches and were launched when a vessel was seen in distress. In the early nineteenth century, the Deal luggers were primarily used for smuggling, but there was also some revenue to be had from the Post Office by taking out mail to the sailing ships which were lying windbound at the start of a voyage.

The Deal luggers were put out of business by steamers which no longer lay for weeks waiting for a favourable 'slant' of wind to take them down channel or up the North Sea. The same thing happened in the 1890s to the beach companies which had thrived on shipwrecks, particularly the colliers which were wrecked along the East Anglian coast. The beachmen banded together in co-operatives known under the old terms as

The Deal galley Undaunted, *built in about 1895, on Deal beach in 1981. The traditional craft of the south coast were usually varnished to show off the quality of the wood used* (Author)

'companies'. There were seven companies at Great Yarmouth and others at Lowestoft, Winterton, Palling, Happisburgh, Southwold, Thorpeness, Aldeburgh and Orford. The prime craft of each company was its beach yawl. These huge 70ft open two-masted dipping luggers were credited with 14 knots on a broad reach. The merchant seamen hated these yawls since whenever the wind picked up, out came the 'salvage sharks' in their powerful white-sailed luggers, in search of a poor sailing ship in trouble.

By the early twentieth century pickings from salvaging had become so poor that the beach yawls were left to rot on the open beaches and the task of saving life was continued by lifeboats. One of the best-known coxswains in the long history of the RNLI has been Henry Blogg of Cromer, a crab and lobster fisherman who personally assisted in the rescue of 873 people. He served for fifty-three years in the Cromer lifeboat and retired in 1947 at the age of seventy-seven after thirty-eight years as coxswain. Blogg won his first RNLI gold medal in 1917 when he took the Cromer pulling (rowing) lifeboat out twice in a north-easterly gale to rescue the crews of steamers. The autumn of 1927 saw a succession of severe gales sweeping along the east coast and it was in one of these that Blogg took the new motor lifeboat *H. F. Bailey* out to the steamship *Georgia* which was ashore on the Haisborough Sands.

When the Cromer lifeboat reached the steamer, it was almost dark and a huge sea was running in the roaring gale. The seas were breaking right over the steamer, but Blogg knew that the fifteen men aboard her stood little chance of survival if they were left until the following day. He took the risk of going in over the sandbank with the sea boiling wildly all around and went right alongside the wreck. The lifeboat, which is now on display at Thorpe Water Park, Surrey, was damaged, but it got away safely with the whole crew of the steamer.

8

The Shipbuilders

From earliest times the people around the coast of Britain built ships to supply local needs. Shipbuilding was not really specialised in any one place until the Tudor period, when it developed on suitable sites in southern England. The rise of England as a maritime power in the Elizabethan period was the reason for the expansion of shipbuilding. The shipbuilders looked for a piece of reasonably flat land on which to build their vessels, and this had to be beside deep water so that the vessel could be launched safely. Next they needed a plentiful and cheap supply of timber. For centuries great wooden ships were built with an almost total lack of machinery. All the master shipbuilders and their shipwrights possessed were a collection of simple tools and their own skills. Planks were cut in a saw pit in which one man stood on top to guide the cut and another, on the bottom of the saw, pushed the saw up and down. It was incredibly hard work and sawyers had a reputation for being great beer drinkers.

Shipbuilding was always a highly speculative occupation. The shipbuilder had to construct a vessel which the customer could afford to buy. Often when the ship was being built on a set contract, the price of materials rose during construction and the shipbuilders made a loss. On some occasions the customer could no longer pay for the ships they had ordered when they were completed. Bankruptcy amongst shipbuilders was always high, and shipwrighting in the days of wooden ships was a nomadic occupation.

The builder needed some form of measurement to fix the size of the vessel when discussing a proposed ship with a future owner, and it became the practice to describe a ship's size in tons. The origin of ton came from the word 'tun', meaning barrel, used to transport wine. A ship was described as being able to load so many tuns or the equivalent in size or weight. By the Elizabethan era, ships were usually referred to in tons burden, meaning the number of tons a ship could carry as cargo. The tonnage of the ship became a measurement of cubic space within a ship's hull; it had nothing to do with the actual weight of the vessel. Early tonnage measurements were rather vague and often distorted. Merchants wanted small ships to avoid custom dues and the navy wanted ships to be as large as possible to impress their enemies.

Wooden sailing ships could be built wherever there was a reasonable depth of water in to which to launch them. This is the brigantine Gleaner *being completed at Hugh Town in the Isles of Scilly in 1878. She was the last sizeable ship built in this small bay, open to the Atlantic. The warehouses have been pulled down and there is now no trace of this shipyard* (Author's Collection)

Parliament made many attempts to fix a reliable formula for arriving at a vessel's tonnage, and information on ships' sizes became progressively more accurate after 1660 when better records were kept of the ships of the Royal Navy. A tonnage measurement act was brought in for merchant ships in 1720. A new measurement system was introduced in 1835, which reduced the tonnage by about a third from the previous formula. However, an act of 1854 introduced reliable forms of tonnage measurement, of which the gross ton is the most useful. A ton is the equivalent of 100 cubic feet, and in gross tons this includes all the ship's hull space and deck houses. Net tons are just the cargo-carrying hold space and is roughly the equivalent of tons burden.

In the English fleet which defeated the Spanish Armada in 1588 the average size of ship was 360 tons. These were the largest merchant ships sent by the leading ports around the coast. About a quarter of the English fleet were over 600 tons, while the *Ark Royal*, the flagship, was described as being 800 tons, and was roughly 150ft long.

Not much is known about the size of the *Golden Hind*, the vessel in which Drake sailed round the world, except that she once paid dues on 150 tuns. However, after the famous voyage, Elizabeth I ordered the *Golden Hind* to be placed on display to the public in a dock at Deptford. She was there for nearly 100 years before being broken up, and part of her timber is now in the Great Hall at Buckland Abbey. Measurements taken of the dock in Deptford suggest that the *Golden Hind* was around 75ft overall length which would have been a ship of 100 tons.

The exact origin of the *Golden Hind*, which started the voyage as the *Pelican*, has never been discovered. There is a strong suggestion that she was a prize taken in some previous privateering venture. Certainly she represents the stage in ship development when the carrack, of Mediterranean origin, had given way to the faster and more easily manoeuvrable galleons. A reasonable impression of an Elizabethan galleon is given by the replica *Golden Hinde* which was built in Appledore, Devon, in 1973.

The replica *Golden Hinde* was built to plans drawn up after a great deal of research; it is doubtful whether plans were drawn up for the original vessel. Sometimes a model or half model was made so that the builders and owners were agreed on what the future vessel should look like. The more common method was for an owner to say the particular size of vessel he required for a certain trade. The builder then produced a hull which he thought would meet the owner's requirements. This method of building 'by eye' was common in small shipyards and boatbuilding shops which turned out small traders, fishing boats and yachts, right up to World War I. Indeed, many boatbuilders can still build without plans, although it is seldom done now for decked craft.

The original *Golden Hind* would have been built out in the open by shipwrights using hand tools, while the replica was built in a shed with the use of power tools. The builders of the replica *Golden Hinde* were J. Hinks & Son of Appledore, a family-owned yard similar to many others found round the coast. This yard traces its origins back to Henry Hinks who started boatbuilding in the town in 1844. Henry Hinks won the prize of 100 guineas in a RNLI competition in 1851 to produce a new lifeboat design. The old Hinks Yard was in amongst the waterside houses of Appledore and here they built fishing smacks and pilot cutters, but in the 1930s the yard was mainly producing yachts.

In common with a few other yards during the mid-1960s, Hinks, then run by Alan Hinks, the great-grandson of Henry Hinks, decided to keep to wooden hulls when fibre glass started to make an impact. It was this policy that won J. Hinks & Son their first order from the Hudson's Bay Company to build a replica of their first ship, the square-rigged ketch *Nonsuch*. Largely because of this order, Hinks moved to a new site just west of the little town of Appledore to gain more space.

The original *Nonsuch* had been built by Page at Wivenhoe, Essex, in 1650, and in 1668 a group of merchant venturers with influence at court sent her on a voyage from the Thames to trade with Canadian Cree Indians on the shores of the Hudson's Bay. The replica *Nonsuch* had planks and frames fastened with traditional 'trenals' (treenails). These were wooden pegs driven into hand-drilled holes. Much of the shaping of the wood was done with an adze, a kind of hand-held trimming axe. However, in order to save time, machine-sawn planks and some power tools were used on the *Nonsuch* replica. The significant difference was that the replica *Nonsuch* was built in a covered shed while before World War II wooden shipbuilding took place out in the open and workmen were laid off in bad weather. It was quite usual for a wooden-hulled vessel to be standing for years out in the open before it was completed.

For instance, in 1911, the Harwich barge builder McLearon signed a contract with a Mistley shipowner Fred Horlock to build a large spritsail barge *Redoubtable*, still active as the *David Gestetner*, yet she was not completed and launched for four years. Obviously wooden hulls could have been completed a great deal quicker, but this slow rate of building was a financial safeguard. The builder put his men on to ship repair and maintenance work for which he was paid fairly quickly and only concentrated on building a new hull when this work was slack.

From the Elizabethan period until the mid-nineteenth century—the great wooden shipbuilding era—the River Thames was probably the most continuously important centre of shipbuilding in the British Isles. Timber was not only being brought from the English forests: soft woods came from the Baltic for spars and hard wood came from the East by the eighteenth century. It was not just the Royal Dockyard at Woolwich which made the Thames the centre, but the East India Company was so successful that within nine years of having received its charter, the company had opened its own yard at Deptford. Their first ship, the 1,100-ton *Trade's Increase*, was launched in 1609 and was then the largest British merchant vessel ever built. The *Trade's Increase* proved something of a problem because of her size, and leaked badly.

The East India Company held a complete monopoly over all overseas trade with India from 1600 and the company made vast profits by trading with the Indian sub-continent, but it later divided its shipbuilding activities between the Thames and Bombay. Gabriel Snodgrass was the surveyor of the East India Company who, in 1791, proposed that ships would be stronger with iron knees—brackets which held the deck beams to the side frames. This was done in 1810 and later iron spikes and bolts started to replace the treenails. These iron spikes were highly successful in the Indian built ships because the eastern hard woods did not corrode the iron as fast as English oak, which is more acid.

In 1634, while King Charles I was visiting his dockyard at Woolwich, he instructed Phineas Pett to build a very large warship. The body responsible for marking navigation round the coast, Trinity House, protested vigorously that no vessel of the size proposed could possibly be navigated in English waters. Neither the cost, nor the fact that she might be too large to sail in confined waters, deterred Charles I from having his giant ship. Work started on the ship in 1636 and the following year the 170ft, 1,637-ton *Sovereign of the Seas* was launched. This huge warship was still steered by a whipstaff tiller controlled by tackles and was lavishly decorated with gilded carvings, but she was not just a prestige symbol because she was never defeated in battle. She had cost £65,586 when the usual ship of 40 guns cost about £6,000.

The Pett family were deeply involved in shipbuilding and the Royal Dockyard on the Thames for a century from the time of Henry VIII. Peter Pett, son of Phineas, finally fell from favour ostensibly because he gave lucrative state offices to his relations. However, this was a normal practice and the reason for the Pett's loss of office was more a change in political power at court.

With the restoration of the monarchy in 1660, King Charles II rewarded all those who had aided his return from The Netherlands. One of those rewarded was Admiral Montagu, who became the Earl of Sandwich, and he installed his kinsman and protégé Samuel Pepys on the Navy Board as Clerk of the Acts. Pepys was a highly effective and devoted administrator who later rose to the responsible office of Secretary to the Admiralty. Pepys is chiefly remembered for his diaries which give a colourful picture of England in the seventeenth century.

The Thames was the heart of old London with eight miles of houses running along the shore, none of which had any protection against high tides. In theory the Lord Mayor and his water bailiff controlled the Thames, but in practice this was difficult to enforce among the hard swearing Wapping watermen. When Pepys visited the royal dockyards, he travelled down the Thames in the Navy Board barge but the normal form of transport at that time was a waterman's skiff. Going down the Thames at that time meant passing between banks lined with shipyards and wharves which were only exceeded in size by Amsterdam.

By the mid-seventeenth century Britain's merchant fleet claimed to have 10,000 sail employing 170,000 seamen. Pepys was aware that this outburst of energy had begun only a century before, with the Elizabethan seamen. He devoted a great deal of effort into finding old manuscripts and one of those he rescued was Baker's 'Fragments of Ancient English Shipwrightry'. Pepys also collected and saved many of the builders' models from which the ships were constructed. In those times few people had an education. Pepys tells of seeing a Mayor of Bristol who pretended to read a pass, but it was upside down, and this was a difficulty encountered by shipbuilders who could not interpret a plan, but could work from a half model to see the hull shape. Some of the models Pepys saved had been made to send to the King and the Admiralty to acquire their approval before the ships were actually built. One of the earliest of these superb Admiralty models to survive is of the 100-gun *Prince*, built in 1670. Pepys' great achievement was steering the Royal Navy's affairs through the tricky court politics and establishing sound administration. A well-known master shipwright of the seventeenth century was Sir Anthony Deane who was responsible for building three First Rate ships of war between 1670–5. With the Royal Navy steadily increasing in size, there were periodic demands for new ships, and to meet this demand, timber had to be shipped in from the country ports.

A new dockyard at Harwich was well placed to receive oak from the North Essex villages so that ships such as the Third Rate *Resolution* of 70 guns were built by Sir Anthony Deane at Harwich in 1667. Sawing up the timber to achieve the maximum use of each length and selecting the right tree to buy, was an important part of the shipbuilder's business. Phineas Pett started going a little further north of Harwich into the heavyland Framlingham district of Suffolk on timber buying expeditions. The shipyards in the St Clement's area of Ipswich had long drawn on this area for prime oak. Perhaps it was to avoid established local interest that Pett started shipping oak out through the smaller port of Woodbridge. Pett became very involved in Woodbridge, and it was due to his influence that eleven large ships were built there between 1625–38. One of these was the *Prosperous Mary* which was towed as a bare hull for about eighty miles from Woodbridge to Deptford for fitting out. Peter Pett followed his father as Master Shipwright at Chatham, but continued to steer contracts for small naval ships to Woodbridge builders. This ended when Pett ran into deep political trouble and was thrown out of office.

The King's ships were, when possible, built in the royal dockyards at Deptford, Woolwich, Chatham and after 1650 increasingly at Portsmouth and the depot at Harwich. The Hamble River was, in medieval times, the home of naval ships, but the deeper water of Portsmouth harbour was a better base. In 1495 Henry VII ordered the first dry dock in the country to be built at Portsmouth, sited near the present berth of

HMS *Victory*. However, it was not until 1690 that a major expansion programme at Portsmouth Dockyard turned it into the main Royal Navy base. Before the Industrial Revolution, the royal dockyards were some of the largest centres of employment in Britain. The Government was well aware that well-run dockyards were the basis of Britain's sea power. With the growth of this power, there was a tremendous amount of dockyard building between 1750–1832. While Pembroke Dockyard on Milford Haven was opened principally for shipbuilding and repairs in 1809, Plymouth Dockyard, which was renamed Devonport in 1824, had already been a long-standing base for naval ships in the western Atlantic and the Mediterranean.

Between 1689 and 1815, Britain was at war for sixty-five years, and between the wars there were periods of 'cold war', so for virtually half this period Britain was on a war footing and needed a continual stream of new fighting ships. The demand far outstripped the capability of the royal dockyards and men-of-war were being built for the Crown in many yards round the coast south of the Humber and up to the Mersey. The Navy Board Commissioners placed many contracts on the Hampshire coast in the knowledge that there was a better supply of good oak and other timbers in southern England than other areas.

Between 1690–1820, naval ships were built at thirteen sites in Hampshire outside the Portsmouth establishment, and the best known must be Buckler's Hard on the Beaulieu River. It was also a leading shipbuilding centre in Hampshire after Portsmouth because it was a good place to launch a hull. The hamlet of Buckler's Hard has a very wide 'street' and it is said that this was to facilitate the movement of large logs down to the shipyard. The Master Builder's house was the home of Henry Adams (1713–1804) who, like many of the Hampshire builders, had come down from the Thames to find fresh opportunities on the south coast.

At the height of Adams' lease of the yard he employed about thirty-five shipwrights and other unskilled labourers, making a work force of at least ninety at Buckler's Hard. The practice in Hampshire was similar to that of the east coast contractors who were building for the Navy Board: a bare hull was launched which was then towed to a royal dockyard for fitting out. There is a record of a hull taking four days to be towed by rowing boat from Buckler's Hard to Portsmouth. The hull was of course anchored when the tide was against them and for the men to sleep.

At the time of the War of American Independence, Adams was continually building navy vessels, notably the Third Rate 64-gun, 160ft *Agamemnon* of 1,376 tons in 1781. The *Agamemnon* was known to her lower deck crew as 'Am & Eggs' and earned a place in history as Nelson's favourite ship. He commanded her as captain and then commodore in the Mediterranean between 1793–6. Adams even managed to win the contract to build two East Indiamen. This said much for the quality of the yard's work because the East Indiamen were then Britain's finest merchantmen and the Thames builders had almost a monopoly of their construction. However, Adams was at one time a partner in the yard at Deptford, which has left problems for historians who set themselves the task of sorting out which ships he built in Hampshire and which he built on the Thames.

Hampshire's days as a shipbuilding centre were over by 1815, and already the north of England was rising as a major shipbuilding area. Even though Adams and others built ships-of-the-line, at the peak of the area's activity only 208 shipwrights were employed in Hampshire and the Isle of Wight. In the whole of Britain in 1804, there were only 8,621 shipwrights and apprentices in private yards. The shipwrights were always the highest paid men in the yards and they banded together to protect this position. In 1260 a Guild of Free Shipwrights of London had been formed and they, like many workers' organisations, became over-protective by limiting membership, so a rival Company of Shipwrights of Rotherhithe was started and received a charter in 1605. For many decades there was bitter feuding between these craftsmen's societies, but in 1703 they managed to unite and establish the Shipwright's Hall at Stepney. The two societies later merged into a livery company at London under the present name of the Worshipful Company of Shipwrights.

In times of war, when the demand for ships suddenly increased, there was always a shortage of skilled shipwrights, but in the eighteenth and early nineteenth centuries, many thinking people were deeply concerned at the rate that good timber was being used up. The 100-gun First Rater HMS *Victory*, launched at Chatham in 1769, required at least 3,000 trees for her hull. Of these, about 700 were large, fully mature oak trees. These trees did not come from one place, but the construction of a ship-of-the-line meant clearing at least two hundred acres of prime timber. Had this space been replanted immediately, which seldom happened, it would have taken 80–120 years to produce another crop of oak trees. Even when the oak was felled, it had to be seasoned for about ten years. Shipbuilding demanded the best timber; for sections of the hull like the keel, giant English elm was used because this provided good holding for fastenings and providing it was always immersed it did not 'move'. As there simply were not enough good trees available to keep up with the demands of British yards, imported timber and hulls from the Canadian Maritime Provinces filled the gap, but shipbuilding in Britain during the nineteenth century ran into a crisis through lack of suitable materials.

The desire for larger ships exacerbated the problem, as did the need for ships travelling to the tropics to have their underwater planks sheathed with copper to prevent worm from eating them away. By the 1820s, the use of iron for knees, pillars and deck beams was becoming increasingly common. Several experimental iron-hulled ships were built, but finally the *Great Britain* proved conclusively to the conservative shipping world that iron was stronger than wood. But still the move towards all metal hulls was surprisingly slow. In the 1850s the building of iron steamers on the River Wear at Sunderland was increasing, and the long-established coal-mining districts began to produce more fuel for making iron and then steel. These two factors contributed towards the growth of shipbuilding. However, the shipbuilders of the Thames adapted very quickly to new designs. For example, R. & H. Green at their Blackwall yard built the first British clipper the *Challenger* in 1851. This yard had previously built East Indiamen and then the Blackwall frigates which were the fastest armed merchantmen until they were replaced by the clippers in the China Trade. The Thames Ironworks and Shipbuilding Company at Blackwall switched to new techniques, and it was there in 1860, that the 9,000-ton HMS *Warrior*, Britain's first ironclad warship was built. Brunel had his monster iron *Great Eastern* built at Millwall in 1855, but the cost of transporting materials was beginning to put the Thames' yards at an economic disadvantage. The last large ship launched on the Thames was the battleship HMS *Thunderer* in 1910.

Coal was sometimes referred to by old sailors as being 'black diamonds', with good reason for it helped to amass a great amount of capital in the north-east of England, some of which was reinvested in new ships to carry yet more coal. The expanding coal trade made the River Wear a major shipbuilding centre. Wooden ships were built there, but when iron came in the Wear was able to undercut the wooden shipbuilders in the south of England.

The little country ports like Woodbridge which had been building schooners in early Victorian times were put out of business. The Lime Kiln Yard at Woodbridge launched its last schooner, the *Ellen*, in 1853 and the town saw little building until yacht construction gained momentum just before World War I. Yet the mid-Victorian period was still the age of small ships working to small ports, even in the ocean trades. Wooden hulls suffered a great deal of strain from long ocean voyages, so when there was a great burst of trade to Britain's colonies in the 1870s–80s, there was a tremendous demand for small iron-hulled ships with square rig, which was the best for making use of the ocean trade winds system.

Typical of the iron sailing ships built was the 179ft, 640-ton barque

Clan Macleod (now the *James Craig*) which was launched from Bartram, Haswell & Co's yard at Sunderland in 1874. This yard grew from the venture of seven young shipwrights who banded together in 1837 and set up a business as shipbuilders. The partnership had no capital; the shipwrights just put in their own labour and the venture prospered. These shipwrights could not afford to employ any workmen so they started work at 4.0am in good weather in the summer and worked a fifteen hour day. In the winter they worked the more normal hours of 6.0am to 6.0pm. However, not all the shipwrights wanted to be involved in the management side and the partnership was dissolved, but Haswell had developed enough skill in the management side to borrow capital and start up on his own. Later he went into partnership with R. A. Bartram and they opened the yard at South Dock, Sunderland. This yard was highly unusual because it launched its vessels into the open North Sea, which had a slight advantage as the launching could take place in the worst weather while the numerous yards on the first four miles up the River Wear were sometimes blocked by ice.

The new company of Bartram, Haswell went straight into iron hulls, and the first vessel, the steamer *Ardmore* of Liverpool, was built in 1872. They then established a good relationship with Hine Brothers of Mayport and built several ships for their Australian trade. The reason that owners kept coming back to these yards was because of their reliable delivery dates: for instance, it was only two months from launching before the barque *Clan Macleod* was completely fitted out and had sailed, loaded with coal. The firm of Bartram, Haswell has long since faded away—shipbuilding has long been noted for its financial disasters. It is known that during a trade depression in about 1840, around forty yards at Sunderland went bankrupt. However, William Doxford managed to ride out this bad patch, and his business became William Doxford & Sons Ltd which was Sunderland's largest shipbuilding company. Their early successes included the contract to build HMS *Magician* in 1875. This was a screw corvette with 'composite' hull which had iron frames and wooden planking. This method of building was rather outdated even then, because it represented a type of construction which briefly bridged the gap between wooden and metal hulls. Composite was also important because it could be used by traditional yards which had not learnt plate-iron techniques.

(opposite) The Cunard liner Aquitania, *almost complete on John Brown's Clydebank yard. The keel was laid on 10 December 1911, and the liner was launched twenty-two months later, in April 1913* (National Maritime Museum)

The shipbuilders in the north-east of England built any type of vessel that was needed, but they were among the first to move away from sail to screw steamers. On the Tyne, Wear and Tees the major part of the output became freight carrying vessels, although the splendid liner *Mauretania* was launched from Swan Hunter on the Tyne in 1906. Swan Hunter grew by a series of amalgamations and its first known passenger ship was built in 1865. Over the next eighty-five years, the Tyneside building berths at Swan Hunter & Wigham Richardson Ltd built 216 passenger ships. The building of the *Mauretania* focused attention on the firm and the ship's success was a reflection of the firm's expertise in passenger ship construction. When the *Mauretania* returned to Swan Hunter in 1922 for a recondition, Sir George Hunter, the company chairman, called her the 'Queen of the Atlantic'. The 26-knot *Mauretania* lived up to this title by returning to her western ocean run and continued to be the holder of the Blue Riband of the Atlantic until 1929. She also created a record in 1931 by crossing the Atlantic four times in one month.

The use of iron and steel in ship construction concentrated shipbuilding near the coalfields. The one exception was the rise of Belfast in Northern Ireland as a major shipbuilding centre. In the mid-nineteenth century the town had a flourishing textile industry, but no real port for trade. Belfast is some fifteen miles inland at the head of Belfast Lough, and to create a port there a navigable channel was cut in the River Laggan. The mud from the channel created an island on the east of the channel and this was named Queen's Island, in honour of Queen Victoria's visit in 1849. Later a small shipyard was started on Queen's Island and in 1854 Edward Harland became the manager there.

The growth of Belfast shipbuilding was largely due to the fact that it was cheaper to move bulk materials by water than on land by rail. This meant that Belfast could import its raw materials from the industrial centres of western Scotland and the north-west of England more cheaply than the Thames yards. Also the textile industry employed women and girls so that several members of a family could find employment in the town. People flowed into Belfast in search of work and this gave the shipyard a reliable source of labour. Edward Harland took into partnership his chief draughtsman and two managers to form Harland & Wolff, the great Belfast shipbuilding firm. This team, a Yorkshireman, a Hamburg Jew and two Ulstermen, worked together for twenty years between 1874–94. It was the inventive engineering genius of Harland which created the three 270ft 'Bibby's coffins' steamers in 1859 which were the forerunners of a whole generation of long, lean-hulled steamships. Harland & Wolff later persuaded the Liverpool White Star Line to abandon their Australian routes and enter the North Atlantic with a 'long ship' liner, built to the length to beam ratio of about ten to one instead of the usual eight to one. This progressed to the 470ft, 14-knot, compound-engined *Oceanic* (I) which entered the North Atlantic trade in 1871.

The building of very large and heavy hulls caused problems on Queen's Island due to the ground sinking. To overcome this, thousands of tree trunks were fully sunk into the ground and the surface sheeted with heavy boiler plates. The White Star Line continued to return to Harland & Wolff for its new liners, and the firm also built all types of sailing merchant ships. To increase its financial backing to expand Queen's Island, Harland & Wolff became a joint-stock company. As well as shipbuilding, all sorts of allied industries sprung up in Belfast, particularly marine engines. When Sir Edward Harland died in 1895, Harland & Wolff were in the grips of a strike, yet thousands of shipyard workers turned out in the rain to walk behind the coffin to the city cemetery.

The fortunes of the Belfast shipbuilder fluctuated with the demand for ships. In 1970 Harland & Wolff launched a 250,000-ton tanker for Esso; at that time some 8,000 people were employed in shipbuilding and 4,000 in marine engineering in Belfast. While most of the world's new tonnage was being built in Japan, Harland & Wolff managed to win an order for four identical tankers from Shell. The first of the 313,000-ton, single screw, 15-knot oil tankers was the *Lampas* in 1975. Four years later Harland and Wolff's 840-ton crane *Samson* lifted the small steel trading schooner *Result* out of the water on the first stage of her eight-mile journey by land to the Ulster Folk & Transport Museum at Cultra. The 102ft *Result* had been built lower down Belfast Lough on the County Antrim shore at Carrickfergus. In the mid-nineteenth century wooden shipbuilding was being carried out in the Carrick yard, when it was owned by Robert Johnson who later employed his son-in-law Paul Rodgers as shipyard manager. Rodgers had a great talent for designing yachts and schooners, and eventually took over the yard. His first vessel was the wooden schooner *Accrington Lass*, built for Fleetwood owners in 1874. Rodgers was noted for the repetition of successful lines in later vessels. This was in an age when most builders of small sailing vessels were working virtually by eye or from a model rather than from hull drawings.

In 1885 Rodgers, who had been using steel frames in his wooden hulls for several years, switched to all metal hulls. Between 1874–93 Rodgers built twenty-nine vessels at Carrickfergus, mostly schooners, but also two barquentines and two steamships. His most important customer was James Fisher & Sons of Barrow-in-Furness for whom he built twelve three-masted topsail schooners between 1880–92. During the latter part of this time, Rodgers was experiencing difficulties in financing his yard and was forced to go out of business before the *Result* was completed. The schooner was completed to the highest classification, Lloyd's survey 100 AI, by Robert Kent & Co of Ayr, who replaced the old patent slip and deepened the finishing dock at Carrickfergus, only to bankrupt themselves.

The firm which built, between 1885–95, more merchant sailing ships than any other concern in the world was Russell & Co who had three yards on Clydeside, two at Port Glasgow and one at Greenock. Their speciality during this time was building four-masted barques, and it is said that Russells once had thirty new sailing ships in their yards at some point of construction. In 1892 records show that Russells built twenty-nine new sailing ships. Russells were swallowed up by the Scott Lithgow group, but the construction of 2,000-ton barques on the Clyde tailed off once the balance was tipped in favour of steamers after the introduction, in 1897, of triple expansion engines fed by high pressure boilers. Before this, steamers were still too hungry on coal to be economic on long ocean voyages, but this breakthrough enabled a steamer to carry in three years the same tonnage that a sailing ship could carry in ten years. Inevitably sailing vessels disappeared rapidly.

Shipbuilding had now become closely linked with heavy engineering to

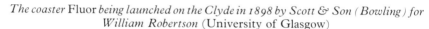

The coaster Fluor *being launched on the Clyde in 1898 by Scott & Son (Bowling) for William Robertson* (University of Glasgow)

Wood Skinner's Bill Quay yard, Newcastle-upon-Tyne, in about 1889. The steamers Tonsberg, Angelus, Skarpsno *and* Active *can be seen under construction on the slipways* (National Maritime Museum)

supply the engines and machinery, and the two industries progressed together. Sir Charles Parsons invented the turbine, a form of marine engine which used steam under high pressure to drive angled blades on propellers. The world's first turbine vessel was Parsons' experimental 100ft launch *Turbinia*, built at Wallsend-on-Tyne in 1894. The Admiralty eventually became interested in the new form of propulsion, and Admiral Fisher showed great faith by ordering the first two turbine destroyers, *Viper* and *Cobra*, in 1899. It was the success of these that convinced Admiral Sir John Fisher, the great naval administrator, to include turbines in the new breed of capital battleship starting with HMS *Dreadnought* in 1906.

Dennys of Dumbarton fitted a turbine in the Clyde ferry *King Edward* in 1901. She was a great success and Allan Line of Glasgow built the turbine liner *Victorian* for the Canadian services in 1905. Cunard fitted turbines to the liner *Carmania* in 1905 which proved faster than her sister ship *Caronia* with a quadruple-expansion engine. Following this Cunard ordered the express liners *Lusitania* and *Mauretania* to be built with turbines.

By 1900, yards in the Clyde and the north-east of England were producing about 80 per cent of all new vessels built in British yards. Belfast was thriving and so too was Barrow-in-Furness, where the industry was coming under the control of Vickers who built all types of ships, but later specialised in submarines. A fall-off in world trade in 1907 caused fewer orders from foreign shipowners and 8,000 shipbuilders found themselves out of work in Sunderland. However, trade recovered, and in 1912 Doxford launched the *Cairnross* on the Wear which was the first pure cargo ship to have turbine machinery. She was 7,800 deadweight tons which was a typical size of merchantman being built then.

When Doxford launched two 540ft, 10,064-ton gross tankers in 1913 and 1914, they were the largest ships that had been launched on the Wear. In 1914 a total of seventy-four new ships were launched from Wearside yards. When World War I broke out in 1914, many shipyard workers left to join the army. This led to a cronic shortage of skilled labour in the shipyards, and in 1915 only thirty-one ships were built. This mistake was not repeated in World War II when shipyard work became a reserved occupation to prevent conscription into the forces. The shortage of shipping due to the success of the German Navy's submarine campaign in 1917 almost starved Britain into defeat. The world war forced Britain to evolve the standard ship, built under mass-production methods. World War I saw two main types being built: the 400ft, 8,175-ton, single screw 'A' type standard cargo ship and the 'B' type of standard ship which was about 100 tons smaller. Both types carried the prefix *War* in their name.

During World War I, Thompson's built ten standard ships. The firm of J. L. Thompson & Sons was founded in 1846, but the Thompson family had been building wooden sailing ships on the Wear since 1819. They started constructing iron steamers in 1871 at their yard at North Sands, Sunderland. Thompsons, Doxfords, Laings and Crowns were the firms to remain partly active through the inter-war years on the Wear. A brief mention of the numbers of ships gives a clear picture of shipbuilding in Britain during the Depression. In 1918 sixty ships were launched on the River Wear and this fell dramatically to only three in 1930. By 1939 the number had only risen to nine, and grass grew on the berths where ships had been built in Victorian times. The humming, hammering sound of riveting no longer echoed down the Wear and the streets of the town were full of men who had 'signed the book' at the employment exchange.

In the 1930s British shipbuilders created the National Shipbuilders Security Ltd with their own capital. The intention of this organisation was to buy up small yards and concentrate production in the efficient and progressive yards. The NSS closed and dismantled 116 building berths on the Wear in three years, and a total of 684 in Britain. This was bitterly opposed by many local councils who saw little hope of employment ever being brought back into their towns. Of course until there were orders for new ships, there was very little that anyone could do. However, in the late

1930s the Government started making available subsidies for construction to the owners of cargo liners, tramp steamers and coasters so orders started to come in slowly.

In the late 1930s there was also a slight build-up of naval vessels as the Government became more alarmed by Hitler's ambitions. The 22,000-ton aircraft carrier *Ark Royal* was built by Cammell Laird at Birkenhead in 1935 and two years later the Admiralty building programme included six 36-knot, 348ft 'Kelly' class fleet destroyers. When World War II began, every yard went into full production and on the River Wear all previous shipbuilding records were broken: in the five years of World War II, the yards along just four miles of narrow river produced over a quarter of the total output of Britain's shipyards.

During World War II the largest number of submarines that the German Navy managed to place in the North Atlantic at any one time was sixty, but the result was that over 3,000 merchant vessels and over 100 naval vessels were sunk in the Battle of the Atlantic. In the first nine months of the war 150 Allied ships were sunk. In September 1940, a British Merchant Shipbuilding Mission went to the United States to order new merchant ships. The Mission took to America the plans of the *Dorington Court*, built and designed by J. L. Thompson & Sons at Sunderland in 1939. In the United States these plans were used as a basis for producing what became known as the standard 'Liberty' ship, while British yards rushed through standard 'Empire' and 'Victory' ships.

The war brought about other radical changes to shipbuilding. Swan Hunter's had one woman naval architect before the war, but generally speaking before 1939 there were no women working in the shipyards. During the war a large percentage of the workforce became female, although it seems that most were quite happy to leave this rough work when peace time came. There was also an increase in the use of prefabrication and welding.

The method of constructing iron and steel ships had been to fasten the plates to the frame with rivets. The usual practice was to drill out the hole and put in the rivets which had been heated red hot. The outer side of the plate had been countersunk so that the rivet head could be hammered flush and the other end was also hammered in to make it hold. Even this did not make a watertight fit so the ends had to be further flattened when the rivet had cooled.

The first all-welded hull was the SS *Fullager* built by Cammell Laird at Birkenhead in 1920, but the Depression seems to have halted the widespread adoption of welding. The necessity to mass produce hulls caused welding to be adopted on a great scale by the end of World War II. This was hastened by the use of women in the shipyards because they found welding easier than riveting, even though automatic tools were used for hammering. Although Whites of Cowes did some of the experimental work with welded hulls early in World War II, they accepted the order to build what was probably the last riveted hull to be constructed in a British yard. This was the Trinity House tender *Winston Churchill* in 1962. It seems that the conservative approach of Trinity House at the time led to them insisting on the tried and tested method of hull riveting.

The American-built Liberty ships became the best-known example of mass-produced vessels of World War II, but the desperate shortage of tonnage led the British yards to Standard Ships in both world wars. After World War II there was a tendency to use a series of standard hulls in order to reduce costs. By 1979 over a hundred SD 14 cargo ships had been built to the same design on the River Wear. The Bartram South Dock yard built fifty-four SD 14s in unbroken sequence while Austin & Pickersgill built them continually for ten years.

Yards which relied on orders for one-off ships were finding it increasingly hard to survive. In 1976 the bulk beer carrier *Miranda Guinness* was launched at Bristol, the last in a long line of ships built in the shipyard founded by James Martin Hilhouse in 1760. The original yard was on the North Bank of the River Avon, but in 1820 Hilhouse & Hill moved to the Albion Dockyard, a ten acre site on the south side of the Floating Harbour (which was built in the original course of the Avon). The yard became Charles Hill & Sons, and it was one of the daughters of the family, Favell, who officially named the barque *Favell* when she was launched in 1895. This was the last square-rigged sailing ship built at Bristol and she was constructed for Hill's Bristol City Line.

While the straight-stemmed, single tall funnel steamers replaced the sailing ships in the ocean trades, there was competition amongst shipbuilders to produce a type of vessel to replace the schooners in the coastal trades. The steam driven engines used too much coal to be economical in small cargo vessels, but the new oil powered internal combustion engines seemed to offer a better source of power. In 1905 James Pollock, who had started a firm of naval architects in London, pioneered the fitting of hot-bulb oil engines in coasters. His son, Walter Pollock, started a shipyard in about 1915 at Faversham, Kent, which concentrated on building small motor vessels.

Walter Pollock started in 1934 the 'Landina' class of motor coaster which became very popular. Before the yard closed in 1970, when it was run by Walter's son Marshall Brook Pollock, it was also building tugs. Strangely James Pollock & Sons Ltd are remembered for two of their most unsuccessful coasters, the 125ft, concrete-hulled *Molliette* and *Violette* in

1918–19. The technique of concrete hulls reinforced with steel was first discovered in 1848, but it was the steel shortage of World War I that forced the adoption of ferro-cement hulls.

Walter Pollock designed the *Molliette* and the *Violette* as auxiliary coasters that could load about 300 tons. They were rigged as three-masted schooners, besides having centrally situated 120hp two-cylinder Bolinder engines. Both coasters proved thoroughly troublesome: the *Molliette* was run down and sunk in the River Colne, while the *Violette* finished her brief trading career by getting stuck after colliding with Southend Pier in 1921. Her hull was towed back to Faversham, but in the mid-1970s she was still lying at Hoo on the River Medway. Although there were considerable problems with the design of these early ferro-cement craft, there is little doubt that the material itself is very strong and durable.

Due to the effective German submarine campaign, 150,000 tons of reinforced concrete shipping were built in Britain and America in 1917–22. Yards were set up all over Britain to produce ferro-cement hulls, at such places as Barrow, on the River Wear, Blackell's yard at Thornaby-on-Tees and Whitehall on the River Esk above Whitby. Some reinforced concrete steamers took coal across the North Atlantic, while the Admiralty ordered twelve ferro-cement ocean-going tugs powered by triple expansion engines and twin boilers working on forced draught. It does not seem as if any of these ferro-cement vessels survived the run-down of shipping which followed in the 1920s. However, six of these tugs were used commercially with two concrete lighters to take coal from the Tyne to the continental ports.

Building in ferro-cement was largely a necessity created by the war. Shipbuilders have to be very flexible and produce what circumstances demand. The growth of coaster building on the River Medway is linked with the expansion of the fleet of Crescent Shipping Ltd. The company's flag, the crescent in a red background, was the house flag of the Gill family whose fortunes began with George Gill, who started as a builder of sailing barges at Chatham, Kent, in 1858. In search of more space, Gill moved to Bridge Yard, Rochester, and it was there in 1887 that Gill & Sons built the barge yacht *Dinah*. This little barge is still afloat, but the paddle steamers *City of Rochester* and *Lady of Lorne* which were very much the pride of Gill's productions, have long since been broken up.

Through a series of mergers, the Gill yards became part of the largest sailing barge-owning company on the east coast, but at the Quarry Yard, Frindsbury, they continued to repair and build their own sailing barges. The 73-ton *Cabby*, launched from the Quarry Yard in 1928, was the last full-sized wooden barge to be built. There was then a gap of thirty-three

The coastal vessel Rohoy *being launched at the Quarry yard, Frindsbury, on the River Medway in 1965* (Crescent Shipping)

years before a steel motor coasting vessel, *Rock*, was launched from Quarry Yard. Building continued after this but none of the new motor craft bore much resemblance to the sailing barge, instead the square counter sterns of these Medway coasting craft show a clear resemblance to the old concrete coaster *Molliette* which had been launched at Faversham some forty years previously.

Crescent Shipping's repair and building yard at Frindsbury was not affected by nationalisation of the major part of the British shipbuilding and marine engineering industry in 1977. Not many shipowning companies operate shipyards; the two enterprises are usually totally separate, but as well as Crescent Shipping, another east coast shipping company, F. T. Everard & Sons of Greenhithe, have their own repair yard. The firm was started with a single sailing barge in the 1880s and the best-known sailing barges they built were *Hibernia* and *Cambria* in 1906; the latter is now open to the public in St Katharine's Dock, London. Everards started to create a fleet of motor coasters by purchasing existing vessels. Many of their new coasters since the 1930s have been built in Humberside by the Goole Shipbuilding & Repairing Company Ltd, a long-established firm which became part of the Swan Hunter group.

The growth of interest in restoring traditional sailing craft has saved some old barge building yards on the east coast from extinction. For underwater work, a flat-bottomed barge can only be worked on while it sits on 'blocks', as it is only then, at low tide, that it is possible to get underneath. Cook's yard at Maldon became the mecca for people wanting to restore barges. The yard appears to have been started in 1894 by two cousins, James Woodward, who did the actual barge building, and Walter Cook. They built the *Dawn* (1897), *Lord Roberts* (1900), and *British King* (1901), which are all still afloat, before the partnership broke up, Walter Cook continuing with barge repairs. Walter's son, Clifford, continued to run the yard until, by the late 1960s when he retired, it was one of the last barge repair yards. Then two barge enthusiasts bought the yard and Clifford Cook stayed as technical adviser to pass on the skills he had acquired in a lifetime of repairing wooden sailing barges.

Alf Last, one of the shipwrights at the yard, worked in the collection of weather-boarded sheds on the banks of the Blackwater all his life. He went there when he was fourteen and Walter Cook told him he could have the job on a trial period. Fifty-one years later, Alf Last remarked to the author one day that he never was told if he was going to be kept on permanently.

The Dock End Yard at Ipswich is another place where traditional skills are kept alive. Used since World War II, the slip was originally part of the neighbouring St Clements Yard where, until 1885, fast barquentines and

Shipwrights making a new windlass knee in the hold of the sailing barge Ethel Ada. *This barge was built at Paglesham, Essex, in 1903 and as most of the timbers were in a poor state seventy-five years later, a major rebuild was required to save her* (East Anglian Daily Times)

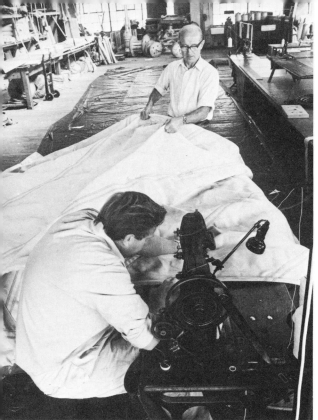

Sailmakers at Whitmores, Ipswich, finishing off a new jib for the sailing barge Dannebrog *in 1978* (East Anglian Daily Times)

The anti-submarine carrier HMS Ark Royal *being launched from Swan Hunter's Wallsend yard, Newcastle-upon-Tyne, in June 1981. The British invention 'ski jump ramp' for flight take off can be seen clearly. This carrier was the fifth Royal Navy warship to bear the name* Ark Royal. *With the other two Invincible class vessels, these are the largest warships built for the Royal Navy since the 1950s, but the Government has decided not to put this carrier into commission yet* (Swan Hunter)

brigantines were built for the deep sea trades. After this small type of yard had lost deep sea work, they concentrated on sailing barges. In about 1900 Pauls, the owners of mills at the head of Ipswich Wet Dock, bought the Dock End Yard and six barges were built here, ending with the *Jock* in 1908. Because the Ipswich mill barges carried grain, a highly perishable cargo if it became wet, the barges had to be very well maintained at the Dock End Yard and a high percentage of those left afloat were once from Ipswich.

Below Ipswich Docks on the River Orwell is another active barge repair yard run by Ruben Webb at the delightful riverside hamlet of Pin Mill. The steady increase in the number of traditional barges has kept the repair yard business going, but Cook's yard at Maldon, run by Barry Pearce, has carried the revival a step further by building a new clinker bawley, *Marigold*, completed in 1981 on the lines of the *Lilian*, built in 1864, which has also been restored. The smell of fresh-sawn timber and the sight of men working skilfully attracted many to watch the new bawley taking shape.

While Cooks, Webbs and the Dock End Yard are commercial enterprises, the Dolphin Barge Yard Museum at Sittingbourne, Kent, is fulfilling the dual role of being a place where barges can be repaired and saved, and also where the public can visit a traditional yard. In 1971, when the Dolphin Yard was first opened as a working museum, it was just a few derelict buildings beside the narrow Milton Creek, where there had once been a major barge building area. From 1836 it is believed that around 500 barges were built on the two miles of Milton Creek and most of them served the cement and brickworks along the creek. Burley's Dolphin cement works was simply one of many, and the yard beside it repaired and built barges to carry away its products. The last of eight barges known to have been built there was the *Charles Burley*, in 1902, and after that only repair work was carried out. As the cement works closed, the barges disappeared and the yards became abandoned. When the Dolphin Yard reopened, it was in the middle of this abandoned industrial landscape.

Ship- and boat-building are particularly vulnerable to the laws of supply and demand. In the nineteenth century the availability of home-produced steel gave British shipbuilders a tremendous advantage. More efficient use of manpower and more flexible attitudes in foreign yards have produced tough competition for British shipyards. The idea of placing the nation's shipyards under state ownership was first seriously suggested by the Labour Government in 1945, when it was a political aim rather than a practical need. In the following thirty years the competition from foreign yards forced shipbuilders to ask for state support to keep them going. Between 1967–73 the volume of world trade doubled and shipyards were able to get orders for new ships. In 1973, after the oil crisis, there was a dramatic drop in the number of new ships ordered. The boom in building tankers ended almost overnight as oil prices rose steeply.

The Government was already giving cash grants to keep some yards open and was encouraging shipbuilding firms to group together to become more competitive. In 1974 a Labour Government won the election and decided to push ahead with nationalisation of the United Kingdom shipbuilding industry. This was bitterly opposed, but eventually it became law in March 1977. One major shipbuilding company that was not taken over by the Government was Harland & Wolff in Belfast, which had already come under the control of the Northern Ireland Office.

The shipbuilding industry became the state-owned British Ship-builders which has its headquarters at Newcastle-upon-Tyne, but nationalisation allowed the twenty-seven companies to divide into eleven

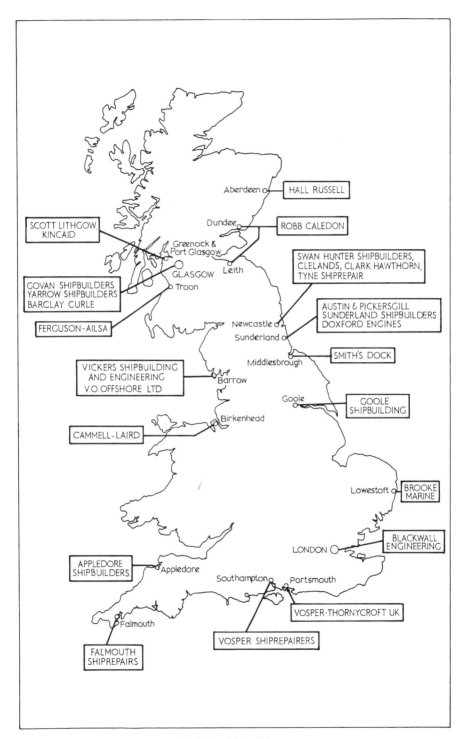

British shipbuilders

groups and continue operating more or less independently in their specialised fields. Nearly £200m has been spent on updating shipyard facilities. For example, the Pallion Yard of Sunderland Shipbuilders and the Appledore Shipbuilders in North Devon have been completely rebuilt as undercover ship factories with new building docks and outfitting shops. Covered building halls and berths have been built in the British Shipbuilders' yards in major centres in north-east England, Clydeside, Merseyside and Barrow-in-Furness. Many small firms in Britain also came under the state ownership.

In 1979 the Conservative Government was elected and they agreed to continue to subsidise British Shipbuilders along the same lines started by the Labour Government in 1977. One of the groups within British Shipbuilders which is making a determined effort to remain economically viable on its own initiative is Vosper Thornycroft, who have yards near Portsmouth and Southampton. These were originally two rival firms which built high-speed craft for the Royal Navy. Ships launched recently for the Royal Navy have included the destroyers *Nottingham*, *Southampton* and *Gloucester*, all built to the Ministry of Defence standards which dictate that a ship must last for thirty years and be capable of fighting a major action for twenty years after launching.

This Royal Navy standard, and the group's record for delivering ships ahead of contract date, has won a continual stream of orders from foreign navies. Good working relationships with the Brazilian Navy in 1970 led to orders for ten years' work. Vosper Thornycroft have specialised in small high-speed coastal craft, a type that many smaller countries need and can afford.

In 1980 British Shipbuilders produced virtually all the new warships built in the United Kingdom, and had in hand work for completing a further forty-three warships. In all, during 1980, the corporation had 70,168 employees, produced 57 ships of a total 405,726 gross tons, and of these, 27 vessels of 173,928 gross tons were for British owners. With good leadership and a co-operative work force, the British Shipbuilders should make a large contribution to the balance of payments and general prosperity in the future. At the same time this will give interesting industrial work to the thousands who work in the yards up and down the country.

9

Harbours and Docklands

There is always a special air of excitement and tension when a ship comes into port. For a short while that ship and her people become part of the port and its activities. Each port has a special purpose, but as the pattern of trade, fishing or warfare alters, so too do the ports which serve their special needs. The result is that every port is unique and has been shaped to suit the ships and men which visit it.

As one approaches London from the sea with marshland on both sides, there is little to indicate the extent of the port's size. To the north is the low coast of Essex, while to the south is the rising land of Kent. The River Thames is certainly a mighty estuary, but it is only after passing miles of endless, grimy dockland that one realises that this was once a giant amongst the world's ports. London's size and strength grew because it was a good centre for trade with markets on the European mainland. London was within reasonable distance of the European market cities but was just out of reach for a quick attack in troubled periods. Once the King and his court had settled in London in the late Saxon period, nothing could stop it growing as the social and cultural centre of the British Isles.

Between the medieval period and the Industrial Revolution, the Thames was the major shipbuilding centre. The great attraction of the Thames was that ships could lie off at anchor in deepwater in a sheltered river. This natural advantage is often forgotten; of course the Thames has been dredged, but it should be remembered that over the years most of Britain's ports and harbours have been almost totally created by great engineering feats in building harbours, breakwaters and docks. Long before all this activity created ports all round the coast, the Pool of London was one of the few places where a great number of ships could lie in safety. From the Elizabethan age, the Pool was the base for ships carrying the cargoes of the great merchant trading companies, first in the Tudor wool trade, then the Company of Merchant Adventurers and into the Muscovy, Levant, Hudson's Bay and East India companies. The usual custom was for the ships to lie at anchor and the cargoes to be ferried ashore in barges to warehouses. When the Great Fire of London swept along the north bank in 1666, many of the Tudor warehouses were destroyed.

After the Great Fire there was a change to using coal for house fires so that the risk of fire caused by wood sparks could be reduced. This obviously increased the trade in coal from the North of England. A spell of bad weather, particularly a south-west gale, often held up the collier fleet and the capital ran short of coal. Once, after gales in 1837, 741 colliers all arrived in the Thames at the same time. As well as rows of tubby collier brigs lying in tiers in the Pool, there were the foreign seagoing merchantmen in the Lower Pool, below the present Tower Bridge. By the eighteenth century, three-quarters of England's foreign trade passed through London. The result of all this shipping was inevitably appalling congestion and delays.

In order to handle their trade, the London merchants had to build more wharves further down river. They built enclosed wet docks where, by fitting lock gates, the water level remained constant and the ships could lie afloat beside the quays. Pepys referred to a wet dock at Blackwall in 1661 and plans to build another at Deptford on the south bank. It was there, with an entrance into Limehouse Reach, that the Great Howland Wet Dock was dug in 1696. As this was out on the open marshland, protection was given by planting three parallel rows of trees which saved many ships from damage in the great storm of 1703. Because this dock later became the base for whalers, its name was changed from Howland to the Greenland Dock, but it was closed in 1970.

After the success of the Greenland Dock, another company purchased forty-five acres of marshes to the north and started to build a further set of docks. These companies eventually linked up in 1878 to create the Surrey Commercial Docks which, with its labyrinth of docks, locks and timber ponds, became the great timber importing centre. From the dock shed surrounding the docks came the sweet smell of timber freshly felled in the forests of Norway and the Baltic countries. Every piece of wood was carried ashore by hand. The 'deal porters' used to walk down a springy plank with a pile of deal timbers on their shoulders. There was quite an art in this because the plank whipped and if the porter got out of step it was possible to be thrown off balance into the water. In 1939 there were some 1,500 deal porters in the Surrey Commercial Docks and a similar number of stevedores, to say nothing of the number of administrative staff. This was just one set of docks, and by that time the dockland had spread for miles along the north bank of the Thames.

The Surrey Commercial Docks seem to have been a stable place of employment with almost a family atmosphere, and it was known for six generations of the same family to work those docks. Most of the clerks lived in the area and the Dock Superintendent had two of the best pews in the parish church of St Mary, Rotherhithe, which showed his importance in the area. There was also a Surrey Club and Institute, a place for

The General Steam Navigation Company's 1,220-ton steamer Cormorant, *seen from Tower Bridge, crossing alongside the Irongate wharf, now demolished and replaced by the Tower Hotel. The bows of the vessel are pointing towards the entrance to St Katharine's Dock and behind that are British & Foreign wharf and Carron wharf. Out in the Thames are the lighter roads. The* Cormorant *was built at Hull in 1927*
(Hugh Perks)

everyone to relax in the evenings. Across the Thames, in the London and Millwall dock companies, the atmosphere was much more 'them and us' and there seem to have been more labour disputes.

There were wharves, jetties and docks all along the north bank of the Thames as it wound its way to the open estuary; the only dock complex on the south shore was the Surrey Commercial. On the north bank, starting from Tower Bridge, were St Katharine's Dock, then the London Docks, which were first opened in 1805, the Regent's Canal Dock, a small basin at the beginning of the Grand Union Canal, and the West India Docks, originally opened in 1802 and later added to so that they cut off the Isle of Dogs, a peninsula made by a bend in the Thames. Continuing east were the small Poplar Docks, which led into the Blackwall basin at the entrance of the West India Docks, and the East India Dock, quite small compared to the other complexes, but important historically. The East India Company had a monopoly to trade with the East from 1600–1813 and then with just China until 1833. In 1793 the Company had thirty-six 1,200-ton East Indiamen and forty smaller ships trading to the East. For this fleet they created their own dock, work on which started in 1804, and it was opened two years later as the East India Dock. The other upper river dock complex above Bow Creek was Millwall Docks which was opened in 1868 on the outer end of the Isle of Dogs. Millwall specialised in grain handling with a central granary, which by 1969 could hold 24,000 tons, enough then to supply London's needs for a week.

Over a century before this, another dock company built the Royal Victoria Dock, opened in 1855, with a lock near Bow Creek opening out into Bugsbys Reach. This was followed by the Royal Albert Dock in 1880, joining up the eastern end of the Royal Victoria Dock, but with a new lock opening into Gallions Reach.

The most attractive of the upper river docks is St Katharine's which was opened in 1828 in what had been a slum area between the Tower of London and the London Docks. The engineer responsible for St Katharine's Dock was Thomas Telford, while Philip Hardwick was the architect. It was only a small dock, lined with high, brick warehouses, but its proximity to the City of London made it popular for luxury goods. Through these warehouses, packed spices, wine, fine carpets, mercury, marble and even ostrich feathers were passed. The Ivory House, between the East and West Dock, was a warehouse built in Italianate style in 1854.

Imposing brick-built warehouses continued for several miles along the banks of the Lower and Upper Pools. Because of this concentration of warehouses and factories, the area was very heavily bombed during World War II. After this, trade dwindled and new cargo handling methods made other ports more attractive as industry moved away.

When the author first went up the Thames on a sailing barge in 1956, to load sunflower seeds from a steamer lying at Bellamy's, a wharf in the Lower Pool, there was not much shipping above Bugsbys Hole off the West India Dock's entrance. By 1967, the trade had virtually gone from the Pool which was still lined with high, brick warehouses with names like Metropolitan, Colonial, Continental, St John, Morocco and Orient. These names gave an indication of just how widespread trade had been in the Thames.

It was the same with the docks: the Surrey Commercial dealt with seasonal timber; the West India Docks were the centre of trade with the Caribbean in sugar, rum and hard wood, although Silvertown Wharves on Woolwich Reach later became the centre for sugar imports; the East India Docks were mainly concerned with tea, silk and goods from the East, but when this trade contracted the dock was given over to coastal and European trade.

Tramp steamer discharging into lighters in London Docks. All the bags were handled several times and the work was physically demanding. The loaded lighters could be used for storage until being towed to one of the numerous riverside warehouses. This scene was replaced by containerisation which mushroomed into worldwide use in the 1960s. Containers had actually been used on the Liverpool–Belfast and Liverpool–Isle of Man services before World War II, but the forming of the large ocean-going container services run by consortia such as OCL, ACT and Atlantic Container Line ended most hand-discharged cargoes (Port of London Authority)

Only the small St Katharine's Dock and London Docks were without railway links, but in most cases goods discharged in London could be delivered by rail to any part of the British Isles. A considerable part of London's tonnage was stored and moved in lighters, a system which grew up because they did not have to pay to use the docks. The development of the spritsail sailing barge was encouraged largely through the tremendous volume of trade which was discharged directly over the sides of ships and then taken to other ports. This was cheaper than putting goods through warehouses and using rail.

In 1968 St Katharine's was officially closed; it reopened in about 1974 as a major tourist centre with the 800 bedroom Tower Hotel and the London World Trade centre replacing some of the warehouses. Around the same time, many of the early nineteenth-century warehouses were pulled down, which completely changed the character of the Lower Pool.

Before the great dockland era, the Thames was already a colourful tideway. One of the Wapping warehouses had a large E on its front to mark that this was the site of the Execution Dock. Here pirates were hung and their bodies were left to hang in chains at low water mark for three tides. One of the most famous pirates to suffer this fate was Captain Kidd in 1701. While enough of the warehouses have gone to change the character of the river, at least the waterside pubs have survived, notably the Mayflower and the Angel on the Bermondsey bank and the Prospect of Whitby on the North Shore at Wapping.

The name 'Prospect of Whitby' came from a Yorkshire ship built in 1777 which used to trade regularly with building stone to this wharf. So frequently was she there that the inn was renamed Prospect of Whitby in 1790. Originally this was the Devil's Tavern which dated from 1520 and had been the haunt of thieves and smugglers. The landlord of Prospect of Whitby in the late eighteenth century apparently also ran a nursery and is credited with being the first person to grow fuchsias in this country. The original plant was given to him by a sailor.

In Victorian times the firm of Jamrach's on Ratcliff Highway used to buy any wild animal which sailors had managed to keep alive on their voyage home. The Ratcliff Highway was the centre of a notorious sailor-town which extended from Wapping east beside the Thames to Shadwell, St George and Limehouse around the West India Dock gates. So many orientals settled in Limehouse that it became known as Chinatown. The area around Ratcliff Highway was one of human degradation; there were pubs, boarding houses, brothels and opium dens which many Christian people and social workers fought to suppress.

Although much of the thirty miles of the River Thames below Tower Bridge to the sea was lined with wharves and jetties, the real dockland

Wapping waterfront in 1856. The topsail schooner Express *of Alnmouth has her square topsail drying and one yard 'cock-billed' at an angle to allow the cargo to be hoisted out of the hold* (Port of London Authority)

was hidden from the river, often behind high walls built to try to stop theft which took place on a vast scale. The Port of London was made up of some 600 independently owned wharves and four large, highly competitive dock companies. Because of the competition from the new Royal Docks, the East and West India dock companies joined forces to build a new deepwater dock in 1886 down near the mouth of the Thames at Tilbury. An Act of Parliament in 1909 created the Port of London Authority and put the river and all the enclosed dockland under its single control. On the day the PLA finally took control, the directors of the Surrey Commercial Dock Company flew the company flag at half mast and drank the remainder of the company's 'liquid' assets.

The PLA took over not just the largest dock complex in the world, but also one of the largest human problems. Work in the docks depended on how many ships were there to be unloaded, and dockers had been employed on a casual day-to-day basis to unload ships. When there were

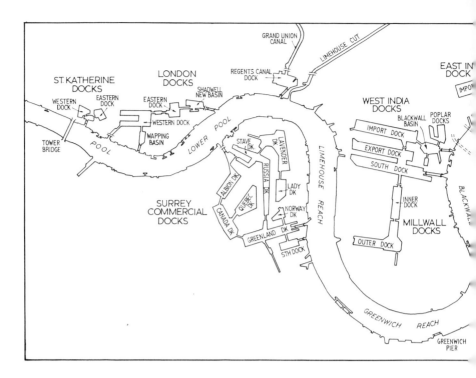

fewer ships, there was less work, but the men naturally wanted a permanent income. When one realises that in 1914 the London docks and wharves employed around 100,000 men, the size of its problems can be seen. What happened in the docks affected the prosperity (or lack of it) of much of east London. The dockers first fought for a set scale for their labours in the 1889 Great Strike in which they demanded and won a 'tanner an hour' (this was 6 old pence or 2½ new pence), but since the casual labour system remained, men still flocked to the dock gates every morning in the hope of a day's work. This had been worse in the sailing ship era because bad weather often held up the ships at sea. Steamers arrived more regularly, but after World War I the world trade depression meant that there were fewer ships coming in. In the 1930s there were appalling scenes of violence at the dock gates, with dock police fighting back hundreds of men who were trying to seek a few dozen jobs.

The size of the London docks continued to grow with the opening of King George V Dock in 1921, next to the Royal Albert. The Royal Group of docks, which consisted of Victoria, Albert and George V were linked by locks and then comprised the largest docking system in the world. They had 235 acres of water and about 13 miles of quays.

Although the King George V Docks could take liners drawing 38ft of water and even took the 36,655-ton liner *Mauretania* in 1939, vessels of

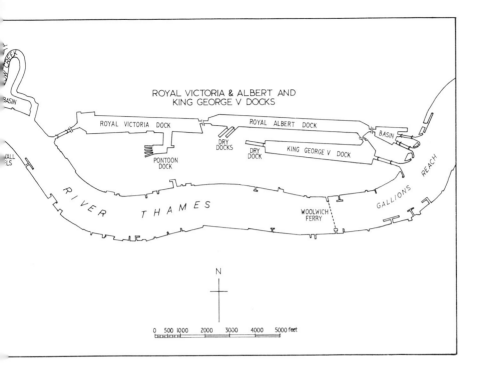

ROYAL VICTORIA & ALBERT AND
KING GEORGE V DOCKS

ROYAL VICTORIA DOCK

ROYAL ALBERT DOCK

BASIN

DRY
DOCKS

DRY
DOCK

KING GEORGE V DOCK

PONTOON
DOCK

REACH

RIVER THAMES

GALLIONS

WOOLWICH
FERRY

N

0 500 1000   2000   3000   4000   5000 feet

this size and length did not normally go right up the Thames. The smaller ships of the Blue Star, Royal Mail and Ben lines did use the King George V Dock, but in 1929 the PLA enlarged the Tilbury Dock so that they could take the larger P & O liners.

In the early 1930s Ford was expanding its plant at Dagenham but the most rapid development was taking place nearer open sea at the oil refineries on or near Canvey Island in Sea Reach. American oil was first landed near Shell Haven, a creek on the Essex shore, in 1880; but since then jetties and tank storage areas have spread along the marshland. In the middle, beside Hole Haven, is the Lobster Smack, a pub that took its name from the lobster smacks that used to deliver their catch here for storage before it was taken to London. These riverside pubs thrived in the days when up to a couple of hundred sailing barges and coasters were sometimes held up in Sea Reach waiting to start a passage. To the deepwater sailors who swept past up river to their dockland homes or the dubious delights of sailortown, these pubs were of little interest, but to the coastal sailor and bargemen places like the Lobster Smack and the Ship & Lobster, across the river just below Gravesend, were definite landmarks.

London's growth was due to its role as a trading centre: commodities of every description passed through on their way to other destinations. The

273

only British port seriously to rival London was Liverpool, which at its height had 600 acres of enclosed water docks and some 35 miles of quays. Until the depression of the early 1930s, Liverpool handled a fifth of all Britain's foreign trade. Liverpool first rose to importance as the chief trading link with Ireland after the old medieval port of Chester was closed by the silting up of the River Dee. Liverpool merchants quickly developed trade with North America and the East and by 1796 the town had grown to be the commercial centre of north-west England, North Wales and eastern Ireland.

Liverpool's situation at the entrance of the River Mersey was ideal for trade in the Irish Sea and across the Atlantic. The industrial towns of the Midlands and south Lancashire increasingly sent their manufactured goods for merchants to export through Liverpool's growing dock system. The port began to expand rapidly through the infamous triangular trade: ships took cotton and manufactured goods out to the west coast of Africa, then made the 'middle passage' across the Atlantic packed with wretched black slaves and returned to Liverpool with sugar and rum. Shipowners who disapproved of the slave trade sent their vessels to North America and then down to the West Indies. The result was the same: a great influx of wealth.

Liverpool had an individual style of dockland architecture based on classical designs which was largely started by Jesse Hartley. He was born at Pontefract in 1780 and had become an expert in bridge construction by the time he was appointed as Liverpool Dock Engineer in 1824. He pushed the dock system north along the Mersey, building strong warehouses and docks of stone, brick and iron which looked as if they would stand for ever. A mile away across the narrow channel, Chester merchants and landowners were financing the building of a rival set of docks at Birkenhead, but Liverpool had a head start, not only with the docks, but also with railway links to the industrial areas.

Many merchants considered that too much capital was being invested in Liverpool docks and refrained from supporting Hartley's plan for an enclosed high security dock. Instead London built St Katharine's Dock and captured the high value goods trade. It took seventeen years before Liverpool built a rival dock, the totally enclosed Albert Dock which was opened by the Prince Consort in 1845. This 7 acre dock, surrounded by warehouses, was on a grand scale and was Hartley's greatest achievement. Both Liverpool and Birkenhead docks came under the control of the Mersey Docks and Harbour Board as early as 1857.

As the docks grew, so people flocked in to the rapidly spreading city of Liverpool in search of work or better prospects. In 1847 alone 300,000 poor and desperate Irish landed at Liverpool. Many 'took ship' for

America, including some young men bent on building business empires. The Brocklebank Line, the oldest shipping company in Britain, grew from the enterprise of Daniel Brocklebank who between 1770–5 built four ships in New England before returning to his native Whitehaven in Cumberland. Brocklebank ships traded to the West Indies, America, Ireland and Russia, and with this widespread venture the move to Liverpool in 1820 was a natural one. Daniel's grandsons Ralph and Thomas pushed into new trades and by 1844 they had forty-four ships. As a shipowner Ralph Brocklebank had nothing to lose from dockside 'crimps' who virtually sold seamen to the ships in exchange for the first month's pay, but nevertheless he fought to stop crimping in Liverpool.

The shipowners could not completely escape from the tough, hard world of the waterfront. John Bibby, a ship broker who had created his own fortune, died after being mugged for his watch. Frederick Leyland was furious with Samuel Plimsoll for trying to improve conditions on the cattle ships. To prove his point he brought a lawsuit against Plimsoll and won. Then there was Alfred Holt who started five different business ventures which were not entirely successful. On the sixth occasion he plunged into shipping just as the freight rates soared at the start of the Crimean War; when he died in 1911, aged eighty-two, his Blue Funnel Line had over fifty very modern steamers through being in the forefront of ideas and technology.

While the shipping magnates of London took little interest in Thames Dockland which had brought their wealth, the Liverpool merchants commissioned some solid Victorian and Edwardian architecture to give Merseyside respectability. Right in the centre of the Liverpool water-front, near the Pier Head landing stage, the Liver Building was completed in 1911. It was possibly the world's first reinforced-concrete frame building, and stands with the art nouveau version of the mythical 'Liver' bird on its towers as a symbol of Liverpool's importance in world trade. Another of the Pier Head group of buildings is the new headquarters of Mersey Docks and Harbour Board, started in 1907 and deliberately intended to be a display of magnificence and importance.

Liverpool reached a point where there were 460 acres of docks and 27 miles of quay with a further 181 acres of water and 9 miles of quay on the Cheshire side. In 1914 the Cunard Line added the last great symbol of mercantile success with the Cunard Building in the centre of the Pier Head group. On a smaller scale in adjoining streets other offices with stone façades swelled the ranks of Liverpool's architectural heritage. The shipping gentlemen of Liverpool never lacked imagination when it came to new ventures and by the end of the nineteenth century had the wealth to indulge their tastes. One of these imaginative ideas was the overhead

The 24-knot Cunard liner Aquitania *in the River Mersey, with the Liver Building in the background. The* Aquitania *joined the Liverpool–New York service in 1914 and had a working career of thirty-five years. During this time she steamed nearly 3 million sea miles and carried 1,200,000 passengers. When she was finally withdrawn, she was the last 4-funnelled liner in the world* (Cunard)

railway round the dock area which was built in 1893, but this was later dismantled.

It was the conventional railway which brought most of the export goods to Liverpool, but Lancashire cotton interests wanted to cut out this expense and load straight onto the ships. To achieve this, the Manchester Ship Canal, dug from the Mersey near Ellesmere Port for $35\frac{1}{2}$ miles to Manchester, opened in 1894. The trade from the textile industry soon resulted in this inland port becoming one of Britain's most active.

Although the ship canal made Manchester the fourth largest British port in trade value, it did not pay any return to investors for over twenty years. Ships of 10,000 tons could get right up to Salford Docks just outside the city of Manchester, while the docks at the Mersey end, at Eastham, have been rebuilt to take tankers of up to 30,000 tons.

Few industrial ports in Britain are sited on natural harbours: generally industry grew up and the nearest arm of the sea was shaped into a port. However, trade preceded industry in the Clyde: as early as 1668 the Glasgow magistrates, aware that their town was losing trade because of the difficulties of getting up the shallow River Clyde, started a new Port Glasgow 20 miles downstream. A vigorous trade developed with the New World in tobacco, sugar and cotton, but when the Lanark coalfields poured out cheap fuel, steel manufacturers and then shipbuilding spread in a narrow ribbon along the south shore. Coal also triggered off the growth of Newcastle-upon-Tyne, but like the Clyde the River Tyne had to be dredged and rocks blown out before it could take sizeable ships.

The Industrial Revolution naturally caused some established ports to expand. As an outlet for the industrial towns of the East Midlands and Yorkshire, Hull grew to be Britain's third largest port, although the tonnage handled never came near that shipped at London and Liverpool. The medieval port of Kingston-upon-Hull, which is the city's official name, stood at the mouth of the River Hull. This was later known as the Old Harbour and was lined with mills and warehouses. It is very narrow with a fast running tide so the Humber keels and visiting Thames barges did not have room to manoeuvre under sail. Instead they drifted up on the tide and were controlled by their anchors just touching the bottom. The Thames barges used to do this in their own waters, particularly when going above the London bridges, but Hull's Old Harbour was often, even in the mid-1950s, jammed by drifting barges.

Hull's first dock, the Queen's, was opened in 1778 when the port was a whaling centre. The dockland expanded to 10 miles of quays and 236 acres of enclosed dock. The great docks of Hull were the Alexandra Dock, completed in 1886, and the later King George V Dock. The deepwater fishing fleet and coal exports accounted for much of the work, but a great deal of wheat was also imported.

Hull was like London in that a great deal of its trade was discharged into barges and taken on to smaller ports. In the case of London, sailing barges moved these vast tonnages to coastal ports; the Humber billyboys, round-bowed ketches, took some cargoes to the Wash ports but most of the Hull trade went inland. The Humber keel was the local barge which was developed for this trade.

The Humber keels had a single square sail which allowed them to sail in the waterways as well, reaching Hull, Immingham and Grimsby. Imported goods were taken inland and coal returned. When bound inland the keel skippers thought of the waterways ahead as being a left hand laid flat on the ground: the Humber was the arm, the thumb pointed up through Hull's Old Harbour to Beverley and Great Driffield; the first finger was the River Ouse to Selby and York, the next to Goole, Wakefield and Leeds, the third finger was the River Don to Sheffield and the little finger led to Lincoln.

The River Humber is noted for its very strong tides, but the largest rise and fall of tides, up to about 40ft, is in the Bristol Channel. The city and port of Bristol prospered on foreign trade from early times. In medieval times, trade from the River Avon to France and Spain made Bristol the commercial centre of the West of England. The Bristol merchants were always searching for new markets, and in 1496 the Italian John Cabot sailed from the city in an attempt to find a route to China.

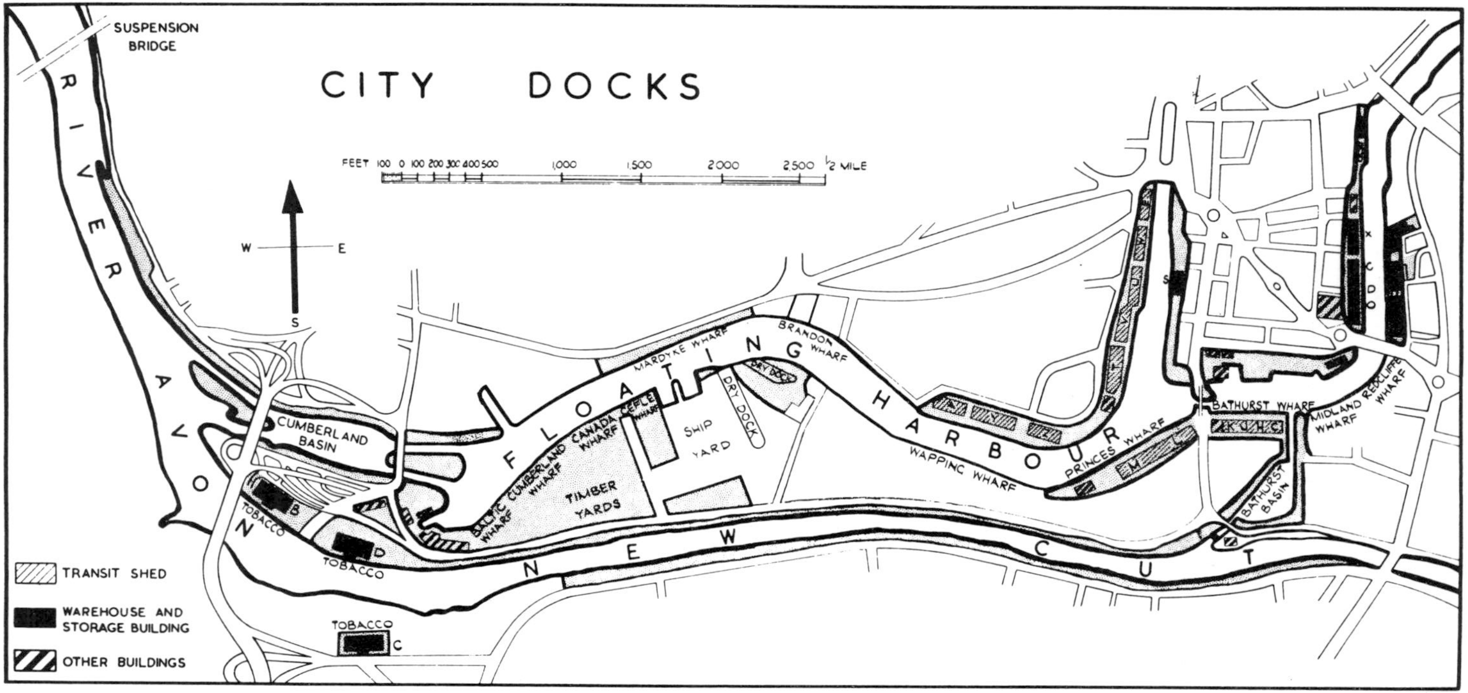

CITY DOCKS

SUSPENSION
BRIDGE

FEET 100 0 100 200 300 400 500   1,000   1,500   2,000   2,500 ½ MILE

RIVER AVON

CUMBERLAND
BASIN

TOBACCO D

TOBACCO B

TOBACCO C

FLOATING HARBOUR

NEW CUT

WAPPING WHARF

PRINCES WHARF

BRANDON WHARF

MARDYKE WHARF

CANADA WHARF

BATHURST WHARF

BATHURST
BASIN

MIDLAND WHARF

RICHMOND
WHARF

DRY DOCK

SHIP YARD

TIMBER YARDS

TRANSIT SHED

WAREHOUSE AND
STORAGE BUILDING

OTHER BUILDINGS

Bristol Docks

The wooden barque Maria, *a West Indies trader, in City Docks, Bristol, in about 1872. On the right is the Severn Shed, which is still standing; it was then the Coach & Horses Inn, which was the basis for Spyglass Inn in* Treasure Island, *and subsequently the Sailors Home* (Port of Bristol Authority)

The Merchant Adventurers Society of Bristol received its charter in 1552, at a time when London was attempting to monopolise the hoped-for trade with the North American colonies. Much later, in the eighteenth century, Bristol received great wealth from the infamous triangle trade, taking slaves across the Atlantic and returning with sugar. There was deep concern at Bristol that the end of the trade in slaves would ruin the port's prosperity. Slavery did not, however, end in the British Empire until 1833, and by this time Bristol was well established in sugar and tobacco trades so that there was little economic hardship. The real difficulty was for vessels of any size to negotiate the tortuous River Avon to Bristol. The railway age with Brunel's great schemes and the liner *Great Britain* seemed destined to make Bristol an even greater port, but the Great Western Railway Company chose a very wide gauge track with the result that they could not link up with other railway companies. Goods from the Midlands could go through the interchange sheds at Gloucester, but this meant delays and extra expense. Here at Gloucester there was a set of docks and warehouses used by inland waterway traffic and connected with the River Severn by the Gloucester and Sharpness Canal. However, neither Gloucester nor Bristol ever offered a very good outlet for the industrial towns and instead trade went through London,

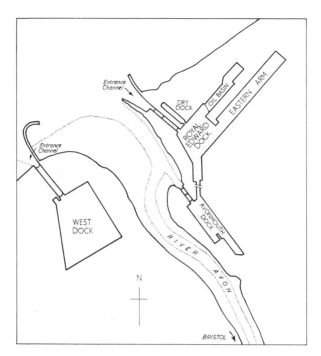

Avonmouth Docks

Liverpool or Hull. Bristol still remained the commercial centre of the
West Country but Bristol City Docks were not developed any further. In
1877 new docks were started at Avonmouth, at the mouth of the River
Avon. Two years later more docks were opened on the south bank of
Avon mouth, near Portishead. These were not so successful, but Avon-
mouth has spread and is now a main import centre in western Britain.

In the nineteenth century some of the most active dock construction
took place in the coal ports of South Wales. This had begun in the
previous century when ironmasters from the Midlands moved down to
the valleys of south-west Wales because coal was easily mined there to
feed their furnaces. The iron had to be shipped across the mouth of the
River Severn to Bristol from where it was exported, mostly to America.
The problem of land transport was overcome by the building of
the Monmouthshire Canal in 1794 which led down the Usk Valley to
Newport. Moving iron was a slow business: for instance, an ironmaster at
Blaenavon still had to send the iron over the hills on horse-drawn
tramways to the canal. The port of Cardiff, then little more than a few
wharfs at the entrance of the River Taff, began to expand when the
Glamorganshire Canal was opened in 1798 to bring iron down from
Merthyr Tydfil ironworks. Further west the Swansea Canal was opened

280

to bring iron from the Swansea Valley to Swansea, although copper smelting was also important. Copper was first imported from Cornwall, later Spain and then from the west coast of South America.

The ironworks and collieries were all on a small scale in the valleys until the arrival of the railways which were able to move goods in far greater quantities than ever before. At the same time railways all over the world started developing a huge appetite for the best Welsh steam coal. At first, ships were loaded while sitting on the mud in the entrances of rivers, but this was a slow arrangement. The Marquis of Bute, a Scottish laird, controlled much of the Rhondda, two valleys which soon became the world's greatest coalfield and which were connected by the Taff Vale Railway with the port of Cardiff where the coal was loaded onto ships. The Marquis of Bute poured in a vast amount of capital to build the Bute West Dock, opened in 1839, and an East Dock in 1859. Even then a Customs' officer was recorded as saying that, 'Coal will never be of any importance to South Wales.' He could not have been more wrong—for the next eighty years the ports could not export coal fast enough to keep up with world demand.

A constant source of delay was caused by the ship loading system at Cardiff. However, the Marquis of Bute who controlled much of the Rhondda, the railways and the rapidly growing town of Cardiff, was in no hurry to invest more capital in the coal trade which he largely monopolised. In 1880 over 4 million tons of coal went through Cardiff, but the shipowners were complaining, as they had done for decades, about the delays and congestion. In the valleys the collieries were working on short time because insufficient railway trucks were being returned from Cardiff Docks. By 1887 over 6 million tons of coal a year were being exported from the Bute Docks, but this was not enough for the colliery owners.

Lord Plymouth, who had considerable mining interests in the valleys of Gwent and east Glamorgan, decided to bypass Cardiff and build a new port at Penarth. Since Plymouth's railways had to cross the Taff Vale Railway lines, the Marquis of Bute managed to delay this for some time, but a new coal port was eventually established.

It was David Davies, a tough Welshman from Montgomeryshire who had made a fortune as a railway contractor and colliery owner, who really established a rival to Cardiff. Davies dammed the channel behind Barry Island to create two new docks which were lined with coal hoists. They were opened in 1889. By 1900 Barry Docks were exporting over 7 million tons of coal a year, but at the same time Cardiff Docks were running into financial troubles. The Marquis of Bute tried to sell them, but because the old docks were too small for tramp steamers, he was forced to build the 52 acre Queen Alexandra Dock which, when opened in 1907, was the largest walled dock in the world.

South Wales reached its peak in about 1913, with 4½ million tons being shipped from Penarth and 10 million tons from Cardiff; Barry had taken the lead with 11 million tons, to say nothing of the vast tonnage shipped from Newport, Port Talbot and Swansea. There were also smaller tonnages going out through Llanelli, Saundersfoot and collieries above Milford Haven. However, Cardiff, because of its early development by the Butes and its links with the Rhondda, was the centre of the coal trade.

Most ships which left a European country for any part of the globe hoped to load Welsh steam coal as the outward freight. Dealings on the Cardiff Coal Exchange were very competitive, as they were throughout the mining business, and often shippers undercut their rivals with fractions of a penny to win a valuable contract. Just as men from all over Wales and England had migrated to work in the coalfields, so men from all over Britain moved to establish and work on Cardiff's shipping fleet. In 1920 there were 132 shipowners in Butetown owning over 600 tramp steamers, mostly built on the Tyne and the Tees. While the residential area around Penarth is reputed to have been the home of ten millionaires, this still did not include men like the Marquis of Bute and Lord Plymouth who became extremely wealthy from the coal trade.

The story of Butetown, the area between the docks and the centre of Cardiff, was a very different one. The Coal Exchange and shipowners'

The coal hoists in No 1 Dock of Barry Docks in 1891 (Welsh Industrial & Maritime Museum)

offices were situated there, but it was really a degrading sailortown. Around Bute Street in an area known as The Bay, or Tiger Bay, there were pubs, crimping lodging houses, dance halls and brothels which gave Cardiff one of the worst reputations in the world. In 1908 The Bay was called 'the dumping ground of Europe' because of the runaway sailors who settled here with their women. Well over forty different ethnic groups settled in The Bay; men of every nation from South Africa to Scandinavia settled in these strange dark streets of Victorian houses. It is said that sailors who came out of the docks in the morning with their discharge pay started drinking in the pubs at the bottom of Bute Street and finished up penniless at the brothels later that night.

While coal was 'king', Cardiff and the ports of South Wales were boom towns, but World War I robbed them of world markets which they never won back. In the collieries there had been much bitterness between the miners and the pit owners who had generally treated them with complete indifference. In the 1920s this animosity developed into long and damaging strikes. These strikes showed the determination of the miners and what sacrifices they were prepared to make but at the same time they lost the outside coal market for South Wales. In 1938 Penarth Dock closed and has since been filled in. While the world looked to oil as a new source of power and foreign coal became cheaper, coal exports from Cardiff dropped to 3 million tons in 1939. In 1931 the Town Dock at Newport was filled in, but the two Alexandra Docks lower down the Usk were still exporting coal. It was here at about that time that Richard Duke, then a fifteen-year-old apprentice, came to join his first ship, the *Panama Trader*, a tramp steamer loading 8,000 tons which belonged to a subsidiary of Houlder Brothers. Loading took nearly a month as the work could only continue as the trains brought lines of trucks down from the collieries. Each truck was turned over on the coal hoists (sailors called them chutes) and the coal fell down a chute into the ship's hold. When the *Panama Trader*'s holds were full, coal was piled up on the decks. This was to save the owners buying expensive coal in foreign ports. If the ship hit a gale in the North Atlantic then this coal was sometimes washed off and lost, but if the weather was reasonable then the deck crew, apprentices and watch keeping officers spent the first fortnight wheelbarrowing it off the decks to replenish the bunkers.

The *Panama Trader* was a month on passage to a South American port which was the destination of most South Wales coal in the 1930s. A month was spent discharging the coal and she then came back with grain to Newport, bunkering at Las Palmas in the Canary Islands on passage. At Newport the steamer joined the other idle tramps lying in the centre of the docks and all the crew except the apprentices were paid off. Supplying bunker steam coal to ports all over the world had been an important part of the coal trade, but as more ships switched to the cheaper oil, the trade died away. Nationalisation of the coal-mines after World War II prolonged the working life of unprofitable pits, but it did not create new demands for coal. Without the competition of the coal factors, prices rose so that it was impossible to export steam coal, although some demand was still there. Also the coal seams were becoming increasingly difficult to work which made it expensive to mine. One by one the collieries in the valleys stopped and scrap dealers started to cut up the coal hoists at the docks. Most coal exporting finished in the 1960s which left whole areas of empty dockland in South Wales. This represented a vast dock area because between them Barry, Penarth and Cardiff had some seven miles of quay. In 1980, when American coal was actually being imported, only a few docks remained. Two coal hoists survived at Barry and more at Swansea, while at Port Talbot the old coaling dock had been filled in and a new steel handling port built.

In 1979 Cardiff had only four shipowners, Evan Thomas Radcliffe, Graig Shipping Company, C. M. Willie and W. Reardon Smith & Sons, and the remaining docks were just handling a little general cargo. Much of the infamous Tiger Bay has been pulled down but off Bute Street the Welsh Industrial and Maritime Museum were recording and saving much of the maritime past of Cardiff and Wales. An important local vessel was the 55ft pilot cutter *Kindly Light* which was built for the Barry pilot Lewis Alexander in 1911. The coal ports had developed so fast that they did not have any spare resources to develop much ship and boat building. The *Kindly Light* came from Fleetwood, although most pilot cutters were built on the Bristol Avon or in North Devon. In about 1908 there were around 100 independent pilot cutters which cruised off Lundy Island putting pilots on to the incoming steamers. Steam pilot boats were introduced at Swansea in 1898 and they replaced the port's unique pilot schooners. Steam was introduced to Cardiff pilot boats in 1912 and Newport in 1920 but the Bristol pilots, who lived and worked from the village of Pill, amalgamated in 1918 and put a pilot steamer into service in 1922.

Coal transformed South Wales into an industrial area and it did the same for the north-east coast of England, particularly the River Tyne. Newcastle lies some 10 miles up the River Tyne with Gateshead on the south shore of the narrow river, while at the seaward end are Tynemouth and South Shields. To make the Tyne deep enough for ocean-going ships, rock had to be blasted out and the whole river dredged. Originally the coal was brought down from the pits in horse-drawn waggons on waggonways to the coal staiths beside creeks and loaded into keels, the local double-ended barges, to be taken down river to the colliers. Later coal drops (loading places) were built above Newcastle Bridge at such places as Lemington, Bell's Close and Ouseburn. One of the first of these mechanised coal drops was one built in 1814 at Wallsend to William Chapman's patent, for coal from Coxlodge Colliery. With this method the 'chaldron' truck was run from the collieries down over the brig's deck and the door in the truck bottom opened.

The aim of the coal drops was to speed up loading and reduce the amount of handling to minimise the fragmentation of the coal which lowered its value. The keelmen and 'casters', coal shovellers, saw quite rightly that the new coal drops would kill their employment, so when new fast coal drops were fitted at Sunderland there was a riot. The drops were burned down and troopers had to be called in to restore order until tempers cooled. However, everywhere the colliers were expanding and taking on more labour, which enabled redundant casters to find work, so the drops became a normal part of every coal port. The volume of coal exports was so great that a new harbour was built on the Durham coast at Seaham in 1828.

By then the massive wooden coal drops were an imposing feature of every harbour from Amble to Hartlepool. Coal drops for bunkering steamers were a feature of most ports, except the smaller ones where it was carried aboard in sacks. Many ways were devised for handling coal in bulk at the coal ports. At Dundee, Granton, Alloa, Silloth on the Solway Firth, and Middlesbrough, powerful cranes were used to swing 30-ton railway trucks over the ships and tip the coal into the hold. The South Wales ports, which were the main coal exporting areas, naturally had the greatest number of coal hoists. Most of these hoists were made by Vickers-Armstrong at Elswick, Newcastle-upon-Tyne.

In 1923 the railway companies in South Wales paid the coal shippers to alter their hoists to take a larger 20-ton truck. The hoists were further modified and fitted with a huge 'Norfolk Spade' which forced the coal out of the truck. These huge spade devices were needed because coal sometimes stuck in frost and also the new electricity generating stations needed the small 'washed duffs' coal which again tended to stick. Cardiff seems to have taken the record for coal hoists because in Roath, Queen Alexandra, Bute East and West Docks there were twenty-eight coal-loading appliances. There were many different types, including some huge movable coal hoists in Queen Alexandra Dock, while the Lewis Hunter hoist with the anti-coal breakage system in Roath Dock was considered the most successful way of minimising coal damage.

There were many different ways of loading coal. At Garston on the Mersey, a unique system enabled a truck to run out on a Vickers

Coal being discharged from a small trader at Whitby in about 1898. The loose coal was shovelled into sacks in the hold. This cannot be seen, but the boy in the background is helping to operate a hand winch which hoisted the full sacks up to the deck level, and the men then carried them ashore on their backs (Frank Sutcliffe)

extension over the ship's hatch. The truck was then fixed rigid to the extension which was then pivoted so that the coal fell into the hold. Vickers erected conventional coal tips along the Manchester Ship Canal at Ellesmere Port, Runcorn and on either side of the canal at Partington. At Goole in Humberside there was a hoist which lifted not railway trucks, but 60-ton barges which had come down the inland waterways.

Not far away, Keadby was sited, with coal tips for the coastal craft. The trade from here started in 1793 when the Stainforth & Keadby Canal was opened enabling keels to bring coal down from Stainforth Colliery. In the 1930s spritsail barges which belonged to Everards of Greenhithe, Goldsmiths of Grays and the London & Rochester Trading Company (now Crescent Shipping of Strood) came regularly to load coal for gas works at Colchester, Dartford, Chatham, Faversham, Margate and Folkestone, as well as some gas works on the Sussex and Hampshire coast. In the 1950s Everard's barge *Will Everard* took many coal freights from Keadby to Harwich gas works.

It was in the hope of attracting export coal from the Nottinghamshire and Derbyshire coalfields that the $9\frac{1}{2}$ acre Alexandra Dock was built at King's Lynn between 1867–9. To construct the new dock the medieval Fisher Fleet was dug out as the entrance and lock gate, and the fishing fleet moved to the present Fisher Fleet. The dock was officially opened by the Prince and Princess of Wales (later King Edward VII and Queen Alexandra) who came round from London in the steamer *Mary*. Queen Alexandra seems to have had more docks named after her than any other member of the Royal family. Despite the new dock, King's Lynn expanded as a general cargo port rather than a coal port.

The coal ports had to load as quickly as possible but at the unloading ports most of the work was done by hand in the age of sail. The coal was 'jumped' or 'whipped' out of the hold in wicker baskets which were filled by shovel. The baskets were attached to a rope which passed round a pulley in the rigging and down to men standing on a raised stage. The men jumped down from the stage and the jerk on the rope shot the basket up to the deck level. Other men swung the basket sideways and it was tipped into a waiting cart or lighter. To discharge coal in this way minimal harbour facilities were needed; in fact colliers were often discharged on open beaches. In Victorian times the Norfolk seaside town of Cromer was supplied with coal discharged on the open beach during the summer. The Cromer-owned colliers *Commerce* and *Ellis* used to run ashore in fine weather and at low tide horses and carts went out to collect the coal. These colliers were sometimes hauled up the beach for the winter. The last cargo of coal was landed at Cromer in 1887. The whole operation depended on good weather, but this was a common practice all round the coast.

Sometimes colliers would discharge on the beach to avoid paying harbour dues, as happened at Whitstable in Kent. In the early nineteenth century, coal landed on Whitstable beach had to be taken by horse and cart up a hill some 300ft and inland to Canterbury. This was expensive and several engineers drew up plans for a railway tramroad between the towns. When the Canterbury & Whitstable Railway was opened in 1830, it was the first steam railway in southern England. In spite of this auspicious beginning, the railway was not a financial success and became a minor branch of the South Eastern Railway in 1844.

On the English Channel there were long stretches of coast without any harbours so beach cargoes were a normal practice. The collier brig *Lamburn* traded regularly to Hastings beach for thirty-three years, while the brig *Pelican* was in the same trade for forty-one years, mostly it seems with coal from Seaham. Both *Lamburn* and *Pelican* were actually built on Hastings beach and were finally lost there when ashore discharging. The wreck of the *Pelican* in 1879 marked the end of the Hastings beach trade. Usually the crew laid out a heavy anchor astern to haul the brigs off the beach, but when a severe November gale sprung up the *Pelican* had not cleared the beach and the pounding damaged her beyond repair.

The brig *Bee* brought coal to Eastbourne and came ashore on the open beach to discharge. The artist John Constable sketched colliers ashore at Brighton where three brigs were wrecked on the beach in 1807. The practice of discharging coal on the beach ended at Brighton in 1830. Just over half a century later, in 1882, the town made history by being the first in the world to have electric street lighting. The need for coal to fire power stations triggered off an even greater expansion of the coal trade, particularly from the north-east coast of England.

The early steam bulk carriers were largely pioneered in the London coal trade in the 1840s. The screw steamer *John Bowes*, built at Jarrow in 1852, was the first successful steam collier and many subsequent vessels were modelled on her.

By the 1880s it was quite normal to transport bulk coal cheaply by sea so it made good economic sense to site power stations on a deepwater harbour. The power stations on the Upper Thames called for a special type of collier which had no superstructure, lowering funnels and telescopic masts so that they could pass safely under the bridges. These 'up river' colliers were known as 'flat irons' and the first ones were the *Vauxhall*, *Westminster* and *Lambeth*, built in 1878. At one time there were forty-seven special 'upper river' ships working to wharves above London Bridge. Early colliers loaded between 2,000–2,500 tons of coal and were turned round very quickly. Blyth was one of the chief loading ports for 'electric light' coal. Colliers were berthed beside huge timber coal staiths and whole trainloads of coal were sent down chutes in a short space of time. The West Blyth staiths were fed by a retractable belt, while the Bates Colliery at Blyth had great conveyors taking coal to colliers. The conveyors of Jarrow were still operating in 1978, but most others, like one still at Pelaw Main staith on the south bank of the Tyne, had long fallen silent.

On the Thames, Wandsworth Gas Works was the highest point a collier could reach; thereafter coal had to be delivered by rail. London once used 13 million tons of coal a year and three-quarters of this arrived by sea. Of the great quantity of coal arriving in London every year, 4 million tons were used by the power stations. This was brought by independent shipping companies to supply municipal-owned power plants. However, in 1948, a sensible piece of nationalisation brought the power supply under one authority which eventually became the Central Electricity Generating Board. In its early stages the CEGB chartered fifty colliers to feed its power stations, much of the management being undertaken by Stephenson Clarke, a firm with a great deal of experience in the bulk coal trade. It seems that the first of the six colliers that the CEGB had built was the 3,345-ton *Cliff Quay* by Wm Pickersgill at Sunderland in 1950. In 1979 the CEGB had four steamers and six motor ships but the oldest and last coal-burning collier was *Cliff Quay* which ran from the north-east ports with 4,500 tons of coal to Ipswich or the Thames power stations.

The nineteenth century was naturally the great age of dock building. Although most large ports had acquired their basic layout by World War I, some ports such as Southampton and London continued with even larger projects in the inter-war years. In World War II most dock areas were very heavily bombed, but after the war the major ports were very busy bringing foodstuffs and raw materials into a country which was living on the edge of starvation.

In the 1950s profound changes affected the way that cargoes were handled at the ports. Firstly bulk cargoes, then containers, replaced the traditional hand stowed cargoes. Reliance upon the railway was gradually diminished by the incursions of the road haulage industry for non-bulk loads. The old established ports were in need of a complete rebuild to make them capable of keeping up with new cargo handling techniques. This might have been achieved but for the appalling record of work stoppages at London and Liverpool which discouraged both private enterprise and the state from investing in improvements. Besides the dockers simply refused to accept any development. A situation was created whereby higher wages and low productivity killed the future of the Upper Thames docks and wharves.

Within two decades of the disastrous London dock strikes of the mid-1950s, the area of East London from Tower Bridge to Essex was virtually a ghost town. This covered some 7 miles of river and 5,000 acres in Wapping, Shadwell, Limehouse, Poplar, Millwall, Silvertown and across the river to Rotherhithe on the south bank. Attempts to revitalize the dockland were, in the main, badly handled, and bulldozers were sent in although some of the Victorian pubs did survive the destruction of an area rich in industrial architectural heritage. The dockland area also had some very good churches including Hawksmoor's St Anne's of Limehouse and St George's-in-the-East. Also in Limehouse is the run-down but architecturally splendid Seamen's Mission. On the north bank of the Pool of London stands Billingsgate Fish Market, built in 1876, which like the others has managed to survive into the 1980s.

The Pennington Stacks in London Docks were not so lucky, although they were probably some of the best examples of Georgian dock buildings in Europe to survive the Blitz of World War II. The stacks were almost a quarter of a mile of brick-groined vaults in which wine barrels were once stored beneath the quays, but they were destroyed by heavy lead weights being dropped through the granite roofs, and then filled in. What is more the nearby St Katharine's Dock had already proved that such dockland architecture could be adapted for a new purpose. Even the St Katharine's Dock scheme was not welcomed by the local council and it took a decade for the scheme to be accepted.

While the workers in the great nineteenth-century ports argued about whether they would continue to unload ships, new ports sprang up to take their place. The Port of Felixstowe on Harwich Harbour in Suffolk was one of Britain's most outstanding industrial achievements of the 1960s. The original Felixstowe Dock was dug by an army of Irish labourers in 1886 in the mouth of a dammed marsh creek. The new dock offered an easier link with Europe and was intended to rival Parkeston Quay across the harbour at Harwich. This quay was created by the Great Eastern Railway Company by building $2\frac{1}{2}$ miles of earth bank and reclaiming 600 acres of foreshore. It took its name from the company's chairman, Charles Parkes, and the quay was East Anglia's first real deepwater berth which quickly became a major passenger link with northern Europe.

Felixstowe Dock was a very useful base for Naval maintenance in World War I and again in World War II for the 'little ships' in Naval and Air Force coastal operations, but as a port it remained something of a white elephant until H. Gordon Parker, a corn merchant, bought it in 1951. Parker appointed Ian C. Trelawney as manager and between them they turned the little dock into a major port. While the dockers in the established ports held up freights, Felixstowe Dock offered quick turn round and little theft or damage. When containers and roll-on, roll-off ferries linked to road transport came in, the quayside workers of Felixstowe and many other smaller ports accepted them without hesitation.

In the 1960s there were many changes in the pattern of cargo handling. Oil became very important and Milford Haven, because of the tanker jetties, handled the fourth largest tonnage of ships in Britain. Felixstowe also built a tanker terminal, but it was really the new quay along the harbour shore with the quick turn round containers and roll-on, roll-off facilities which attracted European and then world trade. What was happening at Felixstowe caused other similar east coast ports to start offering the same facilities. Felixstowe's near neighbours, Harwich and Ipswich, also expanded and the three became known as the Haven Ports which were of considerable importance in Britain's export trade.

This ebb and flow in the fortunes of ports is naturally nothing new. Before rail and road transport, most ports were situated at the head of navigable rivers to serve as wide an inland area as possible. Ipswich was a classic example of this type of port. During the Tudor and Elizabethan periods, wool and general trade with Europe brought considerable wealth to the Ipswich merchants. Some merchants were able to build mansions in the surrounding countryside, but others lived in the narrow streets back from the Orwell 'keys'. After the opening of the new wet dock in 1841, this area was gradually taken over by industry, particularly the huge mills. However, some of the fine merchants' houses have survived in Fore Street, and in an unlikely setting between warehouses and a ballast yard there is one of the last Tudor merchant's warehouses which is still operating as a place of business, as the coal merchants, Isaac Lord.

The original Tudor house was built in about 1550 and stood on an enclosed courtyard, part of which was destroyed by World War II bombing. The door under the archway could be closed at night to prevent thieves from entering. The merchant, his family and servants lived in a half-timbered house forming one side of the courtyard. Another part of the surrounding buildings was a half-timbered warehouse where he had his sale room to display goods to customers. On the river end there was a small dock where ships, or at least small barges, could get right up to the warehouse. This dock was filled in when the Neptune Quay was built on what was then the tidal River Orwell and is now the wet dock.

Since the 1950s there have been major changes in Britain's ports. Many of the great nineteenth-century ports with their massive docks have declined. However, London, largely due to the new facilities at Tilbury, is still a large and thriving port. Closer ties with Europe have resulted in the expansion of several east coast ports and their container facilities.

Felixstowe, Southampton and London have been well placed for container trade because container ships on a regular run can call and then proceed to European ports. These ships do not necessarily deliver all their containers to one port in the way that general cargo vessels do with bulk cargoes. Other changes effected by new techniques in cargo handling are in the short sea ferry work where the new roll-on/roll-off ships have decks where lorries drive straight on and off at their nearest port of call. It is a different aspect of seafaring where occasionally men are injured in parking lorries rather than in the more usual dangers of seafaring. There is also a considerable increase in rail ferry traffic, enabling wagons to carry loads to their final destination without the need for costly re-loading at the docks.

Milford Haven has grown to be a major port, at least in the tonnage discharged from tankers, because it is a good natural harbour. Another good natural harbour, Falmouth, has not attracted shipping on the same scale because it is so far from the large centres of population and southern Britain already has other tanker ports. The ports and harbours of Britain have had to change over the centuries and their fortunes continue to change as cargo methods and patterns of trade alter. These changes have taken place fairly rapidly since the late eighteenth century when ships grew in size and the volume of trade increased. The single-storey merchant's warehouse gave way to the huge brick warehouse. Between 1771–1819, the East India Company built a brick, 6-storey complex of warehouses in Cutler Street to handle their London trade; it was then one of the largest industrial buildings in the world. In the nineteenth century tall, brick warehouses became a feature of every port, while ocean-going ships were berthed afloat in enclosed wet docks rather than lying at anchor and being discharged by lighter.

Most of the enclosed docks were completed before World War I, only a few of the very large ones being built in the inter-war years. After World War II Britain's docking system was still just adequate, but the growth in the size of bulk carriers and container ships meant that port facilities had to be increased in size as well. Some port authorities, such as Bristol, had already been forced to create new discharging berths for large ships near deep water in the 1950s. In most cases it was too expensive and often physically impossible to enlarge enclosed docks, so new deepwater berths were constructed on natural sites, often with the channels dredged deeper.

The opening of new deepwater berths has closed many of the nineteenth-century wet docks, but the volume of trade has not declined. Being an island race, it is vital to Britain that the ports remain a productive commercial link with the rest of the world.

Gazetteer

AVON

Bath

A very attractive inland city on the River Avon. Soon after the beginning of World War II, the Admiralty moved some of its design and administrative offices to Bath, to avoid the heavy bombing in London. One of the buildings they took over in 1941 was the Empire Hotel. This and other buildings around Bath are still used by the Ministry of Defence (Navy) for administration.

Bristol

A city which grew up around the River Avon and was based largely on ocean trade. In 1400 Bristol was the second largest port in Britain with a regular trade to Ireland, France, Portugal and Spain, based on cloth made in the Cotswolds. The desire for more markets made it easier to persuade Bristol merchants to fund John Cabot on his voyage in 1497 which led to the definite discovery of the North American mainland. In 1552 the Society of Merchant Venturers of Bristol received its royal charter and started to promote the Newfoundland fisheries and eventually trade with North American settlements.

By 1650 Bristol had strong trade links with the Caribbean and Virginia which led to involvement in the supply of slaves for the sugar plantations. By 1800 Liverpool had become the outlet for factories in Manchester and Birmingham, and had become the leading port on the west coast. As ships grew larger they had difficulty in coming up the river to Bristol with the fast-flowing tide.

However, the City Docks were constructed in the early nineteenth century and the River Avon re-routed along the New Cut. It sometimes required four tugs, one pulling, one on either side and one guiding the stern, to manoeuvre ships up the Avon. This was naturally expensive and it was not uncommon for ships to go aground and receive severe hull strain and damage when the tide left them stranded.

A new set of docks at Avonmouth were started early in this century, and an industrial complex has grown up around them. The Port of Bristol's river-mouth docks spread north-east along Severnside. The City Docks have slowly declined and had virtually finished by 1973, since when the only regular traffic has been sand suckers discharging sand taken from the seabed to the seaward side of Flat Holme. Very occasionally a heavy lift cargo, which could not be taken from Avonmouth by road, is routed to the City Docks; the rest are visiting naval vessels and pleasure craft.

Bristol City Docks have some of the most attractive quays in Britain, with tobacco warehouses and interesting old buildings such as the Sailor's Home. Near this was the Coach & Horses Inn which was originally the Spyglass Inn in Robert Louis Stevenson's novel *Treasure Island*.

The Bristol maritime business world has contributed two sayings to the English-speaking world: 'Shipshape and Bristol Fashion' referring to anything particularly smart, while 'Paying on the Nail', a phrase for cash payment at the time of business rather than credit payment, referred to the Bristol merchants' practice of putting cash on the flat-topped pillars, the 'nails', at Bristol Exchange.

Since 1979 the Nova Charitable Trust has operated their 92ft sail training schooner *Pascual Flores*, built at Majorca in 1919, from Bathurst Wharf, Bristol. Just round the corner in Bathurst Basin, the Cabot Cruising Club have their headquarters, a former light-vessel now named *John Sebastian*.

On the south side of the Floating Harbour in the City Docks is the *Great Britain* which is slowly being restored to her original condition as a pioneering liner. The *Great Britain* was the first ocean-going ship to be built of iron and the first to rely on screw propulsion as her main source of power. She was designed by Brunel, but none of the Bristol shipbuilders would tackle such a revolutionary project so that a special company was formed which dug a dry dock and constructed the ship themselves. She was named by Prince Albert in July 1843 and floated out of the dock. After seventeen months, she was ready for sea, but her negotiation of the locks into the River Avon was a tricky affair.

The *Great Britain* made four voyages between Liverpool and New York and then on the fifth voyage she went aground on the Irish coast. She was refloated by Brunel, but the bankruptcy of her owners resulted in her languishing for three years at Liverpool. Her most successful years were spent on the Australian run. In 1882 the engines were removed and *Great Britain* became a pure sailing ship. In 1886 she was damaged trying to round Cape Horn and went back to the Falkland Islands. Her repair would have been too costly so she became a storage hulk until 1937, when she was abandoned in a creek until being brought back to Bristol.

The Bristol City Museum has a collection of ship models which include eighteenth-century warships built at

A three-masted barque and other sailing ships berthed in the City Docks, Bristol. The warehouse with the 'To Be Let' sign on it was used in preliminary work in the building of the SS Great Britain *(Port of Bristol Authority)*

Pill on the River Avon in about 1910, with Bristol Channel pilot cutters in the creek. The cutters had letters on their sails which indicated the port for which they carried pilots. Rowles Boatyard can be seen on the right (Port of Bristol Authority)

Bristol, notably HMS *Mars*, a 28-gun frigate of 1778, the privateer *Mars*, HMS *Arethusa*, a 38-gun frigate of 1781 and HMS *Melampus*, a 36-gun frigate of 1785. Another model is of the pilot cutter *Marguerite T*, the original being built by E. Rowles at Pill in 1893 for the Cardiff pilot Frank Trott, who did very well racing in the pilot boat races. In 1912 she was sold and became a yacht. In the mid-1960s there was an attempt by Bristol ship enthusiasts to persuade the City to buy her for preservation, but instead the model of her, as a yacht, was made.

Pill

A village on the River Avon approximately half way between Bristol and Avonmouth. The medieval name for the village was Crockerne or Crewkerne Pill. The word 'Pill' was a local one for creek.

Pill was for centuries the home of pilots who took ships up to Bristol. The Pill pilots jealously guarded their knowledge and rights in pilotage. They fought against attempts by the City of Bristol to

dominate them while, in the nineteenth century, Bristol fought to control the Bristol Channel pilotage, which included the South Wales coal ports. However, by the 1880s South Wales had the right to license their own pilots.

The pilots all operated independently and there was naturally great competition amongst the cutters to put their pilot onto an incoming ship. At Pill the pilot boats were called skiffs, a term used widely in Britain, meaning a small boat, but the pilots from ports on both sides of the Bristol Channel evolved powerful gaff cutters which had to stay at sea in even the worst weather, yet still have a reasonable turn of speed. When sailing pilot cutters were at their height in around 1900, new ideas were introduced from yachting, but from about 1910 until about 1950, cruising yachtsmen were strongly influenced by working boats. Since the Bristol Channel pilot cutters were much admired, those built at Pill had a strong influence on yacht design during the inter-war period.

There were two yards building pilot cutters and other craft at Pill. At the head of the creek, almost under the railway viaduct, Coopers had a dry dock added in about 1885, although it was closed as early as 1905. Edwin Rowles came to Pill in 1887 and had a yard near the creek mouth on the southern side, but this closed in 1910.

Pill was an attractive little village with narrow alleys, but was subjected to some unimaginative development in the 1960s. The head of the creek was filled in and blocks of flats built which did not blend in with the surroundings. However, the creek is the base of a growing number of yachts whose owners are prepared to brave the strong tidal conditions.

Portishead
Small coastal town at the mouth of the Severn where the full range of the tide can be seen. The Bristol Channel has the greatest tide range in the British Isles and at Portishead there can be up to a 45ft difference between high and low tides. The West Dock of Bristol's rivermouth dock, originally known as the Portishead Dock, is on the Portishead side of the River Avon. In 1980 3½ million tons were handled by the Port of Bristol at the Severn mouth.

CAMBRIDGESHIRE

Cambridge
Until the draining of the Fens took place on a large scale from about 1650, small craft penetrated far inland. After the reclamation, small Fen barges were either towed or used square sails. The barges were either 46ft or 27ft long, the distinction being that Fen barges were carvel-built and Fen lighters were clinker-built. Between 1972 and 1974 a group of people raised the Fen barge *Black Prince* from a pit on the River Ouse near Ely, and she is now on display at the Cambridge Museum of Technology in Cheddars Land. Also in Cambridge the Scott Polar Research Institute has a display dealing with voyages into Polar waters.

Duxford
At Duxford in southern Cambridgeshire, the Imperial War Museum has a collection open all the year round which includes a 70ft World War I coastal motor boat and small submarine.

Wisbech
The inland port of Wisbech is linked to the Wash by the River Nene. It has long been a port, but the channel was greatly improved by the building of river walls which controlled the flow of the Nene in 1773 and 1830. Since the end of the nineteenth century, timber has been the largest import to Wisbech. A new quay was built in 1946 and was enlarged in 1967.

CHESHIRE

Chester
Until the sands of the River Dee silted up the channel, Chester was the main port for trade with Ireland. Watergate Street, from Chester Cross, led down to a quayside packed with small ships. In the Victorian period Chester remained the port of register for merchant ships. The river is now used by pleasure craft and there are river trips in the summer.

In 1979 the Merseyside Maritime Museum commissioned the Chester boatbuilders, Taylors, to build the 18ft clinker Dee salmon boat, *Arthur of Chester*. This spritsail boat was the first one of its type built for twenty years and was named after the 73-year-old shipwright Arthur Howard.

Ellesmere Port
The town was given its name as the terminus of the Ellesmere Canal which was authorised in 1793 to link up other canals in Cheshire. From Ellesmere Port, iron ore went by narrow boat to the foundries in Staffordshire, while it was possible for goods to go by inland

Brigs lying in the River Nene at Wisbech in August 1856. Because of slow exposure, early photographers could only take shipping views when the vessels were stationary at low tide (Author's Collection)

waterways right through to Bristol. Later the Manchester Ship Canal passed Ellesmere Port and large docks and warehouses were built here. The Ship Canal here is separated from the Mersey by a massive embankment 140ft wide.

The Canal Boat Museum on the Shropshire Union Canal at Ellesmere Port has a large collection of inland waterway craft. Unfortunately many of the buildings around the canal, particularly the Telford warehouses, were demolished before the museum could save them. However, the warehouses around the Top Basin and pumphouse with its engine are being preserved.

The boat collection includes narrowboats, the Yorkshire 'West Country'

keel *Ethel* and the Mersey flat *Mossdale*, built for the canal company in about 1875. The flat was the double-ended, gaff sloop barge of the Mersey.

Northwich

Inland town and port linked by waterways to the River Mersey. The local salt industry employed Mersey flats, and the Weaver Hall Museum in Northwich covers this trade well. The largest flat built at Northwich was the 78ft *Pilot* by Isaac Pimblott in 1894. She was 'jigger-rigged', a local term for a ketch, and traded to Fleetwood, Menai Strait and Anglesey ports. The yards of Pimblotts and Yarwoods built many coastal vessels for home and export. Pimblotts moved to a larger yard outside the town in 1906 and this closed in 1971.

Runcorn

A growing industrial town at the head of the River Mersey. In the eighteenth century, there was an attempt to turn Runcorn into a fashionable health resort called Montpelier. The growth of such a resort was stunted and finally extinguished by the industry established here during the canal age.

The River Weaver to Northwich and Winsford was turned into a navigation in 1735. In 1773 the Bridgewater Canal was extended to Runcorn, thus making it the outlet for Manchester. This canal system was constantly being improved and the two systems were linked. The Weston Point Basin was built in 1829, and in 1886 the Tollemache Dock was built on Weston Point. By this time a fleet of schooners was owned in Runcorn; some were built by Brundritt in Runcorn. These were chiefly shipping out coal from the Lancashire coalfields and returning with Cornish clay for the potteries in the Black Country. Schooners were owned here until World War II. The 88ft schooner, *Snowflake*, built by Brundritt for J. Foulkes & Co of Runcorn in 1880, is probably still trading as a motor vessel in Yugoslavia.

The small Shaw Museum at Runcorn has photographs of the china clay schooners in the port. In 1840 the Weaver Navigation Company decided to build three churches for the river people. The Navigators Church on Weston Point was built in 1841 and is still used by local people.

Before World War II about 200,000 tons went through Runcorn by water. After 1945 much of the potteries' clay went by road and rail and Runcorn's annual tonnage fell to 32,000 tons in 1959. However, the docks have been improved and the British Waterways Board have done constant work on the Weaver so that seagoing ships can get up to Anderton. By 1971 Runcorn had increased its potential by handling 550,000 tons per year.

Warrington

This was the first place that the River Mersey could be bridged but trade on the river was largely abandoned when the St Helens Canal was built in the 1750s. The intensive building of canals linking the industrial areas stimulated the creation of the Mersey flat, a pointed stern barge which could go up the canal and still sail on an open estuary. Clare & Ridgeways on the St Helens Canal were primarily builders merchants, but they were also amongst the main Mersey flat builders. The 'inside' flats never went out over the Mersey bar, but the 'outside' jigger flats went coasting. One of the last jigger flats to be built was the *Eustace Carey*, by Clare & Ridgeways at Sankey Bridge, Warrington, in 1905.

The St Helens Canal had no overbridges so, with a fair wind, the flats actually used their sails. The railways and the Manchester Ship Canal steadily took away the flats' up-river trade. After about 1910 flats were used by lighterage and chemical companies, but when ICI was formed in 1933 they rejected the use of sailing flats. The *Eustace Carey* was one which dropped out of service because she had been trading to Fleetwood for the United Alkali Company. Her hulk is to be seen abandoned on Widnes marsh. The upper Mersey is now rather empty of craft except for the sailing dinghies of the Fiddlers Ferry Club.

CLEVELAND

Hartlepool

The old fishing port of Hartlepool stands on Heugh headland on the northern side of Hartlepool Bay, just north of the River Tees entrance. It was also used in the mid-nineteenth century as a coal loading port, but an enterprising Stockton solicitor, Ralph Ward Jackson, started to develop enclosed docks across the bay and this triggered off the growth of West Hartlepool. This new town was progressive and expanded more quickly than Old Hartlepool. For over a century the two ports were bitter rivals.

In one gale in 1860 sixty vessels were wrecked or driven ashore with the loss of fifty lives in Hartlepool Bay and the West Hartlepool Town Commissioners, under Ward Jackson, petitioned Parliament to build a 'harbour of refuge' here. However, with the introduction of steam colliers the need for this harbour was reduced and it was never constructed.

The two Hartlepools were also shipbuilding centres. The best known of the shipbuilders was William Pile who had a yard with his elder brother, John, at Sunderland until 1854. William Pile moved to North Sand, West Hartlepool, where he built a series of clipper ships which included *Crest of the Wave* (1853), *Spray of the Ocean* (1854), *Kelso* (1855) and *Lammermuir* (1856).

The Hartlepool Maritime Museum in Northgate covers the town's seafaring past. Particularly convincing is the inside of a nineteenth-century fisherman's cottage. In 1979 HMS *Warrior*, the revolutionary frigate built in 1860, was towed from Milford Haven to the Coal Dock, Hartlepool, to start the massive task of rebuilding her for permanent berthing at Portsmouth.

Middlesbrough

An industrial port created for the coal trade. In Stewart Park, in the park gatehouse, there is the Captain Cook Birthplace Museum. The cottage where Cook was born has been pulled down, but it is planned to build a new museum here eventually.

Stockton was the old port for this area, but in 1830 the Stockton & Darlington Railway was extended to Middlesbrough which triggered off the town's development as a coal exporting centre. In 1850 the first blast furnaces were erected on Teesside, and by 1870 ⅓ million tons of iron were exported to Europe. The Transporter Bridge across the River Tees was opened in October 1911 to form a link to Port Clarence. This village then had a busy coal loading staithe but coal is no longer loaded on the Tees. The Transporter Bridge remains in service.

Redcar

A resort on the south side of the entrance to the River Tees. Fishing cobles are kept along the seafront. The pointed stern or mule coble is a popular type here because it is better coming through the surf in shallow water. There were once 'foying' cobles at Redcar, a term for passenger and general work.

On the seafront is the Zetland Museum which has on display the 30ft *Zetland*, the world's oldest lifeboat. This pulling (rowing) lifeboat was built by William Greathead at South Shields and came to Redcar in 1802. Manned by local fishermen, she rescued 502 lives and was in service until 1880. In the gale when she was last used, twenty-six ships were beached or driven ashore between Saltburn and Coatham, which is only around six miles of coast.

Most of the older lifeboat stations were originally independent and when the RNLI took over Redcar in 1864 they placed the lifeboat *Crossley* here. It was intended to break up the *Zetland*, but the fishermen protested and each gave two shillings to purchase her so that she could remain in service.

Seaton Carew

Now largely a seaside resort with sandy beaches, but in the days of sail the Tees pilots lived here. They used black cobles, while fishing cobles were usually painted bright colours. These pilots rowed or sailed south to the Yorkshire coast seeking incoming ships. The north bank of the Tees, south of Seaton Carew, is another area of golden sandy beaches where sea coal is collected. In recent decades industrial plants have engulfed much of the flat grazing land all along the north shore of the Tees.

CORNWALL and the Isles of Scilly

Bude

The small town developed after a canal leading inland to Launceston was built in 1819–23. The Stapleton family built several wooden coastal sailing vessels here between 1835 and 1878 which were launched sideways into the canal. The *Lady Acland*, built at Bude in 1835, was hauled ashore here in 1903, cut in half and lengthened, and relaunched as the trading ketch *Agnes*. This was the last shipbuilding work undertaken at the Bude yard. The Bude Historical & Folk Exhibition is open down near the canal during the summer. Its exhibits include local shipwreck scenes as between 1824 and 1874 over eighty ships were wrecked on this stretch of coast.

Calstock

Large village on one of the loveliest reaches of the River Tamar, once a busy port with schooners and ketches regularly visiting the now empty quays. The ketch *Garlandstone* was built on the opposite side of the river just above the viaduct in what was then James Goss's Yard; she is now being preserved at Porthmadog.

Charlestown

One of the china clay exporting ports on St Austell Bay. It acquired its name from Charles Rashleigh who started work here in 1791, building the outer harbour and wet dock so that vessels could load in safety. Charlestown now has a Shipwreck Centre display.

Cotehele

On the upper reaches of the River Tamar is Cotehele House, open to the public under the auspices of the National Trust. Also on Cotehele Quay is a small maritime museum which gives a very good representation of local shipping. The Tamar barge *Shamrock*, built by Fred Hawkes at Plymouth in 1899, has been restored and is kept here.

Devoran

A village beside Restronguet Creek inland from Falmouth. Anyone interested in industrial archaeology will be interested to trace the quays of the nineteenth-century mining port which can just be seen, but trade here has now completely ended. John Stephens started a yard here in 1859. The most famous vessel launched was the schooner *Rhoda Mary* in 1868.

Falmouth

There is a large natural harbour with a dry dock for handling up to 90,000-ton tankers here. Boat trips run from Falmouth to the nearby rivers. A small but interesting maritime museum upstairs in the town meeting hall includes a model of one of the sailing mail packets which crossed the Atlantic from Falmouth.

The Maritime Trust's policy is to keep boats in the area where they belong and they have three boats normally moored at the head of Penryn River. These are the 36ft two-masted lugger *Barnabas*, a 'mackerel driver' built at St Ives in 1881, the 24ft Truro River oyster dredger *Softwing*, built at Penpol in 1910, and the 17ft crab boat *Ellen*, built at Penryn in 1882.

From Falmouth a natural harbour known as Carrick Roads extends inland with many attractive creeks leading off it. In the winter the gaff-sailed Truro River oyster boats still dredge oysters under sail here, and in the summer they race very competitively in local regattas.

The steam tug *St Denys* is open to the public at Falmouth. She was built by William Beardmore at Dalmuir in 1929 and has a triple expansion engine which is fitted with Caprotti cam-operated poppet valve gear. The *St Denys* was bought by the Falmouth Maritime Museum in 1981 from Falmouth Towage Ltd.

Fowey

A fine natural harbour like Falmouth which, in the nineteenth century, was a port of call for homeward-bound sailing ships. Schooners trading to Newfoundland were also owned here. There is much of nautical interest in the narrow streets leading down to the water.

Helford

A delightful village around a creek on the Helford River. The roads leading to it, like many in Cornwall, are narrow and parking can be difficult. The nearby Frenchman's Creek, made famous by the novel by Daphne du Maurier, is equally attractive.

The Helford River is packed with yachts and the oyster rights belong to the Duchy of Cornwall. The Duchy's oyster farm, where the oysters are cleaned and packed, is at Porth Navas, a creek on the northern side of Helford River.

Looe

Two fishing villages on either side of Looe River. In East Looe the former Guild Hall is open as a museum.

Mevagissey

A very attractive fishing village on Cornwall's south-eastern coast. Tourism has largely replaced the former pilchard fishing industry which used two-masted luggers. Boatmen run trips along the coast from here.

Newlyn

Now the leading Cornish fishing port. In 1937, when the local council decided to pull down much of the old fishermen's quarter of Newlyn, seven local men sailed the *Rosebud* to Westminster Pier with a petition asking that the village should be left alone. They managed to stop at least some of the houses from being pulled down.

Newquay

Once a small port, but after the beginning of railway passenger services in 1876, it developed into a holiday resort. Today it is well known for surfing beaches. The Newquay Rowing Club have a gig house beside the tiny harbour where they keep the 30ft *Newquay* of 1812, *Dove* of 1820, *Treffry* of 1838, all from the yard of Peters of St Mawes. They also keep the modern 32ft gigs built by Chudleigh of St Mary's, Scilly: *Active* of 1974, *Good Intent* of 1975, and *Unity* built in 1978.

Near Newquay is the fishermen's watch tower, Huer's House, from where a watchman kept a lookout for shoals of pilchard; when he spotted one the cry 'Heva, Heva' went up, Cornish for 'Shoal, Shoal', and the boats encircled the fish with their nets.

Par

Began as a china clay port in 1829 and developed as a main centre. The yard of Benjamin Tregaskin was a noted centre for wooden schooner repairs until World War II.

Penzance

Small seaport on Mount's Bay and one of its two museums, the Museum of Nautical Art, has items taken from local wrecks. These include material salvaged from Sir Cloudesley Shovel's flagship *Association* which was lost on the Isles of Scilly in 1707 with three other ships in his squadron. This was the Navy's worst peace-time disaster. The Admiral Benbow pub is full of nautical antiquities.

Polperro

This village and Cawsand Bay were, in around 1800, noted centres for smuggling on the east Cornish coast. Later it became a successful fishing centre, but in 1891 a severe gale swept heavy seas into the harbour and smashed up most of the luggers and small spritsail boats. Pearce and Oliver, two boatbuilders at nearby Looe, built a new type of boat, the gaff-sailed 'Polperro gaffer'. This name has nothing to do with the Old Gaffers Association, an organisation started in 1963 for owners of veteran gaff-rigged craft and which was largely a reaction against the mass-produced, plastic-hulled yachts.

Polperro is a natural harbour surrounded by stone, white-washed cottages which epitomises the Cornish fishing village. There is a Museum of Smuggling here.

Port Gaverne

A cove near the fishing village of Port Isaac on the north-west coast of Cornwall where trading smacks once came ashore to discharge cargoes.

Prussia Cove

A small cove on Mount's Bay, reached by a track, which in the late eighteenth century was a centre for smuggling where the local leader, Jack Carter, was known as 'The King of Prussia'. His brother Harry stayed mostly at sea with a fast lugger, running contraband from France until the Revenue men managed to seize a cargo. Jack Carter led a party of men to Penzance and broke into the Custom-house to retrieve their goods, but scrupulously left the goods that did not belong to them.

St Ives

A former fishing village on a sheltered bay, now, like so many Cornish coastal villages and towns, largely given over to tourism in the summer but it still retains a strong local character.

The fishermen's quarter was on a neck of land on the seaward side of the bay known as The Island. In 1767 Smeaton built the stone pier which protects the eastern side of the harbour, and on Smeaton's Pier is the little medieval fishermen's chapel of St Leonard.

The luggers here were called mackerel 'drivers' because they drove or drifted on the tide. Before World War I, each of the West Cornish luggers had its own brand of tea mixed to the taste of the

Newlyn, on a sheltered part of Mount's Bay, was a convenient place for Cornish 'mackerel drivers' to land their catch. Here a group of these luggers are seen in about 1902. The fishermen lived in houses clustered round the harbour. In Victorian times most of the fishermen lived within a few minutes' walk of their boats, but after the 1920s the waterside houses of the fishing communities were bought up for holiday homes and other purposes connected with tourism; the fishermen had to move inland (Author's Collection)

crew (or more likely the skipper!). The St Ives fishermen were deeply religious and kept alive their own form of puritanism. The chapels were able to persuade local men to stop fishing on Sundays, but the east country men from Lowestoft, who used these Cornish ports for a few months every year, continued to fish on Sundays. This caused conflict and fights, and in 1877, when two fleets were working from St Mary's in the Scilly Isles, there was a riot. Some of the St Ives fishermen wanted to go to sea on Sunday and this resulted in another scene of violence in 1887. In 1896 the Mount's Bay and Porthleven men forceably boarded Lowestoft smacks and threw all the fish they had caught on a Sunday overboard. This riot spread to Newlyn and Cornish fishermen started attacking the 'east countrymen' whenever they came into port. Finally, two gunboats and 350 soldiers had to be sent from Devonport to restore order.

St Mary's
Hugh Town on St Mary's is the 'capital' of the Isles of Scilly. The St Mary's Museum has the 29ft gig *Klondyke* on display, complete with sails. This Scillonian gig was built by Glyas at St Mary's in 1877 for the coastguards. The gigs *Serica, Bonnet, Golden Eagle, Nornour* and *Slippen* are also kept on St Mary's. From Hugh Town launches run trips to the off islands every day, weather permitting.

St Michael's Mount
A castle on the rock in Mount's Bay which becomes an island at high tide. The castle has two nineteenth-century rowing barges which were used as ferries to the mount.

Tresco
On Tresco, Scilly, there is a collection of figureheads and decorations from shipwrecks at the Valhalla Museum, Tresco Abbey. The 31ft gig *Czar* is kept on Tresco, the 32ft *Dolphin* on St

Martin's and the 30ft *Campernell* on St Agnes. The Bryher gig *Sussex*, built in 1886, was left outside her house and was blown over and smashed by the wind after World War II. She has since been at Feock being rebuilt. The low gig houses are a special feature of the Isles of Scilly.

Truro
The county town of Cornwall stands inland at the head of the Truro River. Small coasters found their way up here until the 1950s, and because it is the administrative centre Cornish vessels are registered here. The County Museum of Truro has some material from the Genoese merchantman *Santo Christo de Castello*, wrecked at Mullion Cove in 1666.

Wadebridge
Situated at the navigable limit of the River Camel. Minerals were exported from here, and commercial shipping at the quay ceased in 1973.

CUMBRIA

Arnside
This village became the port of the area when the railway viaduct closed the River Kent. A Custom-house was built here in about 1845, and ore was shipped in from Barrow for the Leighton furnace. The old Customs warehouse is now the Arnside Sailing Club. The village has become a nationally known name in the traditional boat world because the Morecambe Bay prawners originated here. At high tide, Morecambe Bay is a wide expanse of water, but as the tide goes out this is reduced to just a few narrow channels, and fast, low, half-decked gaff cutters known as 'nobbies' or 'prawners' were used. These Morecambe Bay prawners were principally built by Crossfields of Arnside. Francis Crossfield was a boat-builder at Arnside in 1849, and members of the family had yards in the area

303

building prawners and prawner-type yachts until 1940.

At one time, there were two Crossfield yards in Arnside and the last two builders there were Fred and Will. Crossfield Brothers moved to Hoylake in Merseyside and John Crossfield went to Conwy in north Wales. These Conwy prawners had longer bows to cope with the larger seas off the Welsh coast. However, prawners were used as far south as Aberystwyth and were capable of beating into the narrow Conwy estuary in the worst of gales.

Barrow-in-Furness

The haematite iron ore mined in the Furness district was originally exported through Barrow docks, but in 1841 the first of many ironworks in the area was erected. The docks were created by filling in the channel between Barrow and Barrow Island. The port developed regular services to North America and Belfast in the 1880s, and the exhaustion of local ores has necessitated the import of Spanish and foreign ores since World War II. Shipbuilding came to surpass iron in importance, the first vessel being launched in 1873. Merchant, passenger and naval ships have been built at Barrow but the town is associated most strongly with the construction of submarines, at Vickers. Walney Island, linked by a road bridge between Vickerstown and Barrow Island since 1908, is noted for its good beaches.

Coniston

A former mining village at the head of the 5½ mile long Coniston Water in the Lake District. There is a memorial here to Donald Campbell who was killed on the lake in 1967. He made many attempts on the world waterspeed record here and finally crashed when his *Bluebird* was travelling at 315mph.

Harrington

A small port just south of Workington which was developed in the nineteenth century for the iron and coal trades.

Maryport

Developed in the late eighteenth century by the landowner Colonel H. Senhouse who named the new port after his wife. The port was built for shipping out coal but it has largely silted up and is now used by small fishing boats and yachts. At the head of the harbour there was once a busy shipyard. Ritsons were building sailing ships here in the 1880s, and Williamson built steamers here before World War I. Because the River Ellen was rather narrow, ships had to be launched sideways. Only inshore fishing boats and yachts can be found here now, but in Senhouse Street, near the disused docks and shipyard, there is a Maritime Museum.

Millom

Iron ore from the mine at Hodbarrow was shipped over a jetty built on the open Duddon estuary at Millom. Being a very exposed place, strongly built schooners were specially designed at Ulverston and Barrow to trade here. There were close financial connections between the Hodbarrow Mining Company and Amlwch Mines in Anglesey. William Thomas of Amlwch started a subsidiary yard at Millom in about 1872, and the following year the topsail schooner *Nellie Bywater* was launched here. The three-masted schooner *Cumberland Lassie* was built at William Postlethwaite's yard at Millom. The *Nellie Bywater* was actually in the Millom trade for forty years which proves how strong the hulls must have been. Since Millom was not a port of register, the *Nellie Bywater* had 'Millom, Port of Whitehaven' carved on her stern. Later the Duddon Shipbuilding Company took over the Millom yard and built the 101ft three-masted topsail schooner *Happy Harry* in 1894. This schooner was named after a local character, and because she carried the heavy ore, was low amidships which made her wet in a seaway.

The last wooden schooner to be built at Millom and in the United Kingdom, was the *Emily Barratt* in 1913. She had the pointed stern which was typical of schooners from Lancashire and the north-west coast of England. She was still afloat in 1981, in a derelict state in the Thames, as a houseboat. When the mines and steel smelting works closed, Millom became a depressed area. George Postlethwaite had sold off the remaining five schooners by 1912, but there had also been boatbuilding here as William Anderson built two fishing boats and fourteen yachts between 1890 and 1914.

Today, virtually all trace of the port of Millom has gone, but the Fleetwood sailing trawler *Harriet* was being used as a houseboat. She was built at Fleetwood in 1893 and later worked as a motor vessel until 1975.

Milnthorpe

This village used to claim to be the only port in Westmorland, but after the county boundaries were altered in 1974, it became part of Cumbria. However, it is a very long time since Milnthorpe was a port; there used to be trade to Whitehaven and Liverpool from here until, in 1837, Brunlees built the railway viaduct across the River Kent.

Piel Island

Reached in the summer only by a ferry from Roa Island. It has the ruins of a thirteenth-century castle and the Ship Inn. The eight houses built for the pilots in 1875 are now used as weekend cottages.

Ravenglass

An attractive village on the estuary where the rivers Esk, Mite and Irt meet. The estuary dries out at low water and leaves a difficult entrance. It is believed that the Romans used this tiny natural harbour at the mouth of the Esk as a port to supply Hadrian's Wall. Certainly the Roman fort of Glannaventa was situated here. The last trading vessel to come in to Ravenglass was the *Isabella* with a cargo of guano in 1914.

Roa Island

Reached by a mile-long causeway. There is a pub, the Roa Hotel, and a small village. A jetty now used by the sailing club was once used to ship goods in and out of the area. The Custom-house, built in 1848, is now a church. From 1867 to 1881, a steamer service to Belfast was operated from Piel Pier which had been opened by the Furness Railway in 1846.

Ulverston

A stone tower on the hilltop overlooking the town is a replica of the Eddystone Lighthouse and was built as a memorial to Sir John Barrow, who was born in Ulverston in 1764, and was for some forty years Secretary to the Admiralty. Ulverston was declared a port in 1774 when 70 ships were registered there.

After 1800 shipbuilding started on the banks of the canal leading up to Ulverston. From 1861 to 1878 John and William White built twelve wooden ships here, including the well-known schooner *Millom Castle*, and ending with the *Ellen Harrison*. The Ulverston canal was opened in 1796 and its claim to fame was that it was then the shortest, broadest and deepest canal in the country. The railway company placed a low bridge over the canal in 1845 which meant that vessels had to have their masts lowered to reach the canal head and this greatly restricted its use. The lock gates were cemented up in 1949.

Whitehaven

A pleasant town with a harbour which is used to import phosphate rock from North America. The Public Library & Museum has a good collection of material relating to local shipping.

In the seventeenth century, Whitehaven enjoyed a monopoly in the Dublin coal trade, and developed the tobacco trade from Virginia and Maryland. This trade generated the capital to build more ships, and Lloyd's files reveal that in the forty-three years from 1743, at least 180 vessels were built, of an average size of 1,531 tons. Activity on this scale meant that in the late seventeenth century, Whitehaven was one of the leading ports in the British Isles. There were then five shipbuilding yards here, but the loss of trade to the American colonies hit Whitehaven.

The nineteenth century saw a steady decline in Whitehaven's shipbuilding activities. To try to revive shipbuilding and to maintain the prosperity of the town, the Whitehaven Shipbuilding Co was started by local shareholders in 1869 with Member of Parliament, G. C. Bentinck, as chairman. The company employed about 450 men, which was not justified by the order book and the scale of work undertaken, with the result that after launching 42 vessels of 40,519 tons in total the company went bankrupt in 1879. Again local businessmen rallied round and raised the capital for the shipyard to continue. This time 34 vessels were built, including some fine four-masted ships. However, in 1889, both the *Alice A. Leigh* and the *Englehorn* stuck on the launching berths. This resulted in heavy financial losses, and in 1891 the company was wound up and Whitehaven ceased to be a ship-building centre.

Windermere

A tourist town situated on Lake Windermere which, being over 10 miles long, is England's largest lake. The Lake District started to attract visitors during the Napoleonic Wars when Switzerland was closed to wealthy British travellers. Later, successful industrialists started coming to central Cumbria and buying holiday homes. It was these people who started a class of racing yachts on Windermere and introduced steam launches.

In 1960 sub-aqua divers discovered in Windermere the hull of a clipper-bowed steam launch in about 40ft of water. Further dives revealed that there were other wrecks still intact on the bottom. The reason for this was that the fresh water contained few corrosive agents and allowed wood, iron and even steel to remain intact for a long time. The clipper-bowed launch was brought to the surface in 1962 by the Furness Sub-Aqua Club, and later it proved to be the *Dolly*, a launch of about 1850 which had sunk in the Great Freeze of 1895.

Other boats were salvaged from the bottom of Windermere and there are still some in the deeper water. In 1971 the Windermere Nautical Trust was formed so that steam launches could be saved for the future. In 1976–7 an old sand wharf was turned into Windermere Steamboat Museum and the Steamboat Dock was built over the original quay so that the 9 steamers, all in working order, could be displayed afloat.

Dolly is the world's oldest mechanically powered boat afloat, and has pride of place. The *Esperance*, built on the Clyde in 1869, is the oldest vessel in Lloyd's Yacht Register. She was Flint's houseboat in the Arthur Ransome's classic *Swallows and Amazons*. The museum has a 26ft sailing boat built in 1740 which was found abandoned in a boathouse in 1934, but unfortunately it was badly damaged by fire in 1952. George Pattinson, who was the driving force behind this collection and museum, also found a 1780 hull being used as a henhouse at Southport.

The Lake District attracted speedboats as soon as they were invented, and the Windermere Steamboat Museum has early examples of these, notably the 30mph *Canfly*, built in 1922, which dominated the lake's motorboat activities for many years.

DEVON

Appledore

The North Devon Maritime Museum has a collection devoted to local sailing vessels. The same trust that operates the museum owns the 37ft sailing barge *JJRP*, one of the local barges which loaded sand and gravel at low tide on the banks at the entrance of the rivers Torridge and Taw.

Barnstaple

At the ancestral home of the Chichester family, Arlington Court, which is open in the summer under the auspices of the National Trust, there is a collection which includes sailor-made models, paintings and a model of Sir Francis Chichester's *Gipsy Moth IV*.

Bideford

The town had many trade links with North America until the mid-nineteenth century. Bideford Museum has shipwrights' tools on display.

Brixham

Until about 1350, Brixham was a creek in Tor Bay, but part of the creek has silted up and is now under the main streets in the valley. The present inner harbour was the lower end of the creek. The eastern quay near the fish market was built in about 1760, and the present pier beyond it dates from 1804, although it has been enlarged. The outer breakwater was started in about 1892, but since the work was financed from money raised by fishermen, it was not completed until around 1912.

Even in medieval times, Brixham was a leading fishing port in western England, and Brixham fishermen attended the Yarmouth Herring Fair. In around 1770, Brixham boats were searching out new fishing grounds in the English Channel and the Irish Sea. By 1810 they fished in the North Sea and round the Isle of Man. Brixham played a leading role in the development of the primitive medieval trawl into a highly effective fishing method. The Brixham sailing smacks were noted as good seaboats, and the last one built was *Ruby Eileen* in 1927.

Brixham is still a leading fishing port and the quays are packed with boats between trips. The Brixham History Society Museum has been open in the summer, but it is hoped to turn the 1981 Fisheries Exhibition at the National Maritime Museum, Greenwich, into a National Fishery Museum at Brixham.

It was at Brixham that William of Orange landed in 1688 to begin his invasion of England.

Dartmouth

A beautiful West Country town on the hillside near the mouth of the River Dart. The Royal Naval College stands on the top of the hill and the Maritime Museum in the town has a collection of ship models.

East Budleigh

A village near the south Devon coast where Sir Walter Raleigh (1552–1618) was born at Hayes Barton. He returned here to live in 1587 and built a porch and smoking room to make the house into an E in honour of Queen Elizabeth I. In 1591 Elizabeth I gave Raleigh a castle and estate at Sherborne, Dorset.

Exeter

In 1969 two ex-army officers who had served in the Arabian Gulf, started the International Sailing Craft Association with the object of saving Arab dhows which they had seen trading. This grew into the Exeter Maritime Museum which has acquired a very large collection of working craft from all over the world.

Exeter was a port in medieval times, but the Countess of Devon built weirs which blocked the channel. Between 1564 and 1567 a canal from near Topsham on the River Exe was dug up to Exeter, and this is the oldest locked canal in Britain. The Custom-house on the East Quay at Exeter was built in 1681. The port was finally closed because of the new A38 swing bridge over the canal, which delayed the passage of large ships. The museum now occupies many former warehouses on each side of the basin and there is a ferry linking them. The varied craft on display include *Bertha*, a steam dredger from Bridgwater which Brunel designed in 1844, the steam tug *St Canute*, the Bristol Channel pilot cutter *Cariad*, the Ellerman collection of Portuguese working craft, Arab dhows and a Chinese junk. This junk is a Ha Kau trawler built in Hong Kong in 1980.

Galmpton
A village at the head of Galmpton Creek on the River Dart where Brixham smacks were built.

Hartland Quay
On north Devon's wild, rocky coast there was once a tiny harbour at Hartland Quay which has been washed away. There is now a small museum there in an old stable.

Ilfracombe
Between 1777 and 1888, at least sixty sailing ships were built at this north Devon harbour. However, after 1860, Ilfracombe was developed as a holiday resort which has eclipsed the port. Ilfracombe Museum has a collection of photographs of local sailing craft and some ship models.

Morwellham
Copper, tin and arsenic mined in central Devon in the nineteenth century was brought down by canal and wagonway to Morwellham which was virtually the highest point of navigation on the River Tamar. Schooners and ketches brought in coal and pit props. When the mines closed the port was abandoned and decayed away. In the mid-1970s work started on the restoration of Morwellham Quay and it is now open as an industrial museum with rail trips into the mine.

Plymouth
Much of the old city of Plymouth, standing on a wonderful site between the rivers Tamar and Plym, was destroyed by World War II bombing. It is now a modern city and the largest in the West Country.

Part of the old waterfront does survive near the Barbican around Sutton Harbour at the entrance of the River Plym. The Hoe at Plymouth, where Drake was playing bowls when the news came in 1588 that the Spanish Armada was approaching, overlooks Plymouth Sound. Drake with typical Elizabethan over-confidence said he would finish the game before dealing with the Spanish. No doubt he was equally shrewd in waiting for the tide to turn in his favour before sailing. Plymouth became the principal naval base in the war against Spain.

Plymouth was the final port of call for the Pilgrim Fathers who sailed for America in 1620. The Mayflower Steps commemorate this event. When the United States celebrated her bicentenary in 1976, sailing ships gathered in Plymouth's Millbay Dock for a Tall Ships Race to New York. The Plymouth City Museum and Art Gallery has a good collection of maritime paintings by artists with local connections. During the summer tours are provided around the Devonport naval dockyard, which had come into being by 1696. Devonport was known as Dock until renamed in 1824.

Some fourteen miles off Plymouth Sound is the Eddystone Lighthouse, the fourth to stand on the Eddystone Rock. The first lighthouse was built by Edward Winstanley between 1695 and 1700; he lost his life when it was washed away in 1703. Rudyerd's light built in 1706–9 was destroyed by fire in 1755. The present Eddystone Lighthouse was completed in 1881 to the design of Sir James Douglas, chief engineer at Trinity House, the body responsible for lights on the coasts of England and Wales. Beside the present lighthouse is the stump of Smeaton's 1759 house, which had to be demolished because the rock was crumbling underneath it. Smeaton's tower was re-erected on Plymouth Hoe, where it still stands.

Salcombe
A beautiful little town overlooking the harbour. Like Dartmouth there were many fast fruit schooners owned here until the 1870s, when yachting began to

take over. A small museum on the picturesque waterfront is largely devoted to schooners which raced home with fresh fruit. The National Trust's Overbecks Museum, Sharpitor, also has a display relating to local ships.

The Island Cruising Club, whose green-hulled sailing craft take members on cruises, is based in Salcombe. The club's schooner *Hoshi* was built by Camper & Nicholson in 1908, and is one of the few large Edwardian gaff yachts left active. Another craft is the former Brixham trawling smack *Provident*, built at Galmpton in 1924. She was one of the smaller Brixham smacks, and was bought by the Island Cruising Club in 1951. In 1971 they handed her over to the Maritime Trust, but continue to use her for cruising.

Teignmouth

In common with men from other West Country ports in the eighteenth century, many spent their summers fishing on the Newfoundland Banks. To improve trade, the Harbour Commission was formed in 1853 to dredge the channel, and in 1886 a company promoted the building of the quay. Now a thriving small port and holiday resort.

Topsham

A pleasant little town at the head of the Exe Estuary where there was a thriving port until the railway line from Exeter to Exmouth was opened in 1861. John Holman & Sons built sailing ships here and the Topsham Museum has an exhibition relating to the town's maritime past.

Yelverton

Buckland Abbey was the home of Sir Richard Grenville (1542–91) for nine months until he sold it to Sir Francis Drake (1542–96) when he returned from his voyage round the world in 1581. A large number of ship models are on display.

DORSET

Bournemouth

This was mostly open common land in the 1750s, but the sandy beaches and mild climate began to draw people to this coast and a resort developed. Two piers were built here which, until World War II, were used by paddle steamers for passengers to embark during the summer, in common with most resort piers.

This country once had ninety piers, but when the Victorian Society held a 'Piers of the Realm' weekend in 1977 at Bournemouth, the number was down to fifty.

Bridport

A largely Georgian town with wide streets and pavements dating back to the time when cordage and sail cloth making took place here. The pavements were once the rope-walks where fibre was twisted together to make rope and twine. Much of this was exported in the nineteenth century to Newfoundland fisheries which were then very important to the West Country economy. Most of these lines, net and cordage were used on the Canadian Atlantic coast, but Spanish fishermen visiting St John's, Newfoundland, also bought Gundry's Bridport lines to take back to Spain.

Chesil

A village on the northern end of the Isle of Portland, with grey stone houses and narrow streets, Chesil gives its name to the shingle beach which runs for over 11 miles along the coast. The name Chesil appears to come from the Old English word 'chesil', meaning shingle.

Chesil was the home of the Portland lerret, a double-ended rowing boat used in West Bay. The term 'lerret' is said to have come from a particular boat: a Chesil sea captain, who was master of a Weymouth ship trading to the Gulf of Venice, had built a copy of a boat he had seen there and named it the *Lady of Loretto*. The 20ft lerrets, built on similar lines, were used for mackerel netting and the 17ft boats for crab potting. Wooden clinker boats are still used for crabbing here, although those now built by Nobby Clark on Portland have a transom stern to take an outboard. These boats, however, still have single thole pins on which the oar is fixed so that they hang firmly while the fishermen attend the pots. The Chesil boats are still dragged up the beach on the oar as they were in the Victorian period.

Isle of Portland

An island linked to the mainland at Weymouth by a road behind Chesil Beach. Portland Harbour was created by the construction of a long breakwater across one corner of Weymouth Bay. The breakwater was built by convict labour and took 23 years to complete by 1872. A vast quantity of stone from the Isle of Portland was shipped out, and in the nineteenth century this included stone for the continual building of the royal dockyards at Chatham, ' Portsmouth and Devonport. Portland remains a major naval base with naval establishments on the Fortuneswell side of the harbour.

The southern tip of the island is the Bill of Portland, off which is the infamous Portland tide race which is very dangerous for small ships in bad weather. Some crab boats are kept on the open coast of the Isle of Portland and these are lowered down the cliff into the sea by old quarry cranes.

Lulworth Cove

Cosens & Co of Weymouth and Bournemouth had the excursion steamers *Empress* (1879) and *Victoria* (1884) built with the idea that they should be able to land passengers in shallow waters such as Lulworth Cove. The *Empress* made her last landing in this attractive oyster-shaped cove lined by chalk cliffs and hills in 1955. The last paddle steamer landing passengers 'over the bow' into this cove was *Consul* (formerly *Duke of Devonshire*) in 1964. Launches have taken their place.

Poole

Poole Harbour is an attractive natural tidal basin dotted with islands, the largest of which is Brownsea. Poole is on an arm of the harbour and is now a small commercial port and large yachting centre.

In the eighteenth century, Poole was the centre of Dorset's trade with Newfoundland. English fishermen had gone out to Newfoundland in the reign of Queen Elizabeth I and settled there. Thereafter, the pattern was for the Newfoundlanders to do the fishing and for ships from the 'home country' to go out to buy dried and salted cod.

The Newfoundland trade died out in the 1830s, by which time clay from pits in the Poole and Wareham area was the main trade. This was not a new trade because in 1773 an account tells of 10,000 tons of clay being shipped from Poole, mostly to the Liverpool area, bound for the Staffordshire potteries and to Selby for Leeds potteries.

The largely nineteenth-century buildings along Poole quay are very attractive. The old Custom-house was rebuilt in 1813 after the previous one had been burnt down. Also on the quay is the small, but very good, maritime museum, located in a late fifteenth-century vaulted cellar. This has models with good descriptions on local trading schooners and some maritime paintings. The central exhibits are a 1909 X class racing half-decker and a 14ft National dinghy.

West Bay

A small harbour with largely unspoilt surroundings popular with tourists, although the early nineteenth-century Custom-house indicates that this was an active port. In the 1850s Elias Cox was operating a shipyard on the west side of the harbour, building 300-ton barques for the deepwater trades. Cox had business connections with merchants in St John's and Harbour Grace, Newfoundland, for whom he built ships. The Cox yard closed in 1885, but West

Country schooners remained in the Newfoundland dry fish and salt trade until after World War I. The Atlantic crossings against the prevailing south westerly winds were hard, and the schoonermen's great toast was 'forty days to the westward'. They longed for such a passage but gales often made the passage longer.

Weymouth

Sea bathing appears to have already started at Weymouth by 1748, but it became nationally known because King George III came here in 1789 to bathe in the sea. Royal patronage accelerated Weymouth's popularity as a fashionable sea bathing resort. The sea front has many groups of attractive late eighteenth- and early nineteenth-century houses with good ironwork on the balconies.

Weymouth was also a prominent 'South Country' port sending ships to Newfoundland and in the coastal trade. The town's growth as a naval base also led to regular trade with naval dockyards on the Thames. There is a busy harbour with regular Sealink ferries to the Channel Islands.

Weymouth Museum of Local History, in a former school at the top of the backwater, has many photographs relating to the town's maritime past. A Tudor cottage in Trinity Street is opened as a museum showing a typical Elizabethan house of a ship's captain.

DURHAM

Dene Mouth

A stream runs down here from Castle Eden, and the sea shore at the mouth is an area well known for collecting sea coal. This was because many of the Durham collieries tipped the spoil into the sea and the coal in this was washed along the coast. In 1966 the local coal traders won a court case against Easington Rural District Council to maintain their common law right to gather sea coal. In the days when many collier brigs were wrecked on this coast and on the coast of East Anglia, it was a common occupation to gather sea coal. The salt in the sea coal causes it to burn with a pleasant blue flame.

Seaham

The three coal pits at Seaham produced most of their coal by following seams out under the sea. One of these went out about 3 miles. The harbour was built by the 3rd Marquis of Londonderry, a great nineteenth-century coal magnate, one of whose seats was Seaham Hall, Sunderland. He opposed better schooling in the area and refused to have his mines inspected by government safety officers. The coal drops at Seaham Harbour are reputed to be the last of their type in operation in England.

EAST SUSSEX

Brighton

The beach fishing boats of Brighton were of the same tubby design as all the Sussex beach landing boats, but at Brighton the spritsail-rigged boats with leeboards were called 'hog boats' or 'hoggies'. They were native boats to this coast, but the fishing was slowly pushed out by pleasure resort expansion, although there were still boats kept on the beach in the 1950s.

To the east of Brighton is Brighton Marina, opened by Her Majesty Queen Elizabeth II in May 1979. This was the first man-made harbour reclaimed on a large scale solely for yachts. It was the result of the great pleasure boating boom which started in the early 1960s with the advent of mass-produced plastic hulls. Most small rivers in southern England have, in the last couple of decades, gone from quiet backwaters to yacht-lined maritime roads. The great advantage of Brighton Marina is that yachtsmen can go straight out into the open sea, while most rivers have become very congested for sailing.

The English south coast town of Hastings is one of few places to have decked beach craft; in 1981, the only decked boat with a lute stern left at Hastings was Valiant RX9. *Both of these Hastings trawlers have elliptical sterns. The* Our Pam & Peter RX58 *has 'Hastings, Port of Rye' on her stern, which is a local way of having the home port and place of registration* (Author)

The net shops at Hastings, Sussex, in 1981. These shops are now little used as the fishermen have built more sheds further down the beach. The beach boat Black Cat *has the typical south coast lute stern* (Author)

Eastbourne

In the Victorian period, Eastbourne had a fleet of luggers working off the beach that went to southern Ireland and as far north as Bridlington after herring. The Eastbourne luggers were finer lined than their bluff-bowed Sussex neighbours at Hastings, and the larger ones, which carried steam capstans, had to be hauled up the beach by two horses. The Wiltshire estate owner John Popham was a great enthusiast of the Eastbourne luggers, and had 70ft examples built for both fishing and yachts. However, traders interested in developing the town as a select seaside resort forced the fishermen off the beaches sheltered by Beachy Head.

There is a Coastal Defence Museum in a Martello Tower, and a RNLI Museum on the Grand Parade. The lifeboat station and the longshore fishing boats are at the east end of the town.

Hastings

In the late Victorian period, many fishermen who worked off the beaches of the south coast were forced out by promoters of the new seaside resorts. At Hastings the new resort fortunately grew up to the west of Old Hastings so the town remains a fishing centre. About twenty boats worked off the Stade (a Saxon word meaning 'landing place') in 1981, and the larger ones were decked which is very unusual in beach craft.

The Hastings beach boats are very beamy, which gives them buoyancy for coming through the breaking waves. In the Fisherman's Museum, in a church by the beach, is the lugger *Enterprise*, built at Rock-a-Nore in 1909, which was the last Hastings boat built for sail only. Also in the museum is one of the horse capstans which were used to haul the luggers up the beach until World War II.

The main feature of Stade beach are the net shops (the term 'shop' meaning a place of work). These are tall, narrow sheds thought to date back to Elizabethan times when a high rent on the beach forced fishermen to build on a small land area. Some net shops are 30ft tall and are three storeys high. In June 1961 a fire broke out on the beach and five shops were destroyed and others damaged. These shops were so admired by residents and visitors that public donations enabled them to be rebuilt in the traditional style. Although there are reputed to be forty-three net shops left, few are now in regular use because the fishermen have built more huts further down the beach.

The hulk of the Dutch East Indiaman *Amsterdam* is exposed on very low tides on the foreshore and the Hastings Museum of Local History has a model of a similar ship.

Round the coast of Britain, there were local types of barges. This is at Rye, Sussex, in about 1903. Lug-sailed Rye barges brought cargoes up from the coasters down at the harbour mouth of the narrow River Rother (Author's Collection)

Rye

In the medieval period, Rye was one of the Cinque Ports and then stood on a headland overlooking the sea. Since then the sea has been pushed back to form Romney and Walland marshes, and Rye is now far inland. The walled town still has mainly half-timbered houses and some cobbled streets. One of the many houses with nautical connections is the Mermaid Inn, built in 1420, which much later was the headquarters of the Hawkhurst Gang, one of the many smugglers' bands around Romney Marsh. The Hawkhurst Gang brutally murdered two informers in 1747.

As the River Rother became narrower through silting, ships had difficulty in reaching the Strand Quay so little lugsail barges were used to bring goods up from Rye Harbour. However, because of a good supply of oak from the Weald, Rye continued as a centre for building sailing coasters, including the barge *Convoy* in 1900 which is still sailing. Fishing boats and yachts are still based at Rye and there are attractive warehouses and granaries on the Strand which have been adapted for tourism.

ESSEX

Brightlingsea

Every year at Colchester an Oyster Feast is held to which well-known celebrities are invited. This feast was held as far back as 1667, but the oysters are mainly cultivated in Pyefleet, a creek opposite Brightlingsea.

Brightlingsea is a little town on a creek and is still the base of longshore fishing boats. In the autumn is held the Colne Smack & Sailing Barge Match which is one of the main traditional boat rallies on the east coast. To encourage boats which belonged to the area to stay there, the Colne Smack Preservation Society has leased mud berths in the old yard of Aldous, where many of the smacks were built in around 1900. Smacks and bawleys can usually be seen here.

Burnham on Crouch

A small town which developed in the early part of this century, after the opening of the railway line in 1889, as a yachting centre with easy access from Greater London. The waterfront with its red-brick Georgian houses, clapboard cottages and yacht yards is one of the most attractive on the east coast.

Harwich

A tiny town which owes its importance to being beside Harwich Harbour, the finest natural harbour between the Thames and the Humber. The street layout is medieval with cobble streets and narrow alleys. Some Georgian houses were built for the masters of the sailing packets that went to Europe. There is a crane on the green operated by a treadmill which was built in the royal dockyard in about 1667. The old naval dockyard has now been reclaimed and turned into a European ferry landing. Other Continental ferries run from Parkeston and Felixstowe.

Leigh on Sea

Old Leigh, sandwiched between the Southend railway line and Leigh Creek, is a good place to buy shellfish as the Leigh cockle boats land their catch here. The street is lined with sailors' inns and clapboard cottages.

Maldon

An estuary port not as yet spoilt by modern development or tourism. In 885 the Vikings looted Ipswich, sailed up the River Blackwater and demanded a ransom from the Saxons at Maldon. The result was a battle on Northey Island,

(opposite) The sailing barge Arrow *ashore at Southend in 1961. The Thames Barge Sailing Club, founded in 1948, has operated a number of sailing barges on which members sail. These have been* Spurgeon, Arrow, Asphodel, Westmoreland *and now* Pudge *and* Centaur *(Alan Cordell)*

just down river from the town, in which the Danes defeated the Saxons.

In the early 1960s many people interested in traditional sailing, working craft settled here and made it a centre for the restoration of sailing barges which lie at the Hythe Quay. The yard of Walter Cook & Son usually has barges and smacks under repair.

Mistley

The political adventurer Richard Rigby acquired the Mistley estate in the mid-eighteenth century and tried to turn it into Mistley Spa, a fashionable resort. In 1775 he called in Robert Adam to design buildings for the estate, and some remain. Mistley and Manningtree, further up the river, became great malting centres in the Victorian era, resulting in the construction of tall maltings on the quay. The river dries out at both places at low tide.

Southend-on-Sea

One of the largest seaside resorts in Britain with the longest pier in the world. The first pier was built between 1828 and 1830, but this was rebuilt and added to until it reached its present length in 1898. The tramway was fitted in 1915. In World War II Southend was the assembly point for the east coast convoys, ships' masters being briefed in the pier head rooms. The Prittlewell Priory Museum has some ship models, including one of a Southend fishing bawley.

West Mersea

Reached by land by crossing the Strood, a raised causeway, to Mersea Island. West Mersea is now a crowded yachting centre, but there is also a long-standing oyster industry here and fresh oysters can be bought. Amongst the yachts are some of the oyster smacks which are now mainly kept to take part in the smack races from Essex villages. These include the *Boadicea* CK 213, which was originally built in 1808 and has been rebuilt several times.

Wivenhoe

The pattern in many of the smaller fishing villages in Essex until World War II was for men to go fishing in the winter and then sign on as paid crews on the large yachts in the summer. In 1894 Captain Charles Nottage, a yacht owner, left money in his will to establish an institution where Colneside men could learn navigation. Since then the Nottage Institute at Wivenhoe has run courses for mariners.

GLOUCESTERSHIRE

Gloucester

The city of Gloucester, which is situated on the Severn, grew as a port because it was the farthest point inland that seagoing ships could penetrate. There were, however, severe difficulties with the strong tides and their high rise and fall. Queen Elizabeth I granted Gloucester the right to be a Customs port in 1580, but it was not until the opening of the canal that the port began to grow. In 1793, when canal building in England was at its height, an Act of Parliament was passed to build the Gloucester & Berkeley Canal to allow larger ships to reach Gloucester more easily. The canal had many financial setbacks and its builder, Thomas Telford, suggested it should have the lower outlet at Sharpness, rather than more southerly Berkeley, so that work could be completed and costs reduced. The 16 mile ship canal, with two locks, was finally opened in 1827.

Built in 1810, the main Dock Basin at Gloucester has some interesting quayside buildings. On the Severn side of the Dock Basin is the Alexandra warehouse, the Dry Docks, built in 1843, and a larger one in 1853. At the far end is the Telford warehouse of about 1826, and at the top eastern corner is the huge 6-storey Robinson and Philpotts warehouse. Continuing round is the entrance to the Victoria Dock, and between this and the Barge Arm is the Albert

Reynolds Mill, built in 1840. The Victoria Dock and three 6-storey brick warehouses called Victoria, Britannia and Albert were completed in 1848. It was to this dock that salt came down the Severn from Droitwich and was then shipped by ketch and schooner to Ireland and the Continent. The 63ft steam tug *Mayflower*, built at Bristol in 1861, was berthed here in 1981. She was used for towing barges on the canal until 1963 and then lay derelict until 1972 when a new owner started to restore her.

Gloucester Docks, with their warehouses and mills, are a unique piece of mid-nineteenth-century industrial architecture and some of it was still being used in 1981 by commercial businesses. The dock owners, the British Waterways Board, have pledged to keep the docks' architectural character and create some form of waterside craft village in the buildings that are no longer in commercial use.

There is a regular trade of 1,000-ton tankers coming up to Quedgeley, some 4 miles below Gloucester, while grain is still taken up the Severn to the mills at Tewkesbury.

Lydney

The name 'Lidaneg' in Old English means Sailors' Island. It was to this harbour that small coasting vessels came to load coal from the Forest of Dean in the late nineteenth and early twentieth centuries. Now a forgotten port with crumbling quayside buildings, although the sailing club has preserved one of them.

Saul

There were fourteen yards in Gloucestershire where the open Severn trows were built, but Saul was one of the main centres where they were built and owned. By the 1870s trows had been forced out of much of the inland trade by the railways. The Victorian box trows had raised sides and were ketch-rigged

The 1,000-ton coastal tanker Blakeley *passing through Sellars Bridge bound for the Quedgeley oil terminal on the Gloucester & Berkeley Canal* (Derek Pratt)

for coastal work, which included occasional summer freights to Ireland.

Sharpness
The River Severn estuary, with its strong tide and ever changing channels, has always been a very difficult place for small vessels to navigate. To avoid this stretch of the upper estuary, a ship canal was built from Sharpness to Gloucester. There are 20 acres of floating dock at Sharpness, but 1,000-ton vessels can continue up to Gloucester. The distance by canal is 16 miles while it is some 30 miles up the windy channel of the Severn.

The Severn at Sharpness is well known for its wildfowl. In 1908 the Court of Chancery ruled that if wildfowlers stayed in their boats they were within their rights, but once they stepped on land they became poachers.

GREATER LONDON

Central London
Because London is largely built on marshland beside the Thames, flooding has always been a problem. The Embankment was built at Chelsea in 1874 to protect it from flooding. Above this is Cheyne Walk which has a houseboat colony where many interesting old craft have ended their days. The stretch of Thames above the Pool of London has little shipping. However, it was on these reaches that the Romans chose to establish the settlement that has grown into Greater London. Two Roman boats have been discovered in this area, one on the County Hall site in 1910 and another was discovered during the building of the Blackfriars underpass in 1962. The Blackfriars barge is believed to date from the year AD 200 and was constructed in the Celtic tradition. She is the oldest sailing vessel yet found in northern Europe. Both of these Roman boats and many other interesting items are now displayed at the Museum of London.

Isle of Dogs
The grazing marshes on the western side of the Isle of Dogs became known as Millwall, because of the drainage windmills which once stood on the river wall. With the development of docks in these marshes, two new towns, Millwall and Cubitt Town, were built, the latter being named after Sir William Cubitt who started building here in 1843. In the past this area was famed for its lawlessness. The *Great Eastern* was built at Millwall between 1853 and 1858 and was launched sideways into the Thames after many difficulties.

This dockland area has been radically changed by new housing schemes since World War II, although a few Victorian pubs and terraced houses have survived. The great dock complex is hidden behind high walls and it is quite difficult to see ships; even the river front has many access points closed.

Kensington
The Science Museum in Exhibition Road has an extremely good collection of ship models on display. This includes most types of vessels from liners and battleships to local work boats, and there is also a large model of the Port of London docks. The museum provides a service of selling plans and photographs of vessels to the public.

London Bridges
The medieval London Bridge effectively prevented seagoing ships from travelling any further up the Thames, so the Pool, and then the area below, inevitably became shipping centres. Tower Bridge was opened in 1886, but many of the bridges up river are far older. Richmond Bridge was built in 1777 and the others were built over the following century. The dates of some of the present bridge structures are: Kew Bridge 1903, Vauxhall Bridge 1906, Waterloo Bridge 1944, London Bridge 1973, Wandsworth Bridge 1940, Hammersmith Bridge 1887, Lambeth Bridge 1932, Chelsea Bridge 1937 and Albert Bridge

1873. Before marine engines were introduced, barges bound up river used to drift on the tide through the bridges, requiring great skill and hard work to avoid damage.

London Dockland and the Thames

The Port of London in Victorian times was the greatest port in Britain and indeed the whole world. The main dockland was from above Barking Creek, on the north bank, to Tower Bridge. There was also the Surrey Commercial Dock on the south bank, and most of the Pool of London was lined with warehouses.

After the West India Docks closed in 1980, only the Port of London Authority's Royal Group of docks remained really active of the original upper London Docks, while the privately owned Victoria deep water terminal on the River Thames at Greenwich handles containers. The PLA has developed Tilbury Docks as its major UK container terminal and forest products terminal. The Northfleet Hope riverside container terminal at Tilbury received its first vessel *Encounter Bay* in 1978.

Before the Thames was dredged in the nineteenth century there were sandbanks known as Ham Shelf blocking the navigable channel above Woolwich Reach. This led to King Henry VIII establishing the royal dockyard at Woolwich so that naval ships did not have the difficulty of getting up river to

The Union Castle Company's Llandovery Castle *(II) entering the West India Dock, London. This 14½-knot twin-screw liner of 10,609 tons was built by Barclay, Curle & Company on the Clyde in 1925 for the East African service. The* Llandovery Castle *(II) was broken up in 1953* (Port of London Authority)

Deptford. Woolwich waterfront has been largely dominated by Government activity ever since. The royal dockyard here was building battleships until 1854, but the area was later turned over to the War Department. Woolwich Arsenal, on Gallions Reach, was started in the early eighteenth century as part of the Royal Dockyard. Gunpowder was made at the Royal Gunpowder Factory on the River Lea at Waltham Abbey, Essex, and on the marshes beside Faversham and Oare Creeks in Kent. Powder barges were a common sight on the Thames and the PLA regulations stated that they had to have a red band painted round the top of their hulls. Explosives could only be loaded into lighters or pure sailing barges until 1957, when the PLA relaxed this rule.

Before dredging, large ships could only lie at anchor for discharging in the 'holes' off Blackwall or at Deptford. The large East Indiamen did not go above Deptford and cargoes had to be taken up river to warehouses by barge.

In the course of the great nineteenth-century expansion, the only part not built over within the Port of London was Greenwich. Margaret of Anjou, wife of Henry VI, built the first royal palace here, and Charles II started building another in 1664 to get away from the bustle and smell of London. In 1694 William and Mary gave the palace by the river to be used as a hospital for seamen after the great naval victory at La Hogue in 1692. This was enlarged to become the Greenwich Royal Naval Hospital, which was opened in 1705. It was closed down in 1873 and the Royal Naval College moved from Portsmouth up to Greenwich.

Behind the Naval College, part of the former palace has become the National Maritime Museum which is the museum for all British maritime activities and is probably the most informative museum of its type in the world. It was started largely to record and display material from the Royal Navy, but it quickly spread to cover every field of British maritime endeavour. The museum has far more material in store than on display so exhibits are regularly changed.

Above the National Maritime Museum on the hill top is the Old Royal Observatory which was started by Charles II. In 1884 the longitude of Greenwich was accepted by the world as the prime meridian from which all other time is calculated (Greenwich Mean Time). However, atmospheric pollution caused the Royal Observatory to leave Greenwich Park and move to Hurstmonceux Castle in Sussex in 1949.

By the Thames at Greenwich is the clipper ship *Cutty Sark* which is open to the public. She has been restored to the rig she had in the 1870s when she was in her prime. Launched in the year that the Suez Canal was opened, 1869, she was soon eclipsed in the tea trade by steamers. Her record-breaking period was mainly between 1885 and 1895 when captained by Captain Woodget in the Australian wool trade. Also near the *Cutty Sark* is the ketch *Gipsy Moth IV* in which Sir Francis Chichester sailed round the world single handed in 1966.

Below the Pool, the wharves and warehouses shut off the river from the land and it is only at places like Greenwich and Tower Bridge that it is possible to catch a good glimpse of the mighty River Thames. This is a great pity because it is a very fine river by any standard. Perhaps the best way to see the Thames is to go on a launch trip from near the Tower of London but even then one sees very little of the dockland which is screened by high walls. The reason for this was that stealing from ships and warehouses was once almost a large industry on the Thames, and only by restricting public access could any cargo arrive at its right destination.

The old sailor town around Wapping is now very run down and largely being redeveloped. The London Docks have been filled in and built over, but by the foresight of Taylor Woodrow Ltd, St Katharine's Dock has been saved and is open as a yacht marina and tourist centre. St Katharine's Dock was very small by London standards and was originally opened in 1828. To build the dock, some 11,300 people, which was then about the population of a provincial British city, had to be moved from the old medieval alleys and streets on the site. After World War II, when prolonged dockers' strikes slowly stifled the Port of London, St Katharine's was the first dock to be closed because freights were being taken elsewhere.

The present St Katharine's Dock is a very good example of how a disused industrial site can be given a new purpose without destroying its character. About 2,000 people are employed in the hotels, shops and restaurants. The old St Katharine's Dock was lined with tall, dark warehouses, while the present layout has a more open air.

A sailor warping out of St Katharine's Dock in a sailing ship bound for India or the Far East might well have expected not to see the London River again for a year or more. Today the Eastern Dock, behind the Dickens Inn, has become the safe haven for a unique collection of traditional ships owned by the Maritime Trust. The only way these ships can survive is by donations and the money paid by people to look round them. The latest ship is Scott's polar expedition ship *Discovery*, while the steamer *Robin* represents the type of ship which made up the bulk of Britain's merchant navy prior to World War I. The beautiful topsail schooner *Kathleen & May* is a very good example of a British trading vessel of the late Victorian and Edwardian period, while the *Lydia Eva* is the only survivor of the highly effective, perhaps too effective, steam herring drifter which, until about 1955, was common at the East Anglian and eastern Scottish ports. Also in the Historic Ship Collection is the steam tug *Challenge* and the *Nore* light vessel.

As well as the static collection, the St Katharine By The Tower Company has encouraged other traditional craft to make their base here. In the spring of 1981 there were sixteen Thames sailing barges and one former Brixham sailing trawler lying here. During the summer, many of these go out on charter voyages, but the movement of craft helps to give life to this dock.

South Bank

Cherry Garden Pier in Bermondsey marks the boundary between the Upper and Lower Pool of London. When Samuel Pepys knew the Cherry Garden, it was still out in the country, and became one of the pleasure gardens where Londoners came down river for their recreation. The best known of these public gardens was perhaps Vauxhall Pleasure Gardens where an entrance fee was charged. Some gardens added funfairs and were a centre of London's social life for nearly two hundred years.

Vauxhall Gardens were closed in 1859 and were quickly engulfed by a sea of houses and factories although Tyers Street and Spring Garden Lane mark the approximate site. The Cherry Garden at Bermondsey was also swept under by a tide of bricks and mortar as the Pool of London became lined by brick warehouses five or more storeys high. With the decline of this part of London as an industrial area since 1945, many of these warehouses have been pulled down. By 1981 the Cherry Garden Pier had been closed and was surrounded by open land backing onto high rise flats.

Up river, brick warehouse façades line the south bank of the Thames, and in Shad Thames a creek runs inland. This is also lined with warehouses and they are supplied by lighters from the docks. Above Tower Bridge there are gaps in the cliff of warehouses where some have been demolished. Up stream of the tower of London is Hay's Wharf and another ancient dock cutting into the towering warehouses. Further still, above London Bridge, is St Saviour's Dock which dates from before the creation of the great dock system in the nineteenth century.

At Symons Wharf, opposite the

Tower of London, HMS *Belfast* has been berthed and open to the public since 1971. She was one of two improved 'Southampton' class cruisers, her sister ship being HMS *Edinburgh* which was lost in World War II. *Belfast* played a leading part in helping to sink the German pocket battleship *Scharnhorst* and was at the invasion of Normandy in 1944. She was in active service during the Korean War and finally came out of commission in 1965. The Royal Navy was then going over to missiles so *Belfast* was preserved as one of the last big-gun warships.

Southwark

The Imperial War Museum is primarily concerned with recording military operations in the two major world wars, but it also sets out to portray all aspects of British armed forces. It has many items, documents and photographs in its collection and on display relating to naval matters. One of the maritime exhibits is the 15ft clinker boat *Tamzine* which was one of the smaller craft used to ferry troops off the beaches during the Dunkirk evacuation. Also here is the 40ft *CMB 4*, a torpedo boat built by Thornycroft in 1916, the first boat with a hydroplane hull. She sank the Russian cruiser *Oleg* in 1919.

In 1613, when the first Globe Theatre was burnt down, the watermen were very concerned at the loss of their livelihood in not having passengers to ferry across the Thames. It was claimed that there were thousands of watermen earning a living on the Thames between Gravesend and Windsor and the majority of these lived in Bankside. The popular actor Tom Doggett had a great liking for the Thames watermen and in 1715 he started the Doggett Coat and Badge Race which is now the world's oldest rowing race. The race was originally rowed at the beginning of August in the watermen's wherries, but nowadays light sculling skiffs are used. The original course was against the ebb tide between two public houses about 4¼

miles apart, but now it is a similar distance, with the tide, from London Bridge to Cadogan Pier, Chelsea. Since 1873 the race has been limited to six entrants. The Company of Watermen and Lightermen used to administer the race from the beautiful Waterman's Hall at St Mary at Hill, but the Fishmongers Company have helped to run the race since 1971. In 1977 a new pub, the Doggett's Coat & Badge, was opened on the south bank near Blackfriars Bridge.

Stratford

The Passmore Edwards Museum in Stratford was started by J. Passmore Edwards and opened by the Countess of Warwick, in 1900. This museum, which is a good example of Victorian architecture, has made a determined effort to build up a collection of local material. In 1979 it acquired the spritsail barge *Dawn* which had been built at Maldon, Essex, in 1897 for the 'stacky' trade to take hay and straw from farm wharves to London for the street horses. The *Dawn* traded until 1961 and then became a lighter, but Gordon Swift bought her in 1965 and rigged her out again for sailing in holiday charter work. The Passmore Edwards Museum took the imaginative step of buying the barge to keep her active in charter and exhibition work.

Teddington

The limit of the tidal Thames and the Port of London Authority. A weir was built here in 1811 and Teddington Lock was added later to prevent flooding at high tides. Although there have been discussions since the 1850s about building another flood barrier lower down the Thames, and serious floods, particularly those in 1953, amply demonstrated the need for one, it was not until the late 1970s that the Woolwich Flood Barrier was started.

Victoria Embankment

Along Victoria Embankment on the northern side of the Thames, a number of ships are permanently berthed but are not normally open to the public. These include the *Wellington*, a former naval sloop built in 1935 which is now the headquarters of the Honourable Company of Master Mariners. This Company was registered in 1925 and was the first London livery company started for about two hundred years. In the next downstream berths lie the World War I 'Flower' class naval sloops *Chrysanthemum* and *President* which are used by the Naval Reserve.

The former Humber paddle ferry *Tattershall Castle* which became an art gallery is also berthed beside Victoria Embankment.

HAMPSHIRE

Buckler's Hard
Because of the good supply of local timber, shipbuilding flourished here, particularly during wars with France from 1793 to 1815, when men-of-war of up to 74 guns were built. After this, the Adams family continued building until 1841, but on a very much smaller scale; they produced merchantmen and yachts. There is a model showing Buckler's Hard in 1803, with two men-of-war under construction, at the Buckler's Hard Maritime Museum. The Master Builder's House at the bottom of the unusually wide village street is now a hotel.

Gosport
Part of HMS *Dolphin*, one of the Royal Navy land bases, houses the Royal Navy Submarine Museum and there is an Armament Museum at Priddys Hard. Many Royal Navy craft end their days in the ship breaker's yard at Portsmouth, but the 1,620-ton HMS *Alliance* was saved by the trustees of the Submarine Museum. She is an A class submarine designed at the end of World War II to serve in the Pacific, which meant high surface speeds, in this case 18 knots, for long range. She was given better living accommodation for the crew who were at sea for long periods. *Alliance* was built in 1947 at Barrow-in-Furness, and her seagoing career lasted until 1973.

The Maritime Trust have three of their vessels at Gosport. The 170ft HMS *Gannet*, an auxiliary steam sloop built in 1878, is a hulk on moorings awaiting restoration. The Steam Launch Restoration Group has HSL(S)*376*, an Admiralty harbour service launch, built in 1944, under their care. Also the *Steam Cutter No 463*, built as a tender to the Royal Yacht in 1899, is under restoration at a boatyard.

Portsmouth
The royal dockyard at Portsmouth is not open to the public except where it is possible to walk through to look round HMS *Victory*, but even at this distance, it is possible to see some of the buildings, many of which have plaques on them stating when they were built.

HMS *Victory* was laid down in 1759 and launched in 1765, but her completion and first commission was delayed until 1778. Although she was a flagship from new, it is for her period as Nelson's flagship, from 1803 to 1805, that she is chiefly remembered. When the 2,162-ton *Victory* went to sea fully commissioned in time of war she had aboard 45 officers and 800 seamen and marines. Since 75 per cent of the seamen were forced against their will into the Navy, the marines' principle task at this period was to prevent desertion in port and mutiny at sea.

The guns on the lower deck weighed $2\frac{1}{2}$ tons, fired a 32lb shot with a range of $1\frac{1}{2}$ miles and required a crew of fourteen. It is believed that one reason for the decisive victory at the Battle of Trafalgar was that the Royal Navy's guns were fired by flintlock which allowed a shot to be fired every $1\frac{1}{2}$ minutes while the French and Spanish had fuses that allowed only a shot every 3 minutes. Only one of the guns used at Trafalgar on 21 October 1805 remains on the ship. The other eight surviving guns from Trafalgar are in British museums.

With the advent of steam warships, *Victory* was reduced to a hulk, but in 1922 a public appeal was started to save the ship in a permanent berth ashore. She was opened to the public in 1930 and guided tours are still regularly provided by the Royal Navy. However, *Victory* is the official flagship of the Admiral of the Home Fleet and sometimes part of the ship is closed for official duties. This makes her the oldest commissioned warship in the world.

Also in the naval dockyard near *Victory* is the Royal Naval Museum which has the state barge that carried Nelson's coffin from Greenwich to Whitehall stairs in 1806 as the central exhibit. The Royal Marines Museum is at Eastney Barracks, Portsmouth, and traces the history of the naval army since their formation in 1664. It is hoped that the Tudor warship *Mary Rose* will be placed in a museum in Warblington Street, Old Portsmouth.

Lying on a mooring out in Portsmouth harbour is HMS *Foudroyant*, a 26-gun sailing frigate built at Bombay as the *Trincomalee* in 1817. She replaced the former *Foudroyant* which was wrecked at Blackpool in 1897. The present *Foudroyant* is unrigged and the hull is used by a Trust to train young people. Another unrigged naval ship is the HMS *Gannet* in Fareham Creek. She was built as a naval sloop in 1878 and was used for 'gunboat' duties policing the British Empire. Later she had large deckhouses added, but her owners, The Maritime Trust, would like to restore her to a fully-rigged ship with steam power.

Southampton
The modern port of Southampton was formed because the Cunard, Union Castle and Royal Mail lines adopted it as a passenger terminal. It was at its height as a liner terminal between 1910 and 1960 and Southampton Water was used as a flying boat base in the 1930s. Most of the trade is now container ships and oil tankers to Fawley, but cruise liners still use the port.

Southampton's history is well recorded in the Maritime Museum on Bugle Street. This building was built as a wool warehouse in the fourteenth century. HMS *Cavalier*, built by White at Cowes in 1944 as one of thirty-two C class destroyers built during World War II, is owned by a trust and is at Southampton for restoration. The *Cavalier* was bought by the trust in 1977 because they believe she represented the peak of destroyer design which started in 1893 with the A class.

HUMBERSIDE

Barrow upon Humber
A creek near the Humber ferry port of New Holland. A narrow twisting channel leads up to the old brickworks and Barrow village.

Barton upon Humber
On the south bank of the Humber there is a narrow creek which was a busy port in the nineteenth century. The huge brick maltings, which stood on the east side of the creek mouth, provided regular work for Humber sloops and billyboys.

Also on the east side of the narrow creek are the ropewalk rails of the Hall's Barton Ropery, while at the creek mouth on the west side stands the sheds of Clapson's Yard. This family firm now operates a yacht marina in the entrance of New River Ancholme at Ferriby Sluice, but it once built wooden Humber trading sloops at Barton. In recent years the steel Humber sloop *Amy Howson*, built at Beverley in 1914, has been here awaiting restoration to sail.

Beverley
An inland town with a waterway known as the Beck connecting it to the River Hull. The Humber Keel & Sloop Preservation Society based its fully restored steel Humber keel *Comrade* below the mills at Beverley Beck. This Humber keel, with its square sail, is the only

one of its type under sail. Attempts to preserve others have not been very successful. The wooden keel *Mayday* was allowed to sink in the timber ponds at Goole.

Bridlington

A small harbour around which grew a largely Edwardian summer resort. In the eighteenth century smugglers were as active here as on every part of the British coast. Underground passages under the pier slip lead to cellars in Prince Street and Garrison Street which were presumably intended for bringing contraband ashore unseen by the Customs officers.

Bridlington Bay is sheltered by Flamborough Head and was used as a place of shelter by coastal vessels. Large cobles of up to 45ft were used to run coal out to steamers which were running short of fuel. These cobles were able to carry up to 7 tons each. The big cobles were normally used for trawling and long-lining. Since a large sail area was needed to develop the power to pull a trawl, these Bridlington cobles often became two-masted luggers by having a small mizzen stepped. The motor cobles still working from the harbour are mostly engaged in taking out anglers.

Burton upon Stather

A village near the River Trent which was one of the places where Humber keels, the local inland barge, and the billyboys, the seagoing version, were built and owned. Burton is above the Trent Falls where the rivers Ouse, Trent and Humber meet. In the Victorian period coasting schooners were built and owned here.

Flamborough

A village just inland from the 400ft high chalk headland of Flamborough Head which juts out into the North Sea. The fishing cobles here worked from north and south landings on either side of Flamborough Head. A steam capstan used to haul the cobles up the steep narrow landings, while donkeys carried the catch and gear in panniers back to the village.

In 1895 there were eighty small and thirty large cobles working from the two landings. Some families kept a coble at each landing which could be used according to the weather. The women used to gather whelks on the foreshore for baiting the cod long-lines. In the past Flamborough was very remote and the dialect spoken was almost a separate language. The Flamborough Sword Dance is well known while another old custom was 'Raising the Herring' which required the women to dress up as men and go through the village singing.

Goole

Goole is 60 miles inland from Spurn Head. The port grew up for the export of coal in the mid-nineteenth century. In 1870 there were 457 ships, mostly sailing vessels, registered here.

Goole Library and Museum have a collection of material relating to the port, particularly a collection of paintings by local marine artist Reuben Chappell.

Grimsby

Grimsby was an important medieval port, but the harbour silted up. In 1849 the Manchester, Sheffield & Lincolnshire Railway opened their line down to the Old Dock which had been opened in 1801. In 1852 the Royal Dock was opened on land reclaimed on the south shore of the River Humber.

The railway company offered cheap rates to attract trawling smacks to land their catch from Dogger Bank at Grimsby. By 1860 the port had 315 smacks. The introduction of steam trawlers gave Grimsby another advantage because, being relatively near the mines, coal was cheaper. Grimsby owners went over to steam in the 1890s, and while fishing craft grew in size, they decreased in number. By the start of World War II, there were 240 fishing vessels based here. In 1977 a severe setback was caused by Iceland extending her fishing limits to 200 miles, which deprived the deepwater trawlers of their traditional grounds. The docks were enlarged between 1852 and 1934 by which time there were 140 acres of enclosed water.

A well-known feature is the 313ft high Grimsby Dock Tower, built in 1852 entirely of brick in the Italian style of the Campanile in Florence. The tower was the brain child of W. G. Armstrong with the idea that the water pumped up into the tower would provide the hydraulic pressure to operate the lock gates. The Grimsby Tower is no longer used for its original purpose but a preservation order has been placed on it.

The Welholme Galleries in Grimsby have models of many different types of English fishing boats and also the Doughty collection of marine paintings.

Hessle

A town on the edge of Kingston upon Hull on the north bank of the River Humber with a creek mainly dominated by Dunston's shipyard. In 1981 the Humber paddle ferry *Lincoln Castle* was towed to Hessle and berthed near the Humber Bridge to be opened as a pub and restaurant. The Humber Bridge was opened on 24 June 1981.

Hornsea

Situated south of Bridlington in flat countryside known as Holderness, which extends right down to Spurn Head at the mouth of the Humber Estuary. Over the centuries the sea has steadily eaten away at this coast so that it is believed that about thirty towns and villages which existed in medieval times are now under the sea. Hornsea was a port during the medieval period.

The area once contained a number of meres, most of which have been eroded away. However Hornsea Mere, a freshwater lake about 2 miles long, exists inland from the town and is used for dinghy sailing. Hornsea and Withernsea, further down the coast towards Spurn Head, mark the southerly limit of the coble as the traditional working boat.

Hull

Kingston upon Hull, to give its full name, is a major port about 21 miles inland from Spurn Head. Once an important whaling port, but this had finished by the mid-nineteenth century when it was the home of a large fleet of trawling smacks. These smacks and, after the 1900s, the steam trawlers, worked in fleets with a steam carrier racing with the catch to Billingsgate and other markets. When the fleet system became too expensive to operate and collapsed in 1936, some 60 trawlers and 800 fishermen became unemployed, and at Billingsgate many porters, salesmen and office staff were thrown out of work.

Hull revived after World War II as the home of deepwater trawlers that ranged as far as Arctic waters. In 1961 the Hull vessel *Lord Nelson* pioneered stern trawling with facilities for freezing part of the catch. The *Lord Nelson* and the *Junella*, completed in the following year, were the forerunners of the new distant water trawlers. By the early 1970s, Hull had about 40 freezer trawlers.

Hull, like Grimsby and Fleetwood, was heavily hit by the loss of the Icelandic fishing grounds. Hull's active distant water trawlers had been reduced from 130 in 1977 to only 27 in 1980.

There are plans to turn the Humber Dock, near the Old Harbour, into a yacht marina. One vessel lying here is the smack *William McCann*, built at Hull in 1886 as the *City of Edinburgh*. Like many Humber smacks, she was sold to the Faeroes when steam trawlers were introduced. Fortunately, this smack survived long enough to be brought back to the Humber for restoration. The Maritime Museum at Hull has a large and well-laid-out display on whaling and the fishing industry.

Immingham

There was an important port here on the south shore of the Humber in the thirteenth century. The present 44 acre dock was a case of a railway creating a new town early this century to export coal.

The dock was opened by King George V in 1912. Fison's fertilizer plant is now the largest user of Immingham Docks.

Keadby

Only a hamlet of the River Trent with a coal-loading chute, but it was very well known because so many east-coast craft came here to load coal for the gas works on the south and east coasts. It was also liked because the local people were particularly friendly. The same was true of other smaller ports such as King's Lynn and Harwich—in the larger ports everything had to be locked and guarded against thieves.

The rivers Ouse and Trent meet at Trent Falls and flow into the Humber. Keadby is 17 miles up the Trent, a river which has 94 navigable miles. Trade on the Trent greatly increased with the canalisation of the River Soar in the 1770s, and further canals were built to link up the Trent with inland towns such as the Stainforth & Keadby Canal, opened in 1793.

Steam tugs were used to tow Humber sloops and Thames barges up river. Spritsail barges belonging to F. T. Everard & Son of Greenhithe, Goldsmiths of Grays and the London & Rochester Trading Company of Strood, were trading here regularly up to World War II, in spite of the difficulty of loading at the jetty in the strong tide. Small coasters from the large coastal fleet of Everards continued coming here until the 1960s.

New Holland

New Holland is said to have acquired its name because so much Dutch gin was smuggled in here during the late eighteenth century. The Manchester, Sheffield & Lincolnshire Railway built a line to New Holland in the late 1840s to link up with the ferry to Hull. The 1,500ft ferry pier was designed by John Fowler, designer of the Forth Bridge. In 1979 the Yarborough Arms public house was renamed the Lincoln Castle after the last steam ferry which ran between here and Hull.

Spurn Head

A great curved hook of sand running some four miles out from Holderness into the mouth of the River Humber. Because there is no community living out on Spurn Head, the RNLI maintain a full-time, paid crew for the station here; in most places lifeboat crews are volunteers.

ISLE OF WIGHT

Bembridge

A yachting resort with a small maritime museum. Out in Spithead there are four Victorian forts built to defend the naval base at Portsmouth: St Helen's, Horse Sand, Norman's Land and Spit Sand. When built between 1859 and 1865 they were known as 'Palmerston Follies' after the Prime Minister who commissioned them. These forts were the result of an invasion scare caused by bad relations with France. There was public concern that the new steamships—the abominable invention of the day in the Duke of Wellington's view—could steam 'straight', at speed, to Britain's shores and not have to spend several days beating against the wind across the Channel.

Cowes

Two small towns on either side of the River Medina. Cowes is the 'capital of British yachting' while the large 'Cowes Week' regatta in August is a major sailing event. In Edwardian times it marked the end of the fashionable society's 'season'. The Royal Yacht Squadron has its club house in Cowes Castle overlooking the entrance to the Medina. Yachting became popular on the south coast with the spread of the railways in Victorian times, and yachtsmen settled in Cowes because of the ideal sailing conditions in the Solent. East Cowes is the headquarters of the hovercraft industry.

Just above Cowes on the edge of the River Medina is the Folly Inn. This originated in the mid-eighteenth century as a hull pulled up on the foreshore with a door cut into the sides which was used by local young blades. The inn was later built over the hull, and until about 1979 part of the original *Folly*'s hull was on display in the dining-room floor.

Opposite the Folly Inn on the mud is the hulk of the Cowes ketch *Bee*, built by Hansen in 1801 and trading until 1926. Local tradition has it that she took victuals out to Nelson's ships.

The Solent smack *Fanny* CS 12, built at Cowes in 1872, is still sailing as a yacht on the east coast. She used to work oysters and enter the races during the summer until sold in 1920. Oysters were worked out in the Solent, but in the early 1970s some French oysters were laid and they spread rapidly throughout the Solent. Cowes is now again the centre for Solent oyster fishing boats.

Nab Tower

During World War I someone had the idea that the way to stop German submarines was to sink six towers across the Straits of Dover and put wire nets between them. The Admiralty actually commissioned one of these concrete towers which was built with the sand at Shoreham by 3,000 drafted workmen. After the war, the completed tower was given to Trinity House who placed it, in 1920, 5 miles east of the Isle of Wight where it became the Nab Lighthouse.

Ventnor

A resort on the south coast, the town has a small museum devoted to smuggling. Wooden beach boats are still built here. Before World War II shrimps caught off the Isle of Wight were sought after at Billingsgate and some lobster potting still goes on here. Most of the fishing boats work from Yarmouth and Bembridge, at opposite ends of the island.

Wootton

A very attractive creek on the north side of the island. List's shipyard operated at Fishbourne, on the eastern shore of the creek mouth, until about 1860. Lord

Yarborough had his famous full-rigged yacht *Falcon* built by List in 1824. *Falcon* became a China opium clipper in 1836, and she is regarded as being one of the ships which contributed to the development of the British clipper ship.

A stone tide mill stood at the head of the creek until about 1955; Cowes ketches came in here to load grain and flour which was shipped across to Portsmouth for making hard tack (ships' biscuits) for the Navy.

KENT

Chatham

The first royal dockyard on the Medway was started at Chatham in 1571. In 1620 the site was enlarged and by 1860 it covered 71 acres. This was the birthplace of many of the Navy's great ships including HMS *Victory*. In the late nineteenth century, the dockyard was constantly being rebuilt and enlarged on reclaimed marshland, and new warships continued to be constructed here. Although the dockyard has many listed buildings of historic interest, it is only open to the public occasionally. In front of the Medway House, there is a good collection of ship's figure-heads. Some of the 1811 machinery in the Ropehouse, built in 1785, is still in working order.

Deal

A rare example of a settlement being preceded by an anchorage and the use of the beach: the reason for Deal's growth in the late Tudor period was The Downs, a sheltered anchorage off the town. In the age of sail, ships gathered here in their hundreds waiting windbound for a favourable slant of wind to go up the North Sea or into the English Channel.

Deal was at its peak when The Downs were an important naval base during the Napoleonic Wars. Around 400 men were employed running stores and men out to ships and as Thames pilots.

The Deal Maritime & Local History Museum is housed on the site of the former market garden in St George Road which supplied fresh vegetables to vessels in The Downs. The museum has the Deal galley *Saxon King*, built in about 1890. The Deal galleys were narrow pulling (rowing) boats which worked off the beach attending anchored ships. After their work had finished a few galleys were kept for the Deal Regatta, but the only other galley to survive is the *Undaunted* which is normally kept near the pier.

The earliest record of a Deal galley is in 1770 when they existed in their present name and form, but they were probably established long before that. In 1801, when Nelson was stationed in The Downs, he wrote how a galley had come through the surf on to the beach in conditions which would have swamped an Admiralty built boat. Because of the good reputation of the Deal galleys, naval captains used to buy them. There is little doubt that the boats of Deal greatly influenced small craft design.

The galley was essentially a fast rowing boat, but the other types of Deal craft were sailed. The Deal beachmen worked in co-operative units known as companies which had a set of boats. The largest were 'forepeakers', two-masted luggers up to 40ft long which had a small cabin forward and took pilots out to meet incoming ships. The open 'cat boats', again two-masted luggers, were used for salvaging and taking anchors and chain out to ships in distress. The galley punt, larger than a galley, was a general purpose boat. The introduction of steam tugs by the 1860s meant that ships spent less time in The Downs. After 1900 fishing became the main occupation and the 15ft fore-mizzen punts such as the *Secret* and the *Penny Anne*, which are now owned by the museum at Deal, were more practical for fishing. Boats are still kept on Deal beach and many take anglers out to fish round the wrecks on the Goodwin Sands.

Dover

A major cross-channel ferry port to France and Belgium dominated by a massive castle, built on medieval remains. In 1980 the holder of the 'Blue Riband of the Channel' pennant was the ferry *Herald of Free Enterprise* which crossed from Dover to Calais in 52 minutes 53 seconds at an average speed of 24.7 knots. Dover museum has ship models and a section on the medieval Cinque Ports.

Faversham

In medieval times there was a sea route from Faversham to London south of the Isle of Sheppey but silting and walling up of the marshes have reduced the Swale to a narrow channel. The remains of a Saxon ship were dug up on Graveney Marsh, well back from the sea, in October 1970 and taken to the National Maritime Museum, Greenwich, where there is a replica on display. Faversham now stands inland, a creek port which once had a flourishing coastal trade. The town has many fine old buildings and the narrow creek is lined with wharves. At the head is a small wet dock.

Lower Halstow

Like many creeks, Lower Halstow dries out at low tide, but with the marshland church of St Margaret of Antioch on the west bank, it is a charming waterside area. The brickfields on the opposite bank have been demolished.

Richborough

The River Stour to the attractive Cinque Port of Sandwich became so silted up in the late eighteenth century that the town declined. During World War I it was feared that the German fleet would bombard Dover and Folkestone and cut off the main supply link with France. In 1916 the Government decided to create a third ferry port, inland, in the safety of the Stour.

The 'mystery port' of Richborough was created on some nineteenth-century salt works on the banks of the River

Stour in 1916. By November 1917, three cross-channel ferries were running from Richborough to France and the port was active until 1921. The 1,500 acre site was taken over again by the Government in World War II, and part of 'Mulberry Harbour' was assembled here in preparation for D-Day landings in Normandy on 6 June 1944. Early in 1950 there was an attempt to develop the quays as a commercial port, but with the Ramsgate and Dover harbours thriving nearby it was not successful. It is still possible to see some of the buildings on the marshes beside the Stour.

Rochester

The Rochester Public Museum has a collection of ship models, including some French prisoner-of-war models made in Rochester Castle, models of barges and a fishing bawley.

Romney Marsh

In the late eighteenth and early nineteenth centuries, smuggling of spirits, brandy and tobacco from France was a vast, well-organised industry on Romney Marsh. The lonely marshes were difficult to patrol and were within easy reach of London.

The Coast Blockade, later the Coastguard Service, fought the 'Battle of Brookland' with smugglers near Rye in 1821. In 1828 the 'Battle of Sidley Green' was fought between smugglers armed with poles and the Coast Blockade men armed with cutlasses. One officer was killed and two smugglers died; the rest were captured and sent to New South Wales.

Sheerness

The main town of the Isle of Sheppey. A naval dockyard was opened here in 1665 and later a fortress was added. The dockyard was closed in 1969 but has reopened as a commercial port. Out in the Thames Estuary can be seen the wreck of the *Robert Montgomery*, sunk in World War II and still loaded with live ammunition.

Sittingbourne

The creek was lined with brick and cement works, all of which are closed. A group from the Society for Spritsail Barge Research has taken over an abandoned barge-building yard and opened it as the Dolphin Barge Museum. The idea is to provide a place where barge hulls can be restored by their owners. Also the former workshop, with a sail loft on the second floor and the forge (with barge tillers in the framework), are open in the summer.

LANCASHIRE

Blackpool

This is the north of England's great seaside resort, created entirely to provide pleasure for holiday makers from the mill towns of Lancashire and Greater Manchester. Large clinker-built sloops were designed by William Stoba of Fleetwood about 1890 to take trippers 'round the bay'. Stoba was a foreman shipbuilder who worked in several yards and his designs were very progressive. He was one of few British designers to incorporate successfully centreboards into working sailing boats.

By 1980 Blackpool was receiving 6 million staying visitors a year and some 20 million day trippers.

Fleetwood

In the 1830s the local landowner and MP, Sir Peter Hesketh Fleetwood, envisaged a new port on the southern side of Morecambe Bay between the mouth of the River Wyre and the sea. The original street plan was marked out by the architect Decimus Burton with a plough across rabbit warrens. When the railway opened in 1840, Fleetwood was able to expand into a ferry port for Belfast, but although this took trade from Glasson Dock, which in turn had killed Lancaster's trade, Liverpool continued to be the major port of this coast.

The first lighthouse was built at Fleetwood in 1841. Ships had to lay at anchor in the channel to unload, so in 1869 dock construction began, and by 1900 it was recognised as a port, with large sailing ships coming in to unload.

Smacks from the east coast began to fish from here in the late 1850s, and the Leadbetter family of fishermen moved up from Southport. By 1860 there were thirty-two fishing vessels at Fleetwood and this had increased to seventy in 1876, by which time Fleetwood had overtaken Liverpool as a fishing port which had forty-one smacks, mostly owned in Hoylake. By 1909, when there were about thirty-five steam trawlers at Fleetwood it was one of the main fishing ports in Britain, together with Milford Haven, Aberdeen, Hull, Grimsby and Lowestoft. As well as deepwater trawlers, Fleetwood had a fleet of inshore sailing boats, known locally as half-deckers.

The 64ft *Reliance* had been built by Liver & Wilding of Fleetwood in 1903 to a design by their master shipwright William Stoba. The 40ft Fleetwood cutter smack *Provider*, built in 1904, had a centreboard, but the smacks *Reliance*, *Surprise* and the 68ft *Louie Rigby*, as well as the pilot cutters *Alpha* and *Kindly Light* (now in Cardiff Museum), were all keel boats noted for speed. Stoba also designed some of the traditional yachts seen in Morecambe Bay which had a low freeboard like the prawners. His most successful yacht was the 42ft *Zulu* of 1901 which established a record in 1938 by sailing from Fleetwood to Ramsey on the Isle of Man in 6 hours, 52 minutes.

Glasson Dock

In the 1780s, merchants who were worried by the silting up of the River Lune to Lancaster, financed the building of a dock at Glasson. This was improved and enlarged in 1826 when a canal was opened linking it to the Preston–Lancaster canal. Glasson Dock took trade away from Lancaster's 'out port' Sunderland, but eventually Fleetwood became the port for the area. However, there was some shipbuilding

at Glasson and the well-known 94ft schooner *Englishman* was built here by Simpson in 1864, and Marsh & Nicholson built the attractive clipper-bowed pilot schooner *Falcon* here in 1894 which was wrecked on the Devon coast in 1972.

When the coastal trade finished, Glasson was left as a pleasant place for yachts.

Hambleton

A small residential village on the River Wyre. Mussels used to be gathered here and pearls were often found in them. Pearl mussels were known as Hambleton Hookings. The river is now silted up which discourages large boats.

Heysham

The Midland Railway took a bold step by creating a new port at Heysham between 1896 and 1904. Ferry services eventually linked the port with Belfast, Dublin and Londonderry. Although a good commercial port was created, it altered the channels in Morecambe Bay and many mussel skears were silted over, which put local gatherers out of work.

Lancaster

The ancient port at the head of the River Lune where the castle dominates the little grey stone city. In the late eighteenth century, Lancaster was the main port of the coast until overtaken by Liverpool.

The mid-eighteenth-century Custom house, with its Ionic columns, and the tree-lined quay are a reminder of Lancaster's important past. Lancaster's ancient inn, the Carpenters Arms, and Skerton Bridge were reputedly the haunt of press gangs waiting to grab any unsuspecting country lad and drag him off to serve in the navy. Lancaster still has a Cockle & Mussel Feast in May. These shell fish were once carried by packhorse.

In 1864 the Lune Shipbuilding Company at Lancaster tried to emulate the success of iron shipbuilding yards at Barrow and Liverpool. The 822-ton, full-rigged ship *Wennington* was their first ship, in 1865, and four more sailing ships and four steamers were built before the company was wound up in 1870.

Lytham St Anne's

The first bathing machine appeared on Lytham's golden sands in 1735. It had become an established resort long before the railway reached Lytham in 1864, becoming a fashionable resort for Lancashire's middle class during Victorian times. Prawners worked from Lytham and the local version of the sailing Morecambe Bay prawner had a round bottom to cope with the very hard foreshore. Lytham and St Anne's were quite separate until united in 1922, Lytham being a largely Victorian creation, while St Anne's was predominantly Edwardian.

Morecambe

A flourishing resort which developed from the village of Poulton-le-sands which had been a favourite bathing place in the early nineteenth century. In 1848, the railway arrived here and a wooden jetty was built for steamers. A steamer service to Belfast was started in 1853 and then one to Londonderry; a service to Dublin lasted until 1904. By then small prawner-type pleasure boats used to take out day trippers. Several liners and warships have been broken up at the jetty.

Overton

Pleasant fishing village by the River Lune. Two types of open boats were developed here to work the salmon fishery in the very strong tides. Whammel net fishing was done by staking the net ashore and running out the net from a 20ft whammel boat. The tank boats, so called because they had buoyancy tanks, worked in the confused broken water of the mouth of the River Lune. The whammel boats were built at Overton by Woodhouse & Gardner. In 1981 the Gardner family still had the *Ivanhoe* LR 86, which was built in 1906.

Preston

The 40 acre Albert Edward Dock was opened on the north bank of the River Ribble in 1892. It seems that the council contributed towards this dock which placed a great strain on the town's rates, but the docks did eventually pay.

Sunderland Point

A hamlet on the north bank of the River Lune reached by a road along the foreshore which floods at high tide. In the reign of King William III, the Quaker merchant Robert Lawson developed Sunderland Point for trade with the West Indies and Ireland. The three-floored warehouses have been converted to houses but the quay remains where ships once brought in rum, timber and, it is reputed, the first shipment of cotton to arrive in Britain. In 1787 a Custom house was opened up river at Lancaster and Sunderland Point lost its trade. Small traders discharged freight on the beach, but the hamlet became known as 'Cape Famine'.

By 1900 several mussel boats were working from Sunderland Point. These boats were built by Woodhouse of Overton. Some whammel boats still work from here.

LINCOLNSHIRE

Boston

A very old trade outlet to the North Sea. The River Witham runs to Lincoln from here and the Romans dug a canal, Foss Dyke, to link the Witham with the River Trent further inland. In medieval times the wool trade outlet made Boston a very important town, but the development of trade with North America gave towns on the west coast of Britain a geographical advantage; this exacerbated Boston's decline as the Fens were slowly reclaimed and the town was distanced from the sea.

In the early nineteenth century, there were many attempts to improve the river linking Boston with The Wash. Even the coming of the railways in 1848 failed to save Boston's trade, but in 1884 the Great Northern Railway decided to develop the town for coal export from the Midlands. Three coal hoists were built on South Quay at Boston Docks. A good supply of coal led to Boston becoming a base for North Sea steam trawlers, of which there were thirty-one in 1909. There were also small sailing cutter smacks working in The Wash. One of these, the 54ft smack *Telegraph* built by Gostelow at Boston in 1906, is being restored back to sail in Essex.

Fosdyke
Village on the Welland, one of the four rivers leading into The Wash. Shrimpers still work from here. The Wash sailing smacks, built at Lynn and Boston before World War I, had very narrow hulls, making them ideal for sailing against the wind—much of their time had to be spent beating up the narrow channels.

Saltfleet
While Holderness to the north of the Humber is being washed away, Donna Nook, a spit on the south side, is growing longer. Saltfleet Haven is south of Donna Nook. This hamlet was once an important port and has two fine old warehouses and the Elizabethan New Inn. A Humber sloop last called here in about 1935, with a freight of chalk.

Sutton Bridge
Situated in the Fens on a straight, artificial cut in the River Nene. In 1881 there was a grand scheme to build a dock to rival those at King's Lynn and Wisbech but due to lack of finance it was never completed. The swing bridge which opens to let ships go up to the port of Wisbech was built in 1894–7.

Tetney Haven
The Haile Sand Fort is on the southern side of the mouth of the line of beacons marking the channel across the sand to Tetney Haven.

In this tiny haven are the ruins of a lock at the entrance to the Louth Navigation through which Humber keels and billyboys once took cargoes up to Louth.

Wainfleet
The old word 'fleet' in eastern England generally means a shallow channel. Wainfleet creek is just on Gibraltar Point on the north side of The Wash. Wainfleet All Saints was an important port for wool exports in the medieval period, but even in 1394 there was a complaint that the channel was silting up. By 1774 it had completely silted up and Wainfleet Haven is now a tiny creek.

Wainfleet was the home of large, decked smacks since nearby Skegness, renowned for its bracing air, could only accommodate cobles on its beach. A few cobles worked off the beach here, while fishermen kept larger, decked smacks at Wainfleet. In the early 1970s there was an attempt to restart full-time fishing from here but the increasing seal population in The Wash appears to have been responsible for keeping down catches.

MERSEYSIDE

Birkenhead
The Wirral Museum has galleries of nautical material, notably builders' models from Cammell Laird & Company. This great shipbuilding firm was founded in 1903 with the amalgamation of Charles Cammell (1837) and William Laird (1824) and grew to cover 100 acres with 10 building berths and 7 graving docks. The seagoing monitor *Huascar*, built at Birkenhead in 1865 for Peru, is now in the Chilean Naval Museum in Talcahuano. She fought three important actions, and in 1878 HMS *Shah* attempted to sink her by firing, for the first time in naval history, self-propelled torpedoes. The 158ft gunboat *Uruguay*, built at Birkenhead in 1874, is fully restored at Buenos Aires, Argentina.

Hoylake

Before the River Mersey was dredged, it was the practice for large ships to anchor in the 'Hoye-Pool' off the western end of the Wirral and the goods were taken up river by smaller craft. The pool in the sands is now largely silted up although a few small craft still have moorings. A Victorian octagonal brick tower, now a house called 'Beacon', was originally one of two lighthouses here. The Beacon was rebuilt in 1865, while the earlier lighthouse, which had a coal burning fire, was built in 1761.

About a mile east of Dove Point is the disused eight-storey Leasowe Lighthouse. This was originally built in 1763, but was badly damaged by fire two years later.

Liverpool

A city which grew first through trade with Ireland in the medieval period, replacing Chester, and then in the late seventeenth and eighteenth centuries with trade to North America and the West Indies. The Stanleys (the Lords of Derby) held the Tower of Liverpool in the early fifteenth century and also virtually ruled Lancashire and the Isle of Man. In 1715 the Pool was turned into Liverpool's first wet dock. The slave trade brought great wealth, but Liverpool also provided some of the chief opponents of the trade. Many ship owners thought that the end of slavery would bring ruin to the port but it continued to grow as an outlet for the manufacturing towns.

New canals and railways brought more trade and the population increased from 77,653 in 1801 to 223,002 in 1841. The 'Hungry Forties' saw emigrants from both Ireland and Lancashire pouring out through the port. To be close to the docks, factories sprang up around Liverpool and across the Mersey at Birkenhead.

Liverpool was badly affected by the Depression in the early 1930s. In World War II Liverpool, England's backdoor, was the main port for supplying convoys from North America. This led to heavy bombing in two blitzes by the Luftwaffe. The Picton Library has a good collection of confiscated German aerial photographs of the complete Liverpool dock system which were taken before bombing. Reconstruction of the city after the war has taken away much of its former character.

The best way to see something of Liverpool's 7 miles of waterfront is from one of the Mersey ferries crossing to Seacombe or Birkenhead. The central feature of the waterfront is the Liver Building. Next to the central Pier Head group is the Merseyside Maritime Museum which is situated in part of the disused docks. This includes the Canning Graving Docks, a pair of dry docks built in 1765. The Albert Dock warehouses, which are Britain's largest Grade I listed buildings, have a good view out across the Mersey. The main display centre of the Merseyside Maritime Museum is the Old Pilotage Building, built in 1883 beside the Canning Dock locks.

The museum has many small craft on display, and around the wharfs are many remains of dockside machinery. There is also a hydraulic pumping station between the Canning Half-Tide Dock and Salthouse Dock. The museum also has a unique Maritime Brass Rubbing Centre where visitors can produce their own copies of shipbuilders' plates.

Other places in Liverpool with items of maritime interest include the Dudley Art Gallery, which was the home of a local shipowning family, and the Mersey Dock & Harbour Company offices on Pier Head which have some ship models in the main hall.

Local fishing boats used to work out of 'Cockle Hole', which was built at the South Ferry Basin, probably in the 1820s. It was used until the early 1970s but when the South Docks closed and were made tidal, they moved to the Coburgh Brunswick Docks where there is still a considerable fleet of part-time fishing boats.

Port Sunlight

William Lever, later Lord Leverhulme, started a town and port on the open ground west of the River Mersey in the 1890s for soap manufacture. He created an attractive garden town.

Southport

A resort on the coast which began developing in the late eighteenth century for sea bathing. Although there was a pool out on the sands, Southport was never a port; the name was given so that people knew that it was by the sea and would go there. However, fishermen also settled here and sold shrimps to the visitors. It is believed that around seventy prawners were owned in Southport and Marshside in 1904. The Botanic Gardens Museum at Churchtown has a display on the shrimping and a dugout canoe. In the Edwardian era there was growing interest in yachting on this coast; the 16ft Star Class dinghies were started at Southport in 1906 and eventually raced at West Kirby Sailing Club.

Wallasey

The first steam ferry across the Mersey to Birkenhead started in 1817 and encouraged the development of the Wirral as a residential area; industry followed. Wallasey was at the northern end of the Wirral and was separated from the rest by the River Birket. The lower reaches of this river became the Great Float Dock with Birkenhead on the south side. But the docks were started before this, with the Morpeth in 1847 and the Egerton in 1857.

NORFOLK

Broadland

The name given to a series of rivers and the connecting inland open 'broads', which were dug out in the medieval period for peat to be used as fuel. Within a triangle from Lowestoft, Norwich and Sea Palling are some thirty shallow broads and about 200 miles of river. The main Broads are Hickling, Barton and Wroxham while the largest of these inland lakes is the tidal Breydon Water on the River Yare above Yarmouth. In Victorian times the Norfolk wherries were the sailing barges which carried cargoes to the inland village staithes. In order to preserve one of these boats, the Norfolk Wherry Trust was formed in 1949 and since then has kept the *Albion* sailing with holiday charter parties. The Trust has also leased some marshes on Womack Dyke, near Potter Heigham, where it is to build a headquarters to store and repair wherries.

Burnham Thorpe

One of the seven Burnham villages on the north Norfolk coast. Horatio Nelson was born here in 1758, and his father was the rector of this and Burnham Norton parishes. The church of Burnham Thorpe has a great rood and lectern made of wood from HMS *Victory*.

Cromer

Only a few miles from the gentle reed-lined Broadland is the open North Sea coast of Norfolk. The medieval port of this part of the coast was Shipden, but. after this was eroded away in about 1430, Cromer became a port and in 1580 Elizabeth I granted permission for a harbour to be built. Harbour buildings on this sandy coast were repeatedly washed away: the last Cromer jetty was destroyed by the sea in 1897, since then fishermen have had to work off the beach. The pier was built in 1900–1.

There are beach landings at Caister, Winterton, Sea Palling and Happisburgh, but Cromer and Sheringham have a fleet of full-time longshore boats worked off the beach, mostly after crab.

The railway reached Cromer in 1877 and the railway companies promoted this section of the coast under the name 'Poppyland', in Victorian times.

Great Yarmouth

Amongst Yarmouth's numerous museums and places open to the public in the

A restored ice warehouse at Great Yarmouth. The ice was brought in during the winter and the thatched roof helped to keep it frozen so that the ice could be used by the smacks to preserve their catch. The weathervane is a Norfolk wherry. This type of local barge used to bring ice in from the Broads, amongst other types of work. The Norfolk Wherry Trust keep the wherry Albion *sailing, and also own the hull of the wherry* Lord Roberts. *In 1981 the hulk of the wherry* Maud *was raised from Ranworth Broad for rebuilding* (Author)

summer are the Elizabethan Merchant's House on the South Quay and the Old Merchant's House in The Rows. Since Yarmouth was built on a sandy spit of land between the sea and the River Yare, the space was limited and houses were packed together closely with narrow Rows (alleys) between. Many of the Rows were destroyed in World War II bombing.

Beside the Harbour Bridge is an ice house, originally one of a pair, built probably in the mid-nineteenth century and rethatched in 1980. Wherries brought in ice during the winter from the Norfolk Broads and this was used in the smacks to keep the fish fresh. Later the demand increased and ice had to be shipped in from Norway.

Off the town of Yarmouth lies a sheltered anchorage known as Yarmouth Roads. Around 1859 half the shipwrecks

in Britain were happening on the Norfolk and Suffolk coasts, and in 1860 the Shipwrecked Sailor's Home was opened on Yarmouth seafront. Between 1860 and 1861 nearly 800 men and boys, rescued from about 100 vessels, were helped by the Home. The Sailor's Home was closed in 1965 and opened two years later as the Maritime Museum of East Anglia. The museum has a fine collection relating to the port of Yarmouth, the fishing industry and the East Anglian Broads. It also has a unique collection of about forty early maritime engines.

Horsey

A village between the East Anglian Broads and the North Sea. On the broads' side is Horsey Staithe where reeds are stored for thatching and one of the attractive windmills remains which were used for pumping water out of the marsh ditches. South of Horsey is Hundred Stream, one of the many places on the East Anglian coast which was an estuary in medieval times but has since silted up. The sea broke through here in the tidal surges of 1938 and 1953 when huge inland areas were flooded. The east coast floods of 1953 were the largest natural disasters on the whole of the east coast in modern times. Since then the sea defences everywhere have been considerably strengthened.

King's Lynn

Known locally as Lynn, it received its first name for being persistently loyal to Charles I in the Civil War, when most of protestant East Anglia strongly supported Parliament.

The Custom-house on Purfleet, one of four creeks, or fleets, leading through the town, was built in 1683. The medieval warehouses, the Hanseatic Warehouse and the later Greenland Fishery House make this busy town worth visiting. The last whalers sailed from Lynn in 1822. The original Fisher Fleet, from which medieval fishing boats sailed to Icelandic waters, became the Alexandra Dock lock in 1869 when the present Fisher Fleet was dug. The King's Lynn Museum has many nautical exhibits.

Norwich

An inland port. Pull's Ferry on the River Wensum is one of the medieval watergates in the town wall. In the Castle Museum is a fine collection of paintings of the Norwich School which includes many good maritime views of the early nineteenth century. The Bridewell Museum of Local Industries has a collection of items connected with wooden boat building and wherries.

NORTHUMBERLAND

Alnmouth

A village on a sandy headland with miles of open beaches on either side. An inlet behind Alnmouth which dries out at low tide used to be the base for fishing cobles, and occasionally brigs would come in with timber. However, before the sea broke through the sand dunes in

The 36ft motor coble Joanne D *of Blyth nearing completion at Harrison's Yard, Amble, in 1980. On the left are the planks of another fishing coble taking shape* (Author)

1806 and silted up the harbour, this had been an important port for corn export. It is still used by small pleasure boats.

Amble

Before the present mouth of the River Coquet was formed in a great storm in 1799, it was situated further north. In 1837 a Harbour Commission was formed to improve the harbour for the coal trade. At one time there were twenty-two brigs and schooners owned in Amble.

In 1855 a shipbuilder called Richardson moved to Amble from the Tyne, and amongst his apprentices was James Harrison. In 1870 the firm of James & John Harrison was formed at Amble and by 1976 they had built 396 cobles and are still building them regularly. The yard is now run by John and Hugh Matthews as Harrison & Sons.

The coal trade at Amble seems to have petered out in the late 1960s as the local pits closed.

Bamburgh

A pleasant coastal village dominated by the castle. Grace Darling is buried here and there is a museum devoted to her. She was one of the first national heroines created by newspaper reporting after she had helped her father, keeper of Longstone Lighthouse in the Farne Islands, to rescue people from a wrecked steamer in a rowing coble. The coble on display is believed to have been built for William Darling in 1828.

Beadnell

A small harbour on a sandy bay with adjacent nineteenth-century lime kilns. Motor cobles still work from here for lobsters. Before World War I, cobles used to work off two landings on the shore.

Berwick upon Tweed

The town changed hands between the Scottish and English no less than thirteen times before finally becoming English in 1482. The elaborate defences of the walled town were begun in 1555 and completed under Elizabeth. The River Tweed is famous for its salmon and before the coming of the railways fast smacks raced to London with the freshly caught salmon. The Berwick smacks flourished between 1750 and 1850 (the term 'smack' was usually used to describe a gaff-rigged fishing boat, but it also meant any gaff cutter in the nineteenth century). The Berwick smacks used to race south under a great press of sail and were the clippers of the coast until the first steamers were introduced in 1837. The Berwick Shipping Co ran schooners as well as two steamers. The Berwick yard of A. B. Gowan & Son built the last two schooners *Tweed* and *Teviot* in 1848. In 1872 the company no longer owned ships but became Berwick Salmon Fisheries Ltd, which still exists.

The traditional salmon cobles are still kept at Spittal, on the opposite side of the river to Berwick, but these are quite different to the coastal cobles.

Blyth

This was one of the great north-east coast coal ports. In 1874 around 200 colliers, mostly brigs, were owned here. Lord Runciman, a local sailor who had become a successful shipowner described the era in his *Collier Brigs and Their Sailors*. Later in the nineteenth century, the harbour was considerably deepened to take steam colliers. Dredging of the approach channels began in 1881, and new staithes were commissioned in 1884, 1888 and 1928.

Boulmer

A beach landing where the cobles are taken down to the water by tractor and trailer. When the RNLI closed the lifeboat station, dating from 1825, local people formed their own organisation.

The Fishing Boat pub at Boulmer has a painting of local women dragging one of the old pulling lifeboats along the coast to launch it from a safe place. The women did the pulling so that the men would have the strength to row in a gale.

Old drifters have been turned upside down at the harbour on Holy Island, Northumberland, and used as fishermen's sheds (Author)

Craster

A small fishing village well known for its kippers. The little harbour was built in about 1904 for shipping out stone, but the quarry closed in 1939.

Holy Island

The island can be reached by car over a causeway at low tide but it is well to check the tide-table board on the shoreward end before starting. The sandy island acquired its name for being a haven of Christian culture: the Lindisfarne Monastery was founded here in the seventh century but was destroyed by the Vikings two centuries later.

The tiny village around the harbour is a fishing community, mostly with open lobster boats. In 1887 there were thirty-seven boats owned here, giving employment to eighty-three fishermen. Some of these were the keel boats used for herring, and were eventually turned upside-down and used as sheds around the harbour. The lifeboat *Lizzie Porter* which was stationed at Holy Island between 1909 and 1925 is to be preserved in a Lifeboat Museum in Bristol.

Newbiggin by the Sea

The coble, although not a fast boat, is considered one of the best in the world for coming through breaking waves onto a beach. The size and power of the cobles working off Newbiggin beach earned them particularly high regard. Although one has been lost in the motorboat era, it is believed by fishermen that she was run down by a coaster. The Newbiggin freeholders' rights go back to 1235, and these include the rights of the foreshore so that they can stop people gathering sea coal.

Seahouses

There is a small harbour used by local cobles, and Scottish boats shelter here in bad weather. In a gale the waves and spray carry right over the harbour walls. During the summer boats take visitors out to the Farne Islands, which were bought for the National Trust in 1925.

Seaton Sluice

The harbour was started with a pier in 1660, at the mouth of the tiny Seaton Burn between 60ft cliffs, to load coal. This was improved in 1690 with the construction of a sluice at one end to clear sand by releasing floods of water at low tide. It is badly silted up now and only a few fishing boats are based here, although there were three sailing cobles fishing full-time here in the 1920s.

339

NORTH YORKSHIRE

Filey

Yorkshire's cliff-lined coast has no real natural harbour and the fishermen settled at Filey because the beach was partly protected by Filey Brigg, a headland to the north. Before World War I, the cobles were brought up the beach at Filey on horse-drawn trailers with huge cartwheels, but now, like Redcar, they are brought in on tractor-pulled trailers.

The cobles are taken down onto the beach by a narrow concrete strip known as the Coble Landing. In 1974 there were sixteen beach cobles here. The larger cobles go 20 miles out to sea when long-lining for cod and haddock during the winter. In the summer they are used for laying pots for crab and lobster.

Port Mulgrave

The orderly little harbour of Port Mulgrave was built for the shipment of iron ore in the mid-nineteenth century. A hamlet for harbour workers was built higher up on the cliff.

Robin Hood's Bay

This former fishing village, which was once called Baytown, is said to be the place where the legendary English folk hero Robin Hood retreated. The narrow road leads down steeply between grey stone cottages to the rocky foreshore.

In spite of the solid appearance of the cliffs, this coast has constant problems with erosion. It is believed that since 1760 some 200 cottages have fallen into the sea. In 1975 the concrete retaining wall and the promenade were completed along Robin Hood's Bay sea front as protection. This wall quickly became a popular place for anglers.

Runswick

Like Staithes and Robin Hood's Bay, this former fishing village had to be protected from erosion by a sea wall. Runswick Bay was used for shelter by sailing ships in bad weather.

Scarborough

In 1620 a medicinal spring was discovered on the south shore at Scarborough. By the eighteenth century, there was a thriving spa attracting visitors from a wide area. Since the town's hotels needed good quality fish, Scarborough became the major fish landing centre on the coast, but later the fishing fleet and its hard-drinking fishermen were thought to offend visitors so their use of the harbour was discouraged and many boats moved to the Humber ports.

With the help of the railway promoter, George Hudson, a line to Scarborough was opened in 1845; Hudson was largely responsible for encouraging Scarborough's growth as a resort rather than a commercial port. However, Scarborough did continue as a trading port long after this, and the harbour was largely built from the revenue of ships in the coal trade which sheltered in bad weather. To save space some wooden ships were built with their stern over the water. The last sailing ship to be built in Tindall's yard was the barque *Teviot* in 1859, but deepwater barques were owned here until the 1890s.

Scarborough's fine harbour was used by Scottish, East Anglian and Cornish drifters during the summer as they followed the herring shoals round the coast. The local men used a sailing drifter known as a Yorkshire yawl, which had a lute stern, and for long-lining in the winter they carried a coble, known as a calf, on the deck. The harbour is still used by trawlers.

Most of the old quarter of the town from the harbour to Castle Hill was sadly pulled down in housing clearance schemes, but the old smugglers' inn, the Three Mariners in Quay Street, remains. A secret room with bunks and a secret cupboard with a ladder to a cellar which led to a passage to the harbour, were found.

Staithes

A beautiful village with a creek harbour which dries out. The North Eastern

Railway opened a line through Staithes in 1883, which led to an increase in the number of boats fishing from here. There were also big 35ft mule (pointed stern) cobles which were used for herring drifting from Staithes. No horses were available for launching cobles so the women had to assist them into the water. There were 224 fishermen here in 1887, but this number had been more than halved by 1912 and in the 1970s there were only four motor cobles working from here.

Whitby

The tiny estuary of the River Esk cuts into the cliffs forming one of the most attractive harbours in England. The old town, with its narrow streets, is very picturesque and attracts a large number of tourists. On the south side of the harbour, on the cliff top, is the church of St Mary which can be reached by climbing 199 steps.

Whitby still has an active longshore fishing fleet, using both keel boats and cobles. In the past it was the home of collier brigs and whalers. The best-known whaler captain was William Scoresby (1760–1829) who opened up new Arctic whaling grounds. However, Whitby's best-known navigator was Captain James Cook. He was actually born at Marton, but he came to Whitby and served an apprenticeship on colliers owned by the Quaker shipowner John Walker. During the winter months, the Whitby colliers used to lay up in harbour and Cook lodged at Walker's house in Grape Lane. It seems that Cook's *Endeavour* was built at Whitby by Fishburn in a yard which was eventually filled in by the railway in 1902, while the *Resolution* and *Discovery* came from the Whitewall yard further up the harbour.

The Whitby Museum's shipping gallery has a model of the *Resolution* and memorabilia of Captain Cook, as well as a whaling gallery with exhibits on the Scoresbys, father and son, who were both successful whaling captains.

The first whalers sailed from Whitby in 1753, and over the following eighty-four years, 58 different Whitby ships made 577 voyages after whales. At its peak around 1775, fifteen whalers were owned here, each employing some forty men. The choice of Whitby ships for Cook's voyages was not just because they were good in the North Sea coal trade, but also because they had already been proved capable in the even tougher whaling trade. At one stage Whitby was the second largest whaling port in Britain after Hull.

The Whitby Lifeboat Museum on the West Pier has builders' models of the tramp steamers owned by Headlam & Company of Whitby and the old No 2 pulling lifeboat which was preserved here after it came off station in 1957. Like many fishing communities, Whitby has had at least one lifeboat disaster. In this case it was in 1861 when twelve men were drowned in a particularly severe February gale. In that month no less than 355 ships were lost on what was then Yorkshire's North Riding coast.

The atmosphere of Whitby harbour in around 1890 is very well known through the frequent use of the superb photographs of Frank Sutcliffe (1853–1921). Most of the Sutcliffe photographs of the Whitby fishermen were posed, but they do form a unique record of Staithes, Runswick, Whitby and Robin Hood's Bay. Between 1905 and 1914, Harold Bastin also took photographs of Yorkshire's fishing communities.

York

This city is about 80 miles inland by water from Spurn Head, but the tide comes right up to Naburn lock, 3 miles south of the city. In recent years a Viking trading settlement has been excavated in York, emphasising the town's strong links with Scandinavia.

The wooden Humber keel *Annie Maud*, a typical pre-World War I Yorkshire trader, has been moored within the grounds of York Castle Museum, but she is privately owned and therefore subject to being moved. The Castle

Museum has some maritime material while the National Railway Museum in Leeman Road has a surprising amount of space devoted to the railway-owned cross-channel ferries.

SHROPSHIRE

Coalbrookdale

At this point in the West Midlands, the River Severn runs through a narrow valley. In 1709 a process of smelting iron with clod-coke was discovered here by Abraham Darby, and in the late eighteenth century the ironmongers built furnaces, fanned by great bellows.

This was one of the major birthplaces of the Industrial Revolution. Although far inland, the area's development was facilitated by the ability to ship goods down the Severn and through Bristol to North America and other foreign markets. While the Shropshire coalfields lasted, there was a considerable coal trade on the Severn, largely at Coalport.

The first iron vessel in the world was built on the Severn in this area. She was the barge *Trial* in 1787. Coalbrookdale, Benthall, Ironbridge and Shrewsbury were the normal building places for many of the open Severn trow barges. The word 'trow' probably derives from the Anglo-Saxon word 'trog', meaning a drinking trough, and there are mentions of trows being on the Severn in 1411. The early trows had simple square sails, but by the mid-nineteenth century gaff sails had been adopted. The trows trading to Droitwich were rigged as gaff sloops and took salt down to Gloucester Docks.

By the beginning of this century, the coal mines, clay and iron ore seams which had drawn industry into the Iron-bridge Gorge were virtually exhausted, although one of the eighteenth-century coal pits lasted until 1941. The whole area became one of derelict pits, furnaces and potteries until this important site in the history of human achievement was turned into a series of open air museums.

The museum at Coalbrookdale has many wrought- and cast-iron items on display, including ships' anchors and other early metal fittings used on wooden ships.

One of the aims of the Upper Severn Navigation Trust is to build a replica of one of the 'up-river' trows. One of the last of these was the *William* of Broseley which was trading to Ironbridge in around 1900. The 'down-river' trows evolved into ketch-rigged barges trading to Bristol and even making coastal passages.

The iron bridge across the Severn at Ironbridge was built in 1779 and was the first built of the material in the world. Under its shadow, the ancient craft of coracle building is still practised by Eustace Rogers, the last English coracle maker. The Upper Severn coracle is basin-shaped. They were also used on the rivers Dee, Wye and Teify.

SOMERSET

Bridgwater

An inland industrial centre on the River Parrett which was once busy with coastal cargoes. The dock was opened here in 1841, but much of the trade went from the riverside quays. The trading ketch *Irene*, launched at Bridgwater in 1907, was the last sailing ketch trading in Britain when she finished trading in the 1960s, although she had an engine by then. She is still afloat and was receiving major repairs at Bristol in 1981. The Blake Museum in Bridgwater occupies the house in which Admiral Blake was born in 1599. As well as displays of sea battles, it has a good local shipping collection.

Minehead

The quay was built in around 1616, and in Victorian times schooners for the coastal trade were built at Minehead. The old area of the town is still known as Quay Town. Now mainly a summer resort also used by excursion steamers.

Oakhill
Oakhill Manor, near Shepton Mallet, has a collection of transport models which include some good ship models.

Porlock Weir
A tiny harbour with steep hills rising above it to Exmoor. The dock with a lock gate was formed in a lake behind a shingle ridge. Porlock Weir could take trading vessels of up to 14ft draught and the last cargo was brought in by the ketch *Democrat* in about 1950. Since then it has been used by a few yachts.

Watchet
The early stone quay was improved in the eighteenth century, and by the nineteenth century this was a busy port for schooners and ketches. The West Somerset Mineral Co built a quay in 1860–1 to take 500-ton vessels for loading iron ore from the Brendon Hills bound for Newport for the blast furnaces at Ebbw Vale. A new jetty was opened in 1907, only three years before the iron ore mines were abandoned.

Yeovilton
At the Royal Naval Air Station is the Fleet Air Arm and Concorde 002 Museum. This is mainly devoted to naval aviation history but there is a large collection of ship models.

SUFFOLK

Aldeburgh
The Elizabethan Moot Hall has a small local museum open in the summer. Flourishing longshore fishing with boats working off the beach. The village of Slaughden had eroded away by about 1910, and only the quay remains behind the massive sea defences. The Martello Tower at Slaughden was the first in a chain from the Suffolk coast down to Shoreham in Sussex, built against a threatened invasion by Napoleon Bonaparte. This coast has always been an obvious target for possible invasion. There are numerous concrete pill boxes from both world wars, and radar was developed on Orfordness and at the River Deben entrance at Bawdsey Manor.

On Aldeburgh beach there are two Victorian brick pilot look-outs which belonged to the 'Up-Town' and 'Down-Town' pilots associations. The north look-out is now used by the RNLI and the south look-out is a private home.

Dunwich
There is a small museum here showing how the great medieval port of Dunwich was eroded away: the harbour was destroyed in a great storm during 1328 but the main erosion was between 1550 and 1750. The entrance to Dunwich River moved away to the north and silted up. All that remains is a small creek leading into the River Blyth at Walberswick.

Felixstowe
Landguard Fort, which protected the entrance to Harwich Harbour and was first laid out in 1588, repulsed a Dutch attack in 1677 and was rebuilt from 1753 to 1766. The modern container port of Felixstowe has expanded since 1956, engulfing the 1930s seaplane base and former open marshland.

The Dooley, a public house now surrounded by dockland, was the Ferryboat Inn and is reputed to have many doors so that, in the early nineteenth century, a quick exit could be made from the revenue men and press gang.

Ipswich
Ipswich Museum has a number of nineteenth-century ship models on display. The Ipswich Wet Dock, constructed in 1841, is on the old course of the River Orwell. The Customs-house, built in 1845, is a particularly imposing building, and to the east of this, along Neptune Wharf, is a triangle of exceptional industrial buildings. First is Paul's Home warehouse, then some more typical Victorian brick ware-

houses, followed by Isaac Lord's Tudor merchant's house in Fore Street. None of these are open to the public but it is an interesting area of dockland to walk round.

Ipswich was the last port in Britain to have a fleet of barges working under sail, and a legacy is that the Dock End Shipyard is still active repairing sailing barges and other wooden vessels.

Lowestoft

A man-made harbour considerably expanded since it was first opened in 1831. A busy fishing and commercial port with wharfs in Lake Lothing above the Harbour Bridge. The Maritime Museum is in Sparrows' Nest, a little flint cottage, which is packed with sailor-made models, paintings and photographs, mostly connected with fishing smacks.

Lowestoft Ness is the most easterly point in Britain.

Pin Mill

An attractive waterside hamlet on the River Orwell where sailing barges are still repaired and an annual barge race has been held since 1962.

Shotley

Bloody Point at Shotley, where the rivers Stour and Orwell meet, is believed to have been given its name from a great battle fought here in 884 between the Saxons and invading Danes. The land above the point was open until the Admiralty started to build the HMS *Ganges* Boys Training Establishment about 1905.

The original HMS *Ganges* was the 84-gun ship built at Bombay in 1821 which was towed to Harwich in 1899. When the shore establishment was opened in 1906, the boys were moved ashore, although HMS *Agincourt* was moored off Shotley Pier for a few years. Thousands of boys were trained at *Ganges* for entry into the

A boomie barge and two spritsail barges locking into the Ipswich Wet Dock. This lock was built in 1881, and by 1913 2,000 sailing barges and 600 steamers were entering Ipswich every year (Author's Collection)

The sailing barge Thalatta *visiting Woodbridge Tide Mill, Suffolk, in 1975. This was the first time that a barge had been up to the mill for about fifty years* (Author)

Royal Navy until the establishment was closed in 1976.

Snape
A Viking ship burial was unearthed on Snape Common in 1862. Viking ships have also been found at Ashley Dell, near Lowestoft, and Caister. Snape Maltings is an attractive set of nineteenth-century buildings at the head of the River Alde, now mainly used as a concert hall and shops. Suffolk grown and imported barley was turned into malt here and then shipped to the London breweries by sailing barges and small steamers.

Southwold
Fishing boats worked off the beach in front of the town in Victorian times, but with the coming of power boats, they moved to the River Blyth to the south of the town. The Sailor's Reading Room

on the East Cliff was opened in 1864 and is now used as a club. The walls are covered with old photographs and Suffolk beach boat models. The public are welcome to look round and hopefully make a donation.

The Southwold Museum beside St Bartholomew's Green has more ship models and a good display on the Battle of Solebay, fought in 1672 between an Anglo-French fleet of 98 ships and a Dutch fleet of 75 ships. Solebay is the bay between Southwold and Dunwich. On the 'back' road round to the Harbour Inn at Black Shore is the Southwold Royal National Lifeboat Museum, situated in the old water tower.

Sutton Hoo
In 1939 one of a group of burial mounds on the Sutton Walks, then open heathland on the opposite bank of the River Deben from Woodbridge, was exca-

vated. This revealed a Saxon longship, complete with treasure intended, it is believed, for the King of the East Angles, who died in 624–5. The treasure can be seen in the British Museum, London. The site is not open to the public, but it is possible to walk along the public footpath from the road, which goes past the tumuli.

Woodbridge

A trading port until World War II, but its quayside area is now given over to yacht building and repair yards. The tide mill and granary are believed to have been built in 1793. The mill pond which served the mill was dug out for a yacht harbour in 1962. Woodbridge Tide Mill was restored for opening to the public in 1975 after it had been raised to prevent the ground floor from flooding. All the former warehouses round the Ferry Dock have had to be protected from high tides. Since about 1300, East Anglia has been sinking so flooding has become a more frequent occurrence, but at the same time the estuaries have been silting up so the channels are becoming shallower.

SURREY

Chertsey

The Historical Motorboat Society have agreed with the Thames Heritage Trust to establish a veteran motor boat museum in Chertsey on a 19 acre lake, which has no link with the Thames. The oldest craft owned by this society is a 1908 Vosper teak-hulled motor boat; another early boat is the 35ft Thornycroft motor cruiser *Lorita*, built in 1924.

Kingston

The tidal Thames ends at Teddington (p 322). Kingston is the next town above Teddington and river cruises run from here up to Hampton Court. Two of the larger cruise boats on the freshwater river are the clipper-bowed *Empress of India*, built at Windsor in 1898, which

takes 110 passengers, and the *Windsor Castle*, built in 1920, which takes 175 passengers. These are owned by the Turk family who have been associated with the Thames since the early eighteenth century. They also have period boats which they hire to film companies.

Thorpe

A former gravel pit at Thorpe has been landscaped to form a major leisure centre, which includes Celtic, Saxon and Roman villages and the 76ft Viking longship *Valkyrja*, a replica based on the ninth-century Gokstad ship in Norway, and the 77ft Roman galley *Britannica* which was not based on an actual ship because none have been found, but was designed to represent what is thought to be a typical vessel. Both vessels were built at Appledore, North Devon, and brought round to the Thames by sea.

TYNE & WEAR

Cullercoats

A former fishing village just north of Tynemouth now swallowed up by the resort of Whitley Bay. The Cullercoat fishwives used to carry their baskets inland and sell fish as they went. The village once had a large fleet of cobles and a few are still kept down by the little harbour. Most of the rows of single storey fishermen's houses have been torn down, but a few still remain in Simpson Street. The Cullercoat fishermen's club has also survived. On the sea front is the fishermen's lookout which dates from 1869. Many local men still fish in modern inshore boats from North Shields.

Newcastle

The River Tyne at Newcastle runs through a valley and the quayside area is dominated by the bridges. The present swing bridge at the lower end of the valley was built in 1876 and stands on the site of a Roman and a wooden medieval bridge. There was only one bridge over the Tyne until 1849 when the High Level Bridge was opened for both road and rail traffic. The expansion of the western end of Newcastle and Gateshead prompted the building of the Redheugh Bridge in 1871, which formed a link between the two towns. This bridge was rebuilt in 1901. The King Edward VII railway bridge was opened in 1906 and the Tyne Bridge in 1928, while the construction of the latest Metro Bridge was completed in 1980.

The coal trade, which was the basis of Newcastle's prosperity, reached a peak in 1923 when 21½ million tons of coal and coke left the Tyne. Many seagoing ships berthed above Newcastle to load and in 1924 over 6,000 ships passed through the swing bridge; by the 1980s, it was seldom opened.

The River Tyne Commissioners optimistically expanded the quays in the 1920s to provide twenty-four unloading berths, but by then ships were often discharging at docks nearer the mouth of the Tyne. An unsuccessful attempt to draw fishing boats up to Newcastle had been made in Victorian times by constructing a Fish Market. On the quays are some seventeenth-century warehouses, and leading up the hill through the buildings are traces of a network of ancient narrow stairways to the city centre above. Near the quay is the Guildhall which was rebuilt in the 1650s and became Newcastle's Coal Exchange until nationalisation of the coal industry in 1947.

The Keelmen's Hospital was built in 1701 at Sandgate, the district in which the keelmen lived. Before the Tyne was dredged and improved, the keels were a vital part of the coal trade because they were loaded at the staiths at the head of the river and took the coal down to the colliers which anchored in the lower reaches below Newcastle. The Tyne keel was of medieval ancestry and had a double ended, carvel-built hull and was fitted with a single squaresail until the mid-nineteenth century when a spritsail

and foresail became usual. The keel was a specialist coal carrying craft while the Tyne wherry, a double ended, clinker-built craft, was a lighter used in general cargo work. The keels always loaded 21 tons so that they could calculate their dues, while the wherries could load a capacity of up to 50 tons.

The Tyne & Wear County Museum Service has the last Tyne wherry, *Elswick No 2*, owned by the Maritime Trust, which is kept in the river and is hopefully to be restored. She was a dumb barge which was towed by tugs, while the earlier Tyne wherries were sailed. The museum also commissioned a replica of the Tyne foyboat *Bonny Tyne* in 1977. When the coal trade started to develop in the late medieval period, the practice of foyboatmen assisting ships at the Tyne mouth began, and continued for 300 years until steam colliers and tugs replaced sail. It seems that in around 1800, about 150 foyboats at the two Shields found regular employment helping colliers over the Tyne bar. The boats used were rather like man-of-war gigs, but in the nineteenth century, smaller, 17ft Tyne foyboats were evolved for this work.

There were still some 200 foyboatmen making a living by helping ships moor to buoys and quays in the 1930s, and in the late 1970s the River Tyne Commissioners licensed forty men to carry out this type of work. Powerful motor launches have replaced the sailing and rowing Tyne foyboats, which the *Bonny Tyne* represents, and in 1979 Robsons Boatbuilders Ltd of South Shields built a new type of wooden, diesel powered foyboat, but they still have the traditional black hull with a checkered top plank.

The Tyne & Wear County Museum Service also have on display at Exhibition Park the famous experimental launch *Turbinia* which was built by Brown & Hood at Wallsend in 1894 to Charles Parsons' design. He had pioneered the use of steam turbines in electricity generation and became convinced

The Tyne Dock, South Shields, in May 1909 with the sailing ships Peru, Leon Blum *and* Bayonne *waiting to load coal. Tyne Dock opened in 1859* (National Maritime Museum)

that turbines could be used to power ships. Although *Turbinia* was a success and the Royal Navy ordered two turbine destroyers, turbines were not immediately accepted by commercial shipowners.

This museum also has a very good collection of over 150 builders' and exhibition ship models, including a builder's model of the 485-ton, iron screw collier *John Bowes*, built by Palmer Brothers at Jarrow-on-Tyne in 1852. She was the first successful steam collier in the north-east coal trade, and later colliers developed from her design. The museum also has over 500 original plans relating to merchant ships built on the Tyne between 1853 and 1912, which came from the Low Walker Shipyard of W. G. Armstrong, Whitworth & Company which had a reputation for producing special purpose ships. The Tyneside shipyards also specialised in paddle tugs with side-lever engines. The *Reliant*, built in South Shields in 1907, has been

placed as the central feature in the Neptune Hall at the National Maritime Museum in Greenwich. She was built for the Manchester Ship Canal but was later in operation at Seaham. The paddle tug *Eppleton Hall*, which was built in 1914 and operated on the River Wear and then the Tyne, was sold for scrap in 1968, but San Francisco Maritime Museum bought her, and in 1969–70 steamed her under her own power on a six month voyage of 11,000 miles to San Francisco where she remains in steaming order.

North Shields

In Northumberland Square in North Shields, there is a wooden figure known as the 'Dolly'. The figure is of a Cullercoats fishwife and there has been such a figure in the town since 1814. The first Dolly is said to have been put up in memory of a North Shields master mariner who died fighting pirates off Yarmouth. Somehow a tradition grew up that if a piece of wood was cut from the Dolly, it would bring good luck and the sailor would return home safely. The present Dolly, the fifth in fact, was carved in 1958 to keep this North Shields tradition alive, but people are no longer encouraged to vandalise it.

The North Shields fish quay and market are still very active. On the water front are the high and low lighthouses built in 1805–8 to form a leading line for the harbour entrance. Newcastle Trinity House first put up river lights in 1540.

South Shields

The town is at the eastern end of Tyneside industrial area, while the seafront is a holiday resort. In the harbour mouth, on legs, is the Groyne Lighthouse, while below the pilot's headquarters at the river mouth, under a splendid cast-iron supported roof, is the lifeboat *Tyne*, built in 1833, which saved 1,024 lives before being withdrawn from service in 1887. She is one of the Shields pattern lifeboats which were developed as rowing surf boats from Greathead's *Original*, which was the world's first successful lifeboat, stationed at South Shields.

There were coal loading staiths above South Shields, but in the late nineteenth century the Mill Dam and Corporation Quays were built to attract general cargo and passenger trade. There are old warehouses behind these quays, and from them there is a good view across the Tyne of the ship repair yards and coal loading berths. The Tyne Dock, opened in 1859, was the first to be designed to load steamers with coal.

Sunderland

This great shipbuilding town has been particularly subjected to the trade cycle as world demand for new tonnage fluctuated wildly. The River Wear is still largely dominated by shipyard cranes, notably at Southwick and Pallion, although the two decades before World War I were Sunderland's great era as the most productive shipbuilding town in

the world. The Clyde produced more ships, but they came from yards in several towns.

Just after World War II, 11,000 men were employed in the shipyards on the first 4 miles of the River Wear, but now only two firms, Sunderland Shipbuilders and Austin & Pickersgill, keep alive the 170-year-old tradition.

Like the Tyne, the entrance to the Wear is protected by massive stone piers built in the late nineteenth century. On the Wear's north pier stands the distinctive Roker Lighthouse, built in 1903. The entrance is further protected by two older and much smaller piers, and on the south pier is the attractive pilot house and an iron lighthouse, built in 1865.

Sunderland was also a leading port in the coal trade. The first dock was the Wear, or North, Dock, built in 1837 as a tidal basin. On the south side of the harbour, the far larger Hudson and Hendon Docks were built in the 1850s with their own sea lock. In the south entrance to Wear Docks, Bartram's South Dock Shipyard launched vessels virtually into the open North Sea. This shipyard built fifty-four standard SD 14 merchant ships between 1967 and 1978, after which the hundred-year-old yard was closed down. Over 381 ships had been launched from the yard.

Although not yet on display, the Science Museum at Newcastle has the Sunderland foying coble *Peggy* which was built in 1900. There is a noted collection of maritime paintings, which include over fifty ship portraits from the period 1820 to 1920, at the Sunderland Museum & Art Gallery.

Tynemouth

The mouth of the Tyne is largely dominated by a headland with the ruins of Tynemouth Priory Church and Castle. In the seventh century the Anglo-Saxons first built a monastery here, which was destroyed by Danish Vikings in 865. Some 300 years later the Benedictines founded the Priory. From this area may be had a very good view of the

349

Tyne entrance and inland to the North Shields ship repair yards and the lower reaches of the river.

The mouth of the Tyne is now protected by two massive stone piers which were constructed by the Tyne Improvement Commission. Although this work began in 1854, they were not completed until 1895, but two years later a tremendous gale breached the North Pier and repairs were not completed until 1909.

The pleasant little town of Tynemouth is sheltered behind the headland. It has a wide main street of mainly eighteenth-century houses.

Wallsend

The north shore of the River Tyne from Wallsend up river to Walker has been one of the most productive shipbuilding areas in the world. The first tanker *Glückauf*, built in 1885, and the turbine transatlantic liner, *Mauretania*, launched in 1906, were built here. On 2 June 1981 Swan Hunter Shipbuilders Ltd launched HMS *Ark Royal* from their Wallsend shipyard. Also at Wallsend are the British Ship Research Association and the Lloyds Testing Station.

WEST SUSSEX

Birdham

With the proximity of Chichester Harbour, one of the most attractive sailing areas within reach of London, Birdham was one of the first places to be affected by popular boating as people came and settled in this area.

In 1935 the tide mill near the mouth of Chichester Canal was closed. The mill was turned into a marine engine workshop and the mill pond was converted into the Birdham Pool yacht marina. This was one of the first marinas in Britain created specially for yachts. Chichester Harbour was already starting to be crowded with yacht moorings in the 1950s—the boating boom did not affect most estuary villages in southern England until the early 1960s.

Bosham

An attractive village on a creek which leads into Chichester Harbour. There was a small shipyard building trading schooners here in the 1880s, and small ketches and local Solent barges came up to Bosham Quay. The quay berth later silted up but was dredged out again in 1981. The local channels are now lined with yacht moorings but until the 1920s they were open waters. The building of yacht marinas has been greatly opposed since the 1960s, but had more been built many creeks and estuaries would have been left clear of moorings, giving more room for sailing.

Littlehampton

This was the home of ocean-going ships in the age of sail. Harveys, who were renowned for building wooden sailing ships of great quality, had a yard on the west bank of the River Arun near the road bridge.

Henry Harvey began building wooden sailing ships for deepwater trades in 1848, the last of which was the barque *Goodwood* in 1880. After this, his sons and their successors built coasting ketch barges until their last one, the *Moultonian*, in 1919. The yard was taken over by David Hillyard who built conventional gaff cruising yachts and then specialised in building his own style of motor sailers. Hillyards had pointed sterns, central cockpits and rather flat sides which gave them more cabin space than many post-World War II yachts. Dennis Cullingford became proprietor of Hillyards in about 1964, but within a few years wooden yacht building had stopped because of the impact of the cheaper fibreglass hulls. By 1981 wooden hulls had become an economic proposition again, so Hillyards built a 24ft masthead sloop yacht.

Littlehampton Museum has some paintings and models relating to the town's maritime past, but it is only open on Wednesdays.

Selsey

This was the centre of the South Saxon kingdom for four centuries before the Norman Conquest. Selsey Bill has slowly been eroded away. The shore between Selsey and Bognor is known as The Park after a deer park which was eroded away in the sixteenth century. Pagham Harbour was dammed in 1876 and the sea broke through the shingle bank in 1910. Landowners attempted to halt erosion along this coast with wooden groynes, but the first major scheme with a concrete wall was begun in 1953.

Some gaff cutter smacks worked for oysters from The Park until the late 1930s.

Shoreham-by-Sea

An eastern arm leading off the River Adur forms Shoreham Harbour. In the mid-Victorian period, wooden brigs and barques were built here for general ocean trades. R. H. Penny & Sons of Shoreham purchased their first iron ship, the barque *Cora Linn*, in 1867. Pennys' last ship was the Sunderland-built barque *Alastor* which was in the New Zealand emigrant trade and then general ocean trade until 1895.

On the South Lancing side of Shoreham Harbour, a busy commercial port, there is an interesting collection of World War II Naval MTB and similar craft now converted into houseboats.

Shoreham has sheltered water and yachts are kept on the north bank. The Marlipins Museum in the High Street has a collection of ship models, paintings and photographs.

Worthing

Once a beach fishing station until residential interests discouraged fishermen. However, small open angling boats are still kept on the beach. Along the south coast as far east as Deal, there is a noticeable preference for lute sterns and varnished wooden hulls.

Scotland

BORDERS

Burnmouth

The harbour was built in 1830 at the bottom of a cliff and there is a very steep road leading down to it. The harbour dries out at low tide, and even at high water there are rocks to be avoided in the entrance channel. There is still a small active inshore fishing fleet here.

Cockburnspath

Near the village of Cockburnspath is a tiny harbour in a cove which is used by lobster and crab fishermen. The entrance channel is dotted with sunken rocks. Work on building the harbour at Cove Bay started in 1770 and was completed in 1831.

Eyemouth

The name comes from the fact that the harbour is at the mouth of the Eye Water burn. Benedictine monks fished from here in the thirteenth century, and fishing prospered enough for Smeaton to build the stone north pier in 1768. Further pier building left the harbour quays protected but there is a very difficult, narrow entrance. Once a boat has entered the channel between the rocks, there is no room for it to turn round, however much the sea is breaking around the piers. The harbour was closed for deepening and improvement in the early 1960s and when it opened in 1963 the fishing fleet was encouraged to modernise.

Although haddock fishing was thriving in the late eighteenth century, Eyemouth also became a noted smuggling centre. There were so many underground passageways and secret cellars that it was said that only half the town was above the surface. Coves in St Abb's Head were also used by smugglers. The arrival of the railway in 1846 was a great advantage to the Eyemouth fishermen.

In the mid-nineteenth century, the

351

fishermen stuck persistently to open boats because they were easier and lighter to row without decking. However, in sudden gales these boats were often overwhelmed, causing a high loss of life. The first decked boat built at Eyemouth, and probably on the east coast of Scotland, was launched in 1856. Even the improved decked fifies were still overpowered in bad weather, and the Eyemouth Museum, opened in an old kirk in 1981, is largely devoted to the disaster of 1881 when half the town's fleet was lost in a sudden hurricane force storm. The fleet were at sea shooting their herring nets when a furious wind swept up the coast. In a little over an hour, 45 boats and 189 men were lost. Of the men drowned, 129 came from Eyemouth and the rest from Burnmouth and smaller villages along the coast.

In the colourful and active inshore fleet belonging to Eyemouth in 1981, there was the *Supreme*, owned by the great-grandson of a man who had not gone to sea in his fifie *Supreme* on 'The Disaster Day', a century before, because of a death in his family.

CENTRAL

Bo'ness

The port of Borrowstounness, as it was once known, was the main port of the upper Firth of Forth in the early nineteenth century. Until World War I, timber was still arriving here during the summer from Baltic ports, but thereafter the docks silted up. The Forth & Clyde Canal caused the timber trade to shift to Grangemouth. Great quantities of timber were taken from there by lighters through to the sawmills at Glasgow.

Grangemouth

From the docks at Grangemouth the Forth & Clyde Canal ran through central Scotland to Bowling on the Clyde for 35 miles. It was a ship canal and potentially one of the most useful canals in

Britain, since it could save small seagoing vessels some 400 miles. This canal had thirty-nine locks but it was unpopular because of the number of road bridges which had to be opened for seagoing craft and this caused great traffic congestion in the most densely populated area of Scotland. The canal was closed in 1962. Since there was not enough headroom for inshore fishing craft from the east coast to go through, the closure seems to have been accepted and even the puffer trade which had made use of this canal had already virtually finished by then.

Grangemouth has major oil refineries of over 1 million tonnes annual capacity in 1981 and crude oil pipelines are linked to the 'Forties' oil field.

DUMFRIES AND GALLOWAY

Annan

The Solway Firth is noted for its 30ft high tides and miles of sandbanks, but on a high tide small ships could reach the town of Annan. In the 1850s–60s Benjamin Nicholson built clipper ships for the China trade here. His best-known clipper was the *Annandale* which was built in 1854 with timber from the Annandale Estate. In the mid-nineteenth century, fishermen moved up from the Morecambe Bay area to work the shrimps in the Solway Firth. Local shrimpers built by Wilson at Annan were very similar to Morecambe Bay prawners, and indeed the conditions of narrow channels and fast-flowing tides were very similar. The Annandale Sailing Club on an inland lake has a thriving GP 14 dinghy class.

Cairnryan

The small village of Cairnryan on Loch Ryan became Military Port No 2 in 1941, served by the Cairnryan Military Railway, which was used by King George VI and Queen Elizabeth in 1942 on their way to Northern Ireland. Since the war, many famous ships have ended their days at the shipbreaker's quay at Cairnryan, including the aircraft carriers *Eagle* and *Ark Royal* which were scrapped in 1979–80.

Carsethorn

Now just a hamlet on an exposed part of the Solway Firth. Until World War I, trading schooners were owned here and regularly discharged on the open beach. Back in the mid-nineteenth century, ships came to this beach to take on immigrants, mostly poor crofters, for North America.

Dumfries

Once a small port at the head of the River Nith. Sometimes schooners which traded mostly to Liverpool came up to the dock at the lower end of the town, but a little further down river is Kingholm Quay. Silting was always a considerable problem on the Solway Firth, so at Kingholm Quay water was trapped in a pool above the dock and released at low water so that the silt was washed from the berths. Up until World War II, coasters of around 500 tons came to Kingholm Quay, but it is now silted up with just a few local fishing boats remaining.

The Dumfries Museum has a good gallery of photographs of the schooners which traded from the Solway Firth.

Kirkcudbright

There is a very swift tide which made it a difficult port for the schooners calling at the little dock, which is now filled in, and the quay. In the early 1970s, a large fleet of scallop dredgers, mostly from the east coast of Scotland, used this quay as a base for working the grounds near the Isle of Man.

Portpatrick

On the extreme western end of the county is the small, stone-walled harbour of Portpatrick from which sailing packets once crossed to Northern Ire-land. The distance from Portpatrick to Donaghadee is only about 22 miles but sailing packets sometimes took 24 hours to make the crossing in bad weather. In 1822, in order to speed up communications, the Post Office introduced steam packets. Cattle were also shipped across and were then walked into the English grazing counties.

Portpatrick lost its importance as a port when Stranraer, 6 miles away, became the ferry terminal. Today, the little harbour in the cliff is a favourite spot for yachtsmen coming the 30 miles from Belfast Lough.

Stranraer

Small town at the end of Loch Ryan. The town grew up after the railway reached here in 1863, and a steamer ferry link was established with Larne in Northern Ireland.

Wig Bay

A small bay on the west shore of Loch Ryan. Coastal Command built a huge slip here in World War II, and it is from here that much of the active racing and dinghy sailing in this area of Scotland takes place.

FIFE

Anstruther

The Scottish Fisheries Museum is housed here in a group of former fishermen's houses in Harbourhead. Although the museum is quite small, it gives good coverage of every aspect of fishing and the lives of the fisherfolk. This includes a very modern section which has a memorial with the names of men who have lost their lives recently in the Scottish fishing industry. The museum has tanks in which there are live examples of local fish; fresh seawater is pumped into the tanks from the harbour.

In the museum's courtyard are two small open fishing yawls, and in the harbour is the 70ft fifie *Reaper*, built by Forbes in 1902 and restored in 1980, complete with masts. There is also the zulu *Research* which was worked as a motor craft and now needs a great deal of work to save her. The fifies from around the Firth of Forth had straight stems and sterns, while the zulus from the Moray Firth had raked sterns. The small zulu *Hilda Ross*, built at Sandhaven, is used in the summer to run trips from Anstruther out to the Isle of May. The 55ft zulu *Vesper* was still afloat in 1980, but the last one fishing was the *Violet*, built for the Stephens in 1911; she went drift netting and then seining and long-lining while worked by members of the family from Fraserburgh until she was sold to a Newlyn owner in 1975. The zulu *Radium* has been lying at Bowling for some time; when she stopped fishing in 1964 the youngest member of the crew was seventy.

Burntisland

Formerly a fishing harbour on the Firth of Forth. About 400 boats were landing herring here in 1840; of these 80 belonged to Burntisland and were following the herring north to Caithness. In the nineteenth century, the port became a shipbuilding centre, and the fishing centre moved further east to the East Neuk coast.

Charlestown

A harbour was started here in about 1765 by Charles, 5th Earl of Elgin, as an outlet for the mines and quarries on his estate. When a later Earl of Elgin sold out to the North British Railway in 1860, the port was further expanded so that by 1880 200,000 tons of coal was exported from here. However, when other Forth ports built wet docks, Charlestown, which dried out at low tide, steadily declined. Several stone limekilns could be seen here on the old quays.

Crail

A very attractive little harbour and village at the eastern end of the East Neuk coast. The harbour dries out and fishermen mainly go after lobster and shellfish.

Pittenweem

A small narrow harbour, built in 1830, with attractive, adjacent stone houses. In 1928 Pittenweem had only 6 steam drifters against 32 owned in neighbouring Anstruther and Cellardyke, but in the late 1930s the Pittenweem fishermen introduced herring ring-netting to the Forth. After this, herring drifting from Anstruther declined while the Pittenweem fleet expanded with seiners and general purpose inshore fishing boats. In 1980 Pittenweem had become the main centre of fishing on the East Neuk coast. A daily auction takes place at the fishmarket on the harbour.

Some of the 'top boats', those continually finding the largest catches, such as *Argonaut*, *Forthright* and *Ocean Triumph*, are away for up to six days trawling or seining in the North Sea. Other boats were nephrop (Norway lobster) trawlers, working in areas in the Forth which have a muddy bottom.

In 1980 there were 120 inshore fishing boats in Pittenweem district, although some of these were landing fish at Aberdeen.

Rosyth

There is a Royal Naval base and dockyard here, west of the Forth road bridge.

St Monance

A very small harbour dominated at the inshore end by the sheds of James N. Miller & Sons. This business was started by John Miller at Overkellie in 1747, moved to St Andrews in 1768 and David Miller moved to St Monance in 1779. In 1904 Millers built their last sailing fifie, but they were already experimenting with fitting semi-diesel engines in fishing boats. They then switched to building steam 'liners' (long-liners) for cod fishermen, and steam drifters.

In the inter-war years, the East Neuk fishermen continued to work steam drifters and 'mechanised fifies', so Millers and other local yards built canoe-sterned, motor ring netters for owners on the west coast. After World War II, they built yachts and returned to building wooden fishing boats. In 1975 the first steel fishing boat was built in St Monance.

Tayport

A small harbour on the south side of the Firth of Tay. Formerly timber was shipped in here, and small boats went out after mussels which were sold for bait. In 1980 the harbour was used by sand dredgers. Among the pleasure craft kept here is the fifie *Isabella Fortuna*, which has been restored to traditional appearance with the black sails.

GRAMPIAN

Aberdeen

A busy modern port. The fishing fleet has declined but work serving the North Sea oil rigs has kept many ex-trawlers at sea. The fish market on the Albert Basin was sited near the station for easy distribution of fish. Aberdeen Art Gallery & Museum has a collection of ship models, including one of the steam whaler *Eclipse*, and some of the clipper ships built by Alexander Hall & Sons. In the early nineteenth century, there was fierce competition for the packet trade between Aberdeen, Leith and London, and a group of Aberdonians commissioned Alexander Hall to build a sailing packet to compete against growing steam competition. The result was the 92ft clipper schooner *Scottish Maid*, launched in 1839. She had what became known as the 'Aberdeen bow' and later a 'clipper bow'. The *Scottish Maid* was the forerunner of the British clippers that blossomed into their full form in the 1850s.

Aberdeen stayed in the forefront of the development of clipper ships. Duthie & Son built several medium wooden clippers up to 1,100 tons while another yard, Walter Hood & Co, built a series of clippers for the China tea trade for George Thompson's White Star

Line. These were all very smart with green painted hulls, and included the *Thermopylae* (1868) and the *Patriarch* (1869).

Banff

An attractive old port of grey stone houses beside its harbour at the mouth of the River Deveron. This was the leading trading port of the coast, and records show that in 1838 30,000 barrels of herring were exported from here. Half of these went to Germany and the rest to London, Liverpool and the West Indies. The shallow harbour is now silted up, particularly in the Inner Basin; even before the 1920s, fishing boats had moved across to Macduff.

Buckie

The first house of this seafaring town was built in 1645 and the town grew solely as a fishing station. Men started going out after herring shoals in 1786, while many other ports on the dry, mild coast did not enter the herring fishery until the early nineteenth century. The harbour was started in 1843 when the boats were all still open and the fishermen were resisting the fitting of decks. Single-masted scaffies were replaced firstly by two-masted zulus and then by steam drifters. There is still an active fishing fleet here, and two boatyards at the east end of the harbour turn out new inshore fishing boats for owners in the east of Scotland and Northern Ireland.

Catterline

A village round a cove in a rocky coastline. Apparently the people here were once notorious smugglers, but in Victorian times there were a few fishing boats working from the tiny stone pier.

Elgin

The Elgin Museum has what is reputed to be the only Scottish coracle to survive. On the River Spey these primitive round craft were called 'currachs' and were used until the late nineteenth century for setting nets, spearing fish and for moving logs which were floated down to the Garmouth shipyards. In the tidal Spey below Fochabers, there was pearl fishing, the fishermen finding about one pearl in every hundred mussels opened. In the early 1970s one man was still doing this professionally, but since then it seems that local tinkers sometimes did it unofficially.

Fraserburgh

There was only a little fishing here before 1790, and for a couple of decades thereafter it was limited to white fish, but once herring fishing started, the harbour and town quickly developed. The herring fishery was at its height here between 1870 and 1900, but even in the 1920s there were over a hundred herring drifters owned here. Work on the old harbour started in 1814 and the Balaclava Harbour was started in 1840. As the number of boats increased, this was enlarged with the last piece of breakwater being completed in 1910. Fraserburgh is still a flourishing port because of its proximity to the North Sea fishing grounds.

Gardenstown

An attractive fishing harbour at the foot of a cliff linked by a path to Crovie, another village under the cliff on the other side of Gamrie Bay. Gardenstown was started in 1720 by Alexander Garden.

Garmouth

There is no obviously visible evidence that the village of Garmouth, surrounded by marshland, and the coastal hamlet of Kingston were once the most productive shipbuilding centres of northern Scotland. The course of the River Spey has altered and silted up so the deepwater sites for the launching of ships have gone. However, the reason for the great success of Garmouth in the 1870s–80s was that good quality timber could be floated down the Spey, often for 50 miles from the woods inland.

Garmouth's shipbuilding industry and ownership thrived in an age when much of the world's ocean trades were handled by small ships visiting isolated ports. The best-known shipbuilders here were the Geddies and the Kinlochs. Of the Kinloch brothers, William was the business manager and Andrew supervised construction. They started running the ships they built in the Cape, East and West Indies trades as the Chief Line. This line was known in shipping circles as the Lochie Line. The last vessel built was the barquentine *Moray Chief* in 1888, by which time the steel ships of the Clyde were being built at a more competitive price.

Some of the larger stone houses in Lhanbryde were built for sea captains who sailed in Garmouth ships.

Gourdon

The land near the coast of the Howe of the Mearns is good for farming and this harbour was once an important grain exporting centre. Fishing was also conducted here.

Johnshaven

The village of grey stone houses is at the bottom of a steep hill. The harbour is typical of the little herring harbours built in the nineteenth century along the east coast of Scotland. Johnshaven harbour was probably constructed in around 1820. In Victorian times, before steam drifters started to overfish the herring shoals, there were over a hundred fishermen working from this harbour. Small open boats were still being built and worked from here in the 1980s.

Lossiemouth

As the name suggests, the old harbour is literally the mouth of the River Lossie. Along the banks of the Lossie is the old fishing village, and in 1846 work started on the New Harbour which now extends along the seaward shore and has straight streets leading down to it. The two harbours are entered through a very narrow entrance facing south-east into

Spey Bay. It is a difficult harbour to enter, but has a flourishing fishing fleet and its own market. The Lossiemouth fishermen have a reputation for trying out new ideas. The zulu fishing lugger was devised here, and in 1921 there was a switch to operating Danish seine nets from motor vessels after a miner's strike had prevented the steam herring drifters from working.

Macduff

This small town acquired its name from James, Earl of Fife, who in 1783 had its status raised to a burgh. The harbour, although small, is easily accessible and is a good base for fishing boats. Herring fishing started here in 1815 and continued until the 1950s. Many inshore boats owned in Macduff are now active on the west coast. New wooden hulls are still built in the large shed on the western end of the harbour. Wooden boatbuilding is still active in Grampian because there is a source of good local timber readily available.

Peterhead

Whaling started here in 1788, but after a few decades the emphasis shifted towards inshore fishing, and in 1848 over 400 boats were based here.

By the 1880s, Peterhead and Aberdeen were the main Scottish herring ports. At this time the only ports on the whole of the Scottish east coast which could be entered at all states of the tide were Buckie, Peterhead, Fraserburgh and Aberdeen. The rest dried out at low water. Between 1880 and 1882 Parliament was constantly voting money to improve the harbours all round Britain, and it was at this time that a breakwater was built at Peterhead, mainly by convict labour, of granite from Buchan Ness. In the 1920s, Peterhead ranked as Scotland's third largest fishing port after Aberdeen and Buckie. It is still a major fishing port, and North Sea oilfields are also supplied from here. The Arbuthnot Museum has a good section on Arctic whaling.

Rosenhearty

A pleasant little fishing village which was once a rival to Fraserburgh, 5 miles to the west.

Stonehaven

The harbour at Stonehaven is sheltered from the south wind by Downie Point. The harbour has always had problems with silting. There is much of interest relating to the history of the fishing community in the Tolbooth Museum.

HIGHLAND

Corpach

A village at the west coast end of the Caledonian Canal which links up Loch Lochy, the tiny and very attractive Loch Oich and the deep and long Loch Ness. The canal saves small seagoing craft from having to go north through the Pentland Firth.

The Caledonian Canal, one of the engineering triumphs of Thomas Telford, was started in 1803 and opened in 1822, although it was forty-five years before all the work was completed. Between Corpach and Muirtown, at each end, there are twenty-nine locks. The Caledonian has never been a great success financially as it is not large enough to take ships of any size, but it is widely used by inshore fishing boats and yachts.

Corpach is also the finishing point of one of Britain's toughest offshore yacht races. This is the Three Peaks Yacht Race in which yachts carry mountaineers who have to scale the peaks of the highest mountains in Wales, England and Scotland. The yachts go into Caernarvon for Snowdon, Ravenglass for Scafell Pike and finally Corpach for Ben Nevis.

Inverness

Capital of the Highlands. The name in Gaelic means 'river mouth of the ness' which perfectly describes the town's situation. The quays on the River Ness are still used by coasters.

The harbour at Lybster, from the west, about 1860 (Anthony J. Lambert Collection)

Lybster

A stone pier was built here in 1830 to protect the entrance to this cove and to form a herring harbour. During the season, the harbour was packed with lug-rigged scaffies and the quays piled high with barrels of herring waiting to be shipped out in schooners. In 1881, there were 129 boats owned here. By 1929 this had dropped to 9, and in 1961 it was down to 5 boats. By then, the old curing station was in ruins. The coast was also dotted with empty crofts as the men had to leave the area in search of work.

Flagstones from local quarries were shipped out in the nineteenth century.

Nairn

A small harbour built by Telford in 1820 on the south shore of Moray Firth, now used only by yachts. In 1855, there were 105 boats working from Nairn, mainly after herring. This had fallen to 92 in 1881 and 41 by 1929. However, some of these were steam drifters which would have been far larger than the boats of the mid-nineteenth century.

Thurso

The northernmost town on the British mainland. The fishing fleet work from a harbour in Thurso Bay. On the northern coast of Caithness, around Thurso and Dunnet bays between Scrabster and Castlehill, there are old quarries dotted about. From these thousands of tons of street paving stones which went to towns all over Britain were shipped away by schooners. Below Holborn Head Lighthouse was a loading berth known as the Chains. Here traders lay stern on, their bows held off by their anchors and their sterns made fast to iron rings set in the cliff face. Nearby Dunnet Head is the most northerly point of the British mainland.

Ullapool

A fishing village which was started in the late eighteenth century. Now used as a base for inshore boats going out after the Minch herring. A purser with all the highly technical equipment can take a 100-ton herring shoal in a single night. In 1980 Russian factory ships were coming in here to buy herring.

Whaligoe

A tiny cove in the cliff, there was a small herring curing station down on the beach. It is now ruinous but the 365 steps winding their way up the cliff face to the village are still there. The men returned exhausted after hours of heavy work at sea so the women used to carry the herring up the cliff in baskets.

Wick

Before 1786 Wick merchants were sending cod and salmon to London, but no attempt was made to take any quantity of herring which passed by in shoals every summer. In 1786 the British Fishery Society was formed, and this encouraged boats from the Firth of Forth to go north after herring. By the 1790s, drifters were arriving here in the summer for the herring season. In 1808 the British Fishery Society began building Pulteneytown on the south side of the harbour.

By the 1860s, Wick was like a gold rush boom town during the six weeks of the herring season in July and August, with some 1,700 boats coming here with hundreds of fishermen from all over eastern Scotland. Wick is now the main inshore fishing fleet base in the Highlands.

LOTHIAN

Dunbar

This town was once the main fishing centre on the east coast of Scotland. Before the coming of the railways, sloops were sailing to London regularly with crabs and lobster, while white fish was taken by road to Musselburgh and sold round Edinburgh by the fishwives.

Cromwell allocated money for the building of the first harbour at the east end of the town, and this was replaced by the Victorian harbour to the north-west, near the castle. In spite of the organised marketing system, Dunbar declined as a fishing port during the great herring fishery boom of the late nineteenth century. There are still some fishing boats at Dunbar, but it is now chiefly a holiday resort.

Granton

The large harbour at Granton is the western end of the dock area serving Edinburgh. The harbour was started by the 5th Duke of Buccleuch in 1835 and completed in 1845.

By 1900 Granton and Leith had become bases for steam trawlers working out in the North Sea. At Granton the central jetty had coal sheds and an ice factory to serve the trawlers. In 1928 there were 62 steam trawlers based here, and there is still commercial traffic.

Leith

Although Edinburgh now engulfs the former neighbouring villages of Newhaven and Granton, Leith is the official port of the city. The original harbour was at the river mouth of the Water of Leith, while the docks were created on land reclaimed from the foreshore. Leith Docks are the largest docking complex on the east coast of Scotland. On the west side of the river mouth, the Victoria Dock was built in 1852, the Albert Dock in 1869, the Edinburgh Dock, which is farthest east, was built in 1881 while Imperial Dock, the farthest north, was built in 1901. The port was improved in 1968 by the opening of a new deepwater entrance lock.

Although Leith Docks are much concerned with modern industry, some of old Leith still survives. On The Shore at the mouth of the Water of Leith, there were two famous inns, the Old Ship and New Ship, both of which were in existence in 1680. The Old Ship inn is now a hotel and only the moulded doorway of the New Ship remains. These inns were connected with passenger traffic which was at its height around 1832, when there were 23 smacks on the regular run to London. The Leith smacks could, with a fair wind, cover the 460 miles to London in 50 hours at an average speed of 9½ knots, but their more normal time was about 5 days, although in bad weather they were sometimes weeks on a passage.

Musselburgh

With Fisherrow, on the opposite side of the River Esk, this was a fishing centre. The Fife boats also used to land their catch here and the fishwives of Fisherrow carried the fish into Edinburgh to sell them. The Musselburgh fishwives were noted for their strength, and on Shrove Tuesday there used to be a football match between unmarried and married women. By World War I the fishing industry had moved away from Musselburgh with only a few small open boats remaining.

It was in this area, in 1820, that James Patterson made the first successful machine for manufacturing fishing nets. However, the practice of making nets by hand was widespread amongst longshore fishermen until the 1950s.

Newhaven

Now part of the docking area which extends along the Forth coast north of Edinburgh. Newhaven was established in about 1488 when James III started a shipbuilding yard and ropewalk here. Flemish fishermen are reputed to have settled here to supply Edinburgh with fresh fish. James IV built his warship *Great Michael* here in 1511, and was very keen to have a high proportion of local fishermen to ensure a good crew. The best gunners in Scotland were drafted into the *Great Michael* which weakened Scotland's artillery and contributed to the Scottish defeat at the Battle of Flodden in 1513.

Newhaven managed to retain a strong local character which possibly stemmed from the original Flemish settlers from the Low Countries feeling alien to the Lowland Scots. The Newhaven fishwives retained their own style of dress

into the 1870s; their working costume was a white handkerchief tied round the head, a navy blue bodice and skirt which was gathered up to show a striped blue and white petticoat. These fishwives went round Edinburgh selling fresh fish from creels (baskets) and were noted for their tough bargaining.

In the highly organised late nineteenth-century herring boom, fishermen's wives and daughters from the east coast were employed during the season preparing fish for curing. These Herring Lassies followed the fleet round the coast from Stornoway to Southwold.

North Berwick

A small harbour with a narrow entrance. Only a few boats fish from here, but pleasure boats take passengers round the 350ft high Bass Rock which is about 3 miles off the harbour.

Port Seton

A village and harbour on the south side of the Firth of Forth. The original harbour was built in 1833–4 for shipping coal out, but in the 1870s local fishermen paid ninepence a week into a fund to improve the harbour. In 1980 Port Seton celebrated the 100th anniversary of the opening of this second development and most of the inshore boats stayed in harbour for the centenary weekend. Then about half the port's thirty-two vessels were in the nephrops fishery, a lucrative fishery which started in the Firth of Forth in about 1950. The largest of Port Seton's fifteen trawlers and seiner trawlers in 1980 was the 97ft seiner trawler *Persevere* LH 444, and most of them were white fishing from North Shields and sometimes Peterhead.

Prestonpans

In the twelfth century the monks of Newbattle Abbey established a salt industry here which gave the town its name. The seawater was left in pans to evaporate and the salt was then swept up from the bottom. This method was common practice round the coast in medieval times. Prestonpans held a monopoly in supplying salt to the east of Scotland until the Act of Union with England in 1707 allowed cheaper salt to be bought from English mines.

The houses of the manufacturing and resort town run along the beach, but the harbour is at Morrison Haven about a mile to the west. In the late Victorian period, a fleet of oyster dredgers sailed from here. A 33ft sailing boat ran a regular service carrying sacks of oysters to Newcastle, and the record time for this passage was thirteen hours.

Queensferry

A town on the south shore of the Firth of Forth near the Forth rail and road bridges. As this is a narrow point in the Forth, a ferry used to cross here for at least 800 years. The town's name derived from the frequent use by Queen Margaret of Scotland of the ferry when travelling between Edinburgh and Dunfermline.

The Forth railway bridge was opened in 1890 and the Forth road bridge in 1964. When the road bridge was opened, the car ferry between Queensferry and North Queensferry closed. From the road bridge it is possible to see the now deserted ferry loading hard in North Queensferry harbour on the north shore.

ORKNEY

Kirkwall

The capital of Orkney which was linked, before the coming of steam ferries, with Fife and Aberdeen by the 'Kirkwall Clipper' schooners. Orkney schooners and ketches used to run kelp, dried seaweed, down to the Firth of Forth ports and return with coal.

Scapa Flow

A huge natural harbour, virtually in the centre of the Orkney Islands, affords an anchorage of some 80 square miles of sheltered water. Between 1914 and 1918, the British Grand Fleet was based at Scapa Flow, ready to steam to sea to engage the German High Seas Fleet. This strategic anchorage was the most important sea base in the world, since Britain's domination of the sea depended upon the Grand Fleet.

After the collapse of Germany, the High Seas Fleet was ordered to steam to Scapa Flow and became virtually imprisoned in the anchorage. In 1919 the remaining German crews scuttled the fleet rather than hand it to the British. Scapa Flow was dotted with the masts of eleven battleships, five battle-cruisers, eight small cruisers and fifty destroyers, while British boarding parties managed to prevent the sinking of the battleship *Baden*. The London engineers Cox & Danks later salvaged the fleet over a period of several years, the hulls being towed upside down to Rosyth for breaking up.

In 1939 the Royal Navy returned to Scapa Flow, but with fewer ships than in 1914. However, a German U-boat managed to enter the anchorage and sank the *Royal Oak* with the loss of 800 men. Four days later German aircraft sank the battleship *Iron Duke* which had been Jellicoe's flagship in World War I.

The islands around Scapa Flow were heavily garrisoned throughout World War II, and it was not until 1957 that the Navy finally ended its use of Orkney.

St Mary's

A safe anchorage on the mainland much used by yachtsmen who visit Orkney. After the sinking of the *Royal Oak*, Winston Churchill ordered that the small channel into Scapa Flow should be blocked. To do this 250,000 tons of concrete blocks were sunk to form a barrier linking Mainland at St Mary's to Lamb Holm, Glims Holm, Burray and South Ronaldsay.

Most of the work building this channel barrier, which now carries a road, was undertaken by Italian prisoners of war and they asked permission to turn a Nissen hut into a Catholic chapel. After World War II, the people of Orkney asked eleven Italians to come back and complete the chapel.

Stromness

This town was the last port of call for whalers bound for the Davis Strait, Greenland. The whalers called at Orkney and Shetland to recruit men for harpooning and dismembering the whales. The Hudson's Bay Company ships called for water and Login's Well, at the south end of the town, which was blocked up in 1931, has an inscription saying that it was used by their ships between 1670 and 1891.

Stromness was also one of the ports that the great herring fleet visited, and was the headquarters of Orkney and Shetland defences in World War II.

SHETLAND

Lerwick

It was the Dutch who, in the sixteenth century, developed the great herring fishery around Shetland. Every June, the great fleet of 2,000 busses arrived in Lerwick and based themselves in Bressay Sound, the anchorage off Lerwick protected by Bressay Island. The Dutch fishermen cured their herring aboard their boats, and the Shetlanders also did this at one stage, but the Scottish and English drifters always landed their herring for curing.

In 1702 the French fleet attacked the Dutch busses and their protecting men-of-war, and burnt 150 busses. The Dutch fishery declined thereafter and gradually the Scottish and English boats took over the herring fishery. Although Shetland was remote from mainland Britain, it enjoyed a high degree of prosperity based on fishing even before the offshore oil industry came here.

The town of Lerwick was little more than a village until the beginning of the

nineteenth century, when enterprising merchants developed trade and built the stone houses with loading piers round the harbour.

The inshore fishing in Shetland was controlled by absentee Scottish landlords who claimed the right to coastal waters. This system was broken by Arthur Anderson, a Shetlander born in 1792. He left the islands to follow a business career in London and became one of the founders of the Peninsular & Oriental Steamship Company. Anderson did a great deal to improve life in Shetland before he died in 1862.

As no timber was grown on the islands, all the boats had to be imported from Norway in pieces and assembled. After 1837, boats started to be built in the Shetland Islands, and, although their own types of boat were developed, they retained a strong Norwegian appearance. The 'foureen' had four oars and the 'sixareen' had six oars, and both were very fast under a dipping lug. The Zetland County Museum owns the last 37ft double-ended clinker sixareen and models of local fishing craft.

The early Norse settlement of Shetland is remembered in the Up-Helly-Aa fire festival. This celebration takes place on the last Tuesday in January to mark the end of the long winter nights. The climax of the Up-Helly-Aa is a torchlight procession through the streets ending with the burning of a mock Viking ship.

Fair Isle

About half way between Orkney and Shetland is Fair Isle, the most remote, permanently inhabited island in Britain. There is a weekly boat running to Grutness on the southern end of mainland Shetland. The Fair Isle skiffs used by the fishermen were double-ended open boats very similar to Norwegian craft. A 22ft Fair Isle skiff, rowed by three men using very short, quick chopping strokes, could achieve 45 strokes a minute which made them fast. Before World War I, the men used to go out a long way off the island selling fresh food and hand-knitted jerseys to passing ships. Intricate patterns in Fair Isle knitwear are believed to be Norse in origin.

STRATHCLYDE

Ardrishaig
The building of the Crinan Canal and the introduction of steam 'puffers' were important maritime developments on the west coast of Scotland. The canal, although 9 miles long, enabled puffers and yachts bound from the Clyde to the Highland coast and the western isles to avoid the 130 mile passage round the long Kintyre peninsula which saved at least a day. Ardrishaig is a pleasant village at the eastern end of the Crinan with a small canal basin where yachts are now kept.

Bowling
The entrance to the canal which used to connect the Clyde with the Firth of Forth is situated here, and is used by yachts, but the canal has now been blocked and partly filled in. The yard of Scott & Sons at Bowling built about forty puffers.

Campbeltown
Main town on Kintyre which has an active fleet of inshore boats fishing for white fish, lobster and some herring under quota. Barley for the distillery was delivered by puffer from Kincardineshire.

Clydebank
The Clydeside towns virtually join up, but there were only two major shipbuilding centres on the north bank, Clydebank and Dumbarton. There were dozens of small yards at Clydebank but John Brown & Co are probably the best known because of the liners they built. Here they built the 30,396-ton *Lusitania* in 1907, which at that time was the world's largest vessel.

She was launched at an angle across the junctions of the Clyde and Cart which had to be dredged to make room. The *Queen Mary* was the next spectacular ship, but due to the depression she spent eighteen months in the fitting out berth before she finally sailed on her maiden voyage in 1936. The largest liner ever built, the *Queen Elizabeth*, was over 1,000ft long, and when launched from Brown's yard she was almost the width of the channel.

In the 1960s the Government amalgamated Scotts, John Brown, Fairfield, Beardmore, Stephen and Barclay Curle, to form Upper Clyde Shipbuilders, but demarcation disputes and then the deepening world recession after the 1972 oil crisis, added to the decline of the Clyde shipbuilding.

Corryvreckan
Between the isles of Jura and Scarba is the Gulf of Corryvreckan, the most dangerous stretch of water in the British Isles and one of the most treacherous channels anywhere in the world. For centuries it was believed that Corryvreckan was actually a whirlpool which sucked ships down. In fact it is a massive tide race caused by the current funnelling through a narrow channel which has rapidly changing depths. This results in the white, boiling surface and huge waves even in calm weather. From the northern tip of Jura it is possible to see and hear the roar of Corryvreckan, and it is only safe for vessels to pass through this channel during brief periods of slack tide.

Crinan
A village of character where the Crinan Canal, built between 1793 and 1801, meets the Sound of Jura.

Dumbarton
A town on the north bank of the Clyde which was once an important shipbuilding centre. There were shipbuilding yards here on the River Leven in the mid-eighteenth century, and this con-

tinued as a prosperous industry for the next 200 years.

Many of the early yards were small, and one of these was Scott & Linton which built a few vessels in the 1860s and went out of business while building the famous clipper *Cutty Sark*. She had been ordered by the London shipowner Captain John (Jock) Willis who had commissioned the master figurehead carver, Robert Hellyer of Blackwall, to produce the figurehead and other hull decorations. The *Cutty Sark* was actually completed by Denny Brothers who had started the Leven Shipyard in 1844. In the 120 years of Dennys existence, they built over 1,500 ships and were in the forefront of any new developments. Dennys tended to specialise in cross-channel ferries and motor vessels and this line ended with the Stranraer–Larne ferry *Caledonian Princess* in 1961. The last ship they built was the Ellerman liner *City of Gloucester* in 1963. When this firm closed, there was considerable unemployment in the area. Now much of the waterside area, particularly beside the River Leven, has been landscaped into gardens and the river is used for yacht moorings.

Fairlie

Village with a jetty on the open coast of the Firth of Clyde. In the days of great yachts with professional crews, from the mid-nineteenth century until 1939, the yacht building yard of William Fife of Fairlie was amongst the leading yacht yards. Fife yachts were noted for being particularly well built, although this sometimes made them rather heavy for racing. William Fife (I) was building small craft in about 1865, his son William Fife (II) was a talented designer, and he was followed by William Fife (III).

Girvan

An attractive harbour with an active fishing fleet. The boatbuilding yard and slip of Alexander Noble & Sons is the central feature of the harbour. Alexander Noble came here from Fraserburgh in 1946 and started this business

In the foreground are fishing skiffs at Girvan in about 1900. The topsail schooner Fairy Queen *which belonged to the grain merchant Hutcheson & McCreath, and the Marquis of Ailsa's little steamer* Nimrod *can also be seen* (Author's Collection)

on open ground; it is now a main building centre for the Strathclyde fishing industry. The wooden inshore fishing boats built on the west coast are usually recognisable by their raised foredecks.

Glasgow

The City of Glasgow's deep commitment to transatlantic trade since the eighteenth century encouraged the development of a vast shipbuilding industry in towns on the River Clyde during the nineteenth century.

Lying in the River Clyde in Glasgow centre is the *Carrick*, a sailing ship with painted gun-ports, used by the Naval Reserve. As the clipper *City of Adelaide*, she once made a record passage of sixty-five days from England to Australia.

Glasgow's Museum of Transport is in a former railway station and has a good maritime section. It has a large map showing where most of the shipbuilding yards were situated on the Clyde and a wide display of large models. The paddle steamer *Waverley* is based on the Clyde and is usually kept, between cruises, at Anderston Quay, Glasgow, near the office of her owners, the Waverley Steam Navigation Co Ltd.

Greenock

Until the mid-seventeenth century, this was a fishing village on the lower River Clyde, but because ships had difficulty in getting up to Glasgow, Greenock prospered as a trading centre. In the nineteenth century, the channel up to Glasgow was made deeper but Greenock still remained a centre for industry, particularly sugar refining. Abraham Lyle of Greenock was one of the Victorian merchants dealing in sugar, and he, like many other local businessmen, built up a fleet of sailing ships which were built in Greenock yards. Lyle named his ships after well known capes, such as *Cape York* and *Cape Verde*.

The Greenock shipbuilders were competitive and built whatever the shipowners wanted. In the 1850s to 1860s, the most sought after contracts were for clipper ships in the China tea trade. Robert Steel & Co of Greenock were particularly successful at turning out the clippers which raced back from Chinese ports with tea to catch the early market. Steel's best-known clipper was the *Sir Lancelot* of 1865, which sailed from Foochow against the SW monsoon to the Lizard, England, in eighty-five days. This famous firm went out of business in 1883.

Scott of Greenock also built clippers, but in 1866 they built the steamer *Agamemnon* for Alfred Holt of Liverpool. Holt designed an improved compound tandem engine which greatly reduced the amount of coal used. The *Agamemnon* used $20\frac{1}{2}$ tons of coal in 24 hours and she could, by maintaining a steady speed, complete a passage quicker than a clipper which would have had sudden bursts of speed and then remained almost stationary when there was no wind. When the Suez Canal was opened in 1869, the steamers soon conquered all the lucrative eastern trade. However, sail was still cheaper for hauling low value goods on the long trade-wind routes, and the Clyde builders turned to building steel four-masted barques. In around 1897, the development of steam-driven engines reached a point where they were giving an economic advantage over sail. British shipowners turned their attention to steamships and only a few sailers were built. The last one sailing in the ocean trades for a British owner was the 2,354-ton, four-masted barque *Archibald Russell*, built by Scott at Greenock in 1905. She was ordered by John Hardie, an elderly Glasgow shipowner who preferred to stick to sail. He named her after an old friend whom he had met every day to discuss shipping affairs. The barque *Archibald Russell* ended up under the Finnish flag, and was scrapped at Gateshead in 1949.

Irvine

A small estuary here has an entrance protected by training walls. There used to be a schooner trade from the quay near the tidal yacht moorings. Trading schooners were built here in the 1870s.

Kirkintilloch

Although this town is inland approximately half way along the Forth & Clyde Canal, J. Hay & Sons had a yard here building Clyde puffers which were launched sideways into the now closed canal. The official term for these steamers was 'cargo lighters', but in their regular trading runs in the Clyde and the Hebrides they were generally called 'puffers'. Peter MacGregor & Sons of Kirkintilloch also built puffers, but the last one of this type was the *Chindit*, built by J. Hay & Sons and launched in 1946.

The only puffers normally seen on the west coast now are the *Auld Reekie*, built as the *VIC 27* by Pimblott at Northwich in 1943, and the *VIC 32*, built by Dunston at Thorne, also in 1943. Both of these have been undertaking holiday charter cruises. The letters VIC stand for Victualling Inshore Craft and the original ones were built on the lines of the puffers *Lascar* and *Anzar*, which were built by Scotts at Bowling just before World War II for J. Hay & Son, now part of the Glenlight Shipping Company of Glasgow.

Oban

A resort town with a good harbour. Some of the ferries running to the western isles operate from here, but the real character of the harbour is made by the busy atmosphere of the inshore fishing boats putting in to land their catch. Some of these boats come from the east coast ports of Scotland, but Grimsby stern trawlers sometimes come in for shelter too.

Port Glasgow

The two towns of Port Glasgow and Greenock join up and their shipyards line the Clyde. At least fifty different shipbuilders have operated on this stretch of the Clyde, and there are probably more small yards whose names have been lost. It was on this stretch of the Clyde that Britain's first passenger steamer, the *Comet*, was built by John Wood for his kinsman John Reid. To celebrate the invention of this famous vessel, a replica was built by George Thomson of Buckie in 1962, and this is on display at Port Glasgow on land beside the main Gourock to Glasgow road.

After the mid-nineteenth century, there was a tendency for small firms to amalgamate. Russell & Co was started in 1878, and their three yards were some of the most active on the Clyde. In 1912, like many Port Glasgow companies, this firm was taken over by Lithgow. In the 1960s, before nationalisation, the remaining shipbuilders in Greenock and Port Glasgow were amalgamated by the Government into the Scott-Lithgow group.

Saltcoats

The harbour here was built between 1684 and 1700 for the coal trade between the Clyde area and Ireland. This trade declined in the early nineteenth century, and by 1835 neighbouring Ardrossan had taken most of the trade. In this century, the harbour wall at Saltcoats has been heightened and the area around it has become a summer resort.

Tarbert

An attractive small town with unloading quays for coasters and inshore fishing boats. This was one of the places from which the Loch Fyne skiffs worked. These were fast single-masted luggers with the pointed stern much favoured by Scottish fishermen. The boat types on the west coast were greatly influenced by east coast boats; their design was also aimed at giving them speed because in the summer the men acquired a taste for speed when racing in the vast yachts that sailed in the regattas.

Tarbert on Loch Fyne in about 1903. The Loch Fyne skiffs are waiting for the herring season. Tarbert was the home of A. M. Dickie, a noted yacht builder (Scottish Fisheries Museum)

Tarbert is on a narrow neck of land linking Knapdale to Kintyre. Over in West Loch Tarbert on the Atlantic coast is the quay from which the ferry runs to the Isle of Islay.

TAYSIDE

Arbroath

The first harbour was built of wood here in 1194, but the present harbour was started after several Auchmithie fishermen offered to settle in the town in 1830, providing the harbour was improved. Arbroath is now the busiest fishing port on this section of the coast, with around thirty inshore boats working in 1981. These boats were usually operating out of their home port rather than moving around like many boats from further up the east coast.

The town is famous for its Arbroath smokies which are haddock-flavoured and browned by hanging in smoke from an oak fire. Arbroath and Gourock were well known in the sailing ship age as being places where flax canvas was manufactured; one of the mills remains in operation. The Arbroath Museum is a former signal tower on the coast.

Broughty Ferry

A small harbour which was once the fishing centre supplying Dundee with fish. The harbour is now only used by a few open pleasure boats. Broughty Castle, beside the harbour, is open as a museum, and there is a section on Dundee whaling.

Dundee

A major port on the north bank of the Firth of Tay. Fishing was not very important here, but in 1756 a whaling company was started and Dundee was one of the last British ports to send whalers into the Arctic. In 1883 fourteen whalers sailed from Dundee and seven went north from Peterhead. In 1913 the whalers *Balaena* and *Morning* sailed from Dundee and returned with-

367

out taking a single whale; the whalers had previously made profitable voyages by taking large numbers of seals, and even polar bears, for their skins.

Whalers remained at Dundee because sperm oil was in demand for the processes in the town's jute spinning mills. Jute was imported in bales from Calcutta and Chittagong.

Charles Barrie had two well-known, four-masted barques built for the Dundee–Calcutta jute trade. These were built by Thompson at Dundee and the first was *Juteopolis* in 1891. Later, under the name *Garthpool*, this vessel, although technically registered in Montreal, became the last British square-rigger in the ocean trades until she was wrecked in 1929. The other jute barque, the *Lawhill* of 1892, went on trading under the Finnish and South African flags during World War II.

The Barrack Street Museum in Dundee is largely devoted to shipping, with a good collection of models, navigational instruments and a Victorian racing skiff from the River Tay, while the Central Museum & Art Gallery has some dug-out canoes.

In the Victoria Dock, almost under the shadow of the Tay road bridge, is the 46-gun frigate HMS *Unicorn* which was launched at Chatham in 1824, although her keel had actually been laid in 1794. Even then, she was never fitted out for sea, firstly because Britain was not at war, and later because steam vessels and then ironclads replaced the 'wooden walls' as warships. She was towed to Dundee in 1873 and used as a Royal Naval Reserve training ship until 1968. The Unicorn Preservation Society now own her, and sometimes she is open to the public. The society would like to fit her out as a full-rigged ship as she should have been.

Ferryden
Former fishing village on the southern shore of the River South Esk facing Montrose. The entrance to the Esk is a particularly bad one, with a 6-knot tide roaring over the bar, and this seems to have encouraged men to look for employment ashore.

Montrose
The town has water on three sides, the sea, the River South Esk and the wide Montrose Basin inland. Fishing on any scale finished here just after World War I with the sale of Montrose Fishing Company's steam trawlers. The inland area of water has attracted dinghy sailers, and in 1973 the Montrose Sea Oil Support Base was started on the south side of the harbour. The Montrose Museum in Panmure Place has items dealing with the town's maritime past.

WESTERN ISLES

Castlebay
A natural harbour on Barra with a jetty to which the ferry runs. After 1900, large numbers of drifters from the east coast began calling here, which inspired local men to buy boats and the women to help with curing. The fishing declined during the inter-war depression and the curing stations closed down.

Eriskay
An attractive 3 mile long island between South Uist and Barra, whose inhabitants are dependent on prawn, herring and lobster fishing. The women are renowned for knitting gossamer shawls and fishermen's jerseys with the unique Eriskay patterns of sails, waves and harbour scenes.

Leverburgh
Lord Leverhulme had various disagreements with authorities over developing Stornoway as a fishing port, so he abandoned the town and shifted his attention to Obbe, in the south of Harris, which he renamed Leverburgh. He built piers, kippering houses and roads, and his fishing boats made their first landing here in 1924. Leverhulme died in the following year and his executors abandoned the scheme.

Stornoway

The only town on the Outer Hebrides which evolved where there was an excellent natural harbour. The men of the western isles were traditionally crofter-fishermen, although the men of Lewis, between the seventeenth and nineteenth centuries, hunted pilot whales by chasing them into bays. In 1629, a hundred whales were killed off Stornoway with swords and bows and arrows.

After 1800, Stornoway steadily built up export trades in cattle and cured herring; they were thriving by 1860, although many fishing boats came from the mainland in the herring season. The crofters just did a little fishing with lug-sailed boats which they could afford to operate. By 1912, Stornoway had become one of the main Scottish herring ports with 1,000 drifters, mostly from the east coast, coming here in the season.

In 1918 Lord Leverhulme bought Lewis-with-Harris and set about developing the rich Hebridean fishing waters. He foresaw a diminishing demand for cured herring, and instead opened a canning factory and MacFisheries as a retail outlet on the mainland. Lord Leverhulme's visionary ideas brought much benefit to Lewis, but local crofters were reluctant to become factory workers or serve on the big trawlers, so men were brought from the mainland which rather defeated the object of the scheme.

Following Lord Leverhulme's death, Lewis was sold off into separate estates, and the fishing declined. Between 1959 and 1963 government-sponsored organisers started a fishermen's training scheme; the Highlands & Islands Development Board assisted in financing new boats, and by 1964 Stornoway had ten new inshore boats which were operated in the Minch for herring, white fish and prawns. By 1971 the number of new and second-hand boats owned in Stornoway, Scalpay and Eriskay had increased to around thirty.

Wales

CLWYD

Connah's Quay

A canal and then a railway brought goods from the industrial Midlands to wharfs along the River Dee. Connah's Quay was the last of the ports in north Wales to own schooners, but these finished in the 1940s. Silting closed Connah's Quay as a port just as it had done Chester a century before, and it is now very hard to trace the quay at all.

Conwy

Famous for its suspension bridge built by Thomas Telford in 1826 beside the medieval castle. Small sailing ships in the deep sea trade operated from the quay under the shadow of this bridge. Known as Conway in the sailing ship era.

Llangollen

An inland town at the head of the Vale of Llangollen through which flows the River Dee. Telford built the horseshoe falls here to provide water for the Shropshire Union Canal. The coracles which were made here for salmon fishing were almost square with 'tumble home' sides sloping inwards from the bottom to the gunwale. The coracles were developed by using aluminium struts rather than the traditional willow and hazel withies.

Mostyn

The original Mostyn Quay at the lower end of the River Dee was used only for shipping out coal, but later, iron and steel works were established here. Although the steel works closed down, a new company had developed Mostyn as the port for what is now eastern Clwyd, capable of taking ships of up to 2,000 tonnes. Mostyn and Holyhead are the only commercial ports in north Wales. In common with many other small

369

British ports, a flexible attitude and modernisation has resulted in Mostyn taking trade from established ports.

DYFED

Aberystwyth
A resort and university town in the centre of Cardigan Bay. The small harbour was the home, in mid-Victorian times, of sailing ships in the deep sea trade. The shipbuilding yard stood on the first bend of the River Rheidol. The Ceredigion Museum has a section on maritime affairs.

Cardigan
Schooners could only reach Cardigan on a spring tide so part of the cargo was often discharged at St Dogmaels, from where there used to be a regular steamer service to Bristol.

Carmarthen
In 1860 some 400 men supported themselves by coracle fishing in the River Tywi below Carmarthen Bridge. By 1925 this was down to 25 pairs or 50 men, 12 pairs in 1974 and only 6 pairs were still at work in 1981. The River Taf also flows out into Carmarthen Bay, fished in June and July only by men from Lower St Clears. In 1981 there were still 2 pairs of coracles operating from here.

Cenarth
Situated on the road between Newcastle Emlyn and Cardigan at Cenarth Falls, is a delightful fishing museum. This was started as a private collection of antique fishing tackle, and now has a coracle display which can be visited in the summer. Cenarth was a centre for salmon fishing by a net worked between two coracles. However, angling clubs have virtually managed to suppress this type of fishing in western Britain.

In 1861 there were some 300 coracles on the River Teifi at Cilgerran, Llechryd, Abercych and Cenarth. Because no more licences are issued to the salmon fishermen, the use of coracles has slowly died out. The last licence for coracles on the River Severn was issued in about 1923, so as the men retired or died, this form of fishing ended. The Teifi and Ayron Fishery Board made a by-law in 1935 that coracle fishing above Llechryd Bridge should only be continued by fishermen holding a licence. By 1981 two fishermen, eighty-five-year-old John Davies of Abercych and a Cenarth man were the sole licence holders but they had given up using their coracles. Five pairs, however, still held licences at Cilgerran to fish from coracles below Llechryd Bridge, which was classified as tidal water. Coracles are no longer allowed to be used for fishing on the freshwater rivers of Wales. Welsh coracles are still made of canvas stretched over a wickerwork frame, a method dating back at least a thousand years, although coracles were originally covered in hides. In 1974 the Llechryd builder Bernard Thomas paddled from Dover to Calais in a coracle in $13\frac{1}{2}$ hours.

Dale
An attractive village on a sheltered bay in Milford Haven. Now a yachting centre, Dale was formerly the home port of trading schooners and ketches.

Haverfordwest
The furthermost inland port of Milford Haven and the old county town of Pembrokeshire. The Castle Museum has an interesting display of photographs of local trading vessels.

Llangranog
An open beach with no sign of any connection with shipping, but in Victorian times three traders were owned here, and in the summer coal was discharged on the beach.

Milford Haven
One of the finest natural harbours in Britain. Developed in the late Victorian

Low tide at Tenby, Dyfed, in 1884. The small trawling smack in the centre is registered at Milford Haven. Brixham and Milford Haven smacks landed fish here, but this declined after the Great Western Railway opened a fish dock at Milford Haven in 1888. The open clinker boats on the foreshore are typical of those found all round Britain. Transom boats like these were built until the mid-1950s, but since then they have not usually been replaced (Author's Collection)

period as a fish loading port and in the 1970s was a centre for landing white fish. Because of the deep water, Milford Haven has been expanded since World War II as Britain's major oil importing centre. In tonnage landed, it ranked second after London for the whole of Britain in 1979. A 300 mile pipeline runs from the oil refineries to the Midlands and Manchester to carry refined products to the major marketing areas.

Newport
A sandy bay with a small quay on which warehouses still stand, which was used by trading smacks in Victorian times.

Neyland
One of the inland towns on the 20 mile long Milford Haven. The hulk of the Whitstable brigantine *Sela*, built on Prince Edward Island in 1859, lies near Neyland Point. Neyland Yacht Club, near Great Eastern Terrace, is opposite the point where Brunel's *Great Eastern* lay after one of the transatlantic telegraph cable laying trips.

Porthgain
Little more than a crack in the cliff on the coast of west Wales. A rock crushing plant was built here in 1878 after there was considerable trade to this tiny harbour. The quarries and harbour were improved, and in 1909 12,000 tons of stone and 230 tons of bricks were shipped out. Trade started to decrease from about 1914, but the abandoned stone crushing works were still intact half a century later.

Saundersfoot
A small stone-walled harbour was built here in 1849 as an outlet for coal mined inland. As the railway which opened in the 1830s to serve the harbour had the

unusual gauge of just over 4ft it was unable to link up with the national system and Saundersfoot remained the only outlet for the small mining area. Some coal was shipped to the Solva limekilns, but Thames barges also called to load for East Anglian maltings. The pits began to decline in the 1870s and coal-mining ceased entirely shortly before World War II. The village is now a small resort.

Tenby

Attractive small town on a sheltered part of Carmarthen Bay. This whole stretch of the coast of south Wales had very strong links with the West Country. Brixham sailing trawlers used this as one of their bases and so did the oyster skiffs from Mumbles. Tenby fishermen used open two-masted luggers, and one is being preserved by the Welsh Industrial & Maritime Museum at Cardiff.

GWENT

Monmouth

An inland country town with no link to tidal water, but the Forest of Dean supplied timber for sailing ship spars. This led to Nelson visiting Monmouth, and the town now has a Nelson Museum which has one of the finest collections of memorabilia belonging to Admiral Nelson and Lady Hamilton.

Newport

From the opening of the railway in 1850, Newport developed as a major port for coal export until World War II after which decline was rapid. By 1980 Newport Docks and much of the area of the town which had depended on them was virtually deserted. The Newport Transporter Bridge, opened in 1906, which gives free transport over the River Usk, was still in operation in 1981. This was built to a design by F. Arnedin, who built the famous Marseilles Transporter Bridge, and R. H. Haynes.

The Transporter Bridge at Newport, Gwent, has two 242ft high towers of lattice steelwork joined overhead by a frame from which is suspended a transporter car (Author)

GWYNEDD

Aberdovey

Village on the north bank of the wide, shallow Dovey Estuary. It developed as a port for the local copper and lead mines in the nineteenth century. On the pier is a small museum run by the Outward Bound Sailing School; admission is free but, like the Barmouth Museum, it is hoped that visitors will make a donation to the RNLI.

Amlwch

This is on the north shore of the Isle of Anglesey. The Romans mined copper near here, and by 1770 there was a fleet of ships carrying ore away to smelting works at Swansea and St Helens. As the Mona and Parys copper mines increased production, the tiny creek at Amlwch was enlarged out of the solid rock. Shipbuilding was also developed here in the yards of W. C. Paynter and W. Thomas & Sons. The last Thomas-built vessel was the steel three-masted auxiliary schooner *Eilian* in 1908, and she is one of the last British-built sailing ships still in trade as in 1980 she was trading, albeit as a motor vessel, in the West Indies. Amlwch is now dominated by a large oil discharging jetty.

Barmouth

It is said that Barmouth was given its English name so that merchants in the buying ports could distinguish it from other Welsh slate ports. The fishing port still exists and there is an RNLI Maritime Museum on the quay. This has photographs dating back to the 1860s and records of early rescues.

In the first half of the nineteenth century, Barmouth was a thriving slate port and had yards on the Mawddach Estuary which built small wooden sailing ships. The last of these was the schooner *Glynn* in 1865, after which the Cambrian Railways Co compulsory purchased the land around the harbour to build the coast line. Although cash compensation was high, the arrival of the railway in 1867 effectively killed the port of Barmouth.

Holyhead

In Victorian times the high loss of lives and ships around the British coast worried the public conscience. This resulted in a number of 'ports of refuge' being constructed, not for trade, but as a shelter in bad weather. Holyhead on the outer tip of Anglesey was one chosen for ships bound up the Irish Sea. The building of the massive Z-shaped, $1\frac{1}{2}$ mile long, breakwater started in 1847 and continued until 1873.

Holyhead is a major ferry link port with Ireland and the third largest passenger port in Britain.

Moelfre

A picturesque fishing village on the north Anglesey coast. In 1859 the sailing ship *Royal Charter*, returning to Liverpool from Australia, was lost in a gale in Moelfre Bay. Some 460 crew and passengers were drowned and gold valued at £400,000 went down with her.

Nefyn

A coastal town on the north side of the Lleyn Peninsula. In the sandy bay there is little evidence that there was once a building yard at the western end which was in operation until 1880. It was then known as Nevin, and three barques were built here.

Penmaenmawr

On the open coast of Conway Bay. A jetty was built here from which schooners loaded slate in the summer.

Penrhyn

The industrial locomotive museum at Penrhyn Castle on the Menai Strait has builders' models and pictures of the steam coasters which loaded slate at Port Penrhyn and another slate port, Port Dinorwic. The quarries were nearer these man-made ports than that of Porthmadog so slate was shipped out more cheaply. Lord Penrhyn of Penrhyn Castle owned or gained control of much of the north Wales slate industry. Particularly bitter strikes characterised the relationship between Penrhyn and his quarrymen. The gradual decline of the slate trade since World War I ended schooner traffic to these ports.

Porthmadog

In 1798 a local landowner, William Madock, started to reclaim land at the entrance of the Glaslyn Estuary, and by 1825 the new port of Portmadoc, as it was known throughout the sailing ship era, was busy shipping out slate. A railway was built in 1836, which went over to steam traction in 1863, to bring the slate down from the Ffestiniog quarries. Shipping flourished because

The harbour at Porthmadog in north Wales was created solely to ship out slate. In the 1870s, it was packed with shipping, but by the time this view was taken, in about 1900, the railways had already captured most of the trade (Author's Collection)

The last coal hoist in operation at Barry Docks. The railway truck can be seen being tipped so that the coal shoots down into the hold of the Falcondale. *This photograph was taken in 1974* (Welsh Industrial & Maritime Museum) of the massive slate industry and Porthmadog increased its fleet of small sailing ships in the ocean trades. There were two wooden shipbuilding yards here which specialised in three-masted topsail schooners, although two 300-ton barques, *Ann Mellhuish* and *Henry Jones*, were built here.

Slate exports reached a peak in 1873, when 116,567 tons were shipped out, after which the railways steadily took over the traffic. Demand for roofing slate dropped dramatically after World War I.

The only surviving Porthmadog-built ship is the lower part of the hull of the brig *Fleetwing* in the Falkland Islands, along with the hulks of many other British sailing ships. In 1973 the Devon-built trading ketch *Garlandstone* was brought to the empty Porthmadog harbour and opened as a museum ship. She was berthed by the old slate loading sheds of Oakley No 3 Wharf, in which a small museum was established with a small but very good collection of schooner photographs. Opposite is a luxury housing estate which was developed on the site of David Jones' shipyard. In 1980 the National Museum of Wales purchased the *Garlandstone*, intending to totally restore her, while the Porthmadog Maritime Museum Trust was to provide a new berth at Greaves Wharf.

Pwllheli
A shallow estuary on the north shore of Cardigan Bay now used by yachts and fishing boats. Between 1786 and 1836 nearly 300 small ships were built here; by the time the schooner *W. D. Potts* was built here in 1878, 425 vessels had been launched but the port had by then been surpassed by Porthmadog.

SOUTH GLAMORGAN

Barry
In 1880 this was a village with a population of just eighty-five. Situated 9 miles west of Cardiff with a sheltered deep-water approach, the first dock at Barry was opened in 1889. It covered 73 acres and was the largest enclosed dock in the country. In 1890 over 3 million tons of coal were shipped out in 1,700 ships; in 1913 the total was 11 million. Coal is still exported, but in relatively tiny quantities, and the last coal-loading hoists in south Wales can still be seen. Barry Island is a popular resort. The last passenger steamer called at Barry Pier in 1971.

Cardiff
Still a busy port, but only a shadow of the pre-World War II days when this was the major point of export for steam coal in the world. The port is to the south of the original city and it is possible to walk or drive round the docks.

The Industry Gallery of the National Museum of Wales has maritime collections which include models of tramp steamers owned in south Wales, and some of the types of fishing boats that were once used along the 700 miles of Welsh coast and on the inland rivers.

At the dock end of Bute Street is the Welsh Industrial & Maritime Museum. This museum plans eventually to have its craft based afloat in the Bute West Dock Basin, but until then the 54ft Newport pilot cutter *Kindly Light*, built at Fleetwood in 1904 and now on permanent loan from the Maritime Trust, is on display outside. Also at the museum is the steam tug *Sea Alarm*, built at Sunderland in 1941 as the *Empire Ash*, and operated in the Bristol Channel until 1972 by C. K. King & Co. There is also a waterman's skiff from Cardiff Dock and a Neath Canal narrow boat.

Just to the north of Cardiff, at St Fagans, is the Welsh Folk Museum. This is an excellent open air museum, and housed in part of the modern hall is a collection of Welsh boats and nets connected with the inshore and river fisheries.

375

WEST GLAMORGAN

Mumbles

A pleasant resort on Swansea Bay. The town's older name is Oystermouth, and until 1930 skiffs (smacks) dredged for oysters from here. The smacks were originally kept in the Horsepool, but this was filled in by the railway company in 1892 to make the gardens in the centre of the seafront to encourage visitors.

The company was given permission to fill in the Horsepool on the condition that they built a new harbour for the smacks. However, when the wooden piled harbour needed repairs, the railway refused to do this and the boats were washed away, ending Mumbles' era as a small fishing port. Forty years after this, the oyster dredging stopped. It is possible to trace the harbour and the smack hulks at low tide.

Penclawdd

A village beside the Loughor Estuary from which the cockle gatherers go out at low tide. Horses and carts were still used in 1981 because they could go out into the water and prolong the working time.

Swansea

After Cardiff the second largest city in Wales. The port grew up on the western edge of the major coalfields in the south Wales valleys and became a major port for the export of coal and import of copper with some six miles of quays. The Swansea Harbour Trustees were incorporated in 1854; the dock system comprised the North Dock (1852), the South Dock (1859), the Prince of Wales (1881), the King's (1909) and the Queen's (1920). The North and South docks closed about 1928. In 1977 the Maritime & Industrial Museum was opened in a Victorian warehouse used previously by Coast Lines. Part of the museum is devoted to Swansea and shipping.

Channel Islands

Alderney

In 1847 the British Government, worried by the way France was expanding her naval force at Cherbourg, decided to turn Alderney into the 'Gibraltar of the English Channel'. The original plan was to build a harbour, on the scale of Portland, in Braye Bay, but only one arm of the new harbour, now known as the Breakwater, was actually built. Interest in this work attracted Queen Victoria and Prince Albert to visit the Channel Islands in the royal yacht in 1857. The westerly gales made the work on the harbour slow and very expensive, and the idea was abandoned in 1870, although the Channel Fleet used the harbour into this century.

Guernsey

The main harbour is St Peter Port. In the mid-nineteenth century, the Guernsey ships had their own unique rig. This was barquette which had square sails on the foremast, two square sails and a gaff fore-and-aft sail on the main mast, and a gaff sail on the mizzen. The 240-ton barquette *Matchless*, built on Guernsey by Marquand and De la Mare in 1859, was lost on St Lucia in 1877. Similar vessels were the 206-ton *Carrington* and the 167-ton *Ulysses*.

Guernsey Coaster Company Ltd owned the schooner *Natalla* until she was wrecked on an island in 1924. The last schooner owned here seems to have been *Sydney*, which traded in the 1920s to London and further north to Sunderland for coal. The Guernsey mackerel boats of the late nineteenth century were three-masted luggers similar to the French craft which worked around the island. The 30ft yacht *Try Again*, based on the east coast of England, was a Guernsey sailing pilot boat. She was rebuilt in 1952 but still has the sloping transom and the general hull shape of a Brittany boat.

The Channel Islands have become an increasingly favourite cruising ground for yachts. In 1978 9,501 yachts, mostly French and British, visited St Peter Port. The passenger launch *L'Esprit de Sark*, the cargo vessels *L'Ile de Sark*, *Joanne of Sark* and the *Teresa of Sark* all run a ferry service across to the small island of Sark from St Peter Port.

Jersey

There was no real harbour on this island until St Helier harbour walls were built in 1700. This harbour is in the sheltered St Aubin's Bay on the southern side of Jersey, but there are also small harbours at Gorey and St Aubin's.

In 1828 the paddle steamer *Lord Beresford* was running a regular service between Jersey, Guernsey and Southampton. In 1831 another steam packet, the 350-ton *Lord of the Isle*, was running from Jersey, landing her passengers at Brighton and then going on to London with freight. The Great Western Railway started a ferry service from Weymouth in 1867, and was in fierce competition with the London & South Western Railway operating from Southampton. The present Sealink Ferries run to Weymouth.

In the nineteenth century, there was some wooden shipbuilding on Jersey. The trading smack *Alzina* was built in 1876 to trade to West Country ports. The topsail schooner *Maud* was sheathed with copper for deepwater trading after being bought by a Jersey owner. She was sunk by shell-fire from a German submarine in 1916. Jersey fishing boats like the *Belle Citane*, which are mainly used for potting, sometimes take their catch to Poole.

Sark

Ferries run from Guernsey to La Maseline Harbour, on the east of Sark, which was built in 1949 and opened by the Duke of Edinburgh. Fishing boats use the adjoining Creux Harbour, while in good weather passengers are sometimes landed by boat at Havre Gosselin.

Isle of Man

Castletown

A small harbour at the southern end of the island. The Nautical Museum in Bridge Street was the home of the Quayle family, and on display here is their 25ft open schooner *Peggy*, which was built in 1791. In 1796 the *Peggy* and another Isle of Man boat were sailed to Penny Bridge near Ulverston and taken by waggon to Windermere to race. Later the little clinker schooner was left in the Quayle boat house on the harbour until she was rediscovered in 1935. She is one of the few eighteenth-century open boats still in existence.

Douglas

This is the main ferry port on the Isle of Man, but like all the other ports on this island, the inner harbour dries out at low tide. Sir William Hillary lived in Fort Anne and was deeply concerned about saving life at sea. He was largely responsible for the foundation of the Royal National Lifeboat Institution, and in 1832 built the Tower of Refuge, a kind of mock castle on Conister Rock in Douglas Bay, in which shipwrecked sailors could shelter.

Another of Hillary's schemes was to turn Douglas into a 'Central Harbour of Refuge' for shipping in the Irish Sea. The first pier was built in 1793 and was replaced by the Red Pier in 1832. The Victoria Pier was built forty years later but both were open to the easterly winds. In 1864 a 600ft wooden breakwater was built to Douglas Head, but this was later washed away, and in 1879 the present breakwater or Battery Pier was built. In 1829 the Isle of Man Steam Packet Company was formed and one of their early ships was the 116ft paddler *Mona's Isle*.

In 1930 work started on extending Red Pier to form King Edward VIII Pier, providing two non-tidal berths where ferryboats can lie afloat at any state of the tide. Most of the Isle of Man Steam Packet ships are laid up in the winter. They used to winter at Barrow, but now lie in the Great Float on the Cheshire side of the Mersey.

The Vikings used the Isle of Man between 800 and 880 as a base to raid surrounding parts of the British Isles, and from 880 until 1079 it was ruled by Norse chiefs. A Viking burial containing a 20ft boat and the body of a chief and his weapons was found at Knockydoonee in 1927, and a 35ft Viking boat was found in a grave at Balladoole. Finds from both these are on display in the Viking Gallery in the Manx Museum, Douglas.

To celebrate the Viking colonisation of the Isle of Man, a replica of the Gokstad longship, the *Odin's Raven*, was built in 1979 at Onsoy near Oslo. She was sailed 1,600 miles from Norway to Douglas and can be seen on the island when not on loan to museums.

Onchan

A sizeable community at the north end of Douglas Bay. In Onchan church, Captain Bligh of the ill-fated mutiny of HMS *Bounty* fame, was married to Miss Betham in 1781. She was the daughter of the first British customs officer on the island. Ironically the surname 'Christian', the name of the mutiny's leader, was an Isle of Man name.

Peel

A narrow harbour on the western side of the Isle of Man with a boatbuilding yard at the head. A fishing port and home of the well-known Manx kipper, a herring cured by the smoke from oak chips. Between 1870 and 1880, 113 nickeys were registered here but this type gave way in 1900 to another type of Manx fishing lugger, the nobby. The last sailing fishing boat was built at Peel in 1917.

The Vikings are believed to have first landed at Peel in 798, and to celebrate this, a Viking Festival is held every July. A light-hearted invasion is enacted by local men who come ashore in a mock Viking longship dressed as Vikings and they fight a battle with the 'Celts'.

Port Erin

With the neighbouring Port St Mary, one of the most attractive ports in the island. It was formerly a smuggling centre and then a fishing port from which the Isle of Man 'nickeys' sailed. These were two-masted luggers based on the visiting Cornish herring 'drivers'.

The Cregneash Open Air Folk Museum at Port St Mary has many items connected with the fishing industry, including the home of a fisherman-crofter amongst the stone cottages.

Ramsey

The second largest town on the island where there is a good harbour. The Ramsey Steamship Company was founded here in 1913.

Glossary

a sea sailor's term for a wave

bawley single-masted fishing craft of the Thames Estuary which had a loose footed mainsail

berth a place where any ship lies between voyages. For large ships it means quay space, but for small craft it can be a place in a creek. Seamen also talk of 'getting a berth' in a ship, meaning they wish to be employed on or assigned to that vessel

billyboy a trading ketch of the River Humber ports. They had very bluff bows and leeboards

blue ensign a flag flown by the Royal Navy Reserve and by members of yacht clubs which have been granted an ensign warrant to do so. In the case of yacht clubs, their blue ensigns are defaced with club emblems

blue jacket Royal Navy sailor

bo'sun originally boatswain, a non-commissioned deck officer in charge of organising the daily work of the crew and the running repairs. The equivalent on shore would be foreman or charge hand

clipper fast sailing ship. The term is said to come from horses who made a clipping noise with their hooves

collier ship in the coal trade

crimp a man who procured crews for sailing ships, often by methods outside the law

cruiser a warship designed for scouting duties ahead of the main fleet, very fast, but not as heavily armed as a battleship

cruiser stern pointed stern similar to a warship's cruiser stern

dandy a word used in around 1870 for a ketch, fishing boat or yacht. French fishermen used the term 'Dundee' for a ketch

deep sea ocean voyages

destroyer small, swift warships originally designed to destroy torpedo boats. Nowadays, destroyers are three times the size of World War II destroyers

displacement tons the amount of water displaced by a ship's hull in cubic tons

doble double-ended fishing boat of the River Medway having fish wells amidships. The fishermen said they were double or doble boats

double-ended craft one with pointed bow and stern

flag of convenience in order to enjoy more flexible operating conditions, some ships are registered in a country with which their owners and crew have no connection. They sail under a nation's flag just for their own convenience

flying fish voyage a voyage by sailing ship to tropical waters during which flying fish were seen

fo'c'sle this is a corruption of the word forecastle. The fo'c'sle is the forward end of a vessel. In the case of steamers, the fo'c'sle head is a raised deck in the bows of a ship. The fo'c'sle was also the forward cabin where the crew lived in sailing ships and steamers

fore-and-aft sails any craft which has sails set down the central line of a vessel is called fore-and-aft rigged. All gaff and bermudian craft, and even the topsail schooner with its one or more square sails, are still classified as fore-and-aft

forefoot the underwater section of a craft's hull beneath the bow

foy boat a boat that is plied for hire at a 'fee'. The name foy derived from fee. Passenger and watermen's boats are called foy boats

gig a narrow, seagoing, fast rowing boat. Sails were sometimes used

gross tons measurement of cubic capacity of the ship's closed spaces, including the hold and deck houses

hand a seaman

hard tack ship's biscuit

haul tow a method of dredging oysters from an unpowered boat by kedging

heavy lift cargo a cargo which has to be lifted by special equipment

in irons this is when a sailing vessel is caught head to wind and cannot move

ironclad a mid-Victorian wooden warship coated in iron for protection against shell fire

jolly jack a Royal Navy sailor

kedge a spare anchor. Kedging means laying an anchor out ahead and pulling the vessel up to it as a method of moving a vessel when the wind is insufficient

knot a nautical mile is 6,080ft and a knot is a speed measurement of a nautical mile

lateen a triangular sail set on a long yard on a short mast. Usually used by Mediterranean and Arabian craft

lee-board this is literally a board to prevent a flat-bottomed craft from drifting to leeward (pronounced lo'ward) when beating against the wind. It grips the water below the hull so that the vessel can go about on a fresh tack

liner a passenger ship

little ships World War II small coastal craft, usually high-speed Royal Navy craft

long-lines method of catching cod. Short lines with baited hooks are attached to long surface lines

longshore a fishing vessel or fisherman who works in coastal waters

loose footed a fore-and-aft sail which is only attached to a boom at either end and is loose in the middle

lute stern a transom with a curved extension out over the water. The idea was that the waves lifted the stern

man-of-war a sailing warship

matelot a sailor

MFV motor fishing vessel, usually Scottish

mole harbour protection wall

MTB motor torpedo boat

multi-hull two-hulled craft are catamarans and three-hulled are trimarans

nephrop a prawn-like creature sold as scampi, sometimes called Norway Lobster

net ton one ton equals 100 cubic feet. The net measurement is the cubic space of the ship's earning space, such as the cargo hold, not including engines, bunkers or crew accommodation

one design a class of sailing racing boat which can only be built and rigged to a strict identical design

one off one boat built from a single set of plans. A class boat is one of many boats built from the same design

outport one large port is usually the official place of registration for each section of the coast. Smaller ports within the area are known as outports

packet a passenger ship on a regular run, usually a ferry boat rather than a liner

passage distance at sea covered by a vessel, not including the short distances in the rivers at either end of the voyage

PLA Port of London Authority

punt usually an inland boat with a flat bottom. The term was sometimes used for small, open fishing boats on the coast if they had a reasonably flat bottom

red ensign the only national ensign which can be freely flown by all British vessels. Also worn as courtesy flag by visiting foreign craft

restricted class racing yachts restricted to certain measurements, within which the builder can produce his own hull shape

roads safe anchorage

RRS royal research ship

screw ship's underwater propeller

seeking looking for work, usually cargo or pilotage

ship-of-the-line most powerful sailing warship which fought in the first line of battle

side-winder trawler which hauls her nets onto the deck over the side

silver darling fisherman's term for a herring

square-rigged any sail supported by a yard running across the hull. The 'square' sails are often rectangular in shape. Square-rigged ships are those rigged with the major sail square, namely full-rigged ship, barque, barquentine and brigantine

tacking the nautical term for sailing a zig-zag course in order to make progress against the wind, which is called 'beating to windward'. The tack is the forward lower section of a fore-and-aft sail

tiers a line of craft moored side by side

trade to carry cargoes

training walls built to guide a tide stream. These walls are sometimes built in harbours and rivers to train the current in one direction

tren'als this is literally tree nails, wooden pegs which are used to fasten a wooden boat together

VIC victualling inshore craft

wear ship turning a sailing ship away from the wind to go in the opposite direction. This is often done when beating against the wind, instead of letting the bows pass through the eye of the wind

whaler a ship engaged in hunting whale, also the small double-ended boat from which the whale was harpooned

white ensign the ensign flown by royal yachts and Royal Navy vessels. Members of the Royal Yacht Squadron can obtain permission to fly a white ensign

Select Bibliography

Andrews, Kenneth R. *Drakes Voyages* (Weidenfeld & Nicolson, 1967)
Anson, Peter F. *Fishing Boats and Fisher Folk on the East Coast of Scotland* (J. M. Dent, 1930; reprinted 1974)
Ball, A. SS *Great Britain* (David & Charles, 1981)
Bassett, Ronald. *Battle Cruisers, A History 1908–48* (Macmillan, 1981)
Bates, L. M. *Spirit of London's River* (Gresham, 1980)
Benham, Hervey. *Down Tops'l* (George Harrap, 1951; reprinted 1971)
—. *The Stowboaters* (Essex County Newspapers, 1977)
Binns, A. *Viking Voyages* (Heinemann, 1980)
Bouquet, Michael. *No Gallant Ship* (Hollis & Carter, 1959)
—. *Westcountry Sail: Merchant Shipping 1840–1960* (David & Charles, 1971)
Butcher, David. *The Trawlerman* (Tops'l Books, Reading, 1980)
—. *The Drifterman* (Tops'l Books, 1979)
Carr, F. G. *Sailing Barges* (Conway Maritime Press, 1951)
Clammer, Richard. *Paddle Steamers* (Batsford, 1980)
Clark, Roy. *Black Sailed Traders* (Putnam, 1961)
Coppack, Tom. *A Lifetime with Ships* (Stephenson, 1973)
Corin, John. *Provident and the Story of the Brixham Fishing Smacks* (Tops'l Books, 1980)
Cotton & Fawcett. *East Indiamen* (Batchworth, 1949)
Course, A. G. *The Wheel's Kick and the Wind's Song* (Percival Marshall, 1950)
Craig, Robin. *The Ship Series, Steam Tramps and Cargo Liners 1850–1950* (HMSO, 1980)
Drummond, Maldwin. *Saltwater Palaces: The Hey-day of Steam Sailing Yachts* (Debrett, 1979)
Dunn, Laurence. *The World's Tankers* (Adlard Coles, 1956)
Eames, Aled. *Ships & Seamen of Anglesey* (The Anglesey Antiquarian Society, 1973; reprinted 1981)
—. *Ships & Seamen of Gwynedd* (Caernarfon, Gwynedd Archives Service, 1976)
Emmerson, George S. SS *Great Eastern* (David & Charles, 1981)
England, Richard. *Schoonerman* (Hollis & Carter, 1981)
Finch, Roger. *Coals from Newcastle* (Terence Dalton, 1973)
—. *Sailing Craft of the British Isles* (Collins, 1976)
Greenhill, Basil. *The Merchant Schooners* (Percival Marshall, Vol 1 1951; Vol 2 1957; reprinted David & Charles, 1968; reprinted 1978)
Greenway, Ambrose. *A Century of Cross Channel Passenger Ferries* (Ian Allan, 1981)
Hague, Douglas B. and Christie, Rosemary. *Lighthouses* (Gomer Press, 1975)
Holland, S. J. *Ships of British Oak* (David & Charles, 1971)
Horlock, R. J. *Mistleyman's Log* Chronicles of a barging life as told by A. H. (Chubb) Horlock (Fisher Nautical Press, 1977)
Howard, Frank. *Sailing Ships of War* (Conway, 1979)

Howarth, Patrick. *Lifeboat: In Danger's Hour* (Hamlyn, 1981)

Hughes, Henry. *Immortal Sails* (T. Stephenson & Sons, 1969)

Hume, John R. and Moss, Michael S. *Clyde Shipbuilding from Old Photographs* (Batsford, 1975)

Jackson, Gordon. *The British Whaling Trade* (A. & C. Black, 1978)

Jenkins, A. J. *Gigs and Cutters of the Isles of Scilly* (Integrated Packaging Group Ltd: Isles of Scilly Gig Racing Committee, 1977)

Jenkins, J. Geraint. *Nets and Coracles* (David & Charles, 1975)

—. *Boat House and Net House* (National Museum of Wales, Welsh Folk Museum, 1974)

Kennedy, Gavin. *Bligh* (Duckworth, 1978)

Leather, John. *Spritsails and Lugsails* (Adlard Coles, 1979)

Lipscomb, Commander F. W. *The British Submarine* (Conway Maritime Press, 1975)

Lockett, Alan. *North Western Sail* (Countryside Publications, 1978)

Maber, John M. *The Ship Series; Channel Packets and Ocean Liners 1850–1970* (HMSO, 1980)

MacGregor, David. *Square Rigged Sailing Ships* (Argus Books, 1977)

—. *The Tea Clippers* (Percival Marshall, 1952; reprinted Conway Maritime Press, 1972)

MacKay, Ruddock. *Fisher of Kilverstone* (Oxford University Press, 1973)

Malster, Robert. *Wherries and Waterways* (Terence Dalton, 1971)

Manning, T. D. *The British Destroyer* (Putnam, 1961; reprinted Godfrey Cave, 1979)

March, Edgar J. *Sailing Trawlers* (Percival Marshall, 1953; reprinted David & Charles, 1970)

—. *Sailing Drifters* (Percival Marshall, 1952; reprinted David & Charles, 1970)

McDonald, Dan. *The Clyde Puffer* (David & Charles, 1977)

Miller, William H. *Transatlantic Liners 1945–80* (David & Charles, 1981)

Ollard, Richard. *Pepys: A Biography* (Hodder & Stoughton, 1974)

Oman, Carola. *Nelson* (1947, The Reprint Society by arrangement with Hodder & Stoughton, 1950)

Padfield, P. *Guns at Sea* (Hugh Evelyn, 1973)

Peer, Randolph. *British Battleships 1892–1957* (Putnam, 1957; reprinted Godfrey Cave, 1979)

Perks, Richard Hugh. *Sprits'l* (Conway Maritime Press, 1975)

Preston, Anthony. *Cruisers* (Arms & Armour, 1980)

Ransome-Wallis, P. *North Atlantic Panorama 1900–1976* (Ian Allan, 1978)

Simper, Robert. *British Sail* (David & Charles, 1977)

—. *East Coast Sail* (David & Charles, 1972)

—. *Scottish Sail* (David & Charles, 1974)

—. *Gaff Sail* (Argus Books, 1979)

Slade, W. J. and Greenhill, Basil. *West Country Coasting Ketches* (Conway Maritime Press, 1974)

Stammers, Michael K. *The Passage Makers* (Teredo Books, 1978)

—. *Discovering Maritime Museums and Historic Ships* (Shire Publications, 1978)

Stuckey, Peter J. *Sailing Pilots of the Bristol Channel* (David & Charles, 1977)

Thornton, E. C. B. *South Coast Pleasure Steamer* (Stephenson, 1969)

Trebilcock, R. C. *The Vickers Brothers: Armaments & Enterprise, 1854–1914* (Europa Publications, 1977)

Uglow, Jim. *Sailorman: A Barge Master's Story* (Conway Maritime Press, 1975)
Villiers, Alan. *The Deep Sea Fisherman* (Hodder & Stoughton, 1970)
—. *Captain Cook The Seamen's Seaman* (Hodder & Stoughton, 1967)
Waine, Charles V. *Steam Coasters and Short Sea Traders* (Wain Research Publications, 1976; revised edition 1981)
Wall, Robert. *Ocean Liners* (Collins, 1978)
Walner, Oliver. *Nelson's Battles* (Batsford, 1965)
White, Colin. *Victoria's Navy; The End of the Sailing Navy* (Kenneth Mason, 1981)
White, E. W. *British Fishing Boats and Coastal Craft* (Science Museum, 1950)

PERIODICALS

Coast & Country, Parrett & Neves Ltd. Crown Quay, Sittingbourne, Kent.
Mariners Mirror, The International Journal of the Society for Nautical Research, c/o National Maritime Museum, London.
Sea Breezes, The Magazine of Ships and the Sea. 202 Cotton Exchange Building, Old Hall Street, Liverpool.
Ships Monthly, Waterway Production Ltd. Knottingham House, Dale Street, Burton-on-Trent.
Traditional Sail Review, Anglian Yacht Services Ltd. 28 Spital Road, Maldon, Essex.

Index